STENNER
ON
MUTUAL
FUNDS

STENNER

ON MUTUAL FUNDS

The Complete and Authoritative

Guide to Mutual Fund

Investment in Canada

GORDON STENNER

with William Annett

HarperBusiness
HarperCollins*PublishersLtd*

STENNER ON MUTUAL FUNDS: THE COMPLETE AND AUTHOR-
ITATIVE GUIDE TO MUTUAL FUND INVESTMENT IN CANADA.
Copyright © 1997 by Gordon Stenner.

http://www.harpercollins.com/canada

First edition

The Stenner Multi-Safety Allocation System is a registered trademark.

Canadian Cataloguing in Publication Data

Stenner, Gordon, 1936–
Stenner on mutual funds : a complete and authoritative guide to mutual
fund investment in Canada

"A HarperBusiness book".
ISBN 0-00-255719-3

1. Mutual funds - Canada.   I. Annett, William, 1928–
II. Title.   III. Title: Mutual funds.

HG4530.S73 1997   332.63'27   C97-931230-2

---

97 98 99 WEB 10 9 8 7 6 5 4 3 2 1

Printed and bound in Canada

To my wife, partner and companion, Zenovia,
for her incredible support and encouragement.

To our children: Thane, Lisa, Justyn, Leighton, Vanessa and Tanya;
their partners: Darci, David, Kimberly, Lori, Raymond and Jason;
and their children: Dustin, Chelsea, Vaughan, Chantelle,
Miranda, Thane Jr., Seth, Gabrielle, Justynne (whose arrival was
just in time to meet the publisher's deadline!), Shea-Lynn, and
James — as with Shakespeare's "lean and slipper'd generation,"
our family is our real wealth.

This book is further dedicated to my personal clients, and to all the
excellent, committed financial advisors in the securities industry in
Canada, and to those serious Canadian investors who understand
that an ounce of prevention is still worth a pound of cure.

— G.S.

The Chinese symbol for crisis is always a combination of
two characters — the first meaning "risk"
and the second, "opportunity."

CRISIS = RISK + OPPORTUNITY

Without a proper understanding of risk,
there can be no opportunity for reward.
Indeed, without risk, there can be no reward.
— Gordon Stenner

CONTENTS

List of Figures xiii
List of Tables xv
Foreword xvii
Introduction..xxi
Acknowledgments...xxvii

PART I: FACING YOUR FINANCIAL FUTURE................................**1**

Chapter 1: **The Fun of Funds: The Keys to Successful Investing**...........**3**
The Current State of Financial Planning......................................4
Mutual Funds — Advantages 6
Mutual Fund Investors — Who Are They?...................................9

Chapter 2: **The Mechanics of How (and How Not)**..............................**17**
The Triumph of People's Capitalism...17
Building a Pyramid 19
Sticking to the Rules...27

Chapter 3: **Safety in Numbers: How Mutual Funds Work**....................**31**
The Universe of Funds...31
Opposites Attract 32
Diversification 34
The Stenner Multi-Safety Allocation System Portfolio...............35
Portfolio Dynamics 39

Chapter 4: **Conquering the Phobia of Fluctuation**..............................**40**
Psychology and the Investor 40
Guarantees Aren't...43
The White-Knuckle Syndrome 46
The Worry Factor..49
Know Your Financial Advisor's Style..51
Panic-Proof Investing..54

Chapter 5: **Facing the New Reality**...**57**
Boomernomics 57
Living Longer 60

The Facts of Leverage..62
The Call of Retirement..64
A Shift in the Collective Psyche?..66

Chapter 6:   Investing in Value **69**
The Stenner 15-Point Risk Evaluation Scale...............................70
Is Real Estate a Real Alternative?...94

PART II: SHAPING YOUR PORTFOLIO..**97**

Chapter 7:   Introducing the Stenner Multi-Safety Allocation System................**99**
Multifund Investing: The Four Cornerstones 100
Engineering Our Megafund Portfolio 103
The Model Portfolio..106
Portfolio Maintenance..114
Changes in Your Objective 115
Keeping Your Balance...116
Multi-Advisor Investing..122
Getting Involved 123

Chapter 8:   The Building Blocks **125**
The Magic of Compounding 125
In Search of Income..130
Bonds and Other "Loaner" Vehicles..133
What about Preferred Stocks?...141
Equity Securities...143
Defining Your Druthers...163
Distinguishing among Funds...164
Tough Funds for Tough Times 167
Choosing Your Relatives 169

Chapter 9:   The Challenge: Managing for Reward..**175**
Part I: The Panic-Proofer: Defining and Categorizing Risk 175
Unmasking the Faces of Risk..177
Part II: The B-Factor...191
The Stenner Risk/Reward Spectrum...193

**Chapter 10: Everything You Always Wanted to Know about Risk
                  (And Your Advisor Forgot to Mention)**...**202**
Learning to Love Risk...202
Risky Business...204
Inflation Risk — Protect Those Shrinking Dollars..................209

Chapter 11: Achieving Your Own Comfort Zone **224**
Analyzing Reason and Emotion 224

Legal Protection for Mutual Fund Investors 227
Market Movements and Values 228
Index Funds: Riskier than You Think! 233
A Matter of Interest 236
Dividend Growth — No Trivial Pursuit 239
The Importance of Timing 244

PART III: PUTTING IT ALL TOGETHER **245**

Chapter 12: Taking Control of Your Financial Future **247**
The Money Game 247
The Cost of "Free" 249
Controlling Your (In)Security 252
The Great Financial Planning Flaw 260
The Value of Mutual Funds in Estate Planning 262

Chapter 13: The RRSP: The Great Canadian Tradition **264**
The New Reality 265
Crunching the Retirement Numbers 267
Making Annual Contributions 269
Self-Directed RRSPs 273
Foreign Content Rules in an RRSP 275

Chapter 14: Evaluating Bulls, Bears and Advisors **282**
You Are Known by the Companies You Keep 283
Setting Your Own Investment Style 287
A Fund of Knowledge 289
Why You Need a Pro 292

Chapter 15: Getting *the* Load Off Your Mind **294**
The No-Advice Funds 294
The Illusion of Past Performance 299
Going Back to the Basics 301

Chapter 16: The World in Your Wallet: Investing Globally **302**
Home Truths 302
Worlds of Opportunity 306
A Century of Change 308
Emerging Economies 309
Measuring Investment Value 311
Risk-Adjusted Returns 316
Star Wars: Adjusted Performance and Consistency 319
Risk Adjustment and Performance Consistency 327
A Different Kind of (Shooting) Star 339

Chapter 17: Prospering Despite January and Taxes..................................**340**

    The January Effect..................................340

    Investing Quite Contrary..................................342

    Shedding Tax — Not Tears..................................344

    Mutual Funds and the Tax Collector..................................348

    Stick to Your Principles..................................352

Chapter 18: Unlocking the Power of Mutual Fund Dynamics..................................**355**

    Market Stability..................................355

    Working with the Pros..................................358

    How *Not* to Select a Mutual Fund..................................359

    Psyching the Business Cycles..................................361

    Cherry-Picking Your Mutual Funds..................................362

    The Illustrated Portfolio..................................365

    Rationale for Portfolio Fund Selections..................................369

    Building a Firm Foundation..................................374

Glossary of Investment Terms..................................379

Bibliography..................................391

Index..................................395

LIST OF FIGURES

Figure 1.1: Total Assets of IFIC Members by Type.................................10
Figure 1.2: Canadian Population Growth by Age 11
Figure 1.3: Mutual Funds held by Canadians as a Percentage
             of Household (Financial Assets) 1981-1996 14
Figure 1.4: Mutual Funds as a Percentage of Total Assets per Person 14
Figure 2.1: Stenner Multi-Safety Asset Allocation..20
Figure 3.1: Diversification in Action: Two Investments with Complete
             Negative Correlation 34
Figure 4.1: Time Eclipses Volatility...49
Figure 5.1: Average Household Incomes in Canada (1996)
             by Age Group...61
Figure 6.1: Volatility in Interest Rates 74
Figure 6.2: How Bond Prices React to Market Yield Changes —
             Inversely 75
Figure 6.3: 50 Years of Inflation in Canada...81
Figure 6.4: The Canadian Inflation Rate and the Consumer Price Index
             1986-1997 82
Figure 7.1: Stenner Multi-Safety Asset Allocation.....................................104
Figure 8.1: Years Required to Double Your Money at Various
             Rates of Return...126
Figure 8.2: Asset Allocation through the Business Cycle 134
Figure 8.3: The Growth of $1 Invested in Certain Assets
             Over 71 Years 144
Figure 8.4: A Canadian Comparison: Returns on Bonds, Stocks and
             GICs,Treasury Bills and the Consumer Price Index..........145
Figure 8.5: The Morgan Stanley World Index...161
Figure 8.6: Diversification (International), Return and Risk 171
Figure 9.1: Volatility in 90-Day Treasury Bill Yields and Canadian
             Rate of Inflation/CPI Index...188
Figure 9.2: Mutual Fund Types: A Descending Risk/Reward
             Regression 194

Figure 10.1: Emerging Markets Correlations with the U.S. Market 218
Figure 11.1: The Boring Approach 229
Figure 11.2: The Raging Bull 241
Figure 12.1: Who Had the Better Advice? 250
Figure 12.2: A Systematic Withdrawal Plan 256
Figure 13.1: World Market Trading 268
Figure 13.2: 100% Eligible Foreign Funds for Your RRSP/RRIF 279
Figure 13.3: The RRSP Most Likely to Succeed (1997) 281
Figure 15.1: Investor Behavior with Financial Professionals 295
Figure 16.1: Emerging Markets Life Cycle 310
Figure 16.2: Telephone Lines 310
Figure 16.3: Typical Morningstar Style Matrix 324
Figure 16.4: BellCharts, Inc. Sample Page 332
Figure 16.5: BellCharts Floating Bar Charts 334
Figure 16.6: Midland Walwyn Fund Research Sample 336
Figure 16.7: The Three Dimensions of Mutual Fund Evaluation 338
Figure 18.1: Stenner Multi-Safety Asset Allocation 366

LIST OF TABLES

Table 1.1:   Canadian Mutual Funds by Type, Assets and Market Share 13
Table 3.1:   Diversification and Risk 35
Table 3.2:   The Importance of International Diversification 38
Table 4.1:   Volatility, Individual and Mutual Fund Holdings of Stocks....48
Table 4.2:   Potential Portfolio Re-Balancing for Each Phase of the
             Business Cycle 53
Table 4.3:   Large Cap vs. Small Cap: Best Mutual Funds for
             Changing Markets 56
Table 5.1:   Minimal Reward/Risk Variance: Near-Cash Investments....67
Table 5.2:   Medium Reward/Risk Variance: Income Investments....68
Table 5.3:   Maximum Reward/Risk Variance: Equity Investments....68
Table 6.1:   The Inflation Factor 80
Table 6.2:   The "Best" Time to Invest — It May Not Matter....88
Table 6.3:   Bull and Bear Markets in This Century 90
Table 7.1:   Personal Objectives and Investment Risk 106
Table 7.2:   Maximum Growth Investment Scenario....117
Table 7.3:   Growth Investment Scenario 117
Table 7.4:   Balanced Investment Scenario....117
Table 7.5:   Income Investment Scenario 118
Table 7.6:   Maximum Yield Investment Scenario 118
Table 7.7:   Best Investment Style per Phase of the Business Cycle 119
Table 7.8:   The Best Fund per Phase of the Business Cycle....120
Table 8.1:   The Magic of Compound Interest....127
Table 8.2:   Measures of Market Value 148
Table 8.3:   Canadian Bond Funds 154
Table 8.4:   Canadian Small-Cap Funds....155
Table 8.5:   Canadian Equity Funds 156
Table 8.6:   U.S. Equity Funds....157
Table 8.7:   Canadian Balanced Funds 158
Table 8.8:   Global Equity Funds 159
Table 8.9:   Correlations of Various Asset Types 170

Table 8.10: International Stock and Bond Market
             Correlation Coefficients 170
Table 8.11: World Equity Markets Correlation Matrix (1970-91)..............172
Table 8.12: World Bond Correlation Matrix (1961-91) 173
Table 8.13: World Markets Moving Apart..174
Table 9.1:   How Changes in Interest Rates Affect Bond Prices 190
Table 9.2:   Risk/Reward Fund Category Performance..............................201
Table 10.1: Three Uses for Derivative Instruments....................................208
Table 10.2: A Loss Is Hard to Regain...222
Table 11.1: The Dividend Tax Credit in Action...242
Table 11.2: Dedicated 1995 After-Tax Returns on $1,000 of
             Canadian Investment Income 243
Table 12.1: A History Lesson — Sharp Corrections Are Normal!...........251
Table 12.2: Required Return to Meet Certain Objectives after
             Marginal Tax Rates and Inflation 253
Table 12.3: Trimark Fund — Systematic Withdrawal Plan.......................259
Table 13.1: The Increasing Advantage of Tax Deferral Over Time...........265
Table 13.2: RRSP Quick Reference Summary...270
Table 13.3: Adjusted Cost Base..276
Table 14.1: Growth versus Value 286
Table 16.1: Matrix of Asset Classes/Investment Criteria 312
Table 16.2: Asset Classes: Comparative Risk/Reward................................313
Table 16.3: Matrix of Mutual Fund Types/Investment Criteria 314
Table 16.4: Mutual Fund Types: Comparative Risk/Reward 315
Table 16.5: The Mutual Fund "Risk" Question 317
Table 16.6: Top Canadian Equity Funds...318
Tables 16.7 and 16.7A: Investment Style Matrixes 320
Table 16.8: Stenner Performance Consistency Survey.................................329
Table 17.1: Tax-Deferral Benefits Compound...346
Table 17.2: A Sample C.I. Sector Funds Investment....................................347
Table 18.1: The Stenner Model $300,000 Portfolio 368

FOREWORD

Several years ago, Sir John Templeton characterized the ability of individual investors to participate in the economic growth of nations as "people's capitalism." Those of us who have experienced the bull and bear markets of past decades can certainly attest to the wisdom of Sir John's observation.

With the publication of *Stenner on Mutual Funds*, Gordon Stenner has given the public and mutual funds industry a unique guide. It is my sense that this book will be an important tool for mutual fund shareholders and financial advisors in Canada.

It is seldom that you find an individual who has the tenacity and intelligence to stick with a financial concept, no matter how difficult the environment, because of his personal conviction that his clients are best served by "staying the course." It is even more rare to find an individual who is then willing to share his years of experience and knowledge of the business so that others may better understand the alternatives and profit from this knowledge.

Although mutual funds are a time-proven financial instrument, their popularity has waxed and waned as much as the market they reflect. In his book, Gordon Stenner explores both risk and opportunity as they should relate to the objectives and tolerance of the individual investor, and concludes that financial success and peace of mind can be achieved if certain common sense principles are understood and acted upon.

The opportunities mutual funds present are the very reason Gordon Stenner's book is so relevant and timely. Each day we are faced with myriad choices among literally hundreds of funds, different investment styles, geographical preferences and, most important, varying degrees of risk. It is important that in this highly complex world of investments, we heed the advice of a skilled grassroots practitioner such as Mr. Stenner.

In 1815, financier Nathan Rothschild used a carrier pigeon to learn of Napoleon's defeat at Waterloo — and profited greatly. Would any of us disagree that times have changed? In fact, we are living in one of the most exciting periods in the history of mankind.

The fall of the Berlin Wall in 1989 radically shifted the direction and pattern of global capital outflows. Overnight, three to four *billion* people entered the free enterprise marketplace as both consumers and producers of goods and services. Geo-political shifts since 1989 have redrawn the global economic map. Economic power is shifting eastward, from the Rhine, the Mississippi and the Atlantic to the Yangtze and the Pacific.

At the same time, huge demographic shifts, especially in the major developed countries, are impacting on all of us. The baby boomers are aging. This is the same generation that pushed up the prices of houses in the 1980s and is doing the same to financial assets in the 1990s, as it recognizes the need for additional savings as retirement approaches. These forces are prompting a rethinking and restructuring of retirement and pension programs worldwide.

Individuals have assumed a growing responsibility for their savings and retirement assets. Mutual funds have become their preferred vehicle for seeking higher returns, which exposes their investments to higher risk. Over 85% of the money invested in mutual funds has been invested since 1990, and millions of individuals have become equity and fixed-income investors for the first time.

With more than 30 years in the investment business, Gordon Stenner understands what it takes for investors to profit from this economic revolution. Through this book he has given investors a rare opportunity to take advantage of his wisdom. Most importantly, he imparts his knowledge in a fashion easily understood and applied in the world of investing.

In my experience, the best books are based on the actual experiences of the author. *Stenner on Mutual Funds* only serves to reaffirm this belief. For the conservative, long-term investor, this book should prove invaluable for years to come.

A time of turbulence and change is also one of great opportunity for those who can understand, accept and profit by the realities of a global economy. Once informed, if you don't risk anything, you risk even more.

Thomas L. Hansberger
Chairman, Hansberger Global Investors
Former President, CEO and Chief Investment Officer,
Templeton Worldwide

INTRODUCTION

In one mutual fund's recent annual report, a feature depicted two grandparents introducing their grandchildren to investing. They explained the principles of mutual funds and some of the terminology of investing. My wife and I happened to have just recently bought some mutual fund shares for two of our grandsons, Dustin and Vaughn. They had some questions for us.

"What's a mutual fund, Grandpa?"

Dustin, it means you're a part owner of a lot of different companies that make different stuff. With the money we've saved up and put into your fund, the people who manage the fund then invest in what they consider good businesses. Every year, the fund sends you a report card to answer your questions: How fast did your money grow last year? Did it go in reverse? Did it do better with those companies the managers picked than the other guys' investments did? If the companies make money, the fund does well and so do investors like you. Some day, this could send you to university.

The value of the fund changes every day. This depends on how well its companies' stuff is doing. When you're older, I'll show you how to follow them in the daily newspaper.

"What companies and kinds of stuff do we own, Grandpa?"

One is the company that owns our morning newspaper. One is the company that makes your breakfast cereal, and another that made our refrigerator. And the company that made the Boeing 737 airplane you and Mom and Dad took to Disneyland. And even the Disney company itself that makes all those neat videos you've got.

"Wow! Do we even own part of Mickey Mouse?"

Yes, and Donald Duck and Bugs Bunny and the company that made my car, and the McDonald's restaurant down the street, the Wal-Mart department store where Mom shops, the place where we bought your Super-Tack hockey equipment and even your clothes — these are all some of the companies you own through your mutual fund. If you like them, why not own a chunk of them?

Recently, *The New York Times* and the *Los Angeles Times* have devoted considerable attention to children investing in the stock market. Some people might believe that it's premature to burden children with adult concerns such as saving and investment. But psychologists tell us that children's perceptions are not like those of adults. They see the world in very basic, even symbolic, terms. So many parents and grandparents might conclude introducing mutual funds to their children and grandchildren is a good idea.

What could be a more far-sighted gift to children than teaching them the basic ideas of saving and ownership, and giving them some understanding of how our real world operates?

I'll buy that — for Dustin and Vaughn — and all the other grandkids!

*   *   *

Only a handful of books addressed mutual funds several years ago. Today, keeping pace with the explosive growth in this form of investment, Canadians have been deluged with how-to, why-to, and even when-to, books on mutual funds. These books appeal to people's need to improve their saving, investment and strategic tax programs. Many of them profile individual funds, nudging the investor toward certain ones, particularly those touted as "5 Star" or "Top 10" *past performance* funds.

The size and continuing growth of the mutual fund industry today make mutual funds the greatest investment success story of this century. In fact, 70% of all mutual funds ever sold were purchased over the last five years! Mutual funds now are global in their scope, ranging from Sri Lanka to Chile and from Tibet to Turkey. Offshore stocks and bonds and other domestic sector funds (such as biotech companies), and mortgage-backed securities, have all taken their place alongside more traditional mutual fund media.

The investment world is a minefield fraught with risks. By investing in mutual funds, you may indeed achieve greater rewards than ever before, but you can do so only when you really understand investing and how to manage the risks. In his excellent book, *The Nature of Risk,* Justin Mamis, a veteran Wall Street trader, describes risk as a positive factor in investment because it has an inverse (opposite) correlation with reward. A good insight.

With new types of mutual funds proliferating almost daily, the wonderful world of mutual funds in Canada is daunting, complex and potentially dangerous for the unwary, but can, on the flip side, present a richly rewarding experience for those investors who analyze their own investing personalities first, and then carefully seek to understand the kinds of mutual funds they decide to include in their portfolios.

Adding to the confusion over which funds to buy is the plethora of mutual fund newsletters, seminars, books, newspapers, TV and radio reports, all offering forecasts, theories, trading strategies, past performance numbers, investment cycle strategies, timing devices and crystal balls, Top 10 ratings, Bottom 10 ratings, "secret" research tips, digests and surveys. With digital technology, especially the Internet, this huge complex of information is literally mind-boggling.

Can you use this information to build a successful mutual fund portfolio? Absolutely, you can. But for most people, it will be necessary to ignore most of the media stories that purport to offer models of specific investment advice. Radio and TV programs, and financial publications in general circulation, are often excellent sources of factual information and general investment ideas, as opposed to having specific personal application. As a rule, these sources of information do not take into account individual portfolio needs, nor do they provide consistent follow-up on the securities they mention.

"Financial advice" is always available from personal or business colleagues, bankers, accountants, lawyers, dentists, neighbors, taxi cab drivers and wealthy barbers! As with the media, consider such advice the source of ideas rather than actionable strategies.

Recent polls indicate that investors require and appreciate the hands-on guidance of an experienced financial advisor. Superior long-term success in investments such as mutual funds depends on professional advice, especially since success depends heavily on psychology and human nature. An experienced financial advisor may indeed be your most important investment.

Stenner on Mutual Funds considers the problems that confront you as an investor. You must overcome these or neutralize them before you can realize any rewards. By looking at mutual funds from this angle, you see how easily you could be blindsided while pursuing the gold ring of profits. Constant vigilance is the key.

You'll find no shortcuts to fortune here. I won't join the "fad" parade — those mutual funds that, in the words of Shakespeare, "taken at the crest lead on to disaster!" If everyone else were buying at that point, I might advise you to sell! Similarly, I avoid recommending any specific funds. What I offer is a proven, intelligent approach to balanced investing.

I do refer, from time to time, to specific mutual fund categories and specific funds in order to define or illustrate a point. I emphasize again that I recommend no specific fund, class or group. Expect such recommendations only by engaging the services of a professional, experienced and competent advisor appropriate for your personal investment needs — preferably one who specializes in mutual funds.

As to the merits of any individual mutual fund, to single out individual mutual funds in an industry that in Canada alone now offers over 1,500 funds would be self-defeating for the purpose of this book. Each of these changes its performance against the larger background of shifting securities markets all the time.

I have written this book to present a well-defined road map and a practical process for any investor to follow and also for those in the brokerage and financial-planning field who wish to decrease risk and improve stable returns for their clients.

To invest successfully in today's markets, you need a firm grasp of all the available tools — stocks, bonds, real estate, the mortgage market, and many of the new derivative instruments. To understand them, and to learn how and where to apply each, you must understand the forces that move the prices. You also want to know how to recognize bargains in those markets.

Under the Stenner Multi-Safety Allocation System, we will examine the many securities that are the stock-in-trade of mutual funds. We will also point out the many pitfalls along the way. Only by considering the risks and the shortcomings of investment can you maximize the rewards.

In the process, as one but certainly not the only objective, you'll become familiar with the vital principles of mutual fund investing — return and risk analysis, mutual fund analysis, manager evaluation, international diversification, currency fluctuations, the yield curve, bond characteristics and behavior, market timing, and comparing mutual funds and other investment vehicles.

The Stenner Multi-Safety Allocation System seeks to remove the emotional confusion, anxiety and complexity that so often surround investment decisions. It outlines a logical, experienced, step-by-step approach to investing profitably — how to make decisions based on simple probabilities, using the investment experience of many decades and the necessary number-crunching you need to apply.

The Stenner approach fits the growing sophistication, complexity and volatility of the financial markets and has the ability to adapt to them as they evolve and highlights a broad range of market styles in a single, cost-effective program of investment.

I consider mutual funds the most appropriate investment for the greatest range of people, when used properly. And I'll conclude with a compendium of how you should go about using that medium, and how to avoid mistakes.

Heed the words of the writer of Ecclesiastes on abandoning sound investment: "The man who speculates is soon back to where he started . . . He has been working for the wind. It is all swept away." In other words, a major loss in your portfolio can be more important than a gain.

Whether your assets are large or small, you must play the money game with intelligence and courage. The stakes are high for those who do so. And the risks are just as high and probably higher for those who do not accept this serious challenge.

Finally, every effort has been made to properly credit sources of information. Please write to me, care of the publisher, if an error or omission has occurred. Alternatively, please call me at 1-800-201-2221 (British Columbia residents only) or 1-800-853-2853.

ACKNOWLEDGMENTS

"Of the making of books there is no end," said King Solomon, once considered the wisest man who ever lived. Now, 3,000 years later, despite electronic technology and the information highway, that statement is no less true.

No author writes a book of this kind today without depending on the legacy of the great skill, knowledge and experience of professional analysts and financial practitioners. I could not have written this book without the professional research and financial market data compiled by a number of individuals and organizations, including the financial news media.

My great appreciation is extended to the Bank of Canada, Statistics Canada, BellCharts Inc., the research department of Midland Walwyn Capital Inc., Morgan Stanley and Company, the *Financial Post* DataGroup, the Ibbotson's research organization, the Dalbar Institute, Morningstar Inc., *The Globe and Mail* and the Investment Funds Institute of Canada (IFIC).

I am particularly indebted to Michael Hirsch of New York for his exceptional pioneering work in the area of the multifund portfolio concept, a structured fabric of risk-reduction ideas that I have borrowed heavily upon in this book.

When one contemplates the giants of long-term mutual fund portfolio management, the names John Templeton, Thomas Hansberger and Peter Lynch come to mind. Indeed, Sir John was the first person to pioneer large-scale investment on behalf of individual investors on a global basis. His personal encouragement in writing *Stenner on Mutual Funds* expressed during a meeting in Lyford Cay, Bahamas, in 1987, has been one of the most rewarding moments of my life.

I am most honored by Thomas L. Hansberger, Chairman of Hansberger Global Investors, who contributed the foreword. Mr. Hansberger, a partner with Sir John Templeton, served as President, Chief Executive Officer and Chief Investment Officer of Templeton Worldwide Inc. for a number of years.

My gratitude also to a number of significant investment/mutual fund authors including Ronald W. Ady, Albert J. Fredman, Russ Wiles, Claude N. Rosenberg, Jr., Dr. Mark Mobius, Roger G. Ibbotson, Gary P. Brinson, Dr. John Taylor, Nicholas Murray, Jay Schabacker, Venita Van Caspel, Martin J. Pring, William Donahue and John Bogle, to name a few. We can't forget the demographic dynamics provided by Professor David Foot and the Honourable Garth Turner, nor the data provided by John Kaszel, Director of the Investment Funds Institute of Canada.

And a final tip of the hat to everyone at HarperCollins for their guidance and care, and to freelance editor Kathleen Richards who helped us separate the wheat from the chaff.

Although it would be impractical to name all of the excellent financial institutions in Canada from whom you might seek superior mutual fund investment advice, several other leading brokerage companies, in addition to my own firm, Midland Walwyn Capital Inc., deserve acknowledgment. These are RBC Dominion Securities, Nesbitt Burns, Scotia McLeod and Wood Gundy. There are also many smaller but top-drawer independent broker-dealers across Canada.

I would like to recognize the quiet, yet skillful, members of the Investment Dealers' Association (IDA), who perform a most vital self-regulatory service on behalf of the mutual fund and securities industries and the investing public.

PART I

FACING YOUR FINANCIAL FUTURE

chapter 1

THE FUN OF FUNDS: THE KEYS TO SUCCESSFUL INVESTING

Invest your money in foreign trade, and one of these days you will make a profit. Put your investments in several places — many places even — because you never know what kind of bad luck you are going to have in this world.

—Ecclesiastes 11: 1-2

The explosive growth of the mutual fund industry in recent years parallels a similar one in digital technology. Both have been swift and dramatic. The growing pains that the mutual fund industry and the investing public are experiencing have paid huge rewards, but also have caused widespread confusion and bewilderment. As with high technology, this simultaneous advancement of and the great human benefits produced by the mutual fund industry have come about within a kind of void — few people really understand what this explosion means. So first, let's pause to examine where we are.

THE CURRENT STATE OF FINANCIAL PLANNING

I mentioned a void in our understanding of mutual funds. Many people, inexperienced in investment, and particularly in mutual funds, have little or no understanding of what they should be doing. I'm confronted with this every day as I face prospective clients. Especially prominent are what my friends at the C.I. Group of Mutual Funds and Dan Richards of Marketing Solutions Inc. refer to as "GIC refugees." These are well-meaning lenders who vaguely feel they should be improving their lot but have no idea where or even how to begin.

Stepping into this void are a host of mediocre, well-intentioned practitioners who hang out a shingle as a "Financial Planner," thanks, in part, to the financial deregulation introduced in the last decade. They trundle around in the field of investment fund securities like loose cannons, *often with little or no experience in securities and financial markets.*

Somehow, over the past century, certain financial institutions have created a magnificent public relations image for themselves, forging corporate personae that have been universally accepted. We investors allow them to invest our money while they pay us little for the privilege, and profess that their obvious competence in traditional financial operations, such as spread lending, automatically confers on them similar expertise in every other financial field. Since deregulation, this has included — for them — investment fund securities. More recently, like unsightly weeds in a fine-trimmed lawn, instant "investment consultants" have sprung up behind every financial firm's counter.

In a sophisticated city branch I have seen a "mutual fund consultant" put clients into a Treasury Bill fund *right at the beginning* of a declining interest rate market, when the trend is obvious. This is like shooting one's customer in the foot — by degrees.

The defective portfolios I have witnessed resulting from this kind of well-meaning encounter boggle the mind. The inappropriate market considerations just mentioned are often compounded by the totally inappropriate construction of a portfolio for that particular client. This surpasses incompetent fumbling — it is the tragic misuse of investment funds that can lose these investors a lot of money directly, and even worse, ensure they miss out on important opportunities.

In the hands of a trained surgeon, a scalpel can work healing wonders. That same knife in the hands of an inexperienced amateur can cause irreparable damage.

The business world reacts in true media fashion to losses incurred by the incompetent handling of funds, such as the spectacular administration failure in Orange County in California or traders' even more colossal losses in the Barings Bank and Sumitomo copper trading scandals.

However, almost nothing is ever publicized in those other, more modest but far more numerous cases where the failure to execute a client's trust properly results in losses that may mean writing off a substantial portion of a lifetime's worth of savings. Which is the greater tragedy?

In a book entitled *Confusione de Confusiones*, about the Amsterdam Stock Exchange in 1688, Señor Joseph de la Vega spends a good deal of time playing upon the word "bourse," which means both "stock exchange" and "purse." He asserts that those investors who deal upon the bourse run a good chance of "seeing their bourses picked."

Financial institutions have come a long way since the 17th century, thanks to education and literacy, the self-regulation of the financial industry, and government regulation. We have greatly reduced the dishonest element in our financial institutions. Ridding ourselves of incompetent advisors is more difficult.

But *confusione* marches in lockstep with incompetence, and as a direct result of the proliferation of mutual funds and other securities today. In fact, the title of Señor de la Vega's book might well describe the mutual funds quotation page in any one of our financial dailies. So the growth and complexity in the mutual funds industry requires careful study to educate and to uncover opportunity.

MUTUAL FUNDS — ADVANTAGES

How do we summarize the overwhelming advantages of investing in mutual funds?

The first advantage is *diversification.* I consider the best definition of it "the activating of common sense." It's relatively simple to compare the performance of individual common stocks with that of a mutual fund portfolio.

Safety — that is, the opposite of risk — increases in direct proportion to the degree of diversification in a portfolio of stocks or mutual funds. If you wish to acquire stability, then you must diversify. This is the soundest and primary justification and raison d'être for investing in mutual funds.

Next, there's the value of *continuous professional management.* "Professional" means mature, experienced and alert. In perhaps no other area of life can a person of modest means engage the services of the best professionals in the field, around the world, 24 hours a day, serving his or her best interests, often at no direct cost at all.

Venita Van Caspel, in her excellent book, *Money Dynamics for the 1990s*, provides an insight into the work of a mutual fund's investment committee, which meets daily to determine which stocks should be added, which sold, and ensuring that each holding continues to fulfill the fund's requirements.

"The fund has specialists in the oils, the chemicals, the technologies . . . not only do they read, analyze and project figures on each company in their industry specialty, but they also make on-the-spot studies and conduct fact-finding interviews with the top officers of these companies." (This is what fund manager Peter Lynch used to call tire-kicking.)

Successful investing, says Van Caspel, is a full-time job and the fortunes of individual companies and industries can change rapidly. Besides logging thousands of miles visiting corporations and talking with key people, they also study the industry and the economic and regulatory climate of which each company is a part. The best analysts are those who have both access to the most thorough information and can apply their best judgment and experience. The ideal result is proper selection and constant supervision.

A manager's past performance demonstrates his or her experience and proven capacity. It does *not* indicate that the same manager will achieve the same specific successes in the future. Even though that person may have demonstrated talent, a sense of timing and a high level of experience, only the future can reveal the true measure of a manager's performance.

Low operating costs obviously benefit you as an investor in mutual funds. Economies of scale may reduce your total cost to a level that not even a discount broker can match.

In a single operation, the mutual fund investor acquires instant diversification, constant daily management, the automatic reinvestment of dividends, the compounding benefit, systematic income withdrawal plans (if required), free transfers between funds and usually no front-end purchase costs, as well as automatic investment and tax record-keeping and reporting.

Liquidity is another huge factor for many people. It enables the investor to sell all or part of a portfolio without causing a ripple in the market, which might not be the case in a thinly traded individual security. *Liquidity means readily saleable, for a price.* Large or small amounts of money can be invested in (or withdrawn from) a fund's net asset value at any time, and switches can be accomplished into a different asset class quickly, with little or no brokerage cost.

There is also the matter of *how protected* you are from loss owing to unethical practices. The probability of loss from fraud, scandal or bankruptcy involving a fund's manager has been virtually nonexistent in the past. By transferring the investment risk to thousands of shareholders, mutual fund companies avoid this problem, an especially painful one for people dealing with certain "guaranteed" deposit-taking institutions such as some banks, trust companies, credit unions, insurance companies and cooperatives.

Did you ever consider why the federal governments in both Canada and the United States have long established deposit insurance corporations to give consumers a minimum of protection against the loss of their money by those deposit-taking organizations? In other words, if the guarantee is so great, why does it have to be insured?

THE SAFETY FEATURES OF MUTUAL FUNDS

1. Assets are always held by a custodian, which must be a Canadian bank or trust company.
2. Funds received from clients must be segregated from those of the dealer and remitted promptly to the mutual fund company for investment.
3. The mutual fund manager is prohibited by law from using the fund assets in any way other than making investments expressly for the benefit of the unit holders.
4. Most provinces have established contingency funds against any loss due to fraud or theft.
5. Independent mutual fund dealers or institutions that sell mutual funds must post bonds as insurance against the loss of assets, other than market losses.
6. Under the provisions of the Canadian Investor Protection Fund (CIPF), there is insurance against loss, beyond contingency funds, against fraud or theft, of $500,000 per individual client account which, depending on multiple account structure, may total between $2.75 million and $3.5 million.

Should all of this be construed as a recommendation of mutual funds for the average Canadian investor? You'd better believe it. In the 64 years since the first Canadian mutual fund was created, not a single such fund (and there are 1,500 as I write this) has experienced financial failure.

Is this true of any other investment instrument or corporation in Canada? Unfortunately, no.

MUTUAL FUND INVESTORS — WHO ARE THEY?

Over the past 70-plus years, mutual funds have encircled the world, reaching into every civilized country and attracting people of every occupation and financial circumstance. In the U.S. alone, ownership of mutual funds since the early 1980s has increased from 6% of all households to close to 30% and is growing rapidly. This is convincing testimony to the growth of this investment medium.

According to the Investment Funds Institute of Canada (IFIC), the number of individual fundholder accounts by 1996 was approaching 19 million, or almost 66% of all Canadians.

What does the average mutual fund shareholder look like? A study by the Investment Company Institute of America indicates that the average mutual fund shareholder is mature and nearing middle age (46 years old), and is married and employed. The IFIC does not maintain such figures, but the picture is probably similar in Canada.

Although the number of male investors in mutual funds exceeds the number of females (56% as against 44%), the fact of gender in these figures is not highly significant, since the holdings normally belong to the households involved. But the median investor within these families is employed 72% of the time and is retired 24% of the time. The median household income is $50,000.

The typical mutual fund shareholder household in the U.S. has financial assets of $114,000 in addition to real estate and employer-sponsored plans. Mutual funds loom large in these holdings, accounting for 38% of the total. (Canadian household figures are not recorded by the IFIC; however, the average value of Canadian individual accounts is approximately $10,000.)

What sorts of funds does this average shareholder hold? The average person owns a diversified fund, with a median number of two mutual funds in the portfolio. Seventy-two percent of these portfolios include an equity fund, 50% have money market funds, and 41% hold bond or income funds.

Not surprisingly, 84% of all funds were purchased through a sales advisory channel of one sort or another, with the remainder having been purchased directly from or through a banking institution. In Canada, according to the IFIC, direct and agency sales in 1996 accounted for 8.4% of the market share, while all other sales (91.6%) were made through dealers, brokers, and other financial institutions. (See Figure 1.1: Total Assets of IFIC Members by Type.)

It's evident in recent years that Canadian mutual fund investment on a per capita basis has accelerated faster than in the U.S. It's likely that the numbers are skewed towards the more conservative fixed-income and money market funds with Canadian investors, although the evidence indicates that equity fund investment is gaining in popularity. Also, that same innate conservatism that we see in Canadian investment patterns is likely to continue through a broader diversification into more defensively managed funds.

FIGURE 1.1: TOTAL ASSETS OF IFIC MEMBERS BY TYPE

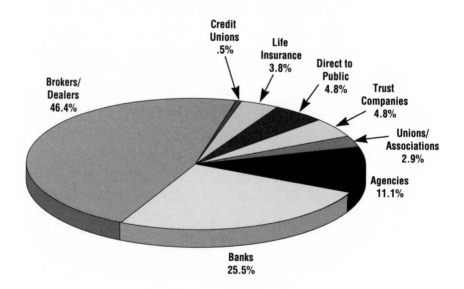

Source: Investment Funds Institute of Canada

One conclusion is inescapable: the degree to which Canadian investors have embraced mutual funds in general — $259 billion as of June 30, 1997, up from $175 billion a year earlier.

Demographically, in Canada the over-50 segment of the population holds 77% of all of the nation's personal financial assets. (See Figure 1.2: Canadian Population Growth by Age.)

FIGURE: 1.2: CANADIAN POPULATION GROWTH BY AGE
1971–1981

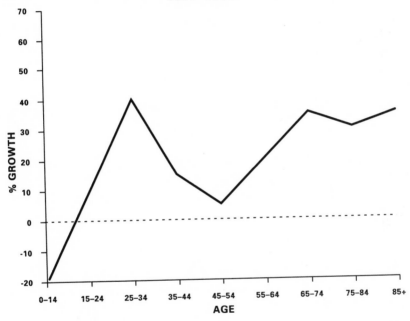

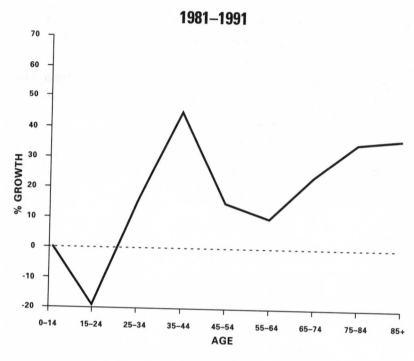

1981–1991

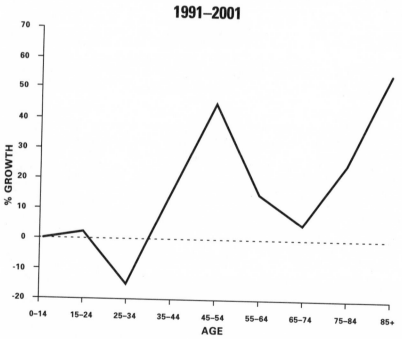

1991–2001

Source: Statistics Canada

This segment is more concerned with savings and investment than the boomer generation. Over 63% of the over-50s own mutual funds, compared to 27% of the general population. Another interesting statistic reveals that among the over-50 segment, 41% are designated as "eager investors," 36% are classed as "reluctant investors" and 23% are considered "independent investors."

Professor David Foot, co-author of the bestseller *Boom, Bust and Echo*, writes, "During the 1990s, the front end of the baby boom will cause the 45-to-54 age category to explode by 50%, while the back end, aged 35 to 44, will increase by 20%. This surge in the population of these age groups is the fundamental underlying cause of the transformation of retailing in Canada."

And, as will see later, the transfer of investment in hard assets such as real estate assets to financial assets, including mutual funds, is snowballing. Table 1.1 shows the total assets represented by the major fund categories.

TABLE 1.1: CANADIAN MUTUAL FUNDS BY TYPE, ASSETS AND MARKET SHARE (JUNE 30, 1997)

FUND TYPE	TOTAL ASSETS (000s)	SHARE OF MARKET
Balanced	$38,061,600	14.7%
Canadian Common Shares	75,147,216	29.4%
Foreign Common Shares	55,326,302	21.4%
Bond & Income	19,544,529	7.6%
Foreign Bond & Income	2,585,983	1.0%
Dividend & Income	10,691,144	4.1%
Mortgage	12,000,981	4.6%
Real Property	344,481	0.1%
U.S. Common Shares	10,535,240	4.1%
Money Market	31,715,739	12.3%
Foreign Money Market	1,682,942	0.7%
Not For Sale	0	0.0%
ALL FUNDS	**$258,636,131**	**100%**

Source: Investment Funds Institute of Canada

FIGURE 1.3: MUTUAL FUNDS HELD BY CANADIANS AS A PERCENTAGE OF HOUSEHOLD (FINANCIAL ASSETS) 1981–1996

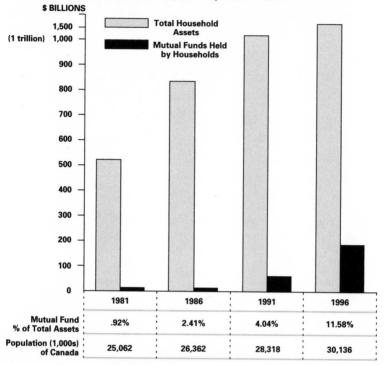

	1981	1986	1991	1996
Mutual Fund % of Total Assets	.92%	2.41%	4.04%	11.58%
Population (1,000s) of Canada	25,062	26,362	28,318	30,136

FIGURE 1.4: MUTUAL FUNDS AS A PERCENTAGE OF TOTAL ASSETS PER PERSON

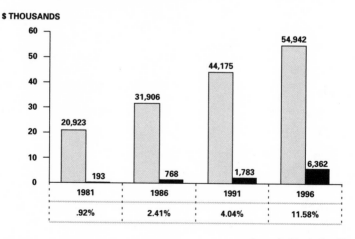

	1981	1986	1991	1996
	.92%	2.41%	4.04%	11.58%

Source: Statistics Canada

STATISTICS ON MUTUAL FUNDS IN CANADA

- Number of individual fundholder acounts in Canada by 1996 — *nearly 19 million* (almost 66% of the entire population)
- Percentage of couples of whom one has a college or university degree — *50%*
- Percentage of adults who hold a college or university degree — *21%*
- Kind of fund most of these investors hold — *diversified, with a median number of 2 mutual funds in the portfolio*
- Of these portfolios, 72% include an equity fund, 50% have money market funds, and 41% hold bond or income funds
- Percentage of mutual fund sales sold as direct or agency sales in Canada — *8.4% of market share* (the remaining 91.6% are sold through dealers, brokers, and other financial institutions)
- Canadians' investment in equity funds as of June 1997 — *$226 billion* (of a total of $259 billion)
- Percentage of the Canadian population represented by people aged 50 and older — *23%*
- Percentage of the nation's personal financial assets owned by this same segment — *77%*

— Investment Funds Institute of Canada

Note: There are over 1,500 mutual funds in Canada.

STATISTICS ON MUTUAL FUNDS IN THE UNITED STATES

- Profile of average mutual shareholder — 46 years of age, married, employed; about 10 years older than the average adult citizen
- Ratio of male investors in mutual funds to females — *56% to 44%*
- Average financial assets of typical mutual fund shareholder household — *$140,000 plus real estate and employer-sponsored retirement plans*
- Percentage of these assets held in mutual funds — *38%*
- Percentage of time these median investors in households holding mutual funds are employed — *72%*
- Percentage of time median investors are retired — *24%*
- Annual median income of these households — *$50,000*
- Chances that an investor's spouse is employed — *68%*

— Investment Company Institute of America

Note: There are nearly 10,000 mutual funds in the U.S.

| # THE MECHANICS OF HOW (AND HOW NOT)

If you search worldwide, you will find more bargains and better bargains than by studying only one nation. Also, you gain the safety of diversification.

—Sir John Templeton

THE TRIUMPH OF PEOPLE'S CAPITALISM

While mutual funds have existed in one form or another in Europe since the 18th century, the first mutual fund in North America (as we know them today) was launched in Boston in 1924. Canadian Investment Fund (CIF), Canada's venerable pioneer, came into being in 1933.

The concept originated in Belgium and Scotland and later led to the formation of investment trusts in the United States, where they helped finance the reconstruction of the American economy after the Civil War. These trusts underwrote railroads, various industries and even farm mortgages. An expanding American economy up to and through the 1920s required financial institutions to grow with it. Mutual funds, which offered another avenue for individual investment, proliferated until the stock market crash of 1929 and the ensuing Great Depression.

Many efficiently managed investment companies did hold their own, surviving the worst of the slumping markets in that catastrophic period.

The first mutual funds offered investors a way to participate in the equity or stock markets. But a new dimension was added much later, in the early 1970s: the introduction of money market funds gave ordinary people the chance to invest in the short-term guaranteed interest rate market, an avenue never before open to them.

The mutual fund concept is deceptively simple. A number of investors pool their capital, it is invested, and they share in the results in exact proportion to their individual investment. Diversification and professional management are thus made available to even the smallest investor. From that elementary concept has evolved a massive industry involved in everything from real estate and commodities to the stock of giant corporations and government bonds and mortgages.

The pooled funds of investors are carefully invested by a professional management group in a range of securities, the diversification of each fund depending on that fund's investment objective — whether it has been organized as a bond fund, a stock fund, mortgage or real estate fund, or a fund devoted to offshore securities. The investor, usually with the advice of a professional financial advisor, chooses the type of fund or funds that best match his or her specific investment objective. In some instances, particularly in the case of larger investors, assets are allocated among a group of diversified funds, creating a *fund of funds* portfolio.

But the simple concept was not so simple to apply in 1924. Bill Griffeth, CNBC writer and commentator, provides a humorous and informative look at the true beginning of open-end mutual funds in North America with the Massachusetts Investors Trust in his book *The Mutual Fund Masters*. Sherman Adams, "a sort of small-time broker" in Boston, conceived the idea of a securities portfolio that combined the growth of equity value and the advantage of a savings bank, enabling investors to draw upon their money at any time. The answer to a small investor's dream!

About 20 years ago, I used the expression "People's Capitalism" to describe what I saw as the future of mutual funds. Where else in

Canada could an investor with only $500 have access to the same rate of return as a multimillionaire? Who could argue with such a concept? Certainly not Karl Marx!

The first fund Adams put together was comprised of 45 stocks with a total value of $50,000. Today's largest *single* mutual fund is a million times that size, with assets in excess of $55 billion!

If Peter Lynch, the former manager of that fund, Fidelity Magellan, can be considered the Mickey Mantle of modern mutual funds, and Sir John Templeton the Babe Ruth, Sherman Adams could be called the Abner Doubleday of this game.

When first approached by Adams, Merrill Griswold, a subsequent trustee of the Massachusetts Investors Trust, recognized the potential and responded by buying $50,000 worth of "this thing." This thing was the embryonic beginning of an industry that now boasts investment in the trillions of dollars in North America.

BUILDING A PYRAMID

My approach to mutual fund investing is what I call the Stenner Multi-Safety Allocation System. It uses a seven-tiered pyramid. It demonstrates the successive steps you must follow as you construct your own portfolio of mutual funds. (See Figure 2.1.)

Here are the levels in descending, logical order:

1. Setting your personal objectives, your overall time horizon and actual financial goals, reducing your taxes, meeting immediate income requirements and estate planning concerns.
2. Writing out a description of your plan for reaching those objectives.
3. Allocating your investment into broad asset classes.
4. Dividing those broad asset classes into specific asset categories.
5. Dividing those categories into market segments and percentages.
6. Adding appropriate domestic/foreign mix formula.
7. Selecting qualified individual mutual funds that fit the above stipulations.

FIGURE: 2.1: STENNER MULTI-SAFETY ASSET ALLOCATION

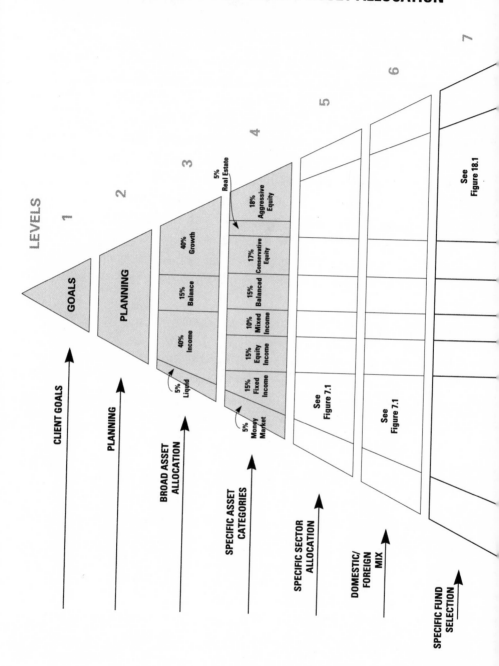

*   *   *

We will complete the first 4 levels now, and add levels 5 and 6 — the specific sector allocation and domestic/foreign mix — at Figure 7.1, and add the final individual fund selection at Figure 18.1.

What does it take to stay ahead? Or, as one humorist said, "What does it take just to get even?" Before going into detail about how to correctly invest in mutual funds, it may be easier to describe how *not* to pick the *wrong* mutual fund. For each individual investor mulling over all the Canadian mutual funds available, there is any number of wrong moves. Some of them are obvious to the professional, but less so to the amateur investor.

The wrong fund is one that does nothing for you as an investor. Worse, it runs counter to your desired objective. These funds may be right for somebody, but do not match your investor personality, profile, objectives or time horizon. A T-Bill fund, except as an interim measure, offers no benefit to an investor of age 30 who wants to pursue growth of capital. A major purchase of an options and futures fund is about as suitable for a retired investor as is a Harley-Davidson for everyday transportation.

Small investors usually make wrong investment decisions at the wrong time. As great opportunities are developing in the valley below, the little guy is losing his breath climbing up the hill. Or as Joe Granville, the fallen Kansas City guru, once put it, "When the rank and file are climbing on the caboose, you'll see me jumping off the locomotive."

Fund managers discern which position to take and which to ignore. Preoccupied with performance, they must resist much of the torrent of information constantly rushing over them. Numbers are important, but, "you have to be comfortable with the style of the fund," says one manager. "If you're nervous about the market and don't like volatility, then it's not a good idea to put money into my fund."

A small investor could hardly secure superior portfolio management when the very rich drove the best investment vehicles — those investors with minimum account balances of, say, $10 million. Through proportionately equal participation in a mutual fund totaling $1 billion or more, a small Canadian investor with $10,000 enjoys equal footing with the most affluent mutual fund investor.

At the same time, smaller investors continue to operate under a number of misconceptions. Here are a few examples of the most common mistakes they make — and many large ones as well — that they should avoid making at all costs.

- Holding unreasonable expectations about making money.
- Failing to do the necessary homework.*
- Failing to diversify.*
- Becoming greedy or nervous at the wrong time.
- Acting on the tip of a relative or friend.
- Failing to cut their losses when things turn sour.
- Failing to commit to investing for the long term.*
- Lacking a sound investment plan, perhaps the most important of all.*

(* An investor can circumvent these general errors by investing in mutual funds.)

Now, we can extend this directory of errors by focusing on the mistakes most often committed by *mutual fund* investors in particular.

1. Chasing last year's top performer. Back issues of consumer money magazines, available at your local library, demonstrate how rarely last year's star mutual funds reprise their stellar performances.

A leading business publication dealt with the danger of depending on mutual funds' past performance, first because sector funds are not truly diversified, but more importantly because hot funds make major advances in a short period of time, then pause before losing popularity and market value. Picking such a fund after it has become "discovered" may be too late in the game.

Apart from fads, avoid the cult of past performance itself. This is a natural mistake. You may be seduced by "top 10 performance" charts in the financial press, but there's often little or no relationship between any fund's rankings from year to year. A fund ranked as one of the "best" one year, or over three years, five years, or ten years, may just as easily appear at the top as at the bottom quartile the following year. Nor does it seem to matter whether a fund achieved its ranking in a rising, flat or falling market.

A single investment theme often dominates. In 1993, for example, the explosive Asian stock market produced unbelievable calendar-year gains. In 1994, Japanese equities were the winners, and Asian stocks the losers, as the bond market registered its worst performing year in modern history. In 1995, both U.S. bonds and equities led the parade with the Dow Jones index as the centerpiece. In 1996, high-tech stocks shot back up in favor, followed by financial and pharmaceutical issues in early 1997. Latin America, Europe and emerging markets also began asserting themselves in 1997.

2. *Picking the most popular category of mutual funds.* This might be entitled "the latest rage" trap. You're not entering a popularity contest. By the time the news gets down to the gossip circuit or hits the media headlines, it's obsolete.

In the late 1960s, we went through the "onics" craze, tacking that suffix on the end of every go-go stock and hot fund. When those darlings went, they went with a bang.

In the early 1970s, the gunslingers — hyperaggressive fund managers who eschewed the traditional practices of fund management — chased electronic and other exotic stocks to unheard of price-earnings multiples. For a while, an unheard-of amount of investors' money chased the gunslingers. Shooting from the hip instead of taking careful aim, these cowboys found themselves outgunned by sober realities, particularly the bear market of 1972-1974.

Early 1983 saw the launching and peaking of numerous high-tech funds. As usual, this craze followed a bull market in such stocks and the corresponding mutual funds that had built up since August 1982. Also as usual, the public's buying mania seemed to coincide with the peaking of that market.

The biotechnology industry funds rocketed to the top of the

charts yet again in 1991. The following year, these wonder funds crashed and burned.

More recently, in 1995, Bill Gates' Microsoft launched its new software program, Windows 95, with the greatest promotional budget in the industry's history — $200 million. On its launch, all the technology industry's stocks unanimously declined on the New York Stock Exchange.

Those items that seem to command the most attention, the most popular demand, are those that are the shortest-lived. This is part of a familiar market phenomenon: "Buy on the anticipation (or rumor); sell on the news."

How often has a friend or neighbor approached you with a sure-fire oil stock? (Let's say it's a junior oil, about ready to bring in three producing wells. It can't miss, and it's trading at $1.50, having steadily risen from 75 cents in recent weeks.) You buy it. Sure enough, the wells are brought in, just as predicted. The stock sells off to 75 cents. Your friend was right. Unfortunately, so was the market.

The mutual fund community always seems able to produce a product that is topical and popular, even hot. But a basic understanding of that sort of commodity is necessary. Any investment becomes most popular precisely when it nears or hits its peak. It happens time and time again, and the slow-learning investors always come back for more punishment.

3. *Going for the fund with the highest year-to-date return.* "It ain't over till it's over," as Yogi Berra used to say. Predicting a fund's performance on the basis of one static point in time is as valid as betting a horse in the backstretch. There are strong starters, and there are strong closers. You can't take a *potential* winner to the bank. Comparing mutual funds within their peer group in a specific calendar year often means very little. Calendar years don't coincide with markets. Markets have minds of their own. No single investor can manipulate or control them.

4. *Predicting future returns on the basis of long-term performance figures.* Mutual funds and fund brokers often pitch investors on long-term records. Nothing could be more questionable, although there are rare exceptions.

A fund with an impressive 10-year track record may never relive those moments of greatness after it loses a hot-shot manager or abruptly changes its investment policy or style. Old news has no bearing on the present and future.

Of course, past performance records are useful if taken in the proper context. That should include solid research into what the fund is doing *now*, and how consistent its past performance was when measured against its peer group, for example.

5. *Choosing a narrow-sector fund* for a large portion of your portfolio over a highly diversified group of funds invested in a wide variety of industries and individual stocks. Sector funds suffer for this lack of diversification and increase your risk.

6. *Concentrating on mutual funds that invest only in stocks or only in bonds.* In 1996, I gave a speech to a West Vancouver service club. A retired banker commented afterward, "Gordon, bonds have had it! I'm putting all of my investments into nothing but equities." I hope he didn't have control over his bank's investment policy! (One bond fund returned 40% in 1996–97.)

7. *Choosing funds for income when what you really need is growth, or vice versa.* This common error has a lot to do with your own time horizon, age and circumstances. Also, your propensity for risk aversion and marginal income tax rate should be thoughtfully considered before deciding which funds are appropriate.

8. *Chasing high yield in an environment such as the current one, mid 1997, of low interest rates.* Obviously, you sacrifice high quality and risk some market loss of capital.

9. *Choosing a fund because of its reputation.* Reputation is very important. But, has a top manager moved to another firm? Has the existing manager changed management style?

10. *Diversifying your portfolio mistakenly* within a single group or family of funds. No one "family" group of funds has all the answers. You get far more selection now, and will have in the future, by diversifying into several family groups.

11. *Trading funds a lot* in and out within a brief period, in hopes of obtaining quick profits. Mutual funds are *not* stocks. They are highly diversified, managed pools of money. They should never be traded like stocks. Also, watch for "realized taxes" on too much realized trading profit.

12. *Choosing funds that rely largely or wholly on market-timing strategies.* No group or individual has, or can, consistently market-time with a high percentage of success. *Modest* market-timing can be good; excessive market-timing is for losers!

13. *Choosing funds that are noted as targets for market-timers and newsletters that advocate a lot of switching.* Again, these are usually dangerous. There is nothing worse than pulling the plug on one fund only to see it rise, and switching to a new fund, only to see it drop in value. Timing service fees are usually significant cost factors.

14. An important error — *buying a fund whose manager has a track record of less than three years.* A brand new fund is fine, *if* the manager is not brand new. A manager's experience and proven track record are very important. You must get to know the manager's history.

15. *Purchasing a fund on the recommendation of a consumer publication or, even worse, a newspaper publication.* There *may* be exceptions to the rule, but generally you want to keep away — far away — from media

hype. Research from several professional reports dealing with the "guts" of a fund — the beta, alpha, standard deviation, micro-economic, and risk-adjusted behavior — will help you. Failing this, get a top-flight financial advisor to help you. That's *their* job.

16. *Buying any fund on the recommendation of a friend, colleague, co-worker or relative.* Unless the relative is Sir John Templeton.

17. *Believing that "no load" means "no charge."* Just as assuming "no GST" means you are not paying the tax in some hidden form. The no-advice, no-help funds can *cost* you plenty. (This subject will be discussed later in the book.)

18. *Purchasing any fund without reading thoroughly and under-standing the basics outlined in its literature and prospectus.* This is tantamount to throwing darts at random to make your choice. To buy any fund this way declares that you assume mutual funds in general perform well, so it doesn't matter which one you buy. There is a dramatic range between funds that perform well and those that don't. The danger of random selection cannot be overstated.

STICKING TO THE RULES

You can avoid all these traps and perils. Insist on several sound portfolio principles. This process will be developed for you in more detail in our final two chapters.

Having described at length what *not* to do in your approach to mutual fund investing, we now turn briefly to what you *should do*, in Stenner's 10 Basic Rules for Successful Investing.

Rule #1: Have a written plan.

Your first move as an investor is as simple as creating a grocery list — to draw up a plan. First, set out realistic personal objectives within a certain time horizon. Then decide how you'll get there. Next, tailor your strategy to your own preferences and personality. A professionally designed risk/reward personality profile questionnaire would help. Along the way, take advantage of strong forces working for you such as the awesome power of compounding capital itself as well as interest. If you're paying income tax, your RRSP purchase is a must and will give you a financial rocket boost. As everyone knows, RRSPs permit you to defer paying tax until you retire, so your RRSP fund grows through the compounding of the retained tax. Putting it down *in writing* is psychologically very important.

Rule #2: Construct a balanced portfolio.

"Balance" in constructing a portfolio of funds is common sense. It is also highly individual. An average person of middle age might divide investments between funds comprised of bonds, mortgages or other interest-bearing instruments and stock and real estate funds, some paying income distributions and some aiming at growth of capital. This balance can be shifted defensively into a higher percentage of bonds to protect the portfolio in times of economic uncertainty or to take advantage of higher interest rates. The reverse could be the case in a booming economy. Over the longer term, the investor would adjust the balance gradually with age, to adopt a more defensive stance. I refer to this process as periodically *rebalancing* your portfolio in numerous asset categories.

Rule #3: Diversify, diversify, diversify.

We all know *the* rule for successful real estate investing: "Location, Location, Location." "Diversification" is *the* word for mutual fund owners. Divide your assets into numerous asset categories and you will mitigate any large risk to your overall portfolio.

Rule #4: Match your investments to your own unique tolerance of risk.

Everyone is different. Your needs, objectives, time horizon, risk to leverage, and personal circumstances are unique. You must measure your risk/reward temperament very carefully. Then, divide and conquer!

Rule #5: Let your own "Time Horizon" dictate your investment choices.

Stipulate different mutual fund categories for different periods of time. "Time" is your best friend or your worst enemy, depending on your ability to select the right investments. Stocks have been the best asset class to own over appropriate periods of time.

Rule #6: Encourage the incredible power of compounding with tax deferrals.

The "eighth wonder of the world!" Your money works for you, while you work. An investment of $167.00 a month, tax-deferred from age 30 to age 70.5 (40.5 years), at 10%, equals $975,000. That's 40 years of compounding of $167.00 per month. Not bad.

Rule #7: Carefully select the best investments.

Most of your mutual fund selections should consider their risk-adjusted behavior. Be objective. Read, read, read. Don't rely on past performance. Avoid the rear-mirror view of investing. Access the best research. Secure the skills of a top-drawer financial advisor who knows mutual funds inside-out.

Rule #8: Manage your portfolio objectively.

This requires discipline and patience. Have a reasoned strategy. Watch your emotions. Don't confuse short-term gyrations with long-term performance goals. Avoid extremes, greed and fear. Insist on a structured portfolio that makes common sense to you.

Rule #9: Exploit investor psychology.

Be contrarian. It's hard to do, but so is becoming rich. The crowd is mostly wrong. The road to success is less traveled. Don't be a sheep — they only get fleeced. The greater the pessimism, the greater the opportunity.

Rule #10: Understand the long-term impact of taxes and inflation on your portfolio.

Taxes and inflation are not your friends. They are losses, every year. "Guaranteed" savings are more often "guaranteed losses," after the tax and inflation bite. Equities (stocks) are your absolutley best answer. Look at the past 70 years! And, they have the answer to inflation and taxes.

chapter 3

SAFETY IN NUMBERS: HOW MUTUAL FUNDS WORK

When should you invest? When you have the money.

— Sir John Templeton

THE UNIVERSE OF FUNDS

William Gross, whose Pacific Management Investment Company of Newport Beach, California, manages over US$60 billion in stocks and bonds for large corporations, states, cities and foreign countries, as well as eight separate mutual funds, was asked in an interview with Bill Griffeth of CNBC if he managed his own personal account. Gross replied, "Actually, I don't. My own money is in mutual funds."

✳   ✳   ✳

In 1875, an English lawyer named Arthur Scratchley (perhaps the origin of the colloquial expression "scratch," meaning legal tender) defined the mutual fund concept: "Whether a man has a large sum or a small sum to invest . . . if he subscribes to a general fund which (assisted by the advice of persons of experience in such matters) would divide its purchases carefully among a selected variety of investments, each member would derive greater benefit with much security from loss by the distribution of the risk over a larger average."

Note Arthur's final line, "security from loss by the distribution of the risk" — an accurate if primitive definition of diversification.

Today's mutual fund industry in Canada should be commended for four particular accomplishments:

1. Mutual funds provide an essential means of diversification that has greatly reduced the risk of owning individual stocks and bonds.
2. Mutual funds provide skilled investment services, such as account information, low relative costs, ease of transactions, efficient record-keeping, liquidity on demand, tax reporting and much more, including great convenience.
3. Mutual funds offer a wide variety of types, asset classes and objectives to meet the most demanding of investors' needs.
4. Apart from the convenient administrative services attached to them, mutual funds provide professional expertise and daily management that, generally speaking, deliver returns reflecting the market segments in which they participate.

OPPOSITES ATTRACT

Diversification by asset class requires more explanation. As is often the case in marriage, business or other relationships, opposites not only attract — they often complement each other. They offset each other's shortcomings and together become greater than the sum of their parts — creating synergy. To secure a balanced relationship among different asset classes, matching — and just as often mixing — are essential to strengthen your portfolio.

The characteristics of one class, such as bonds or other fixed-income securities, differ widely from those of another class. The differences lie in how they will perform in certain markets. Bonds, of course, decline when interest rates rise, which may stimulate certain equities. So bonds and stocks tend at times to be *inverse-related* — they demonstrate an "opposite-behavior relationship."

So an investor who has both securities in a portfolio is employing a balanced approach to the reality of fluctuation. (A rough analogy might be drawn to a wheat farmer who buys call options on the future delivery of his wheat to offset the possibility of declining prices when he sells his cash crop.) Placing bonds in a stock portfolio might be considered a hedge against equity performance. It can be a stabilizer, offering you consistent income distributions monthly or quarterly throughout the bond segment of your portfolio.

An example of inverse-related movement occurred on October 19, 1987, called "Black Monday." As the stock markets of the world crashed, bond, real estate and mortgage mutual funds rose. If opposites don't always attract, they can, and often do, offset one another's moves in the market. A hypothetical illustration of such an inverse-related balance is shown in Figure 3.1.

FIGURE 3.1: DIVERSIFICATION IN ACTION: TWO INVESTMENTS WITH COMPLETE NEGATIVE CORRELATION*

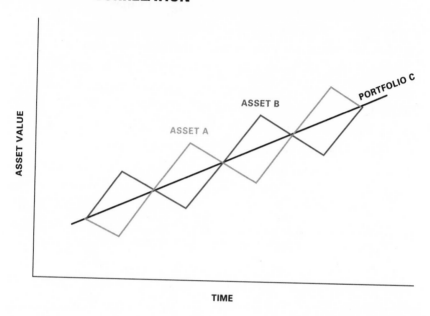

* a hypothetical example

DIVERSIFICATION

To this balance of bonds and stocks, you might add offshore securities that behave in an even more disparate way. This enables you to participate in global economic cycles in different foreign countries which often can differ in their timing, extremity and longevity. This is the last word in the investment principle of "safety in numbers."

An interesting table presented below shows how your investment risk declines as you diversify more and more within your mutual fund portfolio. This is defined as the "relative variability" or "fluctuation of annual returns." The greater the diversification within a portfolio, the lower the risk and the fewer the swings in returns.

TABLE 3.1: DIVERSIFICATION AND RISK

Number of Stocks	Risk Ratio
1	6.56
2	3.77
4	2.38
10	1.55
50	1.10
100	1.04
500	1.00

Source: Major Market Indices, 1970-1995

The variability of return, or risk, is six times higher for the holder of a single stock than it is for someone holding a 100-stock portfolio. Yet a vast number of investors hold only one or two stocks each.

Diversification is equally important within a bond portfolio. If a mutual fund invests strategically in a wide number of bond issues, it achieves this diversification without any proportionate loss in quality or yield.

Certainly, how and by whom your fund is managed is your most important consideration in selecting a fund. Give appropriate weight to the fund's relative rate of return, comparing it with other funds of the same type and peer group, and even to stock market averages.

There, however, comparisons of past performance should end. While a fund manager's achievements to date are definitely worth noting and evaluating, projecting a track record into the present and future can be disastrous.

THE STENNER MULTI-SAFETY ALLOCATION SYSTEM PORTFOLIO

Traditional diversification in a bond/stock portfolio used to be limited to the number of individual stock and bond issues you included in your portfolio. It was therefore diversified on only one level.

Since the early 1970s, stock markets around the world have mushroomed in volume, broadened trading lists, and adopted sophisticated computer systems to execute their transactions. Trading in commodities, derivatives and foreign exchange have snowballed.

In such a world, the overwhelming complexity of traditional blue-chip investing through diversified individual stock and bond portfolios has made it somewhat trickier to analyze and grasp.

In a world where more people can invest so much more readily, individual portfolios must be adjusted much more frequently. Managers must assimilate and weigh a far greater mass of critical information than ever before. And all of these changes have happened over the past three decades, compounding their effect on the way money moves and is made. These changes have revolutionized investing. Mutual funds, in their turn, have evolved to respond to these demands. They are the most liquid and cost-effective way to participate in these domestic and global securities markets.

Getting the Mix Right

Consider the greater advantages of diversifying on *four* separate and distinct levels within a multifund portfolio:

- investment in a mutual fund in the first place, rather than a single security;
- choice of several mutual fund "family" groups, rather than one;
- choice of a variety of mutual fund types rather than a single type;
- ability to build into it hard assets as well as financial assets.

These four levels constitute our *Cornerstone Safety Approach*. Through this strategy you can shape a portfolio around 10 to 20 investment themes, rather than the more traditional one or two. Monitoring a portfolio like this, containing, say, 10 to 15 mutual fund positions, is much easier than keeping track of 30 to 50 separate stocks, 15 to 20 individual bond issues, and a dozen or so different cash equivalents — GICs, term deposits, or other fixed-rate deposits.

With a Stenner Multi-Safety Allocation System multifund portfolio, you consolidate the monitoring and reporting functions into one single, periodic statement. And you win on other counts, too:

1. Conciseness, by including an entire sector, industry, or even national business in a single portfolio.
2. Practical efficiency, managing a complex portfolio or group of portfolios within the grasp of one manager or group, saving yourself an administrative nightmare.
3. Versatility, since you can diversify, invest, divest and rebalance your holdings according to your own level of comfort, within sectors and even whole family groups of funds, in response to market conditions, economic shifts and international developments.

Asset allocation does not attempt to outguess the markets so much as work intelligently with them. It is better to be partially right than precisely wrong.

With 15 to 20 mutual funds in your portfolio, you can obtain indirect ownership in hundreds of specific stocks, bonds, mortgages, real estate, precious metals, currencies, and money market instruments. All of these holdings are constructed in various percentage allocations, according to your own risk/reward profile.

TABLE 3.2: THE IMPORTANCE OF INTERNATIONAL DIVERSIFICATION

Major Market Indices (Best Performing Asset in Boldface)

Year	U.S. Stocks	International Stocks	Cash Equivalents	Real Estate	U.S. Bonds	International Bonds	Moderate Norm
1970	3.9%	10.5%	6.6%	10.8%	**14.0%**	6.5%	5.6%
1971	14.3	**31.2**	4.4	9.2	13.2	15.5	15.9
1972	19.0	**37.6**	4.0	7.5	5.7	9.2	15.7
1973	−14.7	**14.2**	6.8	7.5	0.9	−0.9	−6.0
1974	−26.5	−22.2	**7.9**	7.2	3.4	3.5	−10.3
1975	**37.2**	37.1	5.9	5.7	9.1	14.3	23.1
1976	**23.9**	3.7	5.0	9.3	17.4	11.7	15.8
1977	−7.2	19.4	5.2	10.5	1.3	**33.5**	5.6
1978	6.6	**34.3**	7.1	16.0	−0.5	14.4	11.2
1979	18.6	6.2	9.8	**20.7**	3.4	−8.3	10.6
1980	**32.5**	24.4	11.3	18.1	0.4	9.1	18.6
1981	−4.9	1.0	14.1	**16.6**	7.7	0.9	2.6
1982	21.5	−0.9	10.9	9.4	**33.5**	14.3	18.6
1983	22.6	**24.6**	8.6	13.3	4.8	7.9	15.6
1984	6.3	7.9	9.6	13.0	**14.2**	8.4	9.7
1985	31.7	**56.7**	7.5	10.1	27.1	22.7	30.2
1986	18.7	**69.9**	6.1	6.6	18.6	21.1	24.8
1987	5.3	**24.9**	5.8	5.5	−0.8	20.8	8.3
1988	16.6	**28.6**	6.8	7.0	7.2	4.8	13.4
1989	**31.7**	10.8	8.2	6.2	16.2	−0.4	17.7
1990	−3.1	−23.3	7.5	1.5	8.3	**9.9**	−1.3
1991	30.5	12.5	5.4	−6.1	17.5	15.4	17.6
1992	7.6	−11.8	3.5	−4.6	7.7	**8.9**	3.0
1993	10.1	**32.9**	3.0	0.9	12.8	16.4	13.4
1994	1.3	−8.1	4.3	**6.7**	−5.6	1.3	1.4
1995	**37.6**	11.6	5.4	(e)8.8	23.0	18.8	23.8
Cum. Returr	1761.5	**2345.3**	472.9	774.5	991.5	1211.4	1516.1
Ann. Returr	11.9	**13.1**	6.9	8.2	9.6	10.4	11.3
Std. Dev.	16.4	**22.9**	2.6	6.2	9.4	8.9	9.7

Source: *U.S. Stocks; Standard & Poor's Composite Index; U.S. Bonds; Lehman Long-Term Government Bond (1970–1997); Merrill Lynch 7–10 Year Treasury (1978–1994); Equity MSCI Europe, Asia, Far East Stock Market Index (International) — Gross Dividends (U.S. $); Cash Equivalents: 91-Day Treasury Bill Offering; Real Estate: Frank Russell Company Property Index (1978–1994), Ibbotson & Fall, Journal of*

Portfolio Management, Fall 1979, JMB Institutional Realty Corp., Real Estate, June 1986 (FRC Commingled-Fund 1971–1977); International Bonds: 1985–1994 Salomon Brothers (Non-U.S. 50% H); 1970–1984 composite consisting of Japan, U.K., Germany and France. Moderate Normal Portfolio is 35% U.S. Stock, 15% International Stock, 15% Real Estate, 25% U.S. Bonds and 10% International Bonds.

Note: Almost every year and every decade has had a different star category among these listed asset groups.

PORTFOLIO DYNAMICS

It is the case that mutual fund portfolios must be adjusted more frequently than has been needed in the past. Portfolio managers must assimilate and weigh a far greater mass of critical information over a wider spectrum (like the exponential variables within a chess game) than ever before. And since all of these changes have occurred simultaneously within the past three decades, the effect has been compounded.

The inherent strengths of the open-ended mutual fund are a significant potential solution to most of the contemporary problems of personal investment. Since mutual funds provide, in effect, instant liquidity, tremendous diversification and flexibility, investors are empowered with the ability to cope with volatility.

And in view of the depth of the Canadian mutual fund industry (which, as this book goes to press, offers more than 1,500 individual mutual funds and counting), investors have access to professional expertise unmatched by any other investment media.

The entire range of mutual fund investment alternatives, from the most mundane, conservative dividend and growth stock funds to the most exotic option strategies and high-tech venture funds, can be captured through the selection of less than a handful of funds. By bringing together the two major characteristics of a mutual fund — their liquidity and diversity — an investor can achieve a near-perfect investment vehicle with which to face today's volatile and complex world markets. Such is the purpose of the Stenner methodology of mutual fund investment.

chapter 4

CONQUERING THE PHOBIA OF FLUCTUATION

*A stock market decline is as routine
as a January blizzard in Colorado.*

—Peter Lynch, *Beating The Street*

PSYCHOLOGY AND THE INVESTOR

Investor behavior tends to be consistent. It is also nearly always wrong, except among steel-nerved professionals. And even they are not immune to the epidemics of rumors, hunches and sheer euphoria and despair in their chosen line of work.

Psychology plays a big part in the way you invest your money. There is the overpowering impulse to buy at the top of the cycle because you feel good, matched by its opposite overpowering impulse to sell at the bottom because you're nervous. Stephen Jarislowsky, the veteran pension manager based in Montreal, says investors throw money at him when they should be selling, and seek to redeem their holdings when they should be buying.

Stenner's Law #1: If it is possible for you to make a bad move in a given situation, you will feel an overpowering impulse to make that move.

The psychology of investing is a matter of mind over money. It involves the cold-blooded application of objective market timing and asset allocation, two elements of investing that sometimes seem to clash with one another. Market timing depends on quantity, moving in and out of certain securities and funds before market conditions change, which can alter your portfolio's asset allocation. When inexperienced investors move their assets around too often, and at the wrong time, they lose — usually big time.

There may also be some truth to the idea that Canadians tend to be extremely cautious in the field of finance. Renowned for their "prudence" with money, even for outright parsimony, they have somehow managed to produce such big-time entrepreneurs as Jimmy Pattison, the Reichmann brothers, the Richardsons of Winnipeg, Conrad Black and Paul Desmarais.

To invest well in this day and age requires that you run counter to these traditional Canadian characteristics. Most Canadians, especially those affected by the Great Depression, are still fighting the Dirty Thirties in their minds, still restricting investment by their emotional aversion to risk. Today these people unintentionally increase their chances of losing money in their investments by adhering to these outdated ideas of money and security. They ignore the drastic changes in the way money moves in our economy, and like Diogenes, doom themselves to seek continually a safety and security long gone.

Beyond even this, however, there is an even greater psychological threat to investment success. It is our society's obsession with immediate gratification: the sensual, material and emotional syndrome. We expect love without commitment, benefit packages without production requirements. We refuse to accept pain, sacrifice, discipline and effort. If it feels good, do it. Without assurance that I'll win, I won't play. I want the Canadian dream I see in the movies, the one my parents promised me. And I want it *now*.

Psychoanalyst Aaron Stern brilliantly reveals the nature of immediate gratification as immaturity:

> To attain emotional maturity, each of us must learn to develop two critical capacities: the ability to live with uncertainty and the ability to delay immediate gratification in favor of long-range goals.
>
> Adolescence is the time of maximum resistance to further growth. It is a time characterized by the teenager's ingenious efforts to maintain the privileges of childhood while at the same time demanding the rights of adulthood. It is a point beyond which most human beings do not pass emotionally. The more we do for our children, the less they can do for themselves. The dependent child of today is destined to become the dependent parent of tomorrow.

This sums up the attitude of many investors — demanding more and more of the government in benefits and prepared to contribute less and less. The more we ignore the need for responsible risk in our lives, the greater our future risk will be. You insist on current "guarantees" at the expense of your own future security. This is the New Reality.

Your ability to invest with some uncertainty is the key to your financial independence. A willingness to delay immediate gratification and instant results is the first step in the right direction. Patience is the first virtue. All "value investors," demonstrate patience. It is the hallmark of emotional maturity in all of us. We must grow up, and rid ourselves of the obsession with guarantees and immediate gratification. This liberates us to pursue real financial success.

While you can and should save for the down payment on a house, *saving* for retirement is a self-defeating game — you must *invest* for it. *Saving* means *loaning* your money to an institution. *Investing* means *owning* the institution!

The safety of mutual funds lies in their overall record compared with all other types of investment. Canadian savings accounts, in an average five-year period between 1981 and 1995, earned as much as 15.4%, but also dipped to a low of 0.5%. Dividend-paying stocks in Canada within the same average period yielded as much as 79.5% and as little as -19.6%, compared with real estate's high of 26.4% and a low of -7.1%.

> **Stenner's Law #2:** How do you convert $1 into 10 cents over four decades? Invest it in a guaranteed fixed-rate security.

GUARANTEES AREN'T

A guarantee involves degrees of risk, and perhaps more important, one's *perception* of risk. A perception may be just a peering into a glass, darkly, simply failing to see the real risk lying below the surface. "Guaranteed investments" in an inflationary, highly taxed economy may turn out to be guaranteed *losses*.

The Principal Group fiasco in Edmonton in 1987 illustrates the fallacy of guarantee. *Investors holding the company's "guaranteed investment certificates" lost millions of dollars, whereas investors in the mutual funds Principal handled did not lose a nickel.*

You cannot allow your limited perception of short-term financial events to destroy the reality of long-term equity growth. This latter is achievable and far superior to any guaranteed no-win securities.

The Puritan ethic of "work hard, be thrifty, don't borrow" guarantees financial disaster in today's world. In more sophisticated investment terms, so does the Prudent Man Rule, so dear to the hearts of regulatory agencies that decide whether pension funds or other fiduciary responsibilities have been handled wisely.

If, for example, a portfolio is constructed primarily in government and corporate bonds, it would seem to adhere perfectly to the Prudent Man Rule. It's also likely that the holders and their beneficiaries will "lose" a great deal of value.

Why? Because of the continual battering of inflation and the more substantial loss of opportunity in such a tired old portfolio. Yet in Canada today, you will perceive that both Poor Richard's homilies and the rules of the Prudent Man are difficult to escape. The next time you see a poster or brochure advising you to "Invest in Canada Savings Bonds to Guarantee Your Future," consider this: CSBs are simply a vehicle for the federal government to finance its current budget — and a very expensive vehicle at that, especially for you as a taxpayer. From an investment point of view, the cost to you is even higher.

Such posters may verge on false advertising. Can you name any 10-year period in the last half-century when investing in CSBs has guaranteed your future? CSBs are as safe as a church, a convenient place to park funds temporarily, and certainly better than a savings account in a bank. Just don't confuse them with investments that will guarantee your future.

All fixed-rate investments such as GICs and bonds are subject to a number of risks. There is purchasing-power risk (inflation), a 100% guaranteed tax risk that applies every year. There is interest rate reinvestment risk, there is the uncertainty of future market risk, there is political risk, there can be financial risk, and there is liquidity risk. All of these are associated with guaranteed investments which are loans to institutions and governments, not ownership investments.

Even in absolute terms, there may be evidence of, but little comfort in, safety. The venerable Canadian Deposit Insurance Corporation (CDIC) has come under fire for obviating financial institutions' choice of investments. Dr. John Chant, an economics professor at Vancouver's Simon Fraser University, recently presented a report to the Senate Banking Committee stating that deposit insurance may actually increase the chances of a financial institution's failure since it gives such institutions little incentive "to choose their investments prudently."

But more serious is the effect of the CDIC guarantee on the individual investor's attitude. Institutions with risky investments, said Chant, continue to attract depositors simply because they know that as much as $60,000 of each investor's holdings is covered by the

CDIC. People make their decisions not according to the investment merits of the institution, but because of the insurance guarantee.

Certainly, risks abound in the securities markets. Offsetting such risk is the fact that investment securities offer a satisfactory average return over time, even in the most conservative variety, compared with conventional means of saving. Indexes of investments in the U.S. capital markets over the 71-year period ending in 1996 trace an *average* annual return of 12.6% over that period in small-company stocks. A single dollar invested in such an average at the end of 1925 would have returned more than $4,500 by 1996 — even absorbing and riding through the substantial declines of 1929-30, 1937-39, 1946-49, 1969-75 and 1987-90.

Paradoxically, the ultimate risk — the most damaging source of loss — in investing is that of not assuming any risk at all. Ignorance or naïveté, rather than prudence, usually leads a person to select a "no risk" investment, which is a non-investment. Bank deposits, guaranteed investment certificates (GICs), and other loans produce no capital growth, except to the lender (the bank).

> Risk is the potential for loss. Usually, the greater the potential return, the greater the potential for loss. Still, the potential for loss may not be absolute. That's because of two interlocking elements: volatility and time.
>
> — Bruce Cohen, *The Financial Post*
> 14 February 1995

How can we reasonably estimate the potential for loss in various investment securities over different periods? Potential losses decline over increasing time periods as their "safety factor" increases. For example, measured from 1926 to the early 1990s, in a one-year period, the risk of *any* loss was 31% for the Standard & Poor's 500 Composite Index, 32% for small-company stocks, 23% for corporate bonds, 28% for government bonds, and 0% for Treasury Bills. For a five-year period, those chances of loss had declined to 12% for the S&P, 15% for stocks, 5% for corporate bonds, 10% for government bonds, and 0% for T-Bills. And over a 20-year period, all categories had *zero percent* likelihood of loss.

THE WHITE-KNUCKLE SYNDROME

Volatility in this context is not the risk of losing all your money, unless you panic and run for liquidity. Volatility is the risk that an investment's market value strays from the norm, up or down. Volatility is fluctuation. And the fear of fluctuation may be the greatest fear, the greatest risk, that Canadian investors have to overcome.

Remember that fluctuation almost never need mean "loss." Market fluctuation is normal, healthy and even necessary. You pay a terrific price if you insist on demanding a nonfluctuating investment. The threat of outliving your investment says it all. Relying solely on "guarantees" is a fatal mistake in your current and future financial well-being. A guaranteed investment for most people is a guaranteed *loss* after cost-of living increases, yearly taxation and the lost opportunity cost are factored in.

Professional writers rarely distinguish between risk and volatility, even though short-term swings in the price of an asset (volatility) have little or nothing to do with the long-term safety or risk of an investment.

Let me repeat: fluctuation isn't loss. On the other hand, if you choose to panic, to listen to "media risk" and to confuse your temporary negative emotional state with positive historical performance, and make a panicky decision to sell, *that* can produce a loss. Just don't blame it on, or confuse it with, normal fluctuation. And the answer to a panic-prone personality, if you own one, is knowledge and understanding.

Recall the Latin American stock market plunge of late December 1994–January 1995. Triggered by conditions in Mexico, there was a 50% meltdown in some Latin American markets. Canadian investors understandably were scared stiff and either got out or avoided the Latin American markets and Canadian funds holding their stocks.

But those few investors who had knowledgeable financial advisors didn't panic or run scared. In fact, the smart ones, along with professional mutual fund managers, were taking advantage of this decline to increase their Latin American holdings at bargain basement levels, prior to March 1995. I had publicly recommended it on my money talk show. It took courage and guts, but especially common sense. Right up until December 1995, and through 1996 and 1997, I was still recommending Latin American markets and their corresponding mutual funds.

Was it insanity? Latin Americans seem routinely to shoot their leaders, some clients told me. There's so much corruption there. Weren't Mexican banks dropping like flies?

They neglected the fact that Mexico and Latin America generally were and are in a gigantic and unprecedented revolution toward full democracy and privatization. Inflation, rampant in places such as Brazil, has crashed and burned to around 4% annually. The market crash merely produced unlimited opportunity for alert investors. The same people who buy their heads off when "scratch and save" quality merchandise is marked down 50% run for the hills when it happens in the securities markets.

TIP: Whenever the masses of investors ridicule and avoid deep-discount bargains (where there is underlying quality), it's a key signal to jump into real bargains. I won't dwell on the fortunes of those who ran for the hills in early 1995. But the alert investors who bought Latin American funds throughout 1995 and 1996 have been rewarded over the subsequent two years with some returns of 60% to 100%. As this is written in late-1997, Latin America may still well be the most attractive regional market value in the world.

But you've gotta have heart!

Volatility is not all bad. It can increase the gains made by dollar-cost averaging. These people invest a fixed amount of money in mutual funds at fixed intervals. They systematically buy more units when prices are lower and fewer units when prices are high. A high degree of volatility can lower average costs and lead to increased returns when prices rise. Also, volatility decreases as mutual fund investment increases as a percentage of total common stock holdings. (See Table 4.1.)

TABLE 4.1: VOLATILITY, INDIVIDUAL AND MUTUAL FUND HOLDINGS OF STOCKS

Decade	Volatility	Individual*	Mutuals**
1950s	1.46	88%	3%
1960s	1.44	81	4
1970s	2.04	60	4
1980s	2.06	52	5
1990s	1.52	50	10

*Individual holdings of stocks, as a percentage of total stock holdings.
**Mutual fund holdings of stocks as a percentage of total stock holdings.

Source: The WEFA Group

You will find studying volatility helpful. It may give you an idea of future expectations and keep price fluctuations in perspective. A study of standard deviation — a common measure of volatility — indicates that the asset class of common stocks, measured over 40 years from 1953 to 1992, enjoyed an average annual return of 12%, with a standard deviation of (+ or -) 18%, for a possible gain of 30% or a possible loss of 6% in any year.

The other element affecting these returns is time. The longer you hold equities, the better the probability of their improved returns to you and of reduced volatility. (See Figure 4.1.) Time may heal all wounds eventually — and even a battered investment portfolio.

FIGURE 4.1: TIME ECLIPSES VOLATILITY

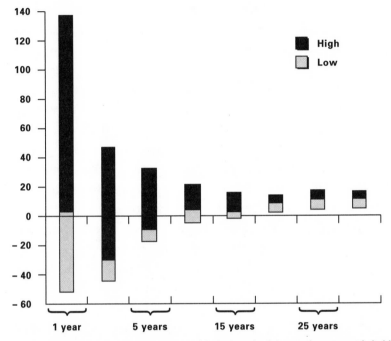

The volatility of the market decreases with the length of time an investment is held.

Source: Twentieth Century Investors

THE WORRY FACTOR

The original word for "worry" comes from the Greek word *merimnao*, a combination of two words: *merizo* meaning "to divide" and *nous*, meaning "mind," which includes our faculties of perceiving, understanding, feeling, judging and determining. Worry means "to divide the mind," to make us unstable in our thought processes.

When it comes to our money decisions, *worry* can divide our emotions, our perceptions and our attitudes. The good news is, you *never* have to worry about your investments. The purpose of this book is to show you why.

Worry can debilitate you and destroy your finances and your physical health. At its most extreme, it can cause heart trouble, high blood pressure, ulcers, arthritis, migraine headaches, nausea, chronic fatigue syndrome and even temporary paralysis.

When it comes to investing your money intelligently and success-fully, you must deal with worry at an early stage. Otherwise, it can render you incapable of action, paralyzed. Worry can divide the mind to the point that it can't make focused, clear decisions.

In a time of low interest rates, these afflicted people will not accept the advice of their financial advisors. They insist their money must be *guaranteed* at all times. They've become investment zombies. Becoming fixated with guarantees will seriously affect your retire-ment peace of mind, as well as erode a huge piece of your capital.

Worry will make you cynical about investing in equities. Worry creates a self-fulfilling prophecy. The slightest comment from anyone — a relative, an accountant, a neighbor — can trigger this response in an investor suffering this kind of inferiority complex. As Job said, "The thing which I greatly feared is come upon me." Only a positive attitude can erase this handicap to an investor's outlook.

In my three decades of advising clients, this is the greatest challenge I face. Self-inflicted phobias are not easily overcome by either a pro-fessional financial advisor or the investor — and sometimes never.

As corny as it may sound, the first antidote to worry is *faith*. "And faith is the *substance* of things hoped for, the *evidence* of things not seen," according to the *Book of Hebrews*, 11: 1-2.

As a financial vehicle, a well-constructed mutual fund portfolio is the best *answer to the investor obsessed with worry. But he or she must understand that any "live" investment fluctuates.* Fluctuation does not necessarily mean loss. GIC vehicles do not fluctuate; nei-ther are they alive. They can produce no capital gain whatsoever. Journalists usually represent "fluctuation" as a negative character-istic. Nothing could be further from the truth. Fluctuation means going "up" as well as down! And the markets typically fluctuate 66% to 75% more up than they do down, historically.

What I call "mind over money" is your psyche as an investor, your awareness of your personal comfort zone and where this should lead in achieving your overall goal. This brings into play basic decisions concerning the *style of your portfolio* — whether the portfolio will strive for maximum growth, moderate growth, moderate income, maximum yield or a balanced approach. Choosing the last of these brings into play portfolio management — asset allocation.

KNOW YOUR FINANCIAL ADVISOR'S STYLE

The active-advisor approach can be fluid. Your advisor may make occasional adjustments (perhaps annually) among the various funds in reaction to corporate developments, and to changes within the industry, the cycle of the domestic economy, and even international developments. At the other extreme, the fund manager in each individual fund may follow a buy-and-hold pattern to try to limit changing the makeup of the portfolio in response to external factors. But the fund manager's changes or the portfolio turnover rate may be more frequent than your advisor's adjustments among the portfolio's funds. An aggressive manager could change (turnover rate) the entire fund portfolio 100% to 250% within one year. A less active manager might turn over, say, as little as 20% of the portfolio.

Substantial arguments can be made for both approaches. The active mode aims to keep the composition of the portfolio most in tune with economic developments, and so do better over any length of time. The opposite argument is that switching too frequently can downgrade the quality of the portfolio. Very generally, sticking with success tends to be more successful than switching for a partial unknown.

Asset Allocation

You and your advisor allocate your overall holdings in percentages among maximum growth funds, growth funds, balanced funds, income funds and other specialties such as foreign and sector funds, according to your own goals and comfort. (See Table 4.2: Potential Portfolio Re-Balancing for Each Phase of the Business Cycle.)

Market Timing — Portfolio Re-Balancing

This refers to strategically allocating assets that will more permanently affect the quality of your portfolio, according to your own taste and objectives, and also according to current market trends and conditions.

Market timing should only represent *modest* adjustments to your portfolio in any given year. You must hang on to the essential core holdings of the portfolio and "weed your garden" at least once each year, perhaps 10%–30% of your overall holdings. You should *never* do wholesale market timing — all in cash, all in equities, all in bonds! That's a huge error many people make and it defeats the whole purpose of asset allocation.

*　　*　　*

A Stenner portfolio depends on both quality control and market timing — such as escalating the proportion of the portfolio in fixed-income fund securities as the interest rate market substantially declines. The former is designed to enhance revenue, the latter to provide defensiveness. If governments stiffen interest rates, these maneuvers can be attractive.

Another difference in asset allocation style may be the extent to which the manager maintains a fully invested position, or retains cash, altering that cash position according to the state of the market. Ideally, the manager should be in the largest cash position at the bottom of a market cycle and fully invested at the top. The discrepancy between this ideal and a static approach to cash inventory also distinguishes between active and passive practitioners of asset allocation.

Superimposed over the active-passive mode of portfolio managers is the basic personalities they bring to their management: by nature are they very bullish, bullish, neutral, bearish, or very bearish? This differs from the active-passive stance. Active-passive determines how managers execute the composition of their client's holdings. Bullish-bearish reflects how they view the market.

TABLE 4.2: POTENTIAL PORTFOLIO RE-BALANCING FOR EACH PHASE OF THE BUSINESS CYCLE

PHASE IN BUSINESS CYCLE	YOUR INVESTOR RISK PROFILE				BEST TYPE OF STOCK FUND	BEST TYPE OF BOND FUND
	CONSERVATIVE	MODERATE	AGGRESSIVE			
PHASE ONE <u>EARLY RECOVERY</u> Economy Expanding Inflation Falling or Low	45% Stock Funds* 45% Bonds 10% Cash	65% Stock Funds 30% Bonds 5% Cash	80% Stock Funds 20% Bonds 0% Cash		Small-Cap Growth	Intermediate
PHASE TWO <u>LATE RECOVERY</u> Economy Growing Inflation Rising or High	35% Stock Funds 35% Bonds 30% Cash	50% Stock Funds 35% Bonds 15% Cash	60% Stock Funds 20% Bonds 20% Cash		Small-Cap Value Natural Resources	Short-Term
PHASE THREE <u>STAGFLATION</u> Economy Slowing Inflation Rising or High	25% Stock Funds 40% Bonds 35% Cash	40% Stock Funds 40% Bonds 20% Cash	50% Stock Funds 20% Bonds 30% Cash		Large-Cap Value	Short-Term
PHASE FOUR <u>RECESSION</u> Economy Slowing Inflation Falling	35% Stock Funds 50% Bonds 15% Cash	50% Stock Funds 40% Bonds 10% Cash	60% Stock Funds 30% Bonds 10% Cash		Large-Cap Growth	Long-Term

*Note: "Stock" allocations may include real estate equity assets.
Both asset classes are "equities."

PANIC-PROOF INVESTING

By now you have psyched yourself up about building and maintaining a good attitude about investing. You will adhere to the careful strategy you build, especially if you have chosen to emphasize active asset allocation in the makeup of your portfolio. You still need a few pointers about panic-proofing yourself. Abiding by these defensive rules will help you hold your course in most markets for the long haul.

Rule #1: *Screw your head on backwards.* Keep your eye on past performance as a guide and to remind you of past mistakes. Also, be aware of hazards that might be overtaking you. Investment is a process that takes place not only within current value and price, but also within the third dimension of time. Time may not heal all things, but it can go a long way toward mitigating risk.

Rule #2: *A strong defence is a good offense.* Establish a strong portfolio along defensive lines and you will protect it better from market turbulence. Rather than investing for highest gain on the upside, you're trying to minimize your losses in bad markets. There are specific strategies you can employ to protect much of your portfolio which we'll be addressing later on.

Rule #3: *Develop an "all-weather" approach.* Equate your panic-proof philosophy with an investment insurance policy. The only premium required is your initial care and feeding of the portfolio with the proper defensive characteristics and the balance of assets to meet *any* market conditions. Unlike life insurance, you don't have to pay premiums for years in order to cash in.

Rule #4: *Smooth out the ride* by employing the reverse of the leverage principle. With leverage you use borrowed or outside capital to expand your financial base. Along the way this creates wide gyrations as your commitments expand and contract. Smooth your way along by employing a mix of safe, stable investments against which you set more aggressive holdings. Less turbulence means more peace of mind.

Rule #5: *Select only the best "risk-adjusted" funds*. I've already mentioned the principle of choosing stocks or a stock for downside strength rather than performance. I can go further — don't invest with an eye *primarily* on upside performance. If you select a mutual fund or portfolio properly, one that will reduce risk when the market declines, the upside will take care of itself. (See Table 4.3.)

Rule #6: *Build a sleep-well-at-night portfolio*. That means one reasonably limited in large risks that would otherwise keep you tossing and turning at night.

Shakespeare would have been an exemplary panic-proof investor:

> Thou hast no figures nor no fantasies
> Which busy care draws in the brains
> Therefore thou sleep'st so sound.

> *Julius Caesar* (II,i)

TABLE 4.3: LARGE CAP VS. SMALL CAP: BEST MUTUAL FUNDS FOR CHANGING MARKETS

	Best Mutual Funds for Economy Slowing Down **LARGE CAP**	Best Mutual Funds for Economy Speeding Up **SMALL CAP**
Focus	Emphasis on large companies well-established.	Emphasis on small, emerging start-up companies.
Company Characteristics	• Reliable sales and dividends • Size of $5 billion and above	• Sales and earnings fluctuate • Dividends are minor • Size of $1 billion or less
Risk	• Usually diversified so risk is low	• Undiversified so volatility of earnings and risk is high
Return	• Moderate returns that include dividends	• No dividends but potential high or low capital appreciation
Performance Periods	• Tends to perform better on a relative basis when economy is slowing down	• Tends to perform better on a relative basis when economy is speeding up

chapter 5 | FACING THE NEW REALITY

Equity mutual funds are Canada's next investment boom.

— Professor David Foot, *Boom, Bust & Echo*

BOOMERNOMICS

In *The Great Boom Ahead*, Harry S. Dent, Jr., wrote: "Two generations ago, Henry Ford's generation ushered in the economy that was
extended to its present maturity by the Bob Hope generation. Baby
boomers are introducing a new economy that will be extended by the
following generation.

"What will this economy look like? It will assume the personality
of the baby boomers at the outset. Throughout our history we've seen
this alternating generation cycle. You will always see an inner-
directed, individualistic, entrepreneurial generation followed by an
outer-directed, conformist, more civic-minded generation. . . . The
baby boom generation is the current example of an inner-directed
generation. So the millennium generation will be the next conformist
generation.

"Each new economy follows the same four-stage cycle of innovation, growth boom, shakeout, and maturity boom."

Currently we have David K. Foot's brilliant book *Boom, Bust & Echo*, a best-seller articulating demographics as "the most powerful and most underutilized tool we have to understand the past and to foretell the future."

"In Canada," says Professor Foot, "the aging of those born between 1947 and 1966 — the baby boomer generation — has changed the economy, driven housing and other markets and transformed social mores and lifestyles. As the boomers enter mid-life, as the 'baby boomers' behind them come of age, and as the 'echo generation,' the children of the boomers, reaches maturity, how will the country change?

"Demographics are about everyone: who you are, where you've been, and where you're going. Demographics explain about two-thirds of everything: which products will be in demand, where job opportunities will occur, what school enrolments will be, when house values will rise or drop, what kinds of food people will buy and what kinds of cars they will drive."

In his chapter on "Demographic Investing," Foot states: "Because there are so many baby boomers, they exert a dramatic impact on markets. The reason is simple: people of the same age tend to have the same needs at about the same time, eyeglasses being one example. Whether you are a boomer or not, you can make money anticipating those needs. That is demographics-based investing.

"The minivan, the wheels of the baby boom, turned Chrysler Corporation into a profitable carmaker. Yet at the time this new vehicle was being developed, Chrysler's stock was worth only US$2 and its management was begging for government help to fend off bankruptcy. At the same time, General Motors and Ford also had minivan prototypes in the planning stages. But Chrysler moved first, launching the Magic Wagon in 1983. In the mid-1990s, its stock has been trading at around US$50."

The real estate meltdown in Ontario was devastating, with the shocking failures of some of the largest office and real estate developers such as Olympia and York, Campeau Corp., Bramalea and Trizec. Because there had been a 30-year trend in real estate did not mean the trend would last forever; the great developers were simply not in touch with the new demographics.

Garth Turner, former Canadian minister of National Revenue, declares in his *1997 RRSP Guide*, "The unfortunate part is that most Canadians have most of their wealth in the wrong type of assets — namely, their homes. With the trend from real assets to financial assets, real estate has a dark future. In a decade, many houses will not be worth the mortgages placed upon them. But tax-sheltered funds, bonds and stocks will explode in value. Mortgage or RRSP? There is no contest."

Professor Foot comments: "Once the bulk of the baby boom generation is in its retirement years, even homes in Canada's most desirable neighborhoods — such as Shaughnessy [Vancouver], Rockcliffe Park [Ottawa] and Forest Hill [Toronto] — will decline in value."

Bill Sterling, chairman and CEO of the large mutual fund and private wealth management firm BEA Associates in New York, is credited with having invented the term "boomernomics." In 1995, during a discussion on my Vancouver radio show, Sterling said: "Competing against each other, baby boomers pushed up the price of cars, furniture and other goods. That helped create double-digit inflation. Competing against each other, they pushed up the price of money. That helped create double-digit interest rates. Competing against each other, they pushed up the price of houses. That helped create a massive bull market in real estate which lasted until the late 1980s, and in Vancouver until about 1993."

As I've said on my Saturday morning radio show over the past three or four years, the days of rapid and huge increases in house prices are gone. The real estate boom was finished five years ago!

"Vancouverites," concludes Foot, "would do well to avoid smugness. British Columbia has had severe recessions in the past and will not be immune from them in the future. Moreover, the prosperity of the real estate industry and that of the rest of us is not one and the same thing. A mere increase in a city's size does not mean that the incomes and well-being of the people who live there also increase. If it did, then the citizens of huge cities such as Mexico City and Calcutta would be wealthier than those of smaller ones such as Vancouver and Geneva."

So where is the best place for Canadians to invest their money today?

Garth Turner: "TIP: you are far better off to invest in the stock market directly through equity-based mutual funds. These are professionally managed funds that spread investors' risk by investing in scores of various stocks in Canada, North America and around the world. Not only will you benefit from the long-term growth of the stock market, but you will be paid income in the form of capital gains, not interest. So, if the funds are ever held outside your RRSP, the income they generate will have much less tax exposure."

David Foot: "Equity mutual funds are Canada's next investment boom."

LIVING LONGER

Most Canadians are forced to ask themselves the same question as they near the age of retirement: "Will my savings, investments and income last as long as I do?"

Canadians have always been diligent in "putting money aside." While Canadians *save* nearly twice as much as their American counterparts do, the opposite is true when it comes to *investing* in stocks and other equity securities.

Now higher taxes, employment insecurity and lower interest rates have forced many Canadians, particularly those of limited means, onto a sort of Procrustean bed.

Canadian investors in particular have been given the painful choice of either stretching their meager incomes from bank interest or GICs to meet their needs, or of seeing the head and feet of their capital lopped off as they sprawl in investment postures they don't understand.

FIGURE 5.1: AVERAGE HOUSEHOLD INCOMES IN CANADA (1996) BY AGE GROUP

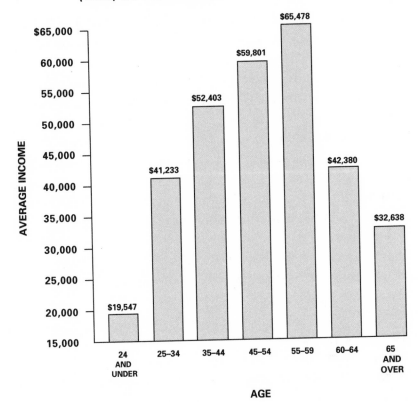

Source: Statistics Canada

Ottawa, too, expects people to stretch their personal finances to accommodate escalating taxation while chopping every tax escape route. And to save the Canada Pension Plan, the federal government is hiking contributions to unprecedented levels.

Peter Cook, the astute financial columnist for *The Globe and Mail*, comments on growing old and insolvent ("Strike It Rich Or You'll Die Poor"): "In the age of the death of social security and the slow extinction of both safe jobs and personal savings, most of us face a pretty horrifying dilemma."

He paints a picture of the disenchanted baby boomer, bereft of a government safety net and without adequate income and investments.

Cook, while dead right in his analysis of the problem, offers no solutions.

He outlines the alternatives available to elderly investors: (1) chasing the highest current past performance numbers; (2) choosing among a huge array of mutual funds — 1,500 or so — utterly unknown to them; (3) entering emerging markets, represented, Cook writes, by the deflated Mexican peso; and (4) counting on savings accounts and GICs, which Cook does not mention precisely. He concludes that "an aging population is rapidly realizing that its nest is devoid of eggs."

Good news is at hand. Peter Cook is right on the money but wrong on mutual funds. Although he does not recommend investing in the hundreds of Canadian mutual funds, even a modest investor can profit from this brave, new universe of multifund, triple-advisor combinations.

Surrendering to the bed of Procrustes — or to Peter Cook's gloomy prognosis — is not the way to get a good night's sleep.

THE FACTS OF LEVERAGE

The field of real estate has long recognized the leverage factor. This principle adapts well to mutual funds. Home buyers know that they can leverage capital appreciation with, say, a 70% mortgage on a $300,000 house. This way their equity of $90,000 actually yields a 33.3% gain when prices in the housing market increase by 10%.

Depending on the available interest rate and other market risks, a mutual fund investor can achieve leverage similar to that of the home buyer by applying borrowed capital to an investment. The relatively low interest rates at the moment may enhance this financial strategy. Whether or not you should borrow to increase the amount you invest in mutual funds is a difficult decision. To make it you must understand fully all of the potential risks associated with leverage. Some of the largest fortunes in history have been made by using leverage. So have some of the greatest misfortunes.

First, understand the risk/reward behavior characteristics of the particular mutual fund you are borrowing for. Second, ask yourself if you can handle a drop in the market. Furthermore, do you have enough cash flow to cover the interest cost of a leverage loan if the market sinks into a prolonged decline? Will your mutual fund portfolio be properly balanced? And are you in a relatively high tax bracket? The higher, the better.

Many investors use a part of their home equity as collateral for a loan to purchase mutual funds. This requires that you hold clear title to your house. One national financial institution will arrange as much as a 200% loan against your mutual fund portfolio. Under such an agreement, you would pay only the interest indefinitely. Revenue Canada permits you to claim this interest expense on your income tax return, unlike regular mortgage interest on your house, which you cannot deduct at all. You greatly increase your market risk, as well as your chances of profiting on such an arrangement as a "two-for-one" loan (200%). Do I recommend such a high-ratio loan? Definitely not! But, the potential for substantially increasing your equity is there. Clearly, so is the risk. If you've decided to leverage, 30% of the equity on a clear-titled house should be excellent for most investors. And, the mortgage interest can be 100% tax deductible!

A final note: According to the Investment Funds Institute of Canada, approximately 20% of all Canadian mutual fund purchases are leveraged.

Stenner's Law #3: Leverage is a two-way street.

THE CALL OF RETIREMENT

We all know that rising unemployment and a shrinking demand for labor have led to widespread early retirement in this age of automation. More and more couples in their fifties are accepting early retirement packages offered by their employers. This accelerated migration from the workforce and regular income underscores the importance of careful, early, knowledgeable and aggressive saving and investment planning techniques.

As a "conservative" investor, your financial success really depends on your definition of two basic, vital concepts: *risk* and *safety*. If you do not understand risk and safety, you can literally destroy your financial dreams.

The old question "Is it guaranteed?" has for many people seeking reasonable income become a trite and meaningless question in today's new financial reality. The real issue is to define "safety" — protecting purchasing power after taxes and inflation — and "certainty," that is, someone guaranteeing that they'll always give you back the purchasing power of your dollar.

With Canadians now living on average several years longer after retirement than their parents or grandparents did, and with the government opting out of the primary support of subsistence pensions, the new reality is quite clear: the loss of our principal in our lifetime is no longer the main risk. The greatest risk is in outliving our money and its purchasing power by not investing in ownership (equity) investments. Given this, the imperative to invest becomes self-evident: only equities and common stocks — preferably those enclosed in mutual fund programs — can produce the growth and the balance over a long term that can meet our future requirements.

This demographic shift, coupled with the advancing juggernaut of national debt and even First Nations land settlements suggests financial disaster on a national and international scale. John Plender of the *Financial Times* of London dubs the whole social change as "the gray crisis." As in hair. As in you and me.

He points out that the "lean and slipper'd" senior citizen of

Shakespeare's day enjoyed the best possible pension scheme — many children. In contrast, Canadians combat a shrinking labor force and declining fertility rates in this age of increasing life expectancy with social welfare and more sophisticated technology. The modern family cannot take care of its own senior members, while it is increasingly called upon to support them. At the same time it must continue to contribute to current and future pensions, at higher cost, for lower payouts.

Many people do not realize that current pension payments do not fund future benefits. Rather, these are applied to current payouts. According to Plender, "the over-generosity of benefits has been further disguised by a monumental failure of public accounting, whereby the real future cost of pension promises does not appear on the face of government budgets."

Currently, Canadian pensioners receive "found money," since they receive an outstanding return even if they themselves made relatively small contributions during their working lives. They now enjoy possibly the best investment in our history.

One group of researchers in the civil service pension fund has determined that if the undeclared liabilities implicit in future pension promises were factored in, public debt would double as a percentage of Canada's gross domestic product.

The aging crisis or "gray crisis" may present the greatest problem we face as a society. It threatens the very basis of our collective protection and stability. If the budgetary and debt problem is not resolved, inflationary and financial havoc could result.

Existing pension and other social schemes were designed for a world of stable prices, long-term employment, and steady industrial conditions. All of those pillars of support have been cracking in recent years. One problem, the incentive to retire early, can be reversed. This would allow healthy older people to work beyond age 65 or 70.

The basic problem posed by the New Reality is that middle-aged people will have to be more active in arranging their own finances as they anticipate retirement. Disaster looms, projecting that problem onto a national level.

Financial analysts in the 1980s were already predicting a windfall of inheritance for the post-boomer generation. Those chickens may or may not hatch, depending on how prudently current seniors guard their capital for their offspring. They may choose to spend it on improving their golf handicaps in Palm Springs and Palm Beach, and in cruising the Caribbean.

The answer may fall somewhere in between these two extremes. Governments at all levels can do a great deal to resolve this whole dilemma according to the degree of social and financial planning they apply to their policies over the next decade. Just recently, the Canadian government has begun to address the CPP problem, considering much larger contributions by working Canadians, reduced benefits for retirees, and overall greater fiscal responsibility in managing the plan. It remains to be seen whether these steps will be enough to save the whole plan. I predict that, unless government gets out of the primary "job creation" business and turns this responsibility over to the private sector, and creates more major tax incentives for the average Canadian investor, the problem will come back to haunt us. It is *small* free-enterprise that creates most of the jobs in this country. This must become the future trend.

A SHIFT IN THE COLLECTIVE PSYCHE?

A shift in the collective investment psyche may be in the works. The proof lies in the mushrooming number of subscribers to new mutual funds.

The individual investor's interest in stocks and bonds, and particularly mutual funds, will grow in leaps and bounds. If we are indeed in the initial phase of a 50-year cycle of comparatively low interest rates, as some analysts suggest, the stock markets of the world will continue to provide the best opportunities for people to create wealth over the longer term.

Consider the series of five-year moving averages in Tables 5.1 through 5.3. These include all major investment categories and their historic rates of return — savings accounts, 90-day deposits, Canada Savings Bonds, five-year GICs, mortgages, bonds, dividend-bearing stocks and real estate, in addition to the indexes of Canadian, U.S., Japanese, European and Pacific growth investments.

The performance reviews draw a compelling picture. The averages range from 15.4% to 0.5% for the highest and lowest one-year return on savings accounts to 130.5% and -41.4%, the highest and lowest one-year return in the Japanese index. Once you accept that you have to seek equities for the most robust growth, you are confronted with selecting from a wide range of investments. Now that we understand *what* the senior investor should pursue, he or she must define *how* to do so. That selection will encompass the mutual fund areas that will best meet that person's income and growth criteria. These I call the New Reality Funds.

TABLE 5.1: MINIMAL REWARD/RISK VARIANCE: NEAR-CASH INVESTMENTS

INVESTMENT TYPE	AVERAGE 5 YEARS Jan. 1/81 to Dec. 31/95 Annual Return	VARIABILITY	
		Highest 1-Year Return	Lowest 1-Year Return
Savings Accounts	6.1%	15.4% Jan./82	0.5% Dec./94
90-Day Deposits	9.6%	19.5% Jan./82	4.6% Feb./94
Canada Savings Bonds	10.1%	19.5% Dec./82	4.3% Dec./94
5-Year GICs	10.5%	17.5% Apr./82	6.2% Feb./94
Inflation	4.1%	12.0% May/82	(0.2)% May/94

TABLE 5.2: MEDIUM REWARD/RISK VARIANCE: INCOME INVESTMENTS

INVESTMENT TYPE	INCOME YIELD Average 5 Years Jan. 1/81 to Dec.31/95	TOTAL ANNUAL RETURN Average 5 Years Jan. 1/81 to Dec. 31/95	VARIABILITY Highest 1-Year Return	Lowest 1-Year Return
Mortgages	12.0%	12.5%	34.8% Mar./83	(2.0)% Jan./95
Bonds	11.5%	14.7%	55.6% Jun./83	(10.4)% Jan./95
Dividend Stocks	6.2%	12.8%	79.5% Jun./83	(19.6)% Jun./82
Real Estate	7.1%	8.5%	26.4% Jan./82	(7.1)% Sept./93
Inflation	4.1%	4.1%	12.0% May/82	(0.2)% May/94

TABLE 5.3: MAXIMUM REWARD/RISK VARIANCE: EQUITY INVESTMENTS

INVESTMENT TYPE	AVERAGE 5 YEARS Jan. 1/81 to Dec. 31/95 Annual Return	VARIABILITY Highest 1-Year Return	Lowest 1-Year Return
Canadian Index	9.6%	86.9% Jun./83	(39.2)% Jun./82
U.S. Index	16.0%	56.9% Jul./83	(22.8)% Aug./88
Japanese Index	18.5%	130.2% Aug./86	(41.4)% Sept./90
World Index	16.5%	69.8% Aug./86	(22.8)% Sept./90
Europe Index	18.8%	112.5% Apr./86	(23.2)% Aug./88
Pacific Ex Japan Index	15.9%	106.8% Mar./87	(31.3)% Nov./82
Inflation	4.1%	12.0% May/82	(0.2)% May/94

Sources: Bank of Montreal, S&P, TSE and CANSIM/STATSCAN

chapter 6

INVESTING IN VALUE

*True value investors pay little attention to market trends
and the predictions of financial experts. Finding undervalued
companies is more productive than reading headlines.*

— Thomas Hansberger

Canadians tend to take their problems to professionals, often out of necessity. If it's a divorce, we need a lawyer. If it's a family crisis, a counselor or minister is asked to help. This is often the case in the investment process. Like those Canadians who employ do-it-yourself divorce kits or seek self-help solutions, such as holistic or homeopathic approaches to healing, a minority of individual investors opt to call some of the shots in building their portfolios. Like driving a sophisticated sports car, it's not necessary to understand *everything* under the hood, although it definitely helps.

Even inexperienced investors sense what should be done, and an *experienced* financial advisor can help them do the right thing. *An individually constructed portfolio is Number One. It must be designed and constructed, it must be defended, and it must be managed.*

THE STENNER 15-POINT RISK EVALUATION SCALE

Designing your portfolio involves (1) placing yourself on the Stenner 15-point risk evaluation scale; (2) looking objectively at your personality profile as you have defined it; and (3) clothing it with the right mutual funds.

Your first job as an investor, whether working closely with a financial advisor or not, is to apply the right criteria in evaluating your potential mutual fund investments. Then you can make the key investment decisions. Most investors lack the qualifications, knowledge or experience to do this for themselves. They lack the "Three Big T's" of Time, Training and Temperament. Your advisor's first responsibility is to ask you a series of precise questions and to listen carefully to your answers and comments. Only after you've completed this process can you and your advisor define and structure an appropriate plan to meet your needs.

The criteria for any investment may involve any or all of these:

1. Risk
2. Potential Profit
3. Volatility
4. Cost
5. Leverage
6. Income
7. Inflation
8. Liquidity
9. Expertise
10. Monitoring
11. Taxation
12. Potential Collateral
13. Potential Loss
14. Market Timing
15. Other Factors: fraud (Bre-X, anyone?), negligence, poor research

Some of these factors carry more weight than others, depending on the individual. A professional advisor can cite general rules, which must be balanced against your individual disposition. Objectivity, safety, appreciation and income are the most critical factors for almost every investor, particularly those in the medium income bracket and who are moderately conservative. An investor with more assets and higher income might opt for leverage and higher profit potential, as well as more attractive tax benefits. A person with a lower income might be more concerned about liquidity.

The financial advisor plays several roles — psychologist, risk management specialist, educator, technician, paralegal, investment tax counselor and market trend analyst. A beginning investor may be confused or uncertain about setting appropriate financial objectives, and so will rely on the advice of a professional financial advisor. The novice investor who examines the detailed discussion of investment criteria that follows, and extracts the five or six most important for him or her, will have gone a long way to designing a sturdy foundation for an individual portfolio.

Those who omit applying this careful self-evaluation are more susceptible to the overtures of product promoters, because they don't know where they stand. The evaluation process insulates you against greed and fear, the enemies of sound investment.

> "Would you tell me please which way I ought to go from here?" asked Alice.
> "That depends a great deal on where you want to get to," answered the Cheshire Cat.
> — Lewis Carroll, *Alice in Wonderland*

For a graphic illustration of these investment criteria, see Chapter 16.

The Risk Factor

Although it's a vague term, "risk management" can be quantified. For example, a bank savings account has a relatively high safety factor, particularly within the $60,000 maximum the Canadian Deposit Insurance Corporation (CDIC) insures. By comparison, the Canadian Investor Protection Fund (CIPF) may protect investors against loss of between $2.75 million and $3.5 million through fraud or financial failure. Here, too, the guarantee applies to the principal only. It offers no guard against inflation, taxation, or the loss of other opportunities and potential profits.

In contrast, commodities offer a low safety factor. Their unusual profit potential might offset this. (In fact, running down our list, commodities show high risk in return for their high potential; they provide no income and no inflation protection and are of doubtful liquidity. They are characterized by their volatility, moderate cost and high leverage. They require a high degree of expertise, extremely precise timing, and constant monitoring. They carry tax implications and collateral possibilities, and could be subject to potentially huge losses as well as a range of other factors from sudden market developments to swift changes to the proverbial price of tea in China.)

Midway between such extremes, better-grade common stocks can best be described as moderate; they offer moderate safety, moderate volatility, good liquidity, and the prospect of above-average returns.

Potential Profit

Savings accounts never appreciate in capital value. They may pay interest, but the principal value of your $1,000 deposit today will still be $1,000 ten years from now. Given a dollar in 2005 worth 80 cents, your $1,000 of today will have depreciated in real purchasing power to $800. A commodities contract, with its low margin requirement, can produce outstanding gains, perhaps 50% per annum. You know the flip side. But we're talking potential here. Residential real estate in a good urban area in a moderate market can appreciate 10% to 15% a year. Moderate, on our scale. Although, let's not forget the over-inflated real estate carnage from 1982 to 1985, where Vancouver residential real estate fell 50% to 60% in 1982 to 1984 alone.

Common stocks can be moderate or outstanding. In the decade

between 1967 and 1977, the Dow Jones Industrial Average increased by a mere 10%, or 1% per annum. Between the fall of 1994 and the summer of 1995, the same average climbed by 50%. You can't buy the Dow Jones, but you can approximate it. Standard & Poor's Index mutual fund contains holdings that closely parallel the listings on the New York Stock Exchange. Invest in that fund, and you'll experience all the thrills and chills of the Big Board.

So, why not throw this book away and buy an S&P 500 or TSE 300 Index fund? As I've already said, the Dow Jones, or the S&P 500, does not uniformly do that well, year over year. A good number of mutual funds do. If there had been an S&P 500 Index Fund in 1967 and you had bought it, you would have kicked yourself for the next decade.

Index funds are a lot like flying on automatic pilot. Personally, I much prefer to hear a live voice announce from the cockpit, "This is your captain speaking. We'll be passing through some turbulence shortly, but it won't last long" . . . something along the lines a skilled financial advisor or mutual fund portfolio manager might say to you.

The Volatility Fluctuation Factor

You may not wish to swing with a volatile market. I've talked about appreciation; volatility refers both to appreciation and its mirror image — depreciation. Canada Savings Bonds (CSBs) provide zero volatility. They provide a modicum of income and a pretty certificate. They enable our federal government to go further into debt. Volatile investments such as commodities and to a lesser degree common stocks can sink as much and as often as they can rise. CSBs do neither. They maintain a static value. If purchasing power itself were also static, CSBs would be a much more rewarding savings vehicle.

All of the other investment securities on the spectrum lie somewhere in between. Figure 6.1 illustrates volatility in bond yields; Figure 6.2 demonstrates how bond *prices* react *inversely* to market yield changes.

FIGURE 6.1: VOLATILITY IN INTEREST RATES

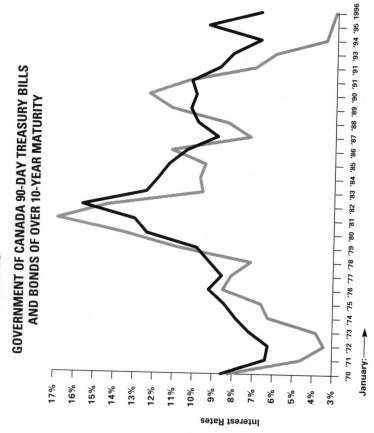

GOVERNMENT OF CANADA 90-DAY TREASURY BILLS AND BONDS OF OVER 10-YEAR MATURITY

90-Day Treasury Bills

Long Canada Bonds

Interest Rates

January:

'70 '71 '72 '73 '74 '75 '76 '77 '78 '79 '80 '81 '82 '83 '84 '85 '86 '87 '88 '89 '90 '91 '93 '94 '95 1996

Source: Bank of Canada

FIGURE 6.2: HOW BOND PRICES REACT TO MARKET YIELD CHANGES — INVERSELY

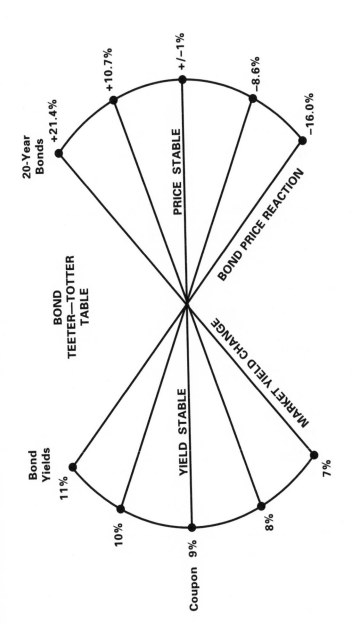

Above figures based on 9% par value bonds.

The Cost Factor

Often investors don't consider this obvious criterion as thoroughly as they should. What does it cost you to have a savings account? Nothing. You just hand over your money to the institution. There are ongoing costs — for example, service charges. Of course, the "real" cost attached to savings accounts is the enormous loss of its value to low yield, lost opportunities and taxation.

Penny Wise, Pound Foolish

How about the cost of real estate? If you have a resourceful real estate agent, you may buy a house with nothing down. Really? What do you call that mountain of up-front, compounding interest? What of liquidity cost? The real estate market goes down, you need your equity, demand is slow . . . what do you do?

The cost of securities transactions? You pay for stocks, bonds and mutual funds, usually through acquisition costs, in the form of commissions, brokerage fees or spreads. (See Chapter 15 on commission costs.) In most cases, mutual funds may be purchased with *zero* front-end cost and on a deferred-cost basis, and typically after six to seven years, redeemed at no cost. No cost to buy; no cost to sell. And a top financial advisor comes with the package.

Oh yes, you can also withdraw up to 10% per annum with a contingent deferred sales charge (DSC) fund over a six- or seven-year period — at no cost. And, there are often unlimited free transfers (that is, no commission is charged) between all funds within each "family group."

According to Oscar Wilde, a cynic is "a man who knows the price of everything, and the value of nothing." That might apply if we were assessing a Renaissance masterpiece; it hardly applies to a mutual fund. In no other sector of financial services are cost and value so closely linked. In the case of mutual funds, knowing the *price* reveals its value. Each dollar of cost reduces the return by that precise amount, although the amount of the return widely varies.

Otherwise, you might conclude that you should always buy the lowest cost mutual fund, which would be foolish.

Lower cost *may* mean higher returns, other things being equal. But, as in most walks of life, other things are not always equal. This is the "free lunch" syndrome. Always ask first of your mutual fund portfolio: "What does it pay?" — not "What does it cost?"

The Leverage Factor

Leverage is a wide-ranging term in the securities markets, and it carries with it a variety of interpretations. In general it means investing — in a house, commodity, the stock market — by putting other people's money to work for you.

"Trading on the equity" is an entrepreneurial term that dates back to the 19th century. Let's say I have a $10,000 investment in a business. I can expand my operating capital by borrowing $100,000 from my mother-in-law, agreeing to pay her 10% on the loan. I in turn am able to earn 15% on the total capital, including her money. I am *leveraging* the equity I have 10 times over.

Of course, if I pay my mother-in-law 15% and am only able to earn 10% overall, I may shortly lose not only my business, but also my mother-in-law, not to mention my wife. This is known as "reverse leverage" — or eventual bankruptcy. "If my outgo exceeds my income, the outcome will be my downfall," as a sage once said.

Everyone is familiar with the principle of leverage applied to residential real estate. You buy a $200,000 house with a downpayment of 25% of the price — $50,000 — and hold a $150,000 mortgage. Your equity in the house is $50,000. If the house goes up in value by 10%, the actual capital gain on your equity is the full $20,000, or 100%. In other words, you now have $70,000 in equity, courtesy of leverage. If the value drops 10%, the amount of equity drops to $30,000, a decline in equity of 40%.

In addition to the leverage you can obtain by borrowing, there is a leverage, less dramatic, produced by market levels. You benefit from the leverage of *dollar-cost averaging* by regularly depositing a fixed sum of money in your investment, regardless of the market's performance. You can buy growth mutual funds at all levels as a matter of routine. Price itself supplies the leverage. Similarly, mutual funds often declare stock dividends that are automatically reinvested. As the market value of those shares moves up, the holders enjoy the automatic leverage of additional shares working in their portfolios. Typically, you'd want to invest in a fairly volatile, aggressive mutual fund for the longer term to acquire more shares when markets are down by using dollar-cost averaging. The more volatility the better during the accumulation stage.

Real-estate operators employ a well-known leverage technique known as "flipping." It may stand as the ultimate legal leverage. A speculator acquires a property and then "flips" it at a profit before having to pay its full, original cost. The leverage base here is zero, so the percentage profit is beyond calculation. But, given a market that moves against the flipper, the flipping of a coin is conservative by comparison.

The Income Factor

Nothing is quite as satisfactory as income — except capital gain. Income makes life bearable for most of us every two weeks. Income in the securities markets is expressed in percentages: 0% in a growth mutual fund or in a non-rental house that you occupy, perhaps 5% in a dividend-paying mutual fund, monthly or quarterly income from a bond mutual fund, a high-yield income fund, and so on. Don't confuse income with the return you gain on the appreciation of your capital. Income is assured in most market conditions; capital gain may or may not happen every year. Taken together, we refer to the two as "total return."

The rate of income is not absolute. Dividends on Canadian stocks are more valuable in the hands of the holder than the equivalent amount of interest income, since the government allows a tax credit on the former. Consider this the government's recognition that the company pays dividends on its shares (equities) after tax, whereas corporations pay interest on bonds (debt obligations) before paying their own taxes.

The Inflation Factor

Venita Van Caspel, in her excellent book *Money Dynamics for the 1990s*, refers to "an investment recommended by many." It is equally applicable to Canadian investors.

If I were to say to you, "I want to recommend an investment for your serious consideration. I know that its record hasn't been very good, but I have faith that it will improve. This investment was selling for $100 in 1957; by 1961 it had dropped to $96; by 1966 to $88; by 1971 to $79; by 1976 to $50; by 1981 to $30 and by 1988 to $26. Today, it is worth about $18, but don't let that discourage you from investing in it, because I understand that it is now declining at a much slower rate."

How would you respond to such a buy recommendation? Before you do, perhaps in language unsuitable for family reading, I want to point out that this investment is recommended by most of our federal and provincial governments, banks, trust companies, insurance companies and credit unions. This investment is a good old Canadian $100 dollar bill as issued in 1957, and represented nowadays with that forlorn icon, the loonie.

On the other hand, you may reply, "Yes, but inflation is running much lower these days than it was five or 10 years ago." True, thanks to the Bank of Canada's initiative since 1991, but so are guaranteed fixed-rate returns! Particularly when you factor in the recent *combined* spousal formula for calculating your tax bracket and Minister of Finance Paul Martin's huge tax grab.

Although the Bank of Canada in recent years has done an outstanding job of mitigating the effects of inflation within the Canadian economy, many people still consider inflation a constant in our lives. No one is more aware of this than investors contemplating parking their capital somewhere for future use. It means little in real terms to say "Here is $100,000 which I will need for my retirement in 2005." The immediate response is, "What will the purchasing power be in 2005?" Table 6.1 illustrates how inflation deflates the purchasing power of one dollar, at various rates of inflation, and over various periods of time. More graphically, Figure 6.3 shows the *real* loss of purchasing power of one dollar ($1) since 1945. Figure 6.4 pictures the Canadian inflation rate and Consumer Price Index (CPI) over the past decade.

TABLE 6.1: THE INFLATION FACTOR

Years from now	If annual rate of inflation is:							
	3%	4%	5%	6%	7%	8%	9%	10%
1	$1.03	$1.04	$1.05	$1.06	$1.07	$1.08	$1.09	$1.10
2	1.06	1.08	1.10	1.12	1.14	1.17	1.19	1.21
3	1.09	1.13	1.16	1.19	1.23	1.26	1.30	1.33
4	1.13	1.17	1.22	1.26	1.31	1.36	1.41	1.46
5	1.16	1.22	1.28	1.34	1.40	1.47	1.54	1.61
6	1.19	1.27	1.34	1.42	1.50	1.59	1.68	1.77
7	1.23	1.32	1.41	1.50	1.61	1.71	1.83	1.95
8	1.27	1.37	1.48	1.59	1.72	1.85	1.99	2.14
9	1.31	1.42	1.55	1.69	1.84	2.00	2.17	2.36
10	1.34	1.48	1.63	1.79	1.97	2.16	2.37	2.59
15	1.56	1.80	2.08	2.40	2.76	3.17	3.64	4.18
20	1.81	2.19	2.65	3.21	3.87	4.66	5.60	6.73
25	2.09	2.67	3.39	4.29	5.43	6.85	8.62	10.83
30	2.45	3.24	4.32	5.74	7.61	10.06	13.27	17.45

FIGURE 6.3: 50 YEARS OF INFLATION IN CANADA

THE PURCHASING POWER OF *ONE* (1945) DOLLAR

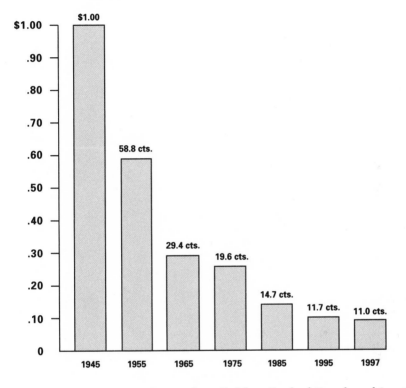

Source: Compiled from Bank of Canada and StatsCan

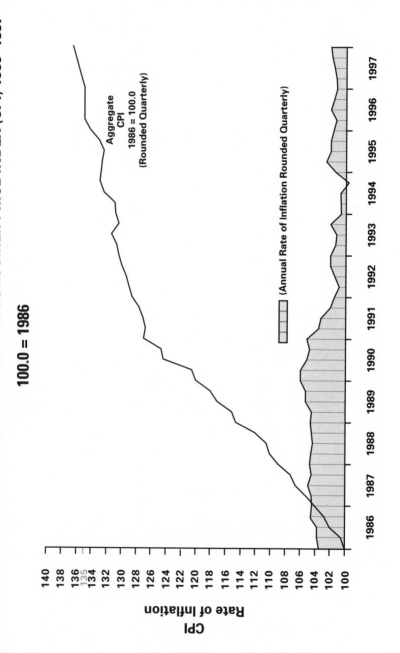

FIGURE 6.4: THE CANADIAN INFLATION RATE AND THE CONSUMER PRICE INDEX (CPI) 1986–1997

100.0 = 1986

Aggregate CPI 1986 = 100.0 (Rounded Quarterly)

(Annual Rate of Inflation Rounded Quarterly)

Source: Bank of Canada Annual Reports 1987–1997

CPI Rate of Inflation

*   *   *

If you can determine a reasonable rate of inflation projected into the future, you can also construct an estimate of the return on your capital *after* inflation. Suppose the best economists predict an average inflation rate of 3% during the next decade. You can project that a 10% gross rate of return will give you a realistic 7% after inflation. Whether or not these estimates turn out to be accurate, the important point is that you should anticipate the 7% figure — not 10%. And you should adjust your planning accordingly to reflect this probable loss of purchasing power.

The other obvious conclusion is that you should constantly look at investments realistically, sorting out those that don't offer the probability of inflation protection — such as fixed-rate certificates of deposit and savings accounts — and those that do — stocks, gold, real estate or commodities.

The Liquidity Factor

Liquidity refers to the ease with which you can convert any security or property into cash. In a bad market, a real estate property may take some time to sell, perhaps many months. This is illiquidity. Savings accounts, on the other hand, give us immediate liquidity, although bankers may hedge at this a bit. Because of their active markets, stock and bond mutual funds can usually be liquidated quickly.

There is another factor in liquidity — that is, the ability to obtain the price you paid, or may want. A fund may be completely marketable or readily saleable, and yet the price level you can obtain for it may be lower than its cost to you or what you might expect for various reasons. So liquidity can be a limited benefit.

The Expertise Factor

To, buy and hold a Canada Savings Bond is straightforward. Purchasing superior, top-drawer common stock mutual funds intelligently, and indeed, other fund categories, however, requires a high level of professional skill and consistently applied expertise in and about the capital securities markets and the wider business world. The expertise, in fact, exceeds the level at which most investors wish to operate. It is the rule, and not the exception, that you will need a financial advisor. Professional research polls indicate that, on average, investors typically do better with a financial advisor than they do acting on their own.

In the case of urban real estate, you might require an even higher level of expertise, perhaps that of a lifelong professional. So you must identify your own position relative to the investment you're contemplating and act accordingly, either independently or with outside expertise.

The Monitoring Factor

This is one of the more important considerations among all investment criteria. Most unsophisticated investors do not have, or do not wish to devote, the necessary time and effort required of investment. Given a savings account, a government bond or two, perhaps a handful of familiar stocks, these investors can limit their attention to reading the financial pages on the weekend, if at all.

At the other extreme, someone holding a commodity option contract must monitor it daily, because options can move quickly — sometimes by 50% or even 100% in a single day. During the Sumitomo copper futures scandal in the summer of 1996, the astute Montreal metals dealer Herbert Black earned $30 million in a single day by shorting copper just as copper prices plunged. In the commodities and option markets, only a full-time professional can adequately monitor the market. To reduce risk very substantially in this high-risk category, a commodities trading option mutual fund may be an answer. Such a fund may have as much as 80% of its portfolio in government Treasury Bills, so the leverage is quite small. This type of product has a *negative* correlation with both stocks and bonds, which adds some "insurance" to a portfolio.

In between the extremes lie most market securities, which require one of two things — either the constant attention of the knowledgeable investor or the engaging of a professional financial advisor to take that responsibility.

The Taxation Factors

Tax considerations in investment are as important as your study of the basic facts relating to the actual investment. High-tax-bracket investors may view tax as their initial consideration. A simple example is the dividend tax credit. Tax shelters, tax deferrals and tax deductions are decisive factors in many portfolios, as are retirement-oriented instruments such as RRSPs, RRIFs and annuities. Mutual funds in most asset classes offer excellent tax efficiencies, but each fund should be measured for its tax characteristics.

The Collateral Factor

The importance of determining the collateral potential of your investment — your ability to borrow against it — cannot be overemphasized. Most banks will loan you a high percentage of the face value on a government bond, perhaps half of that value on equity positions. In the case of mutual funds, the amount of collateral a financial institution will accept depends on the content of your mutual fund portfolio, often 50%. Find out the various rates charged, penalties and conditions before you enter any such arrangement. The collateral value of a security parallels its level of safety and its marketability. In addition, the interest expense against the fund for income-producing purposes can amount up to as much as a 100% tax deduction each year, subject to the minimum alternative tax rule.

As mentioned once earlier, at least one trust company in Canada has offered to loan you as much as 200% against your existing mutual funds — that is, a 2:1 ratio loan. Only monthly interest payments are required on such a loan; you can defer capital repayment for up to 10 years, or even indefinitely.

The Potential Loss Factor

We're not referring to *fluctuation* here but to real loss. Most people shy away from this subject despite the fact that calculating your potential loss on an investment in advance is a healthy exercise. Always construct a worst-case scenario, if only to hedge against your own fallible judgment. The effort will also help you overcome the influence of emotions that could interfere with your investment decisions.

A seasoned investment dealer once said that, before considering any deal, he multiplied the estimated costs or expenses by two, and then cut the suggested profit potential in half. If the deal still looked good, he started to consider it seriously. That's not a bad procedure for any investor to follow. Profit and loss can be quantified and estimated, or at least reasonably approximated. Take into account the unseen erosion of capital through inflation, too.

As noted earlier, for example, a savings account is said to have virtually a zero loss potential. The principal doesn't itself grow, but you do receive interest income. But while the principal itself remains static, its purchasing power shrinks because of inflation. And we haven't even considered the tax bite on the interest income.

More aggressive investments such as commodities and speculative stocks may well boast a corresponding or greater loss potential, to offset their appreciation potential. Often, even real estate can participate in this two-way street. (See Chapter 16 and Figure 16.2, Tables 16.1, 16.2 and 16.3 regarding the quantifying of potential return and loss in various kinds of investments.)

The Market Timing Factor

Some markets are more sensitive to specific timing than others. Think of gold in 1979, for example. The investor needs either excellent advice, a keen sense of the market, or a crystal ball.

To stick with the simplest investments, savings accounts require no attention. Bonds can follow central bank developments and the economy, and stocks can move in cycles. Study notwithstanding, basing an investment program on guessing the major moves of the world's markets is a futile exercise for most investors. The best plan is to define your own objectives, look at your own criteria for compatible investments, buy quality, and stay with it. Don't panic and bail out during the turbulent ups and downs.

When to invest? You can drive yourself up the wall trying to second-guess the market, along with the help of every soothsayer in the land. Of course, you want to buy low and sell high. Every investor wants to do that. How to do it is something else. Sir John Templeton offers an alternative.

There's really no wrong time to invest in a well-constructed asset allocation portfolio, custom designed for your personal comfort zone. (Table 6.2 shows that investing a fixed amount over time at market lows or market highs makes little difference.) But, you may say, what about recessions and investing despite adverse conditions? There have been *eight* recessions or bear markets (measured by two or more consecutive quarters of negative GDP growth) since the Second World War. The average lasted 10 to 11 months. If you remove the longest (17 months), and the shortest (5 months), the average remains the same. However deep the average recession has been, remember that they are relatively short-lived. In this century, there have been 30 bulls, followed by 29 bears. (See Table 6.3.)

TABLE 6.2: THE "BEST" TIME TO INVEST—
IT MAY NOT MATTER

The illustrations below cover the last 25 years and the "Best/Worst" days on
which to have invested 25 different $5,000 net investments totaling $125,000.
The results in each case can be helpful in deciding when to invest.

These are the results of having invested $5,000 in Templeton Growth Fund Ltd.
for each of the past 25 years on the day the market reached its highest point of
the year—*the peak stock prices* each year.

Date of Market High*	Cumulative Investment	Value of Account on December 31
12/11/72	$ 5,000	$ 5,063
01/11/73	10,000	9,039
03/13/74	15,000	12,036
07/15/75	20,000	21,852
09/21/76	25,000	37,398
01/03/77	30,000	55,630
09/08/78	35,000	79,519
10/05/79	40,000	100,303
11/20/80	45,000	134,295
04/27/81	50,000	137,680
12/27/82	55,000	163,393
11/29/83	60,000	224,780
01/06/84	65,000	249,577
12/16/85	70,000	342,650
12/02/86	75,000	415,361
08/25/87	80,000	398,125
10/21/88	85,000	452,200
10/09/89	90,000	552,576
07/16/90	95,000	481,735
12/31/91	100,000	632,962
06/01/92	105,000	733,897
12/29/93	110,000	1,005,203
01/31/94	115,000	1,048,346
12/13/95	120,000	1,201,684
12/27/96	125,000	1,427,872

Average annual compound rate of return: 16.9%

* The market is represented by the Dow Jones Industrial Average of 30 stocks.

These are the results of having invested $5,000 in Templeton Growth Fund Ltd. for each of the past 25 years on the day the market reached its lowest point of the year—*the bottom for stock prices* each year.

Date of Market Low*	Cumulative Investment	Value of Account on December 31
01/26/72	$ 5,000	$ 7,793
13/03/73	10,000	11,001
12/06/74	15,000	15,517
01/02/75	20,000	28,922
01/02/76	25,000	49,021
11/02/77	30,000	66,488
02/28/78	35,000	92,358
11/07/79	40,000	120,669
04/21/80	45,000	162,626
09/25/81	50,000	166,527
08/12/82	55,000	198,286
01/03/83	60,000	273,485
07/24/84	65,000	302,868
01/04/85	70,000	416,547
01/22/86	75,000	505,038
10/19/87	80,000	484,057
01/20/88	85,000	549,487
01/03/89	90,000	671,576
10/11/90	95,000	585,718
01/09/91	100,000	763,509
10/09/92	105,000	884,546
01/20/93	110,000	1,212,178
04/04/94	115,000	1,263,363
01/30/95	120,000	1,391,317
10/01/96	125,000	1,719,702

Average annual compound rate of return: 18.0%

Average annual compound rates of return[†] for periods ended December 31, 1996 are:

1 Year	3 Years	5 Years	10 Years	15 Years	20 Years	25 Years	30 Years	Since Inception
18.4%	12.0%	17.1%	12.4%	15.5%	17.1%	18.1%	17.5%	5.4%

† Simple rate of return.

Source: Templeton Group of Funds

Conclusion: The average anual difference between periodic investing at the worst possible time (highest price each calendar year), and the best possible time (lowest price each calendar year) for 25 years is only 1.1% per annum. So much for wholesale market timing!

TABLE 6.3: BULL AND BEAR MARKETS IN THIS CENTURY

BULL MARKETS					
Beginning		Ending			
Date	DJIA	Date	DJIA	% Gain	Days
09/24/00	52.96	06/17/01	78.26	47.8	266
11/09/03	42.15	01/19/06	103.00	144.4	802
11/15/07	53.00	11/19/09	100.53	89.7	735
09/25/11	72.94	09/30/12	94.15	29.1	371
12/24/14	53.17	11/21/16	110.15	107.2	698
12/19/17	65.95	11/03/19	119.62	81.4	684
08/24/21	63.90	03/20/23	105.38	64.9	573
10/27/23	85.76	09/03/29	381.17	344.5	2138
11/13/29	198.69	04/17/30	294.07	48.0	155
07/08/32	41.22	09/07/32	79.93	93.9	61
02/27/33	50.16	02/05/34	110.74	120.8	343
07/26/34	85.51	03/10/37	194.40	127.3	958
03/31/28	98.95	11/12/38	158.41	60.1	226
04/08/39	121.44	09/12/39	155.92	28.4	157
04/28/42	92.92	05/29/46	212.50	128.7	1492
05/17/47	163.21	06/15/48	193.16	18.4	395
06/13/49	161.60	04/06/56	521.05	222.4	2489
10/22/57	419.79	01/05/60	685.47	63.3	805
10/25/60	566.05	12/13/61	734.91	29.8	414
06/26/62	535.76	02/09/66	995.15	85.7	1324
10/07/66	744.32	12/03/68	985.21	32.4	788
05/26/70	631.16	04/28/71	950.82	50.6	337
11/23/71	797.97	01/11/73	1051.70	31.8	415
12/06/74	577.60	09/21/76	1014.79	75.7	655
02/28/78	742.12	09/08/78	907.74	22.3	192
04/21/80	759.13	04/27/81	1024.05	34.9	371
08/12/82	776.92	11/29/83	1287.20	65.7	474
07/24/84	1086.57	08/25/87	2722.42	150.6	1127
10/19/87	1738.74	07/16/90	2999.75	72.5	1001
10/11/90	2365.10	02/20/97	6927.38	192.9	2324

BEAR MARKETS					
Beginning		Ending			
Date	DJIA	Date	DJIA	% Change	Days
06/17/01	78.26	11/09/03	42.15	−46.1	875
01/19/06	103.00	11/15/07	53.00	−48.5	665
11/19/09	100.53	09/25/11	72.94	−27.4	675
09/30/12	94.15	07/30/14	71.42	−24.1	668
11/21/16	110.15	12/19/17	65.95	−40.1	393
11/03/19	119.62	08/24/21	63.90	−46.6	660
03/20/23	105.38	10/27/23	85.76	−18.6	221
09/03/29	381.17	11/13/29	198.69	−47.9	71
04/17/30	294.07	07/08/32	41.22	−86.0	813
09/07/32	79.93	02/27/33	50.16	−37.2	173
02/05/34	110.74	07/26/34	85.51	−22.8	171
03/10/37	194.40	03/31/38	98.95	−49.1	386
11/12/38	158.41	04/08/39	121.44	−23.3	147
09/12/39	155.92	04/28/42	92.92	−40.4	959
05/29/46	212.50	05/17/47	163.21	−23.2	353
06/15/48	193.16	06/13/49	161.60	−16.3	363
04/06/56	521.05	10/22/57	419.79	−19.4	564
01/05/60	685.47	10/25/60	566.05	−17.4	294
12/13/61	734.91	06/26/62	535.76	−27.1	195
02/09/66	995.15	10/07/66	744.32	−25.2	240
12/03/68	985.21	05/26/70	631.16	−35.9	539
04/28/71	950.82	11/23/71	797.97	−16.1	209
01/11/73	1051.70	12/06/74	577.60	−45.1	694
09/21/76	1014.79	02/28/78	742.12	−26.9	525
09/08/78	907.74	04/21/80	759.13	−16.4	591
04/27/81	1024.05	08/12/82	776.92	−24.1	472
11/29/83	1287.20	07/24/84	1086.57	−15.6	238
08/25/87	2722.42	10/19/87	1738.74	−36.1	55
07/16/90	2999.75	10/11/90	2365.10	−21.2	87

Source: Ned Davis Research

Other Factors

There are many other factors, some unique to particular invest-ments. Is your portfolio portable if you are transferred to Thailand? Owning valuables such as jewelry or art poses the immediate problem of guarding or storing them. And then there is the peren-nial problem of fraud and forgery. Securities certificates are partic-ularly vulnerable. Like all of the other criteria for investment we have discussed, all of these considerations are largely up to each individual. Just be aware of them.

❉   ❉   ❉

Portfolio professional Lynn Hopewell says he earned his reputation by "keeping his eyes off the ticker." Most "value" investment professionals give their clients the same advice. Hopewell recommends to his clients that they create a portfolio that is *good for all markets* and to avoid watching the stock quotations too closely.

In a similar fashion, most value fund managers claim they evaluate situations independent of what may be happening in the market. There is a good argument for such an approach. Stocks listed, say, on the New York Stock Exchange tend to move up or down according to their popularity with the investors, professional and amateur, who in turn decide to buy or sell.

Value investing is known as the "bottom-up" approach to mutual fund stock selection. You examine primarily the internal microeconomic factors of a given security, rather than the macroeconomic trends of an industry and/or the economy, as revealed by the stock market. This method has the added feature that a value professional such as Warren Buffett knows more about his intended target than the market does. (Proof? Buffett is regularly listed as the second-wealthiest American, after Bill Gates.)

Value investors evaluate the anatomy of a company with their backs turned to the ticker tape. They seem to say that, since they are researching in depth, they know better what is happening in a given situation than the varied, often contradictory information fed into the market. They may know that the top of a market is near, because they observe a dearth of good buys around, and not because of a graph.

This is similar to, if not as simple, as a system developed by an acquaintance of mine who is a realtor. Instead of charting the course of residential real estate prices, he maintains a running graph made up of a ratio of listings to actual sales. If the number of listings at any one time exceeds sales for the previous month by more than 6:1, he counts this as a serious sell signal. Alternatively, if the ratio drops below 3:1, he reads it as a buying signal. *Then* he matches his ratio against a chart of residential real estate prices. His system has accurately alerted him to buy or sell since 1979, when he began his monitoring system.

This does not mean that the investor, either professional or amateur, should invest with his head in the sand. On the contrary, read. Read the *Financial Post*, *The Globe and Mail* and the *Wall Street Journal*. Read financial magazines, mutual fund research materials. Discuss your interests with a financial advisor specializing in mutual funds. The point is not to follow all the stocks and mutual funds in the world, but what you want is a feel for what's happening in international business.

Business cycles can forewarn you of broad movements that may affect funds and individual securities. Don't hesitate to rebalance your holdings if the time seems right. Switch from stock funds to fixed income, for example, when interest rates drop. Modestly re-balance from national to international mutual funds as world events dictate, and vice-versa.

With the Stenner Multi-Safety Allocation System approach, you always aim to be in certain markets. The percentage allocation requires periodic changes and rebalancing. You will want to retain your core holdings for the most part.

Foreign stocks and foreign funds can also be highly overvalued as they become faddish and popular. And the risks of international investing are obviously compounded, compared to those closer to home. You can see and hear B.C. Telephone, but Nippon Telephone may be a horse of a different color. In Japanese finance, there often seems to be little if any relation between earnings and price. Nippon Telephone became so overvalued at one point that stockpicker Peter Lynch said, "Not only did the emperor have no clothes, but the people lost their shirts!"

In other parts of the world, contemporary emerging areas such as Latin America and Southeast Asia can show explosive growth. Some mutual funds specialize in fast-moving offshore markets. The enter-prising investor will pay attention to these. Realizing, of course, that what he or she is dealing with is not a kiddies' merry-go-round.

In all things, deciding *when* to buy is just as important as choosing *what* to buy. Hold, of course, until there's a good reason to sell. Perhaps add more to your holding. Once you're fully invested, be patient. Rome wasn't built in a day, and a good portfolio of mutual funds wasn't built in a year. Figure on three to five years to build yourself a solid base.

A seasoned mutual fund manager says, "There have been 40 stock market declines in the past 70 years, and if I had been young and fully invested I would have sold everything on all 40 of those occasions. I would have been wrong 39 of those times. I would only have been right once — in 1929."

IS REAL ESTATE A REAL ALTERNATIVE?

> *More than once prospective clients have told me that real estate has been their best investment. To my question, "What other major investments have you ever owned?" They usually answer, "None."*
>
> — Gordon Stenner

When I show these people the stock market indexes over the past 20 to 70 years compared to a real estate index, they tend to be astonished. That $10,000 invested in Templeton Growth Fund in 1954 would now be worth more than $4.8 million demonstrates to them that they have missed the boat. Few cash investments in real estate have shown this kind of growth — and such fund gains were made without upkeep, maintenance or property taxes.

A number of highly diversified mutual funds have performed better than a single piece of real estate, and with far superior liquidity as well. The real estate market cannot match the immediate redemption feature of a mutual fund.

If you've lived in Toronto or Vancouver, you're no stranger to real estate cycles. In an article entitled "Land vs. Stocks," in *Worth* magazine (February 1997), John Fried writes, "The price indexes compiled by the National Council of Real Estate Investment Fiduciaries [NCREIF] come the closest to doing for land what Standard & Poor's Stock Index does for stocks." But the NCREIF's statistics date back only nine years. During that time, the annualized return has been 21.8% for timberland, 6.26% for farmland, and 3.74% on property. "During the same period, the Standard & Poor's 500 Stock Index has returned an average of 14.8% annually, according to Ibbotson Associates. Land, though, has literally proved more precious than gold bullion, which has returned an average of only 1.7% a year since 1985."

PART II

SHAPING YOUR PORTFOLIO

Chapter 7

INTRODUCING THE
STENNER MULTI-
SAFETY ALLOCATION
SYSTEM

In the morning sow thy seed, and in the evening withhold
not thine hand: for thou knowest not whether shall prosper,
either this or that, or whether they both shall be alike good.

— Ecclesiastes 11: 6

Even in a well-balanced investment program, there can be some potential of temporary market weakness. On the upside, with careful planning
within the right investment media, there can be an unlimited potential.
One senior investment dealer long ago — when the mutual fund concept was in its infancy — recognized this medium as a liberating of
common sense. As a brilliant financial analyst with a leading investment
dealer, he defined mutual funds as "a hedge against one's own judgment." When you buy a mutual fund, or a portfolio of funds, you
invoke first the judgment of a professional manager, and second that of
a financial advisor. That judgment is applied equally, regardless of how
large or how small your holding may be. Surely there is no better bargain in the realm of professional investment counsel and advice.

In undertaking a "balanced" fund of funds (a portfolio of mutual
funds), you have a system of multi-levels (the principle of asset allocation),

multifunds (a variety of different kinds of funds within those levels), and finally multi-managers (whereby each fund is managed by a professional, each group is managed by a management company, and the overall portfolio is managed by a seasoned financial advisor). Throughout the book, we'll be referring to this seven-tiered process as the "Stenner Multi-Safety Allocation" portfolio system.

MULTIFUND INVESTING: THE FOUR CORNERSTONES

My strategy is built on four pillars: John Templeton, Peter Lynch, Warren Buffett and George Soros.

— Heiko Thieme, fund manager
American Heritage Fund

Like a building created by an architect and structural engineer, a multi-layered portfolio has a sound foundation, a solid superstructure, and its various components offset each others' countervailing stresses. Like a solid bridge, it even allows for the regular expansion and contraction of its materials in response to external forces. Put another way, "the sum of the parts is greater than the whole."

Multifund management (Michael Hirsch possibly first coined the term "multifund") has proven itself successful over an extended period of time in many different market environments and for a wide variety of investors, from the rank amateur to the seasoned veteran. This concept has delivered consistently more stable returns even when other approaches to investment have floundered. Common sense suggests a multi-layered approach yields consistency and staying the course in even the most turbulent of conditions. On and after October 19, 1987, Black Monday, the worst equity market crash since 1929, bond funds, mortgage funds and real estate funds generally rose as most stock funds plummeted.

Compactness, efficiency and flexibility provide only part of the answer. The unique feature of the Stenner Multi-Safety Allocation portfolio system is its use of diversification. It works on several separate levels.

If you committed all your assets to a single investment, you would be at far greater risk than if they were deployed among 15 or 20 smaller investments. And if all of your assets were invested in equities (or equity mutual funds), you would be at greater risk than if they were spread across a variety of stock, bond, mortgage, real estate and money market funds. At a third level, if all your investments were committed to strictly investment instruments, they would be at greater risk than those in a portfolio comprised of both financial securities and hard assets such as real estate, oil and gas, collectibles and precious metals. Last, if all of your investments were committed only to the Canadian markets, you would be exposed to greater risk than if they were distributed globally.

Clearly, there is not only safety in numbers, but safety in the kinds of numbers the investor deals with!

The traditional stock and bond portfolio's diversification is limited to the number of different stocks or bonds purchased individually for the portfolio. In other words, diversification exists only on a single level. Our multifund portfolio, on the other hand, achieves diversification in several distinct and separate dimensions, a multiweave fabric, if you will.

Here is where the "Four Cornerstones" come in. We're now putting flesh on the bones of our investment skeleton, breathing life into our structured portfolio. Consider the fixed-income sector. Using four carefully researched and selected fixed-income funds, we gain exposure to:

1. long-term, high-grade (government and guaranteed) bonds
2. short- to medium-term high-grade bonds
3. long-term high-quality corporate bonds, and
4. more junior, higher-yielding corporates.

As investors focused on the greatest yield, we could add a fund invested in convertible bonds or debentures, deep discount issues, strip bonds, mortgage-backed securities, or other fixed-income alternatives. These four major categories include both Canadian and global securities. Why limit your portfolio to less than 3% of the world's markets? That's what you do when you choose only Canadian securities or funds.

Next, we should ideally select a maximum of three or four mutual funds in the aggressive-growth sector. We'll reject the temptation to select the equity-income funds from multifund portfolios strictly on the basis of their past performance. Or by throwing darts at random. We will take the time and painstaking effort (if not hire an experienced financial advisor) to define clearly what the merits of each fund may be, and what makes it unique from every other fund available, particularly those within the same sector.

Within a single portfolio, our multifund approach efficiently represents as many different asset classes, types of securities, and market sectors as we may have the flexibility to choose. Again, the broader the diversification, the greater the safety. We have stressed the importance of identifying clearly each fund candidate's investment qualifications. This enables us to construct the final level, diversifying sectors by investment style.

This step is vital. It ensures that the total sector within our portfolio will not underperform because a single investment style practised by a manager is not in sync with the current market. For example, let's assume that our sector allocation to aggressive-growth funds was proven accurate by subsequent market behavior, but that instead of investing in four aggressive-growth funds, we had chosen only one. If that single fund represented a style out of sync with the investing public's preference at that point, our entire sector might fare poorly. A single high-volatility fund can do that to an entire sector. High-tech funds were the villains in the early 1990s.

The investment performance of one single investor or portfolio manager never determines the success or failure of our Multi-Safety portfolio. The combined expertise of 10 or 15 different money manager professionals, each of whom may exhibit a totally different style or perspective on investing, even within seemingly similar media-published categories, steers our portfolio. We're not talking about multi-overlapping of some fund categories; we are emphasizing multi, distinct-category distribution within single portfolios.

Let's assume that one or two of these managers strike out, making no capital gains or even losing ground. We know that we can seldom see excellent gains through every investment style represented in our portfolio at once. Nonetheless, our portfolio as a whole should do well. When we have 10 or 12 other styles in the portfolio working for us, each managed by a professional with an above-average risk-adjusted, trend-analyzed management record in his or her class, we're minimizing risk while maximizing reward.

ENGINEERING OUR MEGAFUND PORTFOLIO

If we have learned anything, we have learned that it is
time to go to work.

— Lyndon B. Johnson

Until now we have conducted a theoretical discussion of panic-proof mutual fund investing. Now, using this information and applying the principles we've discussed, we move to the actual engineering and analysis of a real practical portfolio of mutual fund securities. In the final stage (see Chapter 18) I will name actual mutual funds, not as specific recommendations, but as an illustration as to how one investor might construct a portfolio of $300,000, for example.

We will follow my seven-step process more generally described previously in our investment pyramid, included as Figure 2.1 (see Chapter 2). This time, we'll provide specific details, adding levels 5 and 6.

FIGURE 7.1: STENNER MULTI-SAFETY ASSET ALLOCATION

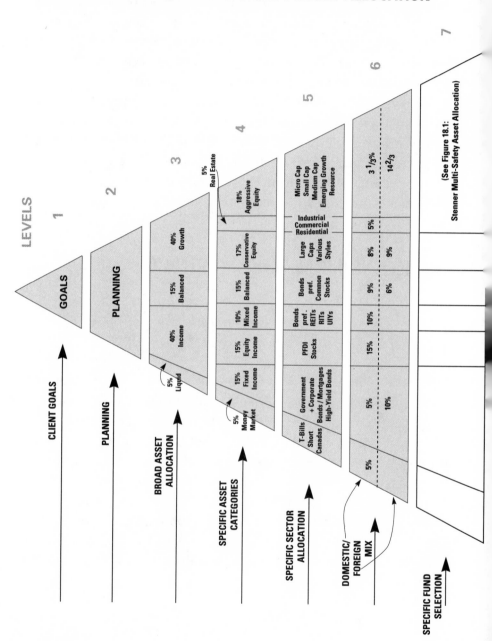

Levels One and Two: Personal Goals and Planning

Clearly understand your investment goals, as well as your ability to understand and accept investment risks, such as fluctuation or volatility. Establish these variables as clearly as you can yourself and with your advisor.

The first and most critical step in putting together a superior portfolio has little to do with actual portfolio construction. Investor, "know thyself." Write down your personal investment goals, both short- and long-term. You will need to decide how much risk you personally are prepared to absorb in return for how much reward.

Your advisor must at the outset question you carefully to determine just what type of individual you are as an investor. What are your investment goals? Are you primarily interested in current income, long-term capital appreciation, or some carefully measured combination of the two?

An investor requiring a high level of current income should not be enticed by the spectacular returns of aggressive-growth funds during a raging bull market. Most such funds, by definition and design, provide little or no current income. They also could cause irreparable capital loss in a temporary market downturn due to an encroachment of capital via the systematic withdrawal of shares in a bear market. If current income is your goal, then you will seek to preserve the capital base that will generate that income.

Many people want and expect "maximum return with minimal risk." Don't we all! Sorry folks, this doesn't exist. Success, to paraphrase John F. Kennedy, may not be achieved in days, weeks or even months. But let us begin.

Many investors, already retired or planning to retire, may often adopt a balanced growth-and-income objective. This middle-of-the-road approach, not too conservative nor too aggressive, will place equal emphasis on growth and income. If you don't require income immediately, let that "balance" act as an anchor within the portfolio, muting risk and providing a measure of safety during equity or fixed-income storms.

The following table illustrates something of the range of personal objectives, through just five investment options.

TABLE 7.1: PERSONAL OBJECTIVES AND INVESTMENT RISK

OBJECTIVE	RISK	FUND MEDIUM
1. Variable rate of current income without principal fluctuations	Extremely low	Bank and short-term Treasury instruments
2. Fixed current income/capital gain potential	Medium/high	Income portfolio
3. Current income/some capital gain potential	Medium	Balanced portfolio
4. Long-term capital and income growth	Medium/high	Growth portfolio
5. Maximum capital gain little or no dividends	High/very high	Aggressive-growth portfolio

THE MODEL PORTFOLIO

Level Three: Broad Asset Allocation

On the basis of your objectives, consider the numerous factors in the global markets, such as developments in various economies, political situations, monetary developments and the securities markets, in terms of how they might affect your investments in the next 12 to 18 months. Then develop a plan in writing, deploying your assets as to growth of capital, income, and liquid or near-liquid investments.

For our specific portfolio, let's assume that the following market factors are in place: The economy is reasonably healthy. It has emerged from a recession 12 months ago. Prospects for sustained economic growth are favorable. The Bank of Canada, as well as the U.S. Federal Reserve Board, are maintaining a fairly reasonable position relative to the growth of money supply. There is no strong indication of an increase in interest rates within the next few months. The recovery may be gaining additional momentum, which might suggest the Federal Reserve and/or Bank of Canada could raise interest rates. But, for the moment, Alan Greenspan has cooled his "irrational exuberance" comments, and Gordon Thiessen is contented.

Nothing of particular significance is occurring on either the domestic or international political fronts. No major tax or spending bills of any major consequence are before our House of Commons or the U.S. Houses of Congress.

Naturally, there are many fundamental and technical assumptions and criteria that must be considered and built into the portfolio's asset allocation, such as the current business cycle, conditions in foreign countries, inflation and the individual investor's disposition toward these factors.

Look too at the securities markets themselves. The Canadian stock market in our scenario is in the middle of a prolonged advance, reflecting a healthy economy. This rally, with its usual expected corrections, has had a broad basis, and most market sectors have participated in it. On the fixed-income side (bonds, mortgages, debentures), the market is also experiencing a significant rally, reacting to lower interest rates. Just recently, the rally in Canadian fixed-income securities has begun to falter, as fears of modest inflation and a rebound in interest rates have surfaced.

In this environment we'll create a *balanced* asset allocation. Since conditions for equity investment appear favorable, we'll allocate 40% of the assets to selected growth investments. Until the upturn in interest rates is confirmed, we need not react. Remember the liquidity and transferability of mutual funds. We'll be able to shift gears quickly if we need to.

We'll devote 40% of the total assets to fixed-income, "mixed income," and equity income investments respectively in relatively equal portions.

Of the remaining 20%, 15% will be slotted into asset allocation (or balanced) funds and 5% kept in highly liquid Treasury Bills and money market funds.

Asset Allocation Techniques

In its Canadian Securities course, the Canadian Securities Institute (CSI) provides an excellent description of the total process of asset allocation, a discipline that has been developed only recently. I have summarized and paraphrased some of its material here.

Once the asset mix is implemented, asset classes will begin to change in value. Dividends and interest will augment cash, and capital gains will increase the equity value. Rebalancing will therefore be necessary. Investment managers limit their rebalancing to minimize transaction costs. Usually an asset class moves more than 5% before being rebalanced.

1. *Strategic Asset Allocation*: The basic policy mix is the strategic allocation, as worked out by the investment manager, reflecting the investor's objectives or those of the individual fund. This long-term mix will be maintained, through monitoring and occasional rebalancing. The stock/bond ratio, for example, may be 10/90, 40/60, or 70/30— or any combination in between. Rebalancing is necessary when market movements cause the mix to stray from the strategic objective.

2. *Constant-weighting Asset Allocation*: Constant weighting involves rebalancing by buying bonds (or bond funds) when they appear to be overvalued. Professional managers tend to increase their cash positions as markets rise and become fully invested at periods when markets are in decline.

3. *Tactical Asset Allocation*: Short-term, tactical deviation from the strategic objective may be capitalized on by the manager, with a view to returning to the long-term mix when markets normalize.

4. *Dynamic Asset Allocation*: The dynamic approach is the opposite of the constant-weighting approach. With the latter, increasingly, equities purchased as the market declines are sold off in favor of risk-free assets as markets rise. The dynamic approach favors selling stocks in falling markets and buying

them in rising markets. These two countervailing strategies bring stability to the overall market.

5. *Insured Asset Allocation*: This strategy assumes a base portfolio value, below which it should not be allowed to drop. If the value drops to or below that base, the portfolio may be managed aggressively; but when the base value is reached, everything is transferred into relatively risk-free investments.

6. *The Integrated Asset Allocation Method*: This technique incorporates all of the strategies listed above, which become part of the overall integrated approach.

The CSI is naturally concerned with the markets for bonds and equities. Our focus is on mutual funds, but the above discussion of asset allocation techniques is no less pertinent.

Level Four: Specific Asset Categories

This imposes a much more detailed structure on the portfolio, determining, for example, whether growth-oriented assets should be invested in aggressive-growth or conservative-growth funds. Also, should the income assets be invested primarily in equity-income funds? Or fixed-income funds (which I have designated "mixed-income" funds)? At this point we must determine the percentage allocations to each asset class. Finally, we'll decide on the type and percentage of money market funds we'll employ for near-cash liquidity in the shorter term.

The short-term view of our investment climate presents a compelling argument for both equity and debt (fixed-income) investments. So, within our sector allocation for the 40% intended for growth, we'll put 18% into aggressive-growth funds, 17% into conservative-growth funds, and 5% into a different type of equity security — real estate.

What about the 40% allocated to income-oriented investments? Because we are attempting to maintain a reasonably moderate, balanced approach, 25% of this allocation will go to fixed-income and equity-income funds, domestic and international, equally divided. We'll allocate 15% to that very interesting high-yield, mixed-income category.

ASSET AND SECTOR ALLOCATION
FOR GROWTH INVESTORS

Growth or maximum-growth investors might allocate both asset and sector investments quite differently. Given our assumed economic and market environment, we could recommend putting, say, 40% of the investment assets in aggressive-growth funds and 20% in conservative-growth for growth investors. We might recommend that maximum-growth investors put 60% into aggressive-growth funds and 20% into conservative-growth funds, the entire balance (20%) going into assorted mixes of income funds.

Since prospects for the equity market remain favorable, 12.5% will be allocated to equity income and 12.5% to a fixed-income category. Further, since our projections for the interest rate environment remain positive, of the 12.5% targeted for fixed income, 7.0% will go into longer-term funds (a mix of high-grade and corporate bond funds) and 5.5% into intermediate term funds.

This assumes a flat yield curve from the intermediate to the long terms. If there is an appreciable yield differential between the two, perhaps only 5% will be placed in intermediate bonds and 10% in longer terms. A "flat-yield curve" means there is little difference between short-term interest rates and long-term rates.

As for the remaining 20%, we repeat that 15% will be placed in asset allocation funds and 5% in a highly liquid general money market fund.

This portfolio may look tilted in favor of equities. We plan to have 18% of the assets invested in aggressive-growth funds, 17% of the assets in conservative-growth funds, and 5% in real estate equity. This would mean 60% of the portfolio would be in equity funds of one orientation or another (40% in equity funds, 10% of the balanced funds currently in equities, plus about 10% in the equity-income segment).

This is not entirely the case. The underlying portfolios of each of the aggressive-growth funds, conservative-growth funds and equity-income funds reveal that some portion of each fund's assets are invested in fixed-income or money market issues, presenting a reasonably even balance between growth and income vehicles.

Our progress to this point:

PRELIMINARY LEVELS:

Level One: Personal Goals
Level Two: Planning
Level Three: Broad Asset Allocation — 40% growth, 40% income, 15% balanced, 5% liquid
Level Four: Specific Asset Categories — 18% aggressive growth, 17% conservative growth, 5% real estate, 15% fixed income (8% long, 7% medium), 15% equity income, 10% mixed income, 15% balanced, and 5% highly liquid

---

Now, on to Levels Five and Six.

Level Five: Specific Sector Allocation

This notes the specific asset categories we selected in Level Two. For example, the money market funds category is broken down as Treasury Bills and short-term bonds.

Level Six: Domestic/Foreign Mix

66% DOMESTIC/34% FOREIGN

Domestic: 5% money market, 5% fixed-income, 15% equity income, 10% mixed income, 9% balanced, 17% growth equity, 5% real estate
Foreign: 10% fixed income, 6% balanced, 18% growth equity

Level Seven: Specific Mutual Fund Selection (addressed in Chapter 18)

There is a wrong way and a right way to select individual mutual funds for any portfolio. The wrong way is to pursue high-flying, media-hyped "hot" funds. The right way is to identify and select consistent managers in each peer group category that have had, or will turn in, above-average performance. We have to go beyond the advertised or historical cumulative performance numbers to understand the unique characteristics of those funds, such as the investment style and philosophy of their managers. We then assemble a group of complementary styles in a single portfolio to provide you with the greatest safety and consistency, utilizing a risk-adjusted performance methodology.

This is our final major stage of the Stenner Multi-Safety investment process, when we select from our core group of mutual funds to create the actual portfolio. It's extremely important that we do not allow any single fund to influence unduly our total portfolio. In addition, each sector has to be invested in funds with a variety of investment styles. This diversifies the portfolio even further.

First, however, let's explore how our safety-first emphasis works.

Safety First

Michael Hirsch, in his original book on *Multifund Investing*, reminds us that if the portfolio has just one more winning style in a given market than it has styles on the losing side, the entire portfolio can show a positive score. For example, Hirsch shows us that if there are 14 well-chosen funds in the portfolio — funds with long-term, above-average performance histories — and if all of them perform proportionately, with only eight of them achieving a gain, the portfolio will still succeed. We derive a safe, consistent return, regardless of the market's direction or our own objective. Why? Because of the safety-first principle of multifund investing.

With the investment world becoming increasingly more volatile and complex, the basic consideration in any portfolio will be reducing overall risk and maximizing safety. By providing five separate and distinct levels of diversification, the multifund portfolio, more than any other, has the essential characteristics for success in a hazardous environment.

OVERDIVERSIFICATION?

Can there be too much of a good thing? Writing in *The Globe and Mail*, Clint Willis of the Reuters News Agency makes a point about overdiversification in mutual funds that should be considered. According to Willis, overdiversification can produce a diminishing return in the very benefit you seek. As overdiversification approximates the entire securities market, a portfolio's performance may suffer . . .

With the proliferation on a global scale of mutual funds of all types, says Willis, there is a tendency for all investors to fall in love with every fund that comes along. The result? Too many funds in every portfolio. "Owning too many funds," he says, "can defeat the purpose of active investing." I believe Willis misses the point. First, each of these fund categories is *weighted differently* by percentage allocation in our Multi-Safety portfolio, and second, we're striving for *increased* stability at all times. There can never be too much of a good thing, but there can be too much of the *same* thing. I believe Willis confuses the two.

A recent study by Prudential Diversified Investment Strategies concluded that a given investor should hold more than one fund in each of the four equity categories, and as many as three each. The reasoning is that, beyond four funds per sector, the performance will be closely correlated with an index fund for that category, which therefore limits the category's own superior performance.

But Willis' argument presupposes that mutual funds — or at least a judicious portfolio of funds — will by definition outperform the market as a whole, a position implicit throughout this book as well. If it were not so, why our preoccupation with balance, selection, allocation, manager agility, and superior risk-adjusted management performance? As a matter of fact, there is a school of thought — the Random Walk Efficient Markets Theory — that maintains that over time the simple purchase of, say, a TSE 300 Index Fund will benefit the investor just as well as a carefully engineered mutual fund portfolio. In fact, the whole point with mutual funds and their managers is not even to attempt to hit the highs and the lows of a given market. Some market timing is desirable, sometimes with relative ease, some involving extensive research. Perhaps the most convincing maneuver of the smart investor is simply to move counter to the mob.

The theory that general market(s) will perform as well as any given segment of it assumes that the market is as much as 100% efficient. If this were so, *value* investors would be out of business. Each stock price would accurately reflect the true value of that stock. Consider the nature of fluctuation in relation to the real value of stocks — at both ends, extreme "bulls" and extreme "bears," we have unrealistic prices not represented by the true intrinsic value of each stock.

The subject (and practice) of "indexing" or simply buying "index funds" has gained considerable attention recently. Index funds, of which the portfolios match the makeup of a standard index, such as the TSE 300 Index or the S&P 500 Stock Index, ignore the experience and skills of a good portfolio manager. Index investing simply adopts the lowest common denominator, mimicking the index. You're depriving yourself of the experienced professional's selection of securities for you, and simply riding the waves of the market. Which is average. To perform better than other investors, you must invest better than other investors.

PORTFOLIO MAINTENANCE

In constructing your multifund portfolio, according to the Stenner Multi-Safety pyramid, I referred to a "top-down" process. Changes at any level of our pyramid trigger changes at all lower levels. If your basic objectives change, you must adjust your sector allocation and mutual fund selections accordingly. If you change your sector allocation, you must alter your mutual fund selection as well.

Modifications should rarely be implemented primarily from the bottom up. The exception can be in the replacement of a "dog" — a consistent bottom-feeder fund — by a superior fund of the same asset and manager style. You can select different funds without affecting sector allocation or personal objectives. You can also reformulate how you arrange your sectors without affecting your asset allocation and personal objectives. And asset allocation can be shifted without changing your objectives.

CHANGES IN YOUR OBJECTIVE

Suppose your employment situation changes — you receive a substantial increase in salary. You now have more income available for investment. Or perhaps you receive a large inheritance. Or, your investments may be associated — like so many Canadians today — with a substantial severance package and early retirement plan, and a need to transfer these funds to an existing RRSP, portable pension, locked-in plan or cash portfolio. Or, an important source of income could be suddenly cut off. You may need to generate more current income or develop longer-term appreciation and greater tax benefits.

As your outlook on life and your temperament change, so do your objectives. Perhaps your risk comfort zone will be altered, suggesting a change in objectives. This shift in turn will affect your feelings about your asset allocation and the overall selection of types of mutual funds. This is entirely natural. A good mutual fund portfolio always maintains core asset holdings, particularly of equities and fixed-income bonds. It has no other absolutes.

KEEPING YOUR BALANCE

The Stenner Multi-Safety Portfolio construction is a live process, not something cast in concrete and then ignored. Even though its primary purpose is to reduce risks affecting your portfolio and to conserve your capital, a significant portion of the time devoted to portfolio management should be spent on upkeep.

For example, an external development affecting the economy, interest rates, or the securities markets may suggest you adjust your asset allocation. A trend you perceive as positive for economic expansion might trigger an increase in your allocation toward growth, while you still adhere to your overall personal objective. Developments with adverse implications for the economy might make you reduce your growth allocation in favor of your income investments.

Events significantly detrimental to interest rates might persuade you to decrease your income investments and move into more liquid investments — or short-term bonds, conservative-balanced, asset allocation hybrids, and money market instruments. Conversely, signs of sharply lower interest rates would call for a reallocation from some of those investments to greater income and equity holdings of varying asset categories.

These reallocations automatically imply shifts in the sector allocation and portfolio categories. If you reduce your growth assets, you'll also have to reduce either your percentage amount to the aggressive-growth sector, the conservative-growth sector, or both. Further changes will be forced in the allocations to specific aggressive-growth funds and aggressive-growth funds in the existing portfolio.

Our final objective is to fine-tune, at least annually, the multifund portfolio so it can deliver what you expect of it. And you will not be hampered in this effort by the potential bias of a large commission each time you undertake a trade from one fund to another within each fund group. Michael Hirsch has fully illustrated how various investment scenarios (horizontal), according to investor outlook (vertical), might vary though three basic investor approaches — Balanced, Income, and

Maximum Yield (see Tables 7.2, 7.3, 7.4, 7.5 and 7.6). Table 7.6: The Stenner Best Fund/Phase Category in The Business Cycle indicates the choice of fund types through the business cycle.

TABLE 7.2: MAXIMUM GROWTH INVESTMENT SCENARIO

Scenario	Aggressive Growth	Conservative Growth	Equity Income	Fixed Income	Money Market
Very Bullish	60%	30%	0%	5%	5%
Bullish	50	25	5	10	10
Neutral	40	20	10	20	10
Bearish	30	15	15	35	10
Very Bearish	20	15	15	35	15

TABLE 7.3: GROWTH INVESTMENT SCENARIO

Scenario	Aggressive Growth	Conservative Growth	Equity Income	Fixed Income	Money Market
Very Bullish	35%	35%	10%	10%	10%
Bullish	25	30	20	15	10
Neutral	20	25	20	25	10
Bearish	15	20	20	35	10
Very Bearish	15	15	10	45	15

TABLE 7.4: BALANCED INVESTMENT SCENARIO

Scenario	Aggressive Growth	Conservative Growth	Equity Income	Fixed Income	Money Market
Very Bullish	25%	30%	20%	15%	10%
Bullish	15	25	25	25	10
Neutral	15	20	25	30	10
Bearish	10	20	25	35	10
Very Bearish	10	10	15	50	15

TABLE 7.5: INCOME INVESTMENT SCENARIO

Scenario	Aggressive Growth	Conservative Growth	Equity Income	Fixed Income	Money Market
Very Bullish	10%	20%	25%	30%	15%
Bullish	5	15	25	45	10
Neutral	5	15	20	50	10
Bearish	0	15	20	55	10
Very Bearish	0	5	10	65	20

TABLE 7.6: MAXIMUM YIELD INVESTMENT SCENARIO

Scenario	Aggressive Growth	Conservative Growth	Equity Income	Fixed Income	Money Market
Very Bullish	0%	0%	30%	55%	15%
Bullish	0	0	25	65	10
Neutral	0	0	20	70	10
Bearish	0	0	15	75	10
Very Bearish	0	0	10	80	10

Source: Michael Hirsch, Multifund Investing

TABLE 7.7: BEST INVESTMENT STYLE PER PHASE OF THE BUSINESS CYCLE

FUND CATEGORY	INVESTOR GOAL	INVESTMENT TYPE	BEST FUND IN PHASE	PHASE
SMALL-CAP GROWTH	AGGRESSIVE CAPITAL APPRECIATION	SMALL GROWTH, HIGH P/E COMPANIES	ONE EARLY RECOVERY	1
SMALL-CAP VALUE	CONSERVATIVE CAPITAL APPRECIATION	SMALL CYCLICAL, LOW P/E COMPANIES	TWO LATE RECOVERY	2
LARGE-CAP VALUE	CONSERVATIVE CAPITAL APPRECIATION	LARGE CYCLICAL, LOW P/E COMPANIES	THREE STAGFLATION	3
LARGE-CAP GROWTH	CONSERVATIVE CAPITAL APPRECIATION	LARGE GROWTH, HIGH P/E COMPANIES	FOUR RECESSION	4

TABLE 7.8: THE BEST FUND PER PHASE OF THE BUSINESS CYCLE

FUND CATEGORY	INVESTOR GOAL	INVESTMENT TYPE	BEST FUND IN PHASE	PHASE
CANADIAN EQUITY GROWTH	CAPITAL APPRECIATION MODEST INCOME	LARGE-CAP STOCK FUNDS OF CANADIAN CORPORATIONS	**FOUR** RECESSION	4
HIGH-YIELD INCOME	HIGHEST MONTHLY INCOME, TAX-PREFERENCED MIXED ASSET INCOME	ROYALTY INCOME TRUSTS (RITs) REAL ESTATE INVESTMENT TRUSTS (REITS) COMMON & PREFERRED DIVIDENDS CORPORATE BONDS	**ONE** EARLY RECOVERY	1
ASSET ALLOCATION	REDUCED RISK, MORE POTENTIAL STABILITY	ADJUSTABLE TO ANY RATIO OF STOCKS, BONDS (SHORT-, MEDIUM-, LONG-TERM) CASH, PRECIOUS METALS, AND OTHER CATEGORIES	VARIOUS	ALL
GOVERNMENT BONDS	LOW RISK, CURRENT INCOME	BOND INSTRUMENTS ISSUED BY CANADIAN GOVERNMENT	**FOUR** RECESSION	4
BALANCED	CURRENT INCOME AND MODEST CAPITAL APPRECIATION	TYPICALLY, FIXED PERCENTAGE OF STOCKS, BONDS AND CASH	**THREE** STAGFLATION	3
GOLD, PRECIOUS METALS	HEDGE AGAINST INFLATION, AGGRESSIVE CAPITAL GROWTH	PRECIOUS METALS, GOLD MINING, STOCKS, GOLD BULLION, SILVER CANADIAN OR FOREIGN	**TWO** LATE RECOVERY	2
GLOBAL BONDS	CURRENT INCOME, CURRENCY HEDGE	BONDS ISSUED PRIMARILY BY FOREIGN GOVERNMENTS AND CORPORATIONS	**FOUR** RECESSION	4

Fund	Objective	Description	Economic Phase	#
AGGRESSIVE GROWTH	STRONG CAPITAL GROWTH	STOCKS, SMALL AND MEDIUM GROWTH	ONE EARLY RECOVERY	1
REAL ESTATE EQUITY	LONG-TERM CAPITAL APPRECIATION	REITs, PUBLICLY TRADED REAL ESTATE COMPANIES HOLDING SHOPPING CENTERS, HOTELS, OFFICE AND APARTMENT COMPLEXES	TWO / THREE	2 / 3
GROWTH & INCOME	CURRENT INCOME PLUS MODEST CAPITAL APPRECIATION	INCOME-ORIENTED STOCKS, TYPICALLY MORE HEAVILY WEIGHTED IN EQUITIES THAN A BALANCED FUND	THREE STAGFLATION	3
SECTORS	SPECIAL SITUATIONS MARKET TIMING	STOCKS IN SPECIFIC INDUSTRIES OR GEOGRAPHICAL REGIONS, UTILITIES, HEALTH SCIENCES, TECHNOLOGY, TELECOMMUNICATIONS, NATURAL RESOURCES	VARIOUS	ALL
MONEY MARKET	SAFETY, PRESERVATION OF CAPITAL	SHORT-TERM, LESS THAN ONE-YEAR BONDS AND GOVERNMENT TREASURY BILLS	THREE STAGFLATION	3
GLOBAL STOCK	CAPITAL APPRECIATION	STOCKS OF BOTH FOREIGN AND CANADIAN COMPANIES (OR FOREIGN AND U.S.)	ONE EARLY RECOVERY	1

MULTI-ADVISOR INVESTING

A professional fund manager oversees the selection and investment of each individual mutual fund and is responsible for its performance within the criteria established for that fund. This is true of an equity portfolio, a balanced portfolio, or a fund of the fixed-income or mixed-income variety.

A specific fund is part of a "family" group of funds. The group — such as AIC, AGF-20/20, Atlas, BPI, C.I., Dynamic, Fidelity, Guardian, Mackenzie, Templeton Global Strategy, or Trimark — includes a broad stable of individual funds running the whole gamut of investment securities from the most conservative to the emerging growth or even speculative funds. The overall management of each "family" of funds is maintained by a professional management committee, made up of numerous professional fund manager analysts.

At the next level is the independent financial advisor, who deals directly with you — the investor. According to your profile, preferences and objectives, your financial advisor first determines the overall diversification of your holdings as to fixed-income, equity income, growth equities, and so on. Your advisor allocates your assets and invests on your behalf across a broad range of individual mutual funds in line with your stated and written risk portfolio and investment requirements. In a real sense, the advisor is the fund company's client, the investor being the advisor's client.

The financial advisor, the group of funds selected, and the professional management of each individual fund in this fashion constitute three distinct layers of professional management. Think of this as a Multi-Safety "safety net."

An investor with total investments of $300,000 might diversify those holdings through 10 or 20 separate and varied mutual funds, each comprised of a portfolio of dozens, or even hundreds, of individual investment securities. This is the asset allocation stage. Within this safety structure you employ an enormous diversity of types of securities, types of funds and types of managers, and maximize chances of achieving your own particular objectives.

First, at the level of each individual mutual fund manager, performance is critical. These pros study the economic cycles, corporate developments and market activity that will influence the securities under their direction. Their sense of timing and selection will determine the strategies that enable them to do as well, and sometimes better, than the rest of the market, maximizing profitability over time.

Second, the group management committee is the important professional factor in the total equation. It supplies the group with its overall philosophy, fine-tunes the approach of individual funds and provides the support systems, research and a source of investment strategy.

Third, the financial advisor becomes personally involved, creating your financial plan and translating your requirements into the actual selection of groups and individual mutual funds. In turn, this person interprets the fund policy and group philosophy to you as investor, to make clear the fundamentals of the market and investment process, and the strategy being adopted, and why specific funds are chosen. All of these market, economic and tax considerations must be integrated with your own personal financial planning needs.

GETTING INVOLVED

What remains is to determine the level at which you as an investor — novice or sophisticate — wish to participate with your financial advisor. How active or uninvolved in the process do you wish to be? This is the unique quality of mutual fund investment. If you as an investor lack the time, training or temperament to understand all the vagaries of investing, you may choose to participate in a modest way, relying more on your advisor's recommendations.

You may turn over the portfolio construction and its management completely to your financial advisor, the fund manager, and the mutual fund "family" group. Or you may elect to participate actively in all determinations — your personal investment profile, the types of funds to be selected and in what balance, the allocation of assets and the frequency of contact and relationship with your advisor. Your advisor is prepared to interpret the plan, process and product for you, and then to guide, instruct and recommend. All this helps make any choice you make a successful one. Obviously, the more ongoing hand-holding, education, research and administration you want, the more you should be prepared to pay. Expect your professional advisor to be paid for his or her time, costs, expertise and diligent work on your behalf.

No other client-professional relationship offers such a complete range of choices to the client. The important point is not what level of participation you undertake, but the fact that *you* can elect any level of involvement that suits you. The question, of course, still begs an answer: Can the part-time novice do as well over time as the full-time professional advisor? Not likely.

chapter 8

THE BUILDING BLOCKS

*Gentlemen who prefer bonds don't know
what they're missing.*

— Peter Lynch

THE MAGIC OF COMPOUNDING

Every investment goal can be enhanced by the interaction of (1) a substantial rate of return, and (2) time. The compounding of assets for any purpose, whether building a capital reserve, saving for a child's education, or accumulating money for your retirement, is an integral, essential part of a disciplined approach to the ownership of financial instruments. (See Figure 8.1: Double Your Money.)

Compounding can be easily illustrated. A mere 2% increase in rate of return (10% instead of 8%) increases the value of $25,000 from $171,200 to $270,000 over a 25-year period. An additional 2% increase (to 12%) increases the 25-year value to $425,000. If we compare the effect of 12% over 8%, the total accumulation is improved by approximately 250%, or $253,800 more! Table 8.1 illustrates the growth of

$10,000 over various periods at selected rates of interest (compounded and reinvested but without taxation.)

FIGURE 8.1: YEARS REQUIRED TO DOUBLE YOUR MONEY AT VARIOUS RATES OF RETURN

THE RULE OF 72

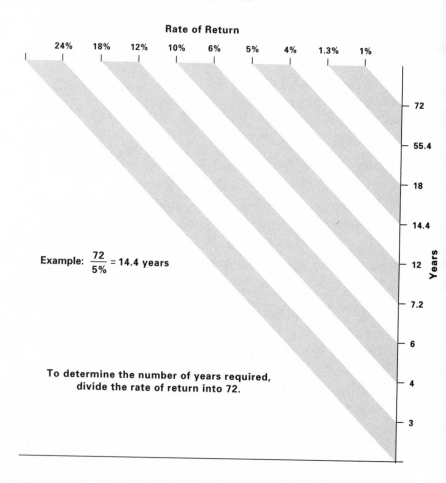

Rate of Return

24% 18% 12% 10% 6% 5% 4% 1.3% 1%

72

55.4

18

14.4

Example: $\frac{72}{5\%} = 14.4$ years

12 Years

7.2

6

To determine the number of years required, divide the rate of return into 72.

4

3

TABLE 8.1: THE MAGIC OF COMPOUND INTEREST

$10,000 NEST EGG

%	Year 5	Year 10	Year 15	Year 20	Year 25	Year 30	Year 35
3	$11,593	$13,434	$15,580	$18,061	$20,938	$24,273	$28,139
4	12,167	14,802	18,009	21,911	26,658	32,434	39,461
5	12,763	16,289	20,789	26,533	33,864	43,219	55,160
6	13,382	17,908	23,965	32,071	42,918	57,435	76,860
7	14,026	19,671	27,590	38,697	54,274	76,122	106,765
8	14,693	21,589	31,722	46,609	68,484	100,626	147,852
9	15,386	23,674	36,425	56,044	86,231	132,676	204,138
10	16,105	25,937	41,722	67,275	108,346	174,493	281,022
11	16,851	28,394	47,846	80,623	135,854	228,921	385,746
12	17,623	31,058	54,736	96,463	169,999	299,597	527,993
13	18,424	33,946	62,543	11,5230	212,304	191,157	720,685
14	19,252	37,072	71,379	137,434	264,618	509,499	981,001
15	20,114	40,456	81,370	163,664	329,188	662,114	1,331,745
16	21,003	44,114	92,655	194,606	408,740	858,494	1,803,135
17	21,924	48,068	105,387	231,055	506,576	1,110,646	2,484,034
18	22,878	52,338	119,737	273,929	626,683	1,433,700	3,279,972
19	23,864	56,947	135,895	324,293	773,878	1,846,753	4,407,006
20	24,883	61,917	154,070	383,375	953,959	2,373,763	5,906,682

Baron Rothschild put it this way: "I don't know what the Seven Wonders of the World are, but I know what the Eighth Wonder is— compound interest!"

The intelligent, ultimately successful investor must understand the nature of the three major categories of liquid financial securities: stocks, bonds and cash reserves.

We want to eliminate some of the mystery surrounding the financial markets. Many individual investors, even those with some exposure to them, continue to regard the financial markets as puzzling, foreboding, even cultish, and driven by unseen and unknowable forces and phantoms.

And it's not simply a matter of the professionals, the well-informed, working contrary to the uninformed. I have experienced situations where seemingly every professional trader on the street was convinced of a certain outcome in the market, only to see the reverse happen. At such times, an observer may be eerily convinced that an "evil troll" is at work beneath the cobblestones of Bay Street and Wall Street, working his machinations to render amateur and professional alike into blithering idiots.

The market is indeed a strange animal and obviously its movements are the product of all investors and traders, big and small, pro and amateur. Over the long term, the basic fundamentals of intelligent investing will determine the successful outcome for financial assets and their owners.

For stocks, returns are historically driven by earnings and the resulting dividends; for bonds and money market instruments, the determinants are basic interest rates and structured discounts (in the case of T-Bills, strip bonds, and zero coupons) over specified periods. Understanding the reality of these forces, not surrendering to the *illusion* of momentary optimism and pessimism, hope and fear, is at the core of intelligent investing.

Trying to build a lifetime investment program around the selection of a handful of individual bonds and stocks is, for all but the most exceptional investor, a fool's errand. The inevitable result is a performance less successful than that of a truly diversified portfolio. (Review Tables 3.1 and 3.2.)

Peter Wallace, former President of Midland Walwyn, Inc., Canada's largest independent investment dealer and mutual fund distributor, divided portfolio investment into three basic stages: *first*, decide on the division of your assets into the major classes of your equities and fixed-income; *second*, decide on foreign versus domestic content, and *third*, determine a mixture of management styles, such as large cap, small cap, growth and value. The wide-ranging possibilities for such diversification are increased in mutual fund investing, compared to conventional securities.

THE MUTUAL FUND GALAXY

Canadian Equity Funds
- aggressive growth
- small cap
- medium cap
- large cap

Global Equity Funds

International Equity Funds

Emerging Market Equity Funds

U.S. and North American Equity Funds
- asset allocation funds

European Asset Allocation Funds
- specific country asset allocation

Foreign Bond Funds

Canadian Balanced Funds
- Canadian asset allocation funds

International Balanced Funds

Canadian Bond Funds

International Bond Funds

Emerging Market Bond Funds

Mortgage Funds

Dividend Funds

Specialty Funds (specific sectors or styles)
- health sciences funds
- technology funds
- telecommunications funds
- financial services funds
- value funds
- growth funds
- blended funds

High-Yield Bond

Gold Funds

Precious Metals Funds

Real Estate Equity Funds

Money Market Funds

Derivative Funds

High-Yield Income

For a more detailed list, see Figure 9.2. And now, let's consider the major building blocks in a solid mutual fund portfolio.

IN SEARCH OF INCOME

As every GIC holder knows, today's low interest-rate environment has replaced former safe and simple sources of income. Canadian investors have been forced to seek higher-income alternatives.

In this changing income landscape, the traditional fixed-income investments offered by the Canadian government are disappearing before our eyes. The Department of Finance forecasts that net new federal bond issues will drop to zero in 1998-99, from highs of over $30 billion in 1993-94. Provincial borrowing is decreasing at an even greater rate as provincial governments act more aggressively to balance budgets.

As new government bond issues decrease, another traditional favorite income alternative, the preferred share market, is also undergoing radical surgery while its supply diminishes. New credit rating policies treat preferred dividends as debt (fixed income) rather than equity income in key ratios. The result is that preferred shares will no longer be a cost-effective method of financing for many companies. According to Nesbitt Burns, companies have retracted $24 billion as at December 31, 1996. In other words, the preferred market has vanished by two-thirds, from $37 billion down to $13 billion (and dropping) since 1987.

As a result, conservative "GIC refugees" are desperately searching for a new form of reliable income offering higher returns, some tax relief and some modest potential growth of their capital. Many have found a brand new source of income in one or several new types of mutual funds offering high-yield monthly distribution of income that are typically composed of Royalty Income Trusts (RITs), Income Trusts (ITs), Real Estate Investment Trusts (REITs), plus some nonperpetual preferred shares, corporate bonds and common stocks. The current monthly income from these trust units within such a fund has ranged from 8% to as high as 14% per annum.

These unique mutual funds offer regular monthly tax-adjusted income, an inflation hedge potential not found in conventional income vehicles, diversification not available in single investment trust units, and full RRSP/RRIF eligibility. A number of these funds are designed to provide reasonably predictable high income while employing the risk control strategy of a professional money manager.

Essentially, a royalty trust is a complex structure, which should be viewed as from a high-yield equity with favorable tax treatment rather than as a fixed-income security. These cash flows are generated directly from the sale of producing oil and gas reserves, of which a part of the systematic income may be partially or fully tax deferred for a number of years. And these trusts are exempt from the traditional exploration risk of oil and gas producers.

Investors must be aware that the income on some of these investments could be reduced over time as oil and gas reserves of the operating company are depleted.

Real Estate Investment Trusts are publicly traded trusts that typically invest in income-producing properties such as shopping centers, apartment buildings, multi-unit industrial buildings, and office properties. They often operate with more conservative balance sheets than those of traditional real estate companies. REITS refrain from raw land or speculative ventures. Revenue growth can occur through rent increases, greater occupancy, redevelopment, expansion of properties, and new property acquisition.

One of the instruments often found in my new category "mixed-income" mutual fund designation is that of high-yield bonds. Although this (lower credit) category can be accessed through some individual bond funds, such as Trimark's Advantage Bond, Atlas Canadian High-Yield Bond or BPI High Income, an income investor can seek out such securities as part of a high-mixed-income trust (RITs and REITs) fund. The selection offered is quite outstanding.

Some commentators refer to high-yield *bond* funds as a subset of fixed-income bonds. I submit that they should be regarded as a new and separate category, distinct from the average bond fund with a different set of parameters — more measured credit risk and more potential higher interest returns than those generated by plain-vanilla bond funds. Over a recent 12-month period, this new bond category produced a 1% to 5.4% better return than the average bond fund. More potential fluctuation of unit value is offset by greater potential reward. This is a growing, popular new category of mutual funds beginning to burst onto the Canadian investment income landscape.

Monthly high-yield mutual funds typically provide an income stream from *four* sources: (1) dividend income from preferred and common shares and investment trust units with significant tax benefits; (2) capital gains from realized gains on the sale of any of the fund's securities, also with preferential tax treatment; (3) interest and other trust revenue from the fund's trust units, corporate and other bonds. While fully taxed, such income is normally higher than dividend income; and (4) return of capital from non-taxable flow-through deductions available to the resource industries. These returns can be used to reduce the adjusted cost base (net cost) of investment of the shareholder's units, creating potential capital gains and, more important, deferring taxation until such time as the fund units are sold by the holder.

It is the opinion of many investment professionals that investment trust units will likely replace the dwindling market for preferred share dividends and dwindling Canadian bond issues. A good high-income fund (mixed-income fund, as I prefer to call it) can permit expert management to take advantage of mixed asset opportunities as they are presented in different periods during the *business cycle*. They can be more defensive in recessionary periods and more aggressive during stronger economic periods. And unlike GIC-type investments, these funds are always available, they are never locked in.

For an excellent example of how high-income funds might be weighted in a typical business cycle inside your portfolio, see Figure 8.2 on pages 134 and 135.

BONDS AND OTHER "LOANER" VEHICLES

Bond prices tend to be less volatile than stock prices, which may lead investors into believing that bonds are stable and provide relative safety and secure income as well. The fact is that bonds swing in price for different reasons than stocks do, but sometimes just as widely. Bonds tend to fluctuate not in response to perceived value, but in relation to prevailing interest rates.

On the other hand, a stock may advance or decline in relation to the fortunes of the individual company as well as in reaction to the fortunes of the company's industry, the general economy or to artificial stimuli, such as the volume in which the individual stock is being bought and sold. But bonds carry their own implicit risks of fluctuation.

The Risks of Bond Investment

1. INTEREST RATE (OR MARKET) RISK. A bond investment always returns a redemption price at par value, however distant, perhaps many years away. Meanwhile, bond prices are susceptible to every movement basic interest rates make. If rates increase, outstanding bonds decline. If rates move lower, bond prices appreciate. Obviously, bonds bearing longer maturities and low coupon rates are especially vulnerable. A stripped bond has even greater market risk if interest rates rise and a greater return if rates decline prior to its maturity date guarantee.

2. CREDIT RISK. Credit ratings reflect whether or not issuers can pay over time or in full. Compare federal and provincial issues, along with municipalities and corporate issues. In the credit world, everything is relative, just as with an individual's credit.

The only Canadian province ever to default on a bond issue was the Province of Alberta in the 1930s. Relatively better credit commands lower coupon rates. As a result, there is a hierarchy of bond values. Federal government bonds rank above provincials, provincials above corporate bonds, and the latter carry a higher credit

FIGURE 8.2: ASSET ALLOCATION THROUGH THE BUSINESS CYCLE

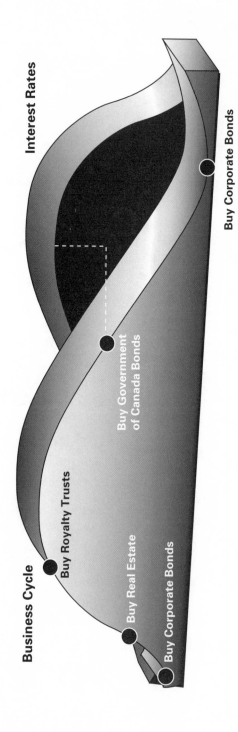

The goal of the BPI portfolio management team is to allocate the best mix of real estate investment trusts (REITs), high-yield corporate bonds, royalty trusts and international corporate and government debt securities at the appropriate period during the business cycle. Your clients will benefit from diversification, liquidity and a monthly income stream With a pre-tax target of 200 basis points over a five-year GIC, after-tax yields will potentially be even greater.

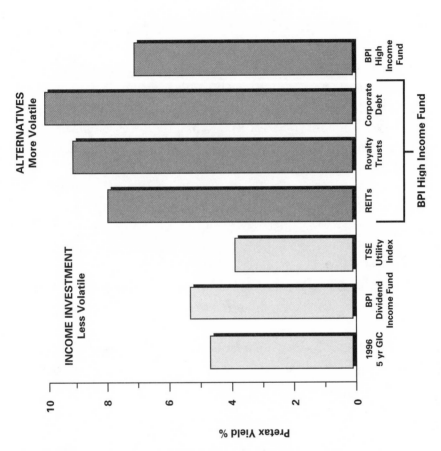

Source: BPI High Income Fund

rating than unsecured corporate debentures. The smaller the coupon, the higher the rating necessary to attract investors.

Within these rankings, some individual government or corporate bonds outrank others. Ontario provincial bonds, or the provincially guaranteed Ontario Hydro bonds, are better credits than those of Prince Edward Island. Bell Telephone pays less for its borrowings than Podunk Machine Works of Pumphandle, Saskatchewan. All of these considerations must be weighed in your investment decisions.

3. PURCHASING POWER RISK. Also known as inflation. If you park your funds in debt securities (which involve fixed dollars), you can be reasonably *certain* that the future interest payments, although dependable, will cost you a lot in purchasing power. Compare this with the effect of purchasing equities, or even bond funds, which partially offset the stagnation of fixed income.

4. REINVESTMENT RISK. You can earn less interest over time if you hold a corporate bond that is refundable by the company. When interest rates drop, the company may call your bond and replace it with one bearing a lower coupon. This can mean lower returns if your bond matures or is called at a lower-interest period and you are forced to replace it with a similar investment that yields less.

5. ROLLOVER RISK. When interest rates decline, lower yields are automatic. This is especially threatening to short-date money market securities.

6. CALL RISK. When interest rates decline, you may find your bond is redeemed by the issuer, beyond your control. A bond fund manager can reduce this risk by holding issues with longer call periods.

7. PREPAYMENT RISK. The risk of having the borrower pay out his obligation in advance makes instruments such as mortgage (bond-like) securities and mortgage-backed securities (MBSs) particularly vulnerable.

8. CURRENCY RISK. When the dollar strengthens, international and global bond holdings in foreign currencies tend to become vulnerable. Professional portfolio managers can offset this risk with sell or buy options and forward contracts.

9. LIQUIDITY RISK. Thinly traded securities can be difficult to sell. Acting according to liquidity and/or illiquidity can mean taking a big hit in price. This shortcoming is more apparent in municipal and junk-bond issues. By definition, you should limit your holdings to large, actively traded issues, such as the better-rated provincials or an Ontario Hydro.

10. EVENT RISKS Credit worthiness may be downgraded because of a specific event, such as a leveraged buyout. RJR Nabisco is a classic example. The imposing of sudden changes in the company's capitalization may benefit the shareholders while it threatens the bondholders.

11. TAX LAW RISK. Changes in taxation legislation, such as a lowering of personal tax rates, can worsen the yields on junior bonds. Or the taxable rate of a realized (sold) capital gain could be altered by the government.

12. POLITICAL RISK. Political actions, in particular fiscal or monetary ones, can affect investment securities immediately and dramatically. When President Ernesto Zedillo of Mexico uncoupled the peso from the U.S. dollar on December 20, 1994, there was an immediate and drastic effect on Latin American and emerging market fixed-income securities.

Political risks, of course, do not apply only to bond investment. Remember the panic that many Canadians felt in the period leading up to the Quebec Referendum on October 30, 1995? Nearly 80% of all the redemptions I saw at this time came from the "no-load" funds offered primarily by the banks, trust companies, credit unions and other financial institutions. All financial markets dislike uncertainty. Even the announcement of another referendum would be enough to spook financial markets, torpedo the Loonie and drive all securities, including Canadian (not international) mutual funds, into a temporary nose-dive.

Hardest hit were "no-load" funds (what I refer to as the "no-advice" funds. For more on these funds, see Chapter 15.) Investors in these generally lack high-quality, personal, ongoing professional advice. Also, because no-loads don't involve redemption charges, many people rushed to redeem these investments. As Garth Turner, former Minister of National Revenue, states in his *1997 RRSP Guide*, "This is why no-load fund investors usually have far poorer returns than the buy-and-hold crowd."

Turner correctly commented, "The day after the referendum, when financial markets rallied dramatically, all those people who sold decided to buy back again . . . in keeping with the typical Canadian strategy of waiting for a crisis to sell low and then buy high!"

Considering all of the above discussion of the shortcomings of bonds, the risks associated with them and their limitations, why should you even consider investing in either bonds or a bond fund?

To begin with, well chosen fixed-income securities and the mutual funds that include them in their portfolios represent a high degree of safety, stability and income. Life insurance companies and other institutions need to invest with certainty against future fixed-dollar commitments. Bonds fit their requirements as few other instruments can. Similarly, a person of a certain age, looking toward a fixed-dollar commitment and a specific date, might find it advantageous to consider the same course.

Bond investment has its values in a much wider sense, too. You can gain certain advantages through *bond funds* over direct bond investment. You can always sell shares of a bond fund, a feature not always available in the case of individual bonds or guaranteed income certificates (GICs). A good global bond fund enables your manager to take advantage of market opportunities as they occur, and also to participate in bond markets outside Canada. You can diversify your bond risk and increase your average gains with greater stability, too. And, we won't forget managed *currency* risk protection, also another

potentially good reason for having global bond funds in a portfolio.
Let's take a longer look at the bond/GIC alternative. Rising
interest rates and a disappointing bond market made many investors
question the wisdom of buying bonds in 1994. GICs offered a 6%
annual return early in that year. With a fixed rate and a set maturity,
GICs sound like bonds, don't they? But consider these two cases:

> If you had invested $10,000 in a bond fund in early 1994, its
> market value would have evaporated by about 4% over the
> ensuing year. That leaves $9,600 of your original investment.
>
> If, however, you had invested $10,000 in a GIC at the
> same time, your GIC, as reported on your year-end state-
> ment, would have grown to $10,600 in value. That is not
> an accurate reading, however, although on the surface it
> would seem to be the case. The same rising interest rates
> would now mean that you could buy an 8% GIC. This
> would make the 6% GIC you had purchased worth less in
> the market, if in fact there was a market for GICs! The
> GIC lost market value; you just didn't see it!

The fact is that the value of a nonredeemable GIC at any given time
cannot be set. A GIC is not liquid, as bond funds are. There is, therefore, no market we can discuss for locked-in GICs. They have value
only at their maturity date. In a way, the value of a GIC between its
purchase and its maturity date may remind you of the emperor's new
clothes. GICs seem stable only because *you* guarantee that you
won't sell them before maturity. Their *unseen value fluctuates* nearly
every day!

GICs and bond funds have different risk profiles. Unlike GICs,
bond funds offer no specific rate of return. This is because while bonds
may mature within the fund, they may also be traded out of the fund
before they mature. The only *specific* return in a bond fund is indicated
when a shareholder redeems the fund's shares at net asset value.

BOND MUTUAL FUNDS VERSUS INDIVIDUAL BONDS

1. *Easy Access:* The bond markets are oriented to professionals and large investors. The smaller investor can employ a *bond* fund to work on his behalf, since transaction costs are relatively high when dealing in small amounts — as is true of any commodity. The professional, including the fund management professional, also knows how to shop around. The small investor doesn't.

2. *Liquidity:* It is easier for a small bond fund holder to redeem money out of a fund without adverse price consequences than if dealing with a small individual bond holding — especially in the case of lightly traded issues, where the dealer's spreads may be quite wide.

3. *Monthly Income:* This can be an important factor for older or retired investors who need the interest from their investments as supplementary income. *Individual* bonds normally pay interest semi-annually. In addition, the more frequent distributions by a bond fund can be used as a reinvested (monthly or quarterly) compounding effect. These distributions of income earnings are paid out automatically, *quarterly*, and often *monthly*.

4. *Ease of Reinvestment:* Convenient reinvestment of interest or dividend income is available with mutual funds, even for small amounts. Beyond the convenience, reinvestment can mean higher compounded returns over time.

5. *Professional Management:* Fluctuating interest rates can make life difficult for the individual bond holder. On the other hand, a professional manager can react to changing conditions and monitor risk factors — in other words, actively manage a bond portfolio.

6. *Diversification:* The dozens or even hundreds of different issues within a mutual fund portfolio allow the bond fund investor the greatest diversification which is unimaginable with a few individual bonds. The individual investor may find a single issue a credit risk. This risk would probably be purged in a bond fund portfolio.

Managers of bond portfolios seek to maintain a core position in major bond asset categories, and at the same time less significant positions in more speculative issues. Since the more speculative positions are more susceptible to market volatility, the managers achieve a sort of balance, whereby the fund can ride out periods of market turbulence. They keep themselves free to take advantage of shorter-term fluctuations.

The "core concept" of a good bond fund is that it aims to outperform individual Canadian bonds of average maturity in both market risk and total return. One international bond fund manager states it this way: "We have designed the bond funds to deliver over time a higher expected return than Canadian bonds and to have less price fluctuation on a daily, weekly and yearly basis. This is achieved by using the benefits of diversification to their maximum and by taking advantage of inefficiencies in the global bond markets."

While a bond fund does *not* have a *specific duration* and set interest rate, it does offer a raft of benefits not available to individual bond holders. Conclusion? Both instruments have their particular benefits.

WHAT ABOUT PREFERRED STOCKS?

Preferred stocks represent a special category. We might include them under the bonds and other fixed-income heading, although in terms of the equity position that they occupy in a company's capital structure, they are more closely related to common stocks. They are stocks in that they represent equity in the company, although of a conditional and preferred variety. My preference is to refer to them as "equity-income vehicles."

Preferred stocks are usually allowed a favored position over the common stock, either in the payment of dividends or in the winding up of the company. Their superior position, however, is limited to a set percentage as to dividend, and also to the payment of their face value on the dissolution or winding up of a company.

On the other hand, preferred dividends are similar in principle to common stock dividends. They both benefit from the dividend tax credit that makes such income preferable to the interest income bondholders receive. Under this tax credit, about 30% to 34% of dividend income becomes tax free each year, depending on the province in which you live.

While the preferred stock is considered a defensive, conservative investment, in some circumstances it can produce capital gains, and therefore can be considered to have added speculative appeal.

Let's say a company has fallen on hard times, so has suspended paying dividends. When the company turns itself around and becomes profitable again, steel-nerved investors may enjoy payment of past missed dividends as a bonanza. The windfall may include considerable capital appreciation in the stock if the price has declined because of missed past dividends. Scouting out these kinds of gains is not recommended for amateur investors.

A typical example is that of Algoma Steel Corp. which, between 1991 and 1995, ran the full gamut from near bankruptcy to recovery. The company's 5.5% *cumulative* preferred shares, whose par value was $25, had sunk to $1.50 by early 1993. By early 1995, they were trading at $23.

That's excellent — *if* you can find the right depressed company. But like buying a used car, you must know what you're doing.

A business professor at New York University once summed up this hybrid security as follows: "Blessed are the preferred shareholders, for they may inherit the company."

EQUITY SECURITIES

"It's so popular, nobody goes there anymore."

— Yogi Berra, commenting on a
famous restaurant in Miami Beach

"What makes a great diamond," says Mario Gabelli, founder and chairman of Gabelli Funds of Rye, New York, "is cut, color, carets, and clarity. . . . So, too, a great stock."

And making money through common stock investment is even more in vogue than ever. Just ask the Russians, Hungarians and Chinese.

Now investors small and large, skinny and fat, the halt and the lame, and of all ages, can secure a well-managed, highly diversified common stock portfolio as one of the best ways to accumulate wealth. With this you can pay for a child's education, finance a business, pay off a mortgage or prepare for your retirement years.

Stock performance is well documented. Stocks have an uncontested history of long-term returns far superior to that of any other asset class. Figure 8.3 traces the course of a single dollar deposited in various U.S. investment media in 1925. Invested in bonds, that dollar would have been worth $33.73 by mid-1996. Figure 8.4 shows a similar pattern: a dollar invested in the Canadian bond market in 1950 would today have a value of $21.67.

FIGURE 8.3: THE GROWTH OF $1 INVESTED IN CERTAIN ASSETS OVER 71 YEARS

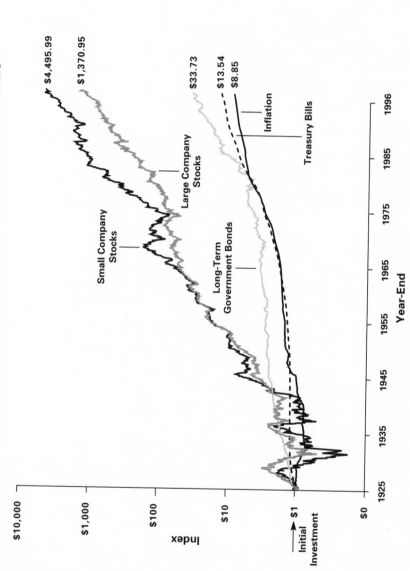

(Includes reinvestment but excludes commission and tax.)

Sources: NYSE, Standard & Poor's 500 U.S. Government Bonds and T–Bills and CPI (U.S.)

FIGURE 8.4: A CANADIAN COMPARISON: RETURNS ON BONDS, STOCKS AND GICs, TREASURY BILLS AND THE CONSUMER PRICE INDEX (CPI)

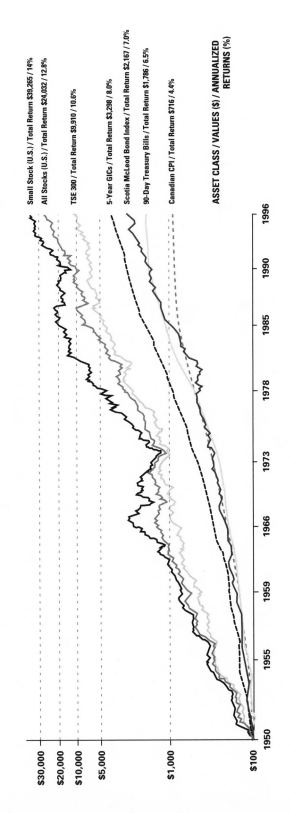

Small Stock (U.S.) / Total Return $39,265 / 14%

All Stocks (U.S.) / Total Return $24,032 / 12.8%

TSE 300 / Total Return $9,910 / 10.6%

5-Year GICs / Total Return $3,298 / 8.0%

Scotia McLeod Bond Index / Total Return $2,167 / 7.0%

90-Day Treasury Bills / Total Return $1,786 / 6.5%

Canadian CPI / Total Return $716 / 4.4%

ASSET CLASS / VALUES ($) / ANNUALIZED RETURNS (%)

Sources: Center for Research in Security Prices, University of Chicago,
NYSE, AMEX, NASDAQ, TSE 300, Scotia McLeod,
Bank of Canada, Statistics Canada

But if you had flipped your 1925 buck into U.S. small-company stocks, it would have weighed in at more than $4,495 in mid-1996, or in Canadian small-caps since 1950, more than $392.

Nor were blue-chip stocks sluggards. A single dollar in such stocks would have swelled to more than $1,370 in U.S. stocks since 1926, or $240 in Canada since 1950.

Stock mutual funds, as distinct from individual stocks or individual portfolios of stocks, without doubt offer the best chance of success, particularly in today's economic climate. Even at the best of times and in the best of hands, however, stocks can act unpredictably, even misbehave badly in ways that even the pros hadn't expected. (After 1994's performance, the same can be said of bonds.)

To minimize your investment's exposure to market volatility, there are income-oriented stocks, such as utilities, some bank stocks and some other blue chips in very stable industries. They tend to be less prone to wide swings. These may be ideal for many people in or near retirement who need regular, ongoing income and not long-range capital growth. The mutual fund comprised of high-income defensive stocks would give these investors even more stability.

Measuring Stock Performance

Securities analysts and mutual fund portfolio managers, and some financial advisors, evaluate individual stocks in several ways. Here are several examples of key ratios to help you determine bargain buys.

The price-earnings ratio (P/E). If a stock is trading at $10 and the company had net earnings of $1 in the last fiscal year, the P/E ratio is 10:1, or 10. Value investors look for stocks trading at low price-earnings ratios, checking that there is no unusual or negative reason for their being abnormally low in price, of course.

Many years ago, Loblaws stock tended to trade at about seven times earnings while its major competitors averaged about 15:1. Was Loblaws an incredible buy, then? Not exactly. Analysts at the time uniformly and vocally criticized Loblaws' management. The company's

---

UTILITIES STOCKS

Many aggressive investors dismiss the yields on utilities stocks as too slight to be worth their consideration. But think about this: your utility bills go up all the time. The companies' shareholders typically collect higher dividends all the time, too. Today's yield should not be the point. Look at *tomorrow's* yield.

The unbroken stream of rising dividends may not be the only goal of an all-equity investment, but it can be one answer to any guarantee-obsessed saver trying to become an investor.

Great North American businesses share their increased profits with their shareholders — *not* their lenders, bondholders, or creditors. Indeed, the shareholders themselves vote for their own increased dividends. *Lend* to the great companies, including utilities and banks, and they'll never pay you a penny more than they promised. Buy stock in those same companies, and you can receive a steady stream of income that may rise even faster than your cost of living does.

---

annual report displayed more four-color spreads of beef tenderloin and colorful bounty of the fields than on the numbers and facts analysts needed to make intelligent financial appraisals. The low P/E multiple persisted for years because Loblaws stock remained unpopular.

Needless to say, the P/E ratio for an equity mutual fund will be an *average* of the ratios for all of its component stocks.

The dividend payout ratio expresses the actual dividend rate compared with the net earnings figure. For example, earnings may be $1 per share and the dividend declared may be 50 cents per share.

The dividend yield measures the annual dividend as a percentage of stock price. When P/E is high, the yield tends to be low. Table 8.2 illustrates some of the extremes of such ratios historically (measures of market risk).

TABLE 8.2: MEASURES OF MARKET VALUE

Ratio	Average Value	Historic High	Historic Low
Price to Book Value (assets minus liabilities per share outstanding)	1.6	4.2 (1929)	0.5 (1932)
Price to Earnings (price divided by earnings per share outstanding)	14.1	28.0 (1935)	6.0 (1979)
Price to Dividends (price divided by dividend per share outstanding)	22.6	38.4 (1987)	6.0 (1932)

Source: Dow Jones Industrial Index

Do Dividends Lie?

The value of dividends, which determines yield, can indicate blue-chip stocks which maximize profits and minimize risk. Dividends represent real money, not just numbers on a balance sheet. An element of certainty, dividend yield has been a measure of value, revealing a company's health that is not necessarily shown by raw earnings and book value.

In addition, dividends have been a bellwether; historically, a dividend yield over 3% has signaled a buying opportunity, while a yield under 3% indicated that the stock was overpriced. In 1982, the Dow Jones Industrial Average indicated an all-time high-dividend yield of about 7%. There followed a five-year bull market. In 1996-97, the TSE 300 Index is showing an average dividend of about 1% to 2.5% as we *may* be entering the final stages of one of the longest bull markets in history.

But this dividend-yield measurement may have currently lost some of its "prophetic" usefulness, particularly in an extended bull market. Have dividends become less reliable as a market barometer?

There are several reasons. First, of course, the TSE 300's relentless rise has reduced dividend yields. Second, the unusually high inflation factor in the late 1970s and early 1980s distorted the yield factor. Third, there has been a fundamental shift in the corporate treatment of dividends. In place of cash dividends in 1996-97 many companies have utilized cash in share buy-back programs, so increasing the value of outstanding stock held by individuals or mutual funds, in effect producing a capital gain benefit rather than one of income. In terms of tax, this is a distinct advantage to the shareholder, since capital losses may be deducted from capital gains. Also, the investor can choose his timing of realized capital gain. Dividends must be reported when earned; capital gain may be deferred over an unlimited period of time.

One estimate places dividends as being only one-third of all distributions in 1996, down from about 80% in the late 1970s. There has also been a trend within companies of building up cash reserves as buffer against future contingencies, rather than increasing dividend payments. Another factor is that Canada's fast-growing technology companies have large capitalizations and thus the need to fund greater development, and so pay little or no dividends. Nonetheless, their stocks — and the mutual funds that own them — represent strong growth potential.

So the new dividend reality is that some dividend yields are declining significantly, often unrelated to the market's direction. I believe we will see a dramatic rebound in dividends paid out in 1998 and 1999 as company share buybacks eventually slow down. Don't count on the old truism that "dividends don't lie." They may well dissemble, because of radically changing dividend demographics. The result of these changes is that conservative current-income investors must now seek solid alternatives, not only to dividends but even to the interest on domestic government bonds, which for different reasons will also become more scarce in the coming years.

BLUE CHIPS

Stocks tend to fit into several categories. In particular circumstances they may encompass more than one category at a time. "Blue chip" signifies a stock of quality, size, and maturity, but it may also be designated as a "growth" stock, an "income" stock, and/or a "defensive" stock. A growth stock may also be speculative.

Blue chips take their name from the most valuable chip in a gambling casino, excepting the $100 black-and-yellow "honey-bees." The stocks are typically those of large, old, and well-established companies, such as those listed on the Toronto Stock Exchange (TSE) or the Dow Jones Industrial Average (DJIA) in New York. Bell Canada, IBM, Coca-Cola, and General Motors are blue chips. They are considered income stocks because of their fairly high dividend payouts. Some can be quite cyclical. Many of Standard & Poor's 500 Index stocks also qualify as blue chips.

Income stocks. The TSE 300 consists of mature companies that pay dividends. This is an area where a competent income mutual fund manager can show superior performance.

Growth stocks. These are stocks of companies with better than average growth prospects. For this reason, their issuing companies tend to pay small or no dividends, ploughing earnings back into their operations to expand as much as possible. Growth investors place a higher priority on current growth and future dividends than on current payout.

Emerging growth stocks are those of companies that are at an even earlier point in the development cycle than growth stocks. Investors seeking unusual capital gains sometimes favor these smaller, untried companies. As you might expect, they are often highly speculative.

Growth and income stocks are stocks of companies that offer investors unusually good prospects for growth at a stage of development from which they feel ready to pay dividends out of their earnings without hampering their companies' ability to grow at a better than average pace.

Cyclical stocks. The companies and industries that issue these are subject to cyclical patterns, for one reason or another, such as changing seasons — they produce winter sports equipment or summer apparel. Another company might engage in cyclical patterns of longer duration, such as parts of the forest industry that expect naturally longer cycles in their sales and earnings.

Defensive stocks. One of these is utilities. Because of their excellent downside characteristics, they are considered safe and defensive — their products are in steady demand.

Speculative stocks sit even lower on the scale of safety than emerging company stocks do. Extreme examples are penny stocks in the mining or oil industries. Occasionally, one of these might soar to great heights, but the vast majority of speculative stocks take their investors for roller-coaster rides at best, and at worst lose huge amounts of their money. Many of these unfortunate investors cash out at the bottom of deep cyclical markets.

Paying Dividends

Let's expand on the subject of the common stock love-hate relationship in general, and stock dividends in particular, by asking two
extremely important questions posed by Nick Murray in his book
Gathering Assets:

1. What do investors hate and fear the most about common stocks?

   If you answered "sudden, unpredictable down-drafts in
   stock prices," you're right, even though such declines are
   often wrongly associated with risk or a fundamental failing
   on the part of the company.

2. What do investors love most about common stocks (next to
   their doubling in value)?

   The *dividend*. And particularly the fact that strong companies regularly increase it. Dividends, like blood pressure, don't lie. Just as mature investors don't cry. So stock
   price appreciation — capital gain — is not always the focus
   in every investment."

Murray continues, "Let's qualify that last statement. Instead of
viewing dividends and capital gains as two different, contending features of investing in blue-chip common stocks, try viewing them as
cause and effect. Common stocks don't increase in value indiscrimi-
nately or because the CEO is a nice guy. Ultimately they rise because
of earnings, the resultant dividends, or even because of the *prospect*
of future dividends."

The stability of dividend-bearing stocks compared to the relative
volatility of growth-oriented equities can be easily demonstrated.
According to BellCharts, Inc. of Toronto, of 124 selected Canadian
equity funds in the period 1991-96, the highest yielded 39.8% and
the lowest 8.3%. By comparison, for 96 selected Canadian balanced

funds (i.e., comprised of bonds and all types of stocks, over the same period), the highest average return was 14.2% and the lowest 9.7%. (See Tables 8.3 to 8.8, particularly 8.5 and 8.7.)

These figures represent the difference. Some investors don't mind living with the greater volatility in order to get an edge in total return. And such a difference compounded annually over five years is impressive. Others, who are more conservative, might accept the lesser return of the dividend funds to live more comfortably through the occasional white-knuckle period.

Some people have trouble sustaining their faith in common stock price appreciation, especially in a bear market period. The final quarter of 1987 really tested these investors. After almost half a decade of unprecedented volatility in common stocks, accompanied by equally extreme growth and profit, the rank and file of investors now finds it difficult to relate stock prices to the value of their corresponding companies.

Everybody likes dividends. They represent one of the greatest bulwarks against loss. They stimulate investors to hold onto their money, without outliving it.

TABLE 8.3: CANADIAN BOND FUNDS
Funds that invest in bonds and other fixed-income securities (3 years: 97 funds; 5 years: 83 funds)

TOP 10 3-YEAR ANNUAL COMPOUND RETURN		TOP 10 RISK-ADJUSTED 3-YEAR RETURN		TOP 10 AVERAGE 1-5 YEAR ANNUAL RETURN	
Batirente-Sec Obligations	9.6%	Dynamic Income Fund	3	Batirente-Sec Obligations	12.6
SSQ-Obligations Canadiennes	9.4	C. I. Canadian Bond Fund	1.98	McLean Budden Pooled Fixed Income	12.4
McLean Budden Pooled Fixed Income	9.3	SSQ-Obligations Canadiennes	1.78892	Optimum Obligations	12.24
University Avenue Bond Fund	9.24	Empire Group Bond Fund	1.78887	SSQ Obligations Canadiennes	12.23
C. I. Canadian Bond Fund	9.18	Batirente-Sec Obligation	1.77	Empire Group Bond Fund	11.81
Optimum Obligations	9.11	University Avenue Bond Fund	1.76	Green Line Canadian Bond Fund	11.79
Empire Group Bond Fund	9.1	McLean Budden Pooled Fixed Income	1.61	Altimira Bond Fund	11.6
Dynamic Income Fund	9.09	Bissett Bond Fund	1.55	Bissett Bond Fund	11.51
Bissett Bond Fund	9.04	Optimum Obligations	1.46	Phillips, Hager & North Bond Fund	11.45
Green Line Canadian Bond Fund	8.8	Phillips, Hager & North Bond Fund	1.44	Desjardins Bond Fund	11.41
BOTTOM 5		**BOTTOM 5**		**BOTTOM 5**	
Top Fifty T-Bill/Bond Fund	2.6	Top Fifty T-Bill/Bond Fund	–2.09	BPI Canadian Bond Fund	4.6
BPI Canadian Bond Fund	2.7	BPI Canadian Bond Fund	–1.2	Top Fifty T-Bill/Bond Fund	5.8
Manulife Vista Bond 2	4.2	Templeton Canadian Bond Fund	–0.89	Pursuit Canadian Bond Fund	6.6
Metlife MVP Bond Fund	4.59	Manulife Vista Bond 2	–0.75	Trans-Canada Bond Fund	6.8
20/20 Income Fund	4.63	20/20 Income Fund	–0.66	Metlife MVP Bond Fund	6.9

Source: BellCharts Inc.

TABLE 8.4: CANADIAN SMALL-CAP FUNDS

Funds that invest in small- and mid-size corporations (3 years: 32 funds; 5 years: 20 funds)

TOP 10 3-YEAR ANNUAL COMPOUND RETURN

Marathon Equity Fund	27.2%
Multiple Opportunities Fund	27
Septre Equity Growth Fund	26.1
Colonia Special Growth Fund	25.9
Millennium Next Generation Fund	21.7
20/20 RSP Aggressive Equity	21.4
BPI Canadian Small Companies	20.5
Pacific Special Equity Fund	20
Guardian Enterprise Fund 'A'	19.6
Bissett Small Cap Fund	17.7

BOTTOM 5

Cambridge Special Equity	0.8
Canada Trust Everest Special Equity	1.5
Industrial Equity Fund Ltd.	2.4
CIBC Capital Appreciation Fund	4
Altimira Special Growth Fund	5.4

TOP 10 RISK-ADJUSTED 3-YEAR RETURN

Sceptre Equity Growth Fund	5.44
Colonia Special Growth Fund	4.35
Marathon Equity Fund	4.09
Millennium Next Generation Fund	4.01
Guardian Enterprise Fund 'A'	3.62
Bissett Small Cap Fund	3.35
Spectrum United Canadian Growth	3.08
BPI Canadian Small Companies	2.89
ABC Fundamental Value Fund	2.79
Mutual Premier Growth Fund	2.75

BOTTOM 5

Canada Trust Everest Special Equity	–1.29
Industrial Equity Fund Ltd.	–0.85
CIBC Capital Appreciation Fund	–0.61
Cambridge Special Equity	–0.6
General Trust of Canada Growth	–0.14

TOP 10 AVERAGE 1-5 YEAR ANNUAL RETURN

Multiple Opportunities Fund	45.7%
Marathon Equity Fund	41.8
Bissett Small Cap Fund	34
BPI Canadian Small Companies	31.1
Sceptre Equity Growth Fund	30.7
Guardian Enterprise Fund 'A'	28.4
ABC Fundamental Value Fund	26.2
Mawer New Canada Fund	25.6
GBC Canadian Growth Fund	22.618
Spectrum United Canadian Growth	22.615

BOTTOM 5

Canada Trust Everest Special Equity	11.4
Cambridge Special Equity	11.6
CIBC Capital Appreciation Fund	12.6
Industrial Equity Fund Ltd.	13.3
Laurentian Special Equity Fund	13.5

Source: BellCharts Inc.

TABLE 8.5: CANADIAN EQUIT YFUNDS

Funds that invest in shares of Canadian corporations (3 years: 145 funds; 5 years: 124 funds)

TOP 10 3-YEAR ANNUAL COMPOUND RETURN		TOP 10 RISK-ADJUSTED 3-YEAR RETURN		TOP 10 AVERAGE 1-5 YEAR ANNUAL RETURN	
AIC Advantage Fund	23.7%	Ivy Canadian Fund	4.68	AIC Advantage Fund	39.8%
Navigator Value Investment Retirement	22.2	Cundill Security Fund	4.6	AltaFund Investment Corp.	26.3
Phillips, Hager & North Vintage Fund	19.2	Optima Canadian Equity Fund	3.93	Phillips, Hager & North Vintage Fund	25.7
Tradex Equity Fund Ltd.	17.4	AIC Advantage Fund	3.86	McLean Budden Pooled Canadian	24.7
Optima Canadian Equity Fund	17	Phillips, Hager & North Vintage Fund	3.83	Tradex Equity Fund Ltd.	23.1
Equitable Life Seg Common Stock	16.9	Navigator Value Investment Retirement	3.78	Scotia Excelsior Canadian Growth	22.9
Scotia Excelsior Canadian Growth	16.8	Equitable Life Seg Common Stock	3.4	Bissett Canadian Equity Fund	22.8
McLean Budden Pooled Canadian	16.7	Tradex Equity Fund Ltd.	3.34	Saxton Stock Fund	22.6
AltaFund Investment Corp.	16.1	Standard Life Ideal Equity Fund	3.32	Guardian Growth Equity Fund 'A'	22.2
Phillips, Hager & North Pooled Pension Trust	15.7	Bissett Canadian Equity Fund	3.22	McLean Budden Equity Growth Fund	21.9

BOTTOM 5		BOTTOM 5		BOTTOM 5	
Cambridge Growth Fund	4.8	Canadian Protected Fund	−2.64	Cambridge Growth Fund	4.5
Canadian Protected Fund	2.1	Cambridge Growth Fund	−2.15	Canadian Protected Fund	4.6
Trans-Canada Value Fund	3.4	Dolphin Growth Fund	−0.69	Dolphin Growth Fund	5.6
University Avenue Canadian Fund	3.6	University Avenue Canadian Fund	−0.57	Admax Canadian Select Growth	7.7
Dolphin Growth Fund	3.8	Trans-Canada Value Fund	−0.55	All-Canadian Compound Fund	8.3

Source: BellCharts Inc.

TABLE 8.6: U.S. EQUITY FUNDS

Funds that invest in shares of U.S. companies (3 years: 75 funds; 5 years: 52 funds)

TOP 10 3-YEAR ANNUAL COMPOUND RETURN		TOP 10 RISK-ADJUSTED 3-YEAR RETURN		TOP 10 AVERAGE 1-5 YEAR ANNUAL RETURN	
Universal U.S. Emerging Growth	20.6%	SSQ-Actions Americaines	5.34	AIC Value Fund	26.5%
McLean Budden Pooled American	20.05	Investors U.S. Growth Fund	5.1	BPI American Small Companies	22.6
Spectrum United American Growth	20.02	Mawer U.S. Equity Fund	4.9	PH & N U.S. Pooled Pension	22.5
SSQ-Actions Americaines	19.9	Green Line U.S. Index Fund ($U.S.)	4.48	Spectrum United American Growth	21.1
AIC Value Fund	19.5	PH & N U.S. Pooled Pension	4.37	McLean Budden Pooled American	20.9
PH & N U.S. Pooled Pension	18.9	Scotia CanAm Growth Fund	4.24	Phillips, Hager & North U.S. Equity	20.8
Green Line North American Growth	18.8	McLean Budden Pooled American	4.204	SSQ-Actions Americaines	20.3
Green Line U.S. Index Fund ($U.S.)	18.3	Canada Trust Everest AmeriGrow	4.201	AGF American Growth Fund Ltd. 'A'	19.9
Canada Trust Everest AmeriGrow	17.78	AIC Value Fund	4.09	Chou Associates Fund	19.7
Fidelity Growth America Fund	17.77	Green Line North American Growth	4.04	Green Line U.S. Index Fund ($U.S.)	19.6
BOTTOM 5		**BOTTOM 5**		**BOTTOM 5**	
Cambridge American Growth	−10.4	Century DJ Fund	−4.21	First American Fund	1.8
First American Fund	−0.1	First American Fund	−3.77	Century DJ Fund	4.6
Jones Heward American Fund	2.4	Cambridge American Growth	−2.93	University Avenue Growth Fund	5.8
Century DJ Fund	4.6	Jones Heward American Fund	−1.02	Admax American Select Growth	8.2
InvesNat Blue Chip American Equity	5.6	InvesNat Blue Chip American Equity	−0.1	Jones Heward American Fund	8.5

Source: BellCharts Inc.

TABLE 8.7: CANADIAN BALANCED FUNDS

Funds with mixed portfolios of stocks and bonds (3 years: 111 funds; 5 years: 96 funds)

TOP 10 3-YEAR ANNUAL COMPOUND RETURN		TOP 10 RISK-ADJUSTED 3-YEAR RETURN		TOP 10 AVERAGE 1-5 YEAR ANNUAL RETURN	
ABC Fully-Managed Fund	16.7%	Ivy Growth and Income Fund	4.51	ABC Fully-Managed Fund	24.2%
Caldwell Securities Associate	14.7	ABC Fully-Managed Fund	3.49	Industrial Pension Fund	19.4
Ivy Growth and Income Fund	13.6	Bissett Retirement Fund	3.38	Saxon Balanced Fund	18.8
Sceptre Balanced Growth Fund	13.3	Saxon Balanced Fund	3.24	Sceptre Balanced Growth Fund	18.4
Saxon Balanced Fund	13.2	BG Private Balanced Fund	3.13	AGF Growth & Income Fund 'A'	17.8
Bissett Retirement Fund	12.85	PH & N Balanced Pension Trust	2.96	Bissett Retirement Fund	16.9
Industrial Pension Fund	12.79	Sceptre Balanced Growth Fund	2.93	Caldwell Securities Associate	16.58
AGF Growth & Income Fund 'A'	12.3	McLean Budden Pooled Balanced	2.82	McLean Budden Pooled Balanced	16.57
McLean Budden Pooled Balanced	12.2	Caldwell Securities Associate	2.8	Maxxum Canadian Balanced Fund	15.7
PH & N Balanced Pension Trust	12.1	Transamerica B.I.G.	2.77	McLean Budden Balanced Fund	15.5
BOTTOM 5		**BOTTOM 5**		**BOTTOM 5**	
Cambridge Balanced Fund	−0.7	Cambridge Balanced Fund	−1.9	Cambridge Balanced Fund	7.4
McDonald Canada Plus Fund	3.7	McDonald Canada Plus Fund	−0.7	BPI Canadian Balanced Fund	8.3
BPI Canadian Balanced Fund	4.7	BPI Canadian Balanced Fund	−0.49	LaSalle Balanced Fund	8.9
Altamira Balanced Fund	5.5	Altamira Balanced Fund	−0.19	Manulife Vista Diversified 2	9.2
Altimira Growth & Income Fund	5.8	Altimira Growth & Income Fund	−0.02	Altimira Growth & Income Fund	9.7

Source: BellCharts Inc.

TABLE 8.8: GLOBAL EQUITY FUNDS

Funds that invest in companies anywhere in the world (3 years: 66 funds; 5 years: 46 funds)

TOP 10 3-YEAR ANNUAL COMPOUND RETURN	
Trimark Fund	15.4%
Saxon World Growth	14.5
Ivy Foreign Equity Fund	14.2
Trimark Select Growth Fund	13.9
OHA Foreign Equity Fund	13.8
Green Line Global Select Fund	13.7
Investors Growth Portfolio Fund	13.6
Canada Life U.S. & Int'l Equity S-34	13
Templeton International Stock	12.8
Fidelity International Portfolio Fund	12.1

BOTTOM 5	
Cambridge Global Fund	–10.9
Spectrum United Global Growth	–3.1
GBC International Growth Fund	1.1
Orbit World Fund	1.3
Admax International Fund	3

TOP 10 RISK-ADJUSTED 3-YEAR RETURN	
Ivy Foreign Equity Fund	4.44
Cundill Value Fund	4.18
Investors Growth Portfolio Fund	3.3
Trimark Fund	3.25
Saxon World Growth	3.08
Green Line Global Select Fund	2.81
Trimark Select Growth Fund	2.79
OHA Foreign Equity Fund	2.69
Fonds de Professionnels Int'l Eq	2.46
Canada Life U.S. & Int'l Equity S-34	2.45

BOTTOM 5	
Spectrum United Global Growth	–3.29
Orbit World Fund	–2.05
Cambridge Global Fund	–1.69
GBC International Growth Fund	–1.63
General Trust International Fund	–1.02

TOP 10 AVERAGE 1-5 YEAR ANNUAL RETURN	
Templeton International Stock	18.2%
Trimark Fund	17.3
MD Growth Fund	17
Canada Life U.S. & Int'l Equity S-34	17.3
Saxon World Growth	16.7
Templeton Growth Fund Ltd.	16.3
Investors Growth Portfolio Fund	15.9
Templeton Global Smaller Companies	15.8
Trimark Select Growth Fund	15.7
20/20 International Value Fund	15.2

BOTTOM 5	
Cambridge Global Fund	–4.6
Spectrum United Global Growth	0.3
Orbit World Fund	3.6
GBC International Growth Fund	4.6
General Trust International Fund	6

Source: BellCharts Inc.

CATEGORIES OF EQUITY FUNDS

For those intent on achieving better than average growth, *aggressive-growth funds* subdivide into micro-cap (capitalization) and small-cap company funds. These include emerging companies with an element of the speculative about them, which demonstrate a better than average potential. There are also *growth funds*, which include mature companies yet focus on strong growth. *Growth and income funds* combine the qualities of a growth fund with good dividend payouts. *Equity income funds* are made up of stocks notable for producing dividend income.

Morgan Stanley & Company reviewed the 25-year performance of the following indexes of stock markets for an average annual growth rate between 1970 and mid-1996:

Canadian Index	— 10.2%
U.S. Index	— 12.9%
German Index	— 12.9%
French Index	— 15.0%
U.K. Index	— 13.2%
Switzerland Index	— 13.8%
Japanese Index	— 17.2%
Hong Kong Index	— 22.1%

Recent years have produced more variations on the equity fund — hybrids, specialty funds, sector funds, diversified funds. And more.

FIGURE 8.5: THE MORGAN STANLEY WORLD INDEX

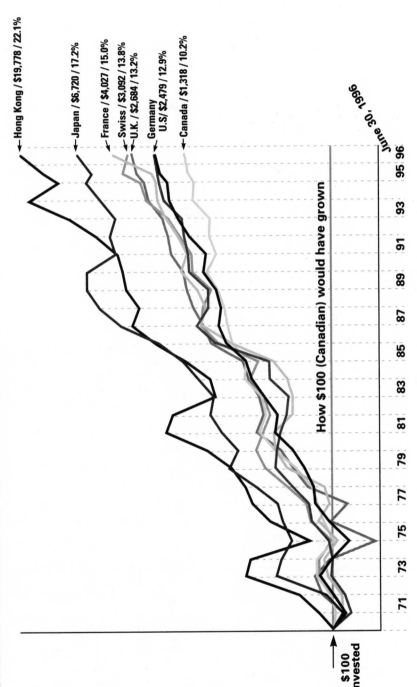

Hong Kong / $19,778 / 22.1%

Japan / $6,720 / 17.2%

France / $4,027 / 15.0%
Swiss / $3,092 / 13.8%
U.K. / $2,684 / 13.2%
Germany
U.S / $2,479 / 12.9%

Canada / $1,318 / 10.2%

June 30, 1996

How $100 (Canadian) would have grown

$100
Invested

Source: Morgan Stanley

Let's examine these equity categories in more detail. Mutual funds in the U.S. have become so popular in recent years that their total number—approaching 10,000—is more than the stocks listed on the New York Stock Exchange. There are more that 1,500 funds in Canada. The Canadian investor today can find a stock portfolio to fit every conceivable investment style, approach, level of risk aversion, investor age and focus.

What is the real value of a stock — and a mutual fund? Not surely, as in the common practice, whatever someone is willing to pay for it — that reflects the market value. The real, intrinsic value of a stock is arrived at by calculating its estimated future benefits, which usually includes its forecast dividends. Analysts then discount these benefits at a rate that takes into account the general level of interest rates and a factor that assesses the level of the stock's risk.

Fluctuations take place above and below the intrinsic value of a stock, prompted by two types of traders: "noise" and "liquidity" traders. *Noise traders* buy and sell in response to conflicting information or emotional impulses — reaction to rumors, tips, or personal superficial research. *Liquidity traders* are passive investors who may sell a stock or mutual fund shares simply because they need the money, or they may invest simply because they have the money.

Index fund managers are liquidity traders, since they make trades without considering the link between price and value. In a climate of inefficient pricing, or that which does not relate exactly to intrinsic value, there are obviously opportunities to outperform the market by skilled managers making bets.

The most obvious evidence of market inefficiencies are the small pockets of obscure, thinly traded companies (small-capitalization companies or "small caps") and investors who overreact to both good and bad news, when there may be considerable noise trading going on.

For this complex of reasons, stocks — and consequently mutual funds — do not sell for exactly what they are worth. When investors panic and stocks trade at depressed price-earnings multiples, bargain hunters grab great opportunities. Markets can be said to be *inefficient* at such times. When investors become wildly optimistic and companies sell at excessively high price-earnings ratios, good money managers cut back on their equity positions.

Inefficiencies are also evident in low price-earnings situations: small-firm and neglected-firm effects, and seasonal effects such as the January Effect. In such situations, the competent mutual fund manager develops a strategy for beating the market; he looks for neglected, poorly researched, out-of-favor *bargain* opportunities.

DEFINING YOUR DRUTHERS

What is the best mutual fund to meet *your* investment criteria? The first place to go, other than to a top financial advisor, is to your local library. Look up all the material there on mutual funds. Second, request and read some literature, shareholder reports, and prospectuses, on various types of mutual funds from a broker or financial advisor. (A bank or trust company will likely have reams of material on their own in-house, captive sales, mutual funds.)

Obtain information from *independent* brokers or advisors who have no axe to grind. This is essential. They probably represent the widest range of funds, not just their firm-sponsored single group. They are most often professionals conducting ongoing research into these funds. Try to discover your comfort zone.

1. **Income** — You may want your investment to produce a steady flow of monthly or quarterly dividend payments. Because of tax credits, too, these can be worth more than a corresponding rate of interest income that's 100% taxable.

2. **Capital gains** — Here you want a fund manager to concentrate on increasing the value of your principal through the capital appreciation the stocks in the fund achieve.

3. **Income *and* capital gains** — Some combination of the objectives and the stocks mentioned in the previous two categories combined in a single fund.

Many funds cite stability of performance or capital preservation (another way of saying *safety*) as another goal. Keep in mind that you can't get all of them at once.

DISTINGUISHING AMONG FUNDS

Now let's broaden the discussion to cover all types of funds, in terms of your *personal objective*: THE BROAD ASSET CLASSES.

Balanced Funds: Both Canadian and International. Balanced funds seek both income and capital gain with a portfolio that typically contains both bonds and stocks.

Bond Funds may be Canadian, short-term, and mortgage, or U.S. and International. The generally accepted objective is a high degree of income and safety, employing bonds and debentures. Mortgage funds have a similar overall objective, employing a combination of commercial, industrial, and residential mortgages, including mortgage-backed securities (MBS). International fixed-income funds may invest in foreign bonds and Canadian government issues denominated in foreign currencies. You can achieve capital gains by trading between varying coupons and maturities, and also through currency fluctuations, although this is a secondary consideration. And we haven't forgotten those high-yield bond funds, a recent new hybrid in Canada, typically paying out a monthly distribution of higher-yield income.

Mixed-Income Funds, a new term I've coined to describe the high-yield income sector, containing Royalty Income Trusts, Real Estate Investment Trusts, and Unit Investment Trusts, are a new breed that offers *high monthly* income with significant tax preference.

Stock funds offer a wide variety and tend to share the objective of long-term growth. They include Canadian Dividend Funds, Canadian Small-to Mid-Cap Emerging Markets, European Funds, Far East, Global, and Specialty Funds. For dividend funds, "long-term growth" refers not as much to capital appreciation as to dividend income, through high-yielding common and preferred shares. Small-cap funds invest in the stock of smaller companies, just as the offshore funds focus on those companies that do business in foreign countries. Specialty funds vary widely, from individual industries, to gold or technology.

The distinctions among the individual categories of funds are not always clear. Many funds fit into two or three categories. For starters, we can look at hybrid, specialty, sector, stock market index, and international categories.

Hybrid funds are not pure equity funds. From time to time some contain a heavy percentage of bonds.

Specialty funds are based on a specific investment focus, such as *ethical funds*, which refuse to invest in liquor, tobacco or companies that promote other "nasty" products, or those that concentrate on a particular region or industry. Be careful of these. The word "ethical" is very generously interpreted. At times it may represent or conceal a political agenda or bias, rather than a real ethical concern.

Sector funds are a specialty fund that focuses on a specific sector or industry, such as health care or high technology.

Stock market index funds closely approximate those stocks included within a particular stock market index, such as the TSE 300.

International funds invest in foreign stocks, usually from several countries. *Global funds* are made up of foreign *and* domestic issues; international funds contain only offshore securities.

General equity portfolios cover a broad category that includes several types of equity mutual funds. These typically invest in various industries in Canada and the U.S. As a subdivision, the aggressive-growth fund is the most prone to risk because of its more active, aggressive stance than that of regular equity funds. This can lead it into more volatile issues. The equity-income fund is the least volatile. These categories break down according to further differences and specialties, depending on the fund's objectives and guidelines established in its prospectus and the style of its fund manager.

Aggressive-growth funds are also termed "maximum capital gains" funds, "capital appreciation" funds, "performance" funds or, a relic of the 1960s, "Go-go" funds. Some are highly volatile and their managers may employ a variety of spectacular strategies — such as leveraging the portfolio by short-selling stocks they feel are due to slump. Many aggressive funds concentrate on smaller, unfamiliar companies.

With fewer assets, the portfolio manager can move around more nimbly. The more reckless of these funds can take the shareholder on an erratic ride, plunging far beneath the overall market in a major sell-off and then streaking upward to outstrip the averages during rallies.

Delivering one's hard-earned money into the hands of these aggressive-growth fund managers is not for the faint of heart. An extreme example of this type of fund is the Multiple Opportunities Fund, a portfolio made up of high-flying Vancouver Stock Exchange (VSE) speculative stock. This fund boasts records as both the best performing and among the worst performing funds in Canada!

Smaller company funds often share some of the characteristics of aggressive-growth funds, but with the distinction that they are usually somewhat more conservatively managed. In the venture capital industry, for example, a "small company" would be one with assets of $5 million or less. These companies can grow at a faster rate simply because their expansion takes place on a smaller asset and revenue base. It's much simpler for a firm with revenues of $10 million to double its market and sales than it is for a company with sales of $10 billion to do so.

Growth funds are generally less volatile in their approach and in the sort of portfolio they manage. As a rule these funds hold stocks of more substantial companies, of which the earnings, and therefore market price, are expected to increase more rapidly than others within their industry or elsewhere in the same market. Their managers set their sights on those companies with well-established earnings records that trade at a reasonable multiple, such as General Electric, Shell Oil, or General Motors. Despite the importance of a strong earnings trend, it is what derives from it — capital appreciation — that the growth fund managers are after, rather than dividend income itself.

Growth income funds focus on capital gains, dividend income and even the growth in future dividends. While still concentrating somewhat on capital appreciation, they are generally less prone to risk because of their more conservative stance.

Equity-income funds offer a special kind of value investing. They look primarily for dividend yields significantly higher than those of an overall market yardstick such as the yields on the TSE Index or the Standard & Poor's 500. When a stock's price falls, its yield increases accordingly.

This type of mutual fund should usually be less volatile than the overall market. It represents one of the lowest-risk approaches to investing in stocks. Remember that high-yielding stocks tend to be especially sensitive to interest rate fluctuations, as are long-term bonds.

Equity-income holdings include better grade industrial, utility, financial and natural resource companies. Some managers hold moderate amounts of convertible securities, bonds, and preferred stocks. As the least risky of the general stock funds, these are what I call "eat-well-sleep-well" stock funds.

TOUGH FUNDS FOR TOUGH TIMES

The Hybrids

We're now concerned about adjusting our portfolio to a more defensive, "bear-proof" arrangement. Not nice, but necessary.

Asset Allocation Funds are a type of balanced fund. When (not if) the economy of a particular country signals a recession, when interest rates tend to drift up, when stock *and* bond markets slide down, consider weighting some of your portfolio assets (*never* most of them) into what I call "all-weather" mutual fund assets. These hybrid funds mix up their stock, bond, and cash positions in single "balanced" portfolios.

These funds tend to keep your nest eggs safe in all kinds of cycles and markets. Spreading their portfolios among a wide variety of different asset classes, they can include domestic and foreign securities, government bonds, precious metals, real estate stocks, mortgages and cash. Asset allocation funds are meant to lower risk while providing favorable total returns. Tony Massies' Global Strategy Income Plus is an example of this category, as are Guardian Growth and Income, Ivy Growth and Income, and Gerry Coleman's new C.I. Harbour Growth & Income Fund. A good country-specific asset allocation fund is AGF's European Asset Allocation Fund.

With some, the asset allocation remains relatively constant. With others, the mix is altered as market conditions change. There are two basic types of asset allocation funds — *static*-allocation portfolios, which hold similar proportions of specific groups and tend to maintain those positions over relatively long periods of time; and *flexible*-allocation portfolios, which can vary their weightings depending on the manager's outlook. A manager has considerable latitude in betting heavily on one asset class or another, seasonally, or in response to general economic cycles.

Balanced Funds are another kind of "tough fund," usually appealing to cautious, conservative investors who seek to preserve their capital. Balanced funds strive for three goals: income, moderate capital appreciation, and capital retention. They hold bonds, convertible securities, and often some preferred stock as well as common stock. The portfolio generally ranges from about 40% to 60% in bonds. These funds are well suited to new investors just getting their feet wet. They use a relatively fixed mix of stocks and bonds, but you can obtain balanced funds ranging all the way from 75% to 25% in favor of bonds to the reverse ratio in favor of stocks.

Convertible Funds consist of bonds or preferred stocks that can be *exchanged* for a predetermined number of the company's common shares, at the investor's option. These are a risk-averse, batten-down-the-hatches, all-weather category of funds. "Convertibles" have split personalities. At times they act like stocks — when the conversion price exceeds that of the stock price — and at other times they behave like bonds (or preferreds). They offer the *downside protection* of a fixed-income (bond) security and the *upside potential* of equities, into which they can be converted. The funds have similar characteristics to a balanced fund, putting greater emphasis on income and safety of capital.

CHOOSING YOUR RELATIVES

Asset allocation is a practical application of the art of diversification. Diversification raises another advantage, which I call *choosing your relatives*. When it comes to choosing a mutual fund portfolio we are faced with an incredible menu of choices. In this instance, you get to choose your very own relatives.

What I mean, of course, is *co-relatives*, because stock, bond and real estate markets often move in opposite directions or in inverse relationships, both domestically and among different international markets. (See Tables 8.9, 8.10 and 8.11.) These differences we refer to as *correlatives*, or the correlation of different markets with each other. For example, the TSE 300 Index moves in a degree of correlation with the Dow Jones Index, Japan's Nikkei Index or that of the Mexican Bolsa. Not all markets move in lockstep, so diversification is a tremendous advantage when you invest through a multifund portfolio.

And the importance of being able to choose your global "relatives" and so balance different strengths in your portfolio cannot be overstated. It may be the only free lunch left in the industry. In a broader sense, the relationship between return and risk through international diversification is illustrated in Figure 8.6.

TABLE 8.9: CORRELATIONS OF VARIOUS ASSET TYPES

	Aggressive Growth	Corporate Bond	Growth	Growth and Income	Precious Metals	Money Market
Aggressive Growth	1.00	0.40	0.99	0.95	0.42	−0.07
Corporate Bond	0.40	1.00	0.43	0.51	0.07	−0.40
Growth	0.99	0.43	1.00	0.98	0.42	−0.09
Growth and Income	0.95	0.51	0.98	1.00	0.39	−0.08
Precious Metals	0.42	0.07	0.42	0.39	1.00	−0.08
Money Market	−0.07	0.04	−0.09	−0.08	−0.08	1.00

TABLE 8.10: INTERNATIONAL STOCK AND BOND MARKET CORRELATION COEFFICIENTS

Value 1.0 = Complete Correlation

Value 0.0 = No Correlation

	Equity Markets	Bond Markets
United States	1.0	1.0
Canada	.63	.82
United Kingdom	.58	.16
Switzerland	.52	.12
France	.49	.45
Australia	.61	.11
Germany	.40	.35
Italy	.42	.37
Japan	.32	.07

Source: Based on data from the DAIWA Institute of Research Ltd.

FIGURE 8.6: DIVERSIFICATION (INTERNATIONAL), RETURN AND RISK

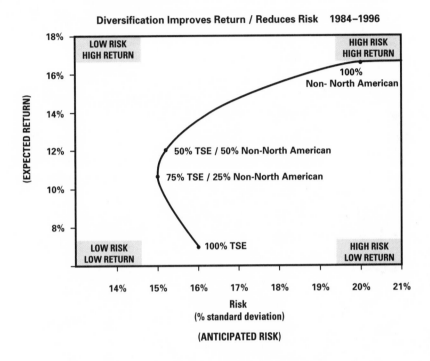

Diversification Improves Return / Reduces Risk   1984–1996

Source: Loring Ward Investment Counsel

A New Take on Distant Relatives

Conventional wisdom has it that the differences between major stock markets have all but vanished, because of computerized trading, arbitrage (buying in one market, selling in another) and the "global economy."

This wisdom is wrong. A 1997 study by Morgan Stanley Capital International indicates that world equity markets are actually moving *apart* independently. That's good news for investors because it means that global diversification is an even more effective way to increase returns and reduce risk.

The Stenner mutual fund portfolio construction insists on such asset allocation taking into account international correlation, or the

TABLE 8.11: WORLD EQUITY MARKETS CORRELATION MATRIX (1970–91) — (U.S. = 1.00)

	AUSTRALIA	AUSTRIA	BELGIUM	CANADA	DENMARK	FRANCE	GERMANY	HONG KONG	IRELAND	ITALY	JAPAN	NETHERLANDS	NEW ZEALAND	NORWAY	SOUTH AFRICA	SPAIN	SWEDEN	SWITZERLAND	U.K.
AUSTRIA	.07																		
BELGIUM	.43	.59																	
CANADA	.71	.21	.37																
DENMARK	.43	.37	.38	.50															
FRANCE	.64	.55	.84	.50	.36														
GERMANY	.24	.83	.68	.14	.43	.69													
HONG KONG	.50	.12	.31	.60	.39	.36	.14												
IRELAND	.70	.79	.89	.68	.63	.93	.88	.55											
ITALY	.51	.61	.68	.32	.26	.75	.62	.31	.87										
JAPAN	.40	.17	.61	.37	.54	.47	.30	.58	.60	.46									
NETHERLANDS	.66	.56	.69	.55	.49	.81	.72	.46	.92	.61	.50								
NEW ZEALAND	.64	.29	.36	.76	.38	.64	.61	.54	.70	.63	-.19	.82							
NORWAY	.37	.33	.28	.57	.14	.28	.10	.09	.72	.20	.28	.15	.00						
SOUTH AFRICA	.37	.35	.43	.36	.10	.59	.38	.23	.44	.44	.61	.57	.10	.32					
SPAIN	.31	.35	.72	.14	.15	.54	.29	.33	.55	.67	.50	.34	.06	.47	.47				
SWEDEN	.44	.34	.61	.29	.52	.59	.58	.09	.72	.57	.42	.51	.17	.40	.33	.52			
SWITZERLAND	.40	.76	.74	.34	.48	.75	.43	.37	.91	.61	.25	.82	.10	.27	.11	.18	.57		
U.K.	.56	.14	.27	.36	.16	.44	.36	.48	.79	.27	.32	.64	-.08	.64	.13	.46	.52	.57	
U.S.A.	.61	.28	.36	.63	.42	.49	.40	.57	.67	.42	.32	.77	.05	.64	.13	.46	.52	.52	.58

TABLE 8.12: WORLD BOND CORRELATION MATRIX (1961–91) — (U.S. = 1.00)

	AUSTRALIA	AUSTRIA	BELGIUM	CANADA	FRANCE	GERMANY	IRELAND	ITALY	JAPAN	NETHERLANDS	NEW ZEALAND	SOUTH AFRICA	SWEDEN	SWITZERLAND	U.K.
AUSTRIA	.07														
BELGIUM	.22	.88													
CANADA	.21	.10	.11												
FRANCE	.32	.74	.85	.21											
GERMANY	.13	.90	.87	.15	.69										
IRELAND	.39	.52	.64	.18	.62	.59									
ITALY	.44	.47	.65	.18	.74	.44	.41								
JAPAN	.41	.50	.68	-.05	.56	.58	.63	.47							
NETHERLANDS	.15	.95	.89	.28	.77	.93	.60	.49	.53						
NEW ZEALAND	.42	.46	.52	.15	.41	.34	.47	.32	.51	.40					
SOUTH AFRICA	.25	.32	.26	.06	.22	.28	.01	.40	.03	.27	.30				
SWEDEN	.14	.77	.4	.13	.70	.64	.28	.57	.45	.70	.58	.31			
SWITZERLAND	.14	.89	.85	.10	.67	.88	.53	.35	.65	.76	.41	.24	.65		
U.K.	.42	.34	.47	.11	.40	.41	.90	.32	.60	.42	.46	.02	.15	.41	
U.S.A.	.11	.26	.31	.82	.45	.35	.28	.37	.07	.49	.00	.11	.21	.12	.16

lack thereof. This means the investor of any age or personality can choose his investment "relatives," preferably distant ones, and those low correlations apply to all markets — bond, stock or real estate.

The Morgan Stanley study clearly shows, for example, that the relative movement (correlation) between the U.S. stock market and the rest of the world was significantly wider in the period from 1993 to 1996, compared with the 23-year period of 1970-1992. U.S. movements once explained about 50% of the market movements in the rest of the world; recently, they explained barely more than one-third of global market behavior.

It's interesting that Canadian markets currently show less dependence on U.S. movements. So for Canadian investors, holding a few U.S. equities provides more diversification than before, but not as much as a well-rounded international portfolio.

TABLE 8.13: WORLD MARKETS MOVING APART
Correlation of Monthly Total Returns:
1.00 is Perfect Correlation; 0.00 is No Correlation

	1970–1992	1993–1996
United States	1.00	1.00
Canada	.70	.62
Japan	.27	.11
Rest of the World	.47	.36

Courtesy: Global Strategy Views

Patrick Forrett, an equities specialist at Global Strategy says: "You can actually see that markets in different parts of the world are behaving quite differently. This is something that an individual investor can use quite effectively." In other words, the relatives are moving away! From an investment stability point of view — rejoice! More market inefficiences, more divergent market behavior, less risk and more stability for your overall portfolio.

chapter 9 | THE CHALLENGE: MANAGING FOR REWARD

You cannot help men by doing for them what they could and should do for themselves.

— Abraham Lincoln

PART I: THE PANIC-PROOFER:
DEFINING AND CATEGORIZING RISK

The way you define risk is highly personal, and arbitrary. In 1931, W.C. Fields drove from New York to California in a new Lincoln with $350,000 in cash concealed on his person. He didn't trust banks. Perhaps the rotund comedian thought nothing of assuming the far greater risk of abandoning a secure career on Broadway for the shifting sands of Hollywood!

All investors thread their own way through a minefield of risks, as we have discussed earlier. Of course, the investor also has to trust his own judgment, which is another form of risk.

Fear can be the greatest risk of all to the intelligent investor, and the greatest fear middle-aged investors should harbor is the risk of guaranteed investments because they offer no tax-preferred benefits of capital gains and stock dividends. Nor do they have the ability over time to outpace rates of inflation or taxation by their very nature.

Large windfalls in our generation have become almost routine, if limited. Many of us will acquire a sum of money beyond the slow accumulation of a life of hard work. A death, a divorce or, more commonly, an early retirement may produce an influx of funds and the corresponding obligation of dealing with the event intelligently.

The response of most people is one of fear, or at least anxiety, akin to the emotion a rookie wide receiver feels as he watches the quarterback launch a football in his direction — the fear of dropping the ball.

Panic, if you like.

If you've been patiently investing $5,000 a year from a carefully shepherded budget and are suddenly confronted with the necessity of investing $100,000 all at once, you naturally treat this sudden wealth with great respect.

Or the opposite may be true — you might want to adopt a much riskier approach to investing than you've previously followed.

Avoid both of these extremes. If you've been following a well-planned investment program, stay the course. Concentrate on preserving your new capital and gradually develop an investment program of safety, asset mix and growth potential. Keep paying attention to all of the risks outlined in this chapter.

*   *   *

The risks we have talked about so far are those of commission *and* omission. Your investing in a declining company or industry would be an error of commission. Failing to invest in a sound growth situation can be an even more costly error of omission. Whatever the win-lose probability in any market, *not being in the market makes winning absolutely impossible.* This guaranteed loss is truly the greatest risk of all!

A seasoned broker once said, "People will forgive me if I sell them a mutual fund that goes down. But if I advise them against a fund that goes up, I never hear the end of it."

Remember this basic rule: the degree of risk increases with the degree of potential gain or profit. There are no absolutes. Every one of us has an individual level of risk tolerance, just as each of us has a personal idea of what degree of profitability we require.

Armed with such a profile, the investor then confronts an incredible array of mutual funds, each bearing its own distinctive risk profile. First, let's categorize some of the risks.

UNMASKING THE FACES OF RISK

THE PRUDENT MAN RULE

Do what you will, the capital is at hazard — all that can be required of a trustee to invest is that he should conduct himself faithfully and exercise sound discretion. He is to observe how men of prudence, discretion and intelligence manage their own affairs, not in regard to speculation, but in regard to the paramount disposition of their funds, considering the probable income, as well as the probable safety of the capital to be invested.

— Justice Samuel Putnam, Massachusetts, 1830

Justice Putnam's message is equally valid today. Manage your affairs with prudence, intelligence and discretion. Don't speculate. Consider the probable income as well as the probable safety of your capital. Recognize that you cannot avoid risk in one form or another, the exposure to erosion through inflation, or possible theft or loss.

The Risk of Inflation

The intelligent investor must focus on money's real or after-inflation return. The inflation rate is really a form of double taxation. You must bear the inflation loss and pay tax on the inflated income you make on the investment as well. Real return is more than just a statistic — it is central to your security. It is all that really matters.

The inflation rate reduces the average nominal return of all asset classes. The relative rewards of common stocks are greatly enhanced through their potential to increase in value. Otherwise, the impact of inflation on the returns of all asset classes is absolute. Result? The return on stocks, adjusted for inflation, surpasses that of other asset classes, such as bonds or mortgages. And your own personalized cost-of-living index may be somewhat higher than the national average indicated by Ottawa.

The overwhelming lesson to be derived from this simple example is this: *Today's investors face the greatest financial risk in exposing themselves to the loss of their purchasing power.* The greatest threat to your money lies in your not risking anything. If you conserve your capital through what you perceive as safety, you will outlive that capital, not the other way around.

The Frustrated Investor

In the money-management business we sell bottom line and peace of mind. Peace of mind is more important than the financial bottom line; a client may not make as much money as those who have a greater risk tolerance, but he'll sleep better at night.

You may at times have blamed your broker or advisor for an investment that didn't work out well. Or an insurance policy may not have been what you expected. A good friend may have slipped you a hot tip on a great stock that hit the skids and hasn't seen daylight since.

There's enough risk to be faced even in conservative investing. And ignoring risk can cost you dearly by the time you reach retirement, if you can afford to do so. You can't hide from risk. *The greatest risk of all is the unwillingness to assume reasonable risk.* Without some risk, your chance of accomplishing nothing is 100%.

Prudence doesn't mean locking up money in term deposits and GICs. We've already seen that to do so is to guarantee loss. That's definitely not prudent!

Frustrated investor or potential one, this book seeks to supply you with practical solutions to your frustration. And how do I evaluate successful investors? Simply because they have three attributes: (1) they have a clearly defined strategy; (2) they follow risk-management concepts, preserving their assets when markets don't always do well; and (3) they have a solid understanding of themselves, and have structured their investments to suit their situation, resources and personality.

Consistency is king. In major league baseball, a .250 hitter hits three times out of 12, and may earn $2 million a year. A .333 hitter hits four times out of 12, and may earn $6 million a year.

Since a nine-inning game provides about four opportunities at bat, the .333 hitter only has to get *one additional hit in every three games to earn three times* what his .250 teammate is paid.

So it's not important whether you strike out occasionally with a short-term loss in any investment situation. What does count is an overall portfolio with a *consistency rating* higher than the average portfolio.

Try to visualize your principal as having no *intrinsic* value. Zero. Its only value to you or anyone else is in the purchasing power of the income stream it produces. If in the next 10 years, the purchasing power of your "safe investment" declines to one-quarter of its present worth, the income you derive from it will drop to 25% of what it is today. This is the only measurement that means anything. So, rather than earning for you, it will have become a negative quantity, even a liability for you.

The long-term aggregate statistics conceal a fundamental truth, that substantial inflation is largely a modern phenomenon. While the average annual inflation rate was 2.3% over the past 120 years, it averaged 1.2% during the 1872–1925 period. Since 1925, it has averaged 3.1% (2 1/2 times the earlier level). In the past 25 years, it has averaged about 4.5% per annum, or nearly *four times* the average in the 42 years ending in 1925. But since 1991, thanks to the efforts of the Bank of Canada, the annual inflation rate in Canada has been kept well within 1% to 3%.

In a world of rising costs of living, most children of deflation continue to invest in a way that would have made their parents proud, and that ensures that their purchasing power is constantly worn away. Most financial institutions perpetuate this dogma. It's a tragedy. (Revisit Figure 6.3: 50 Years of Inflation in Canada and Figure 6.4: The Canadian Inflation Rate and the Consumer Price Index 1986–1997.)

The only real safety for a person of pre-retirement or retirement age is the preservation of what your money will purchase at some point in the future. *Certainty*, on the other hand, is preserving the numbers printed on your dollar bills, which will gradually shrink and become meaningless. You can demand certainty, but you will be the loser. Safety — the only true safety — is refusing the temptation to avoid risk at any cost.

You can't avoid risk, even walking to the corner store. But you can choose to accept the relatively small risk of owning equity in great businesses, a risk that, over any 15-year period since 1926 has turned out to be zero. The other alternative is to seek nonexistent safety, and end up depending on your children or other relatives in your old age.

Inflation: Slaying the Risk Monster

Abdicating to inflation incurs the greatest risk of all.

Many of us hard-working folks seek "guarantees." The guaranteed return on your investment. It doesn't matter that over the past 97 years or so there have been only three years in which the Consumer Price Index has declined by more than one percent: 1930, 1931 and 1932. Your hydro bill may have risen relentlessly almost every year, symbolic of the constant drain on your guaranteed dollar value — a guaranteed loss in everything you consume.

The risk monster, inflation, has gobbled up almost all the purchasing power of your guaranteed dollars, the Canadian currency, emerging from the jungle of risk to gnaw at your hard-earned savings — reducing a 1945 dollar to its current purchase level barely over a thin dime. So where did we get this popular delusion, even compulsion, that we seek a guaranteed fixed return on the money we loan to government, bank or credit union, thereby sentencing ourselves to a guaranteed loss of purchasing power over time?

We got it from our parents and grandparents, a legacy of the Great Depression. Undisputedly a terrible time, but a freakish time when the values of prudence and saving were consistent with safety because inflation and taxes did not exist! But we can't live in the past, particularly this small segment of Canadian history. To do so, fearfully, is to miss today's boat. Today's investor instead should look foreward hopefully to the future, forgetting the *fatal attraction* of the past's obsession with guarantees.

When Interest Rates Rise — What Do You Do?

Rising interest rates can be like a Japanese sauna bath. In Japan, the common practice is to climb into tepid water and then raise the temperature by slow degrees so that the bather can achieve an extremely hot temperature without suffering shock.

Interest rates can be just as sneaky, but more dangerous. Gradually rising rates are not a pretty thing for fixed-income or fixed-rate investors, because of course they erode the value of the investment. Both bond and stock markets are sensitive to interest rates. You can hold your ground over a short- or long-term rate increase over the next six months. This is "noise." Stay the course, keep your current asset allocation mix and make sure your portfolio has some reasonable balance. You can even transfer some of your investments into money market instruments if rates start to rally slightly. But don't try to "time" the market with most of your portfolio.

What's ahead? I don't think interest rates will "soar" in 1998 or 1999; perhaps a 1%–2% rise throughout the years.

If you think interest rates will rise:

1. Remember, losses are wonderful tax shelters.
2. Stay short and safe.
3. Invest in junk bonds.
4. Invest where interest rates are falling.
5. Retain some of your assets in cash.
6. Maintain a solid asset allocation portfolio.
7. Consider international bond funds.
8. Watch for strong value funds, low-ratio Beta funds.
9. Purchase or switch a portion of your holdings to hedge funds or flexible income or option income funds.
10. Consider adjustable-rate bond funds (a new breed), like adjustable-rate mortgages, but only 100 to 200 basis points above money market funds (1% to 2% better).

At times during different economic cycles it is necessary to invest in alternate fund categories, but these changes are never the thing to do for 100% of your portfolio.

Risk Wars

The U.S. Securities Exchange Commission (SEC) recently backed away from insisting on a single risk measurement to identify the risk of a mutual fund. That is, a single, standardized, quantified risk measurement. The SEC is leaning toward requiring fund companies in the U.S. to include a 10-year bar chart showing annual returns. The problem I see with this approach is that the majority of mutual funds in existence today in Canada and the U.S haven't been in existence for more than four or five years! And will a bar chart provide investors with a false sense of security?

Back in March 1995, the SEC decided to ask the public for ideas on how to represent risk, and received 3,700 responses, 3,600 of them from individual investors. Associate director of the SEC's investment management division Heidi Stern stated: "Investors generally would like to see improved narrative descriptions of risk. . . . We found a quantitative measure was not the best way to present risk. Risk means different things to different people and was apt to be misunderstood."

Jeff Kelley, an editor at Morningstar, Inc. in Chicago, says disclosing risk isn't simple. "We're looking for a magic bullet risk score, but haven't found it." Past performance is a reasonable place to start, he added, but "it's hard to see a performance number painting a picture of risk. There's a risk/reward tradeoff and [performance] only shows the reward."

With the SEC first pushing hard for a single risk measurement, and now backing away from such a position, the idea has been resisted very strongly by the mutual fund industry, which has claimed that any one measure of risk is just too simplistic (and very possibly misleading). We've got a brand-new ball game in seeking to identify risk.

To advance its view, the Investment Company Institute in Washington, D.C. released its proprietory survey covering 650 stock and bond mutual funds shareholders. The result clearly indicated that very few investors prefer a written description and a graphic presentation (bar chart) of returns to assess risk.

To add more (necessary) fuel to the debate over how to identiify risk, respected Boston-based research organization Dalbar Institute says that showing total return is not the way to explain risk. Even 12-month total returns shown in a bar chart will present a misleading picture of risk, according to Dalbar, since the major damage an investor can suffer usually occurs within a few months' time. "Risk to consumers means 'how much can I lose?' It's terrible to use a 12-month bar chart," says Lon Harvey of Dalbar.

In addition to disclosing risk through a bar chart, the SEC is also looking at the idea of requiring *duration* to be disclosed by short-term fixed-income funds. Duration measures a bond fund's sensitivity to changes in interest rates. "Duration is a better measure than maturity," declares Kelley. "After the drubbing bond investors took in 1994, duration is coming to the fore."

As Canadians, we have much to learn when it comes to understanding mutual fund risk. And the American experience is a good place to start — they've been at it much longer than we have.

Equity Risk

Total return risk is partially made up of the risk of volatility, or that of fluctuation. Don't confuse notions of safety with fluctuation. This is another way of saying that volatility risk is a very different thing from risking the loss of your assets. Volatility pertains only to the gains or losses that, as long as the asset has not been liquidated, show up on paper. These are only losses when they are actually realized, or redeemed.

Lost-asset risk goes beyond the risk that stock prices may fall and your portfolio thereby declines in value. It poses the question that, after such a decline in your portfolio's market value, you may be forced to sell your holdings. So, lost-asset risk threatens you only when you liquidate your portfolio. We're not referring here to assets that have an *absolute* risk but those involving *relative* or *probable* risk.

If you're faced with even the remote possibility of having to liquidate all or part of your holdings in the near future, you must follow a specific short-term strategy. Those investors who can sustain their investment portfolio for a longer period follow a very different strategy.

We've already illustrated how widely a common stock can swing, even within a single year. Common stocks collectively are not inherently risky. The degree of volatility within a market varies widely among equities. Unless you hedge that volatility with a large group of holdings managed professionally, as in upper-quartile (top 25% performance) mutual funds or even portfolios made up of numerous asset groups, you flirt with more risk than you need to.

The longer you hold your common stocks, the more their degree of volatility flattens out. You therefore reduce fluctuation the more you diversify your holdings. Volatility is substantially reduced by a longer period in *any* securities category.

Investors who can afford the luxury of automatically reinvesting dividends in pursuit of a long-term goal can lower their total return risk in common stocks. Not only does the difference in returns shrink the longer they hold the stocks, but they also improve the probability of returns over all. The investors who add more capital to their stock holdings and equity mutual funds regularly, in good times and bad alike, can wipe out this risk entirely.

These same investors can also take advantage of dollar-cost averaging.

DOLLAR-COST AVERAGING

By investing a fixed amount at fixed intervals, you purchase fewer units when prices are high, and buy more units when prices are low. Thus, you save money.

Researchers at Wright State College in Dayton, Ohio, have argued against this. Their case is that dollar-cost averaging works over the long term, but only if the stock or fund fluctuates as much as the market does in general — and that putting money in the market in lump sums is better over time. This is to me an ineffective argument, since by definition those who engage in dollar-cost averaging can rarely afford the larger overall amount of cash to invest all at once. Investing a large amount of cash whenever you have it available can be advantageous, but it hardly contradicts the principle of dollar-cost averaging.

Principal Risk

The volatility that produces the return on your capital differs from the total return you see on a common stock investment. This volatility suggests two distinctly separate though similar risks. For example, variations in stock prices tend to overwhelm the steady dividend component of total return over one or two years. Yet reinvested dividends, through the magic of compounding, become a key contributor to total return in the long run *and* provide an automatic dollar-cost averaging effect as they are regularly reinvested.

Remove the compounding of dividend income and the principal risk to your investment increases. Without compounding, the investment reflects solely the rate of capital return. The income effect strengthens the asset's productivity disproportionately. Arranging the reinvestment of ongoing income — from bond, mortgage, dividend income and common stock funds — purchases more shares, without cost to your portfolio, and so reduces your risk and improves your entire portfolio stability. That income ploughed back into your portfolio becomes additional principal, decreasing risk to your holdings.

Income Risk

Most investors do not plan properly for income generation until after they reach retirement. They do not often achieve even the reasonable level of income they want. What's worse, their income tends to decrease steadily over time. Of the three basic asset classes we are dealing with, only common stock, by its steady generation of dividends, has been shown to meet this dual objective of providing a comfortable income stream that increases over the years.

Is it prudent to assume that dividends will continue to rise in the future? We think "Yes." The remarkable record of dividends paid by North American corporations, for example, heavily favors the likelihood of an increasing rather than a decreasing level of dividends. Best of all, this holds true despite the business conditions that can prevail over a short span of the economic cycle.

Let's look at the dividend history of a utility company such as B.C. Telephone. Over the 20 years from 1976 to 1995, an annual dividend on B.C. Tel. common stock was declared each year without interruption, and was increased in each of those years, except for three years, when it remained the same. Allowing for to a two-for-one stock split, that dividend rose from 96 cents per share in 1976 to the equivalent of $2.54 per share in 1995.

Bond Risk

The risks inherent in fixed-income investment such as bonds and mortgages are very complex and differ in nature from those of common stock investment. With bonds, the income risk tends to be significantly lower, while principal risk is somewhat lower. Bond categories vary widely in their maturities, credit worthiness and the size of their corporations or issuing governments, all of which affect their marketability.

Bonds — Total Return Risk

As for common stocks, volatility is the standard measure of total return risk for bonds. In one-year holding periods measured since 1926, the total market value of long-term U.S. government bonds has varied from a high of +40% (1982) to a low of -9% (1967) for a spread of 49 percentage points.

While very large in absolute terms, this spread is only about half of that in one-year stock variations. Bonds lost value in only 18 of the past 69 years. All of the rest registered gains in their value. Dramatic, sudden changes in interest rates can be responsible for much of this high volatility. (See again Figure 6.1: Volatility in Interest Rates and Figure 9.1: Volatility in 90-Day Treasury Bill Yields and Canadian Rate of Inflation/CPI Index).

FIGURE 9.1: VOLATILITY IN 90-DAY TREASURY BILL YIELDS AND CANADIAN RATE OF INFLATION / CPI INDEX

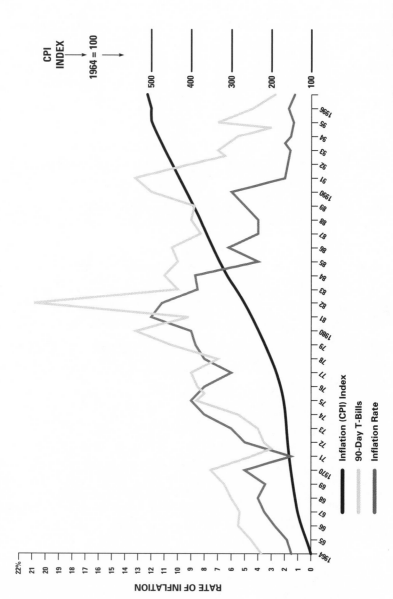

Source: Bank of Canada

Essential Risk

The term-to-maturity of a bond in an investor's portfolio links any changes in interest rates with a change in the value of the capital, the bond itself.

For example, if the government raises prime interest rates by 1%, the value or market price of a bond with a 10-year maturity will decline by about 10%. This will enable it to sell at prices in keeping with currently issued bonds with a higher coupon yield. For a bond with a three-year maturity, the decline in price in the face of a similar interest rate increase would be only about 3%. For this reason, if you know the maturity of a bond, you can quickly calculate the relative effect interest rate changes will have on its market value. (Revisit Figure 6.2: How Bond Prices React to Market Yield Changes, see Table 9.1: How Changes in Interest Rates Affect Bond Prices.

Another example: If interest rates rise by 3%, from 7% to 10%, over a five-year period, and you hold a bond with a 20-year maturity, the market value of your bond will decline. Your total return will be reduced by 5% per annum.

Our focus has been on interest rate risk — that is, bond prices fluctuating through changes in interest rates. These risks are *temporary*, lasting until the bond matures and is redeemed at its stated face value. This applies to both individual bond holdings and those held within a mutual fund portfolio.

Bond Credit Risk

This risk can permanently hurt your principal. Credit risk is a relative term. It occurs increasingly as we proceed down the hierarchy of investment-grade vehicles to high-yield bonds (junk bonds), on which the payment of principal and interest becomes increasingly speculative. It is highly unlikely with federal government bonds, for example.

High-yielding (junk) bonds can represent a substantial opportunity if one wishes to seek a higher level of reward. However, there is a shrinkage of highest quality government debt (bond) availability due to government deficit reduction success, so this investment vehicle is looking very good to millions of investors who crave higher monthly income. These forms of bond securities are best held inside a *managed* mutual fund, with a combination of other high-yield income.

TABLE 9.1: HOW CHANGES IN INTEREST RATES AFFECT BOND PRICES

Source: T. Rowe Price Associates

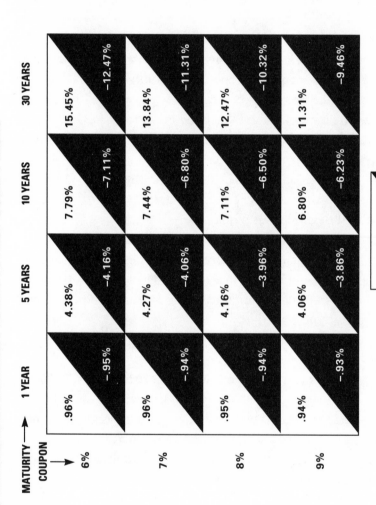

MATURITY → COUPON ↓	1 YEAR	5 YEARS	10 YEARS	30 YEARS
6%	.96% / −.95%	4.38% / −4.16%	7.79% / −7.11%	15.45% / −12.47%
7%	.96% / −.94%	4.27% / −4.06%	7.44% / −6.80%	13.84% / −11.31%
8%	.95% / −.94%	4.16% / −3.96%	7.11% / −6.50%	12.47% / −10.32%
9%	.94% / −.93%	4.06% / −3.86%	6.80% / −6.23%	11.31% / −9.46%

RATES FALL 1%, PRICES RISE BY … / RATES RISE 1%, PRICES FALL …

PART II: THE B-FACTOR

We've talked about several aspects of risk in investing in general and in mutual fund investing in particular. We'll have much more to say about risk factors in Chapter 10. In the meantime, how can we measure risk for ourselves as individual investors?

One key concept in risk measurement is the *"B" (Beta) Factor*, or *systematic* risk. As we've explained, systematic investing, in the form of mutual funds, makes it unnecessary for the investor to become involved in the details of individual stock ownership or other forms of investment. But systematic investing, while useful, supplies the answer to part of the risk puzzle.

"Beta" is a measure of systematic, or *market*, risk. You cannot remove or eliminate systematic (efficient), or controlled, risk through diversification. *Unsystematic* (inefficient) risk, or those factors related to the volatility of each individual stock (say that of a company experiencing poor sales and earnings) can be reduced or removed through the simple process of diversification. The Random Walk (Efficient Market) Theory of simple probability applies in the former case.

Investors are rewarded for assuming systematic risk only, and the B Factor is the only measure of such risk. Investors holding undiversified portfolios of individual securities, incurring unsystematic risk, are not compensated for doing so. These people are on their own. This is why more and more investors are flocking to buy mutual funds under professional management.

Beta provides a measurement of an individual stock's (or mutual fund's) relation to the general market index over time. It reveals the sensitivity of that security to fluctuations in the market. A Beta factor of 1 would indicate that the specific stock would swing in the same range as the general market, while with a Beta factor of 2, the stock would move up and down *twice* as much as the general market would. A fund with a 1.3 Beta behavior has 30% more return and a probability of 30% greater risk than the broad market index; a Beta of 0.7 indicates 30% *less* risk. A stock or fund with a Beta of 0.5 would move only *half* as erratically as the market did. A negative Beta would show that stock would always move in the opposite direction to the general market. When measuring Beta, your fund must be a proper match for the index it is being measured against.

Betas for individual stocks are difficult to determine. You can obtain them from a stock brokerage firm whose securities analysts chart such movements. Once you have arrived at the relevant Beta factor for a stock or mutual fund, you can estimate the return or loss you can expect and measure your relevant risk.

Beta and other technical measurements are really for the professional. Whether your investment is zigging when it should zag or zagging when it should zig, these are some of the risk measurement tools you should know about to help you sleep soundly at night.

But Beta measurement can help in predicting some of a fund's future behavior, provided the same managers are in place and the style has remained the same. Ivy Canadian (0.51) and Guardian Growth Equity (0.75) funds are examples of low-Beta ratio, which can mean a risk factor much less than the market index.

THE STENNER RISK/REWARD SPECTRUM

Figure 9.2: Mutual Fund Types: A Descending Risk/Reward Regression presents 25 types of funds, with numerous subsets. What follows in some detail is a discussion of the major types.

At the lowest level of historic return, and risk, is the TREASURY BILL FUND. The Canadian government, as the senior taxing authority, commands the highest credit rating of any security issuer in the country, which means it can seek financing successfully with the least interest cost. As a taxpayer, you may appreciate that fact. As an investor, you may not. Treasury Bills are issued to finance the cost of short-term government operations, often for a period of 90 days, but sometimes 180 days or even one year.

These funds are therefore constantly rolling over their holdings, so that in a rising interest rate market the investor stands to gain. In a declining rate market, naturally, the reverse is true. Generally, your principal risk never fluctuates. Only the interest rate yield does. T-Bill funds (a subset of money market funds) invest in federal government Treasury Bills and occasionally in the most creditworthy provincial treasuries.

MONEY MARKET FUNDS are made up of short-date Government of Canada bonds, T-Bills, chartered bank certificates of deposit (term deposits) and short-term commercial paper, such as that of retail stores and grain companies. (These are the promissory notes of companies with very high credit ratings.) A highly sophisticated market with relatively low yields combined with a high degree of safety, it is the most stable type of fund available. It is also usually the least profitable and the most boring.

Money market and T-Bill funds are generally used a short-term "parking lots" by investors — temporary, safe, capital-guaranteed holding-tank accounts that are easily accessible.

Canadian government FIXED-INCOME FUNDS seek a high level of current monthly or quarterly income by investing in a mix of federal and

FIGURE 9.2: MUTUAL FUND TYPES: A DESCENDING RISK/REWARD REGRESSION

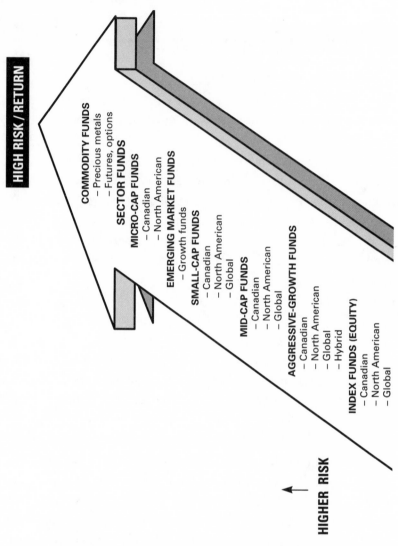

HIGH RISK / RETURN

HIGHER RISK

COMMODITY FUNDS
– Precious metals
– Futures, options

SECTOR FUNDS

MICRO-CAP FUNDS
– Canadian
– North American

EMERGING MARKET FUNDS
– Growth funds

SMALL-CAP FUNDS
– Canadian
– North American
– Global

MID-CAP FUNDS
– Canadian
– North American
– Global

AGGRESSIVE-GROWTH FUNDS
– Canadian
– North American
– Global
– Hybrid

INDEX FUNDS (EQUITY)
– Canadian
– North American
– Global

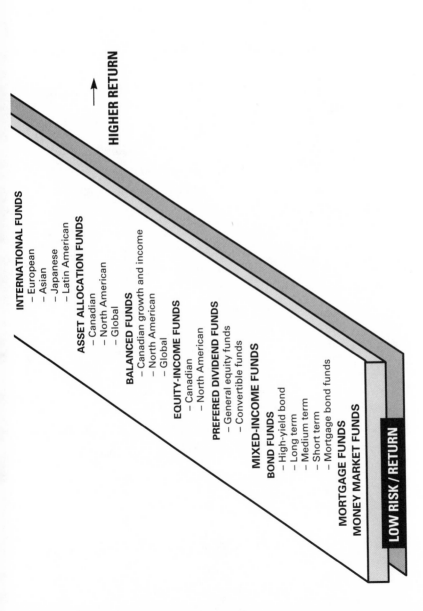

HIGHER RETURN

INTERNATIONAL FUNDS
– European
– Asian
– Japanese
– Latin American

ASSET ALLOCATION FUNDS
– Canadian
– North American
– Global

BALANCED FUNDS
– Canadian growth and income
– North American
– Global

EQUITY-INCOME FUNDS
– Canadian
– North American

PREFERED DIVIDEND FUNDS
– General equity funds
– Convertible funds

MIXED-INCOME FUNDS

BOND FUNDS
– High-yield bond
– Long term
– Medium term
– Short term
– Mortgage bond funds

MORTGAGE FUNDS
MONEY MARKET FUNDS

LOW RISK / RETURN

provincial government bonds and insured short-term guaranteed mortgage-backed securities and government notes. Included, too, may be municipal debentures. While of a lesser credit value, these carry higher coupon yields than federal or provincial issues. The common denominator of all these funds, known as "high grades," is that they seek current daily-interest income and the protection of capital.

CORPORATE BOND FUNDS, like income funds, provide a higher level of income than government bonds do, but with less credit safety. Corporate bonds' quality ranges widely, from that of the largest corporations down to the more speculative issues of medium to small companies. In this hierarchy, as you might expect, the higher the quality, the smaller the coupon income attached.

HIGH MONTHLY (MIXED) INCOME FUNDS typically manage investments in a selection including Royalty Income Trusts (RITs) and Real Estate Investment Trusts (REITs). They typically produce a monthly income stream.

HIGH-YIELD BOND FUNDS consist of lower-rated corporate bonds, as a trade-off for their higher return. The junk bonds prevalent in the U.S. are an extreme example. Canadian High-Yields are becoming very popular. They typically distribute a monthly income stream.

MORTGAGE SECURITIES FUNDS can be invested in National Housing Authority (NHA) first mortgages, Canadian Mortgage and Housing Corporation (CMHC) mortgages, mortgage-backed securities (MBSs), or in residential or commercial issues. The mortgage securities are often insured by the federal government. Mortgages are a type of bond, usually providing less market risk and correspondingly less return.

GLOBAL BOND FUNDS invest in the fixed-income securities of companies and governments worldwide, including the U.S. and Canada. A high priority is attached to current income, with capital appreciation a secondary consideration. Global bond funds invest primarily in bonds of foreign sovereign governments. Allocation is made among countries or geographic regions (such as Europe, Latin America or Asia). Various currencies are often utilized to achieve a high total investment return.

A recent addition is the category FOREIGN BOND FUNDS, also called a HYBRID GLOBAL or INTERNATIONAL BOND FUND, which may invest in an identical portfolio to that described above, but is *never* denominated in Canadian currency.

INTERNATIONAL EMERGING MARKET BOND FUNDS invest in riskier emerging-nation debt securities, such as "Brady Bonds" in Argentina or Bulgaria, for very high bond income.

INTERNATIONAL EQUITY FUNDS must at all times be invested outside Canada in stocks. Predictably, INTERNATIONAL EQUITY FUNDS sometimes offer a higher degree of risk, depending on the country involved.

INCOME MIXED FUNDS seek a high level of current income from income securities, including debentures and preferred stocks, and are a type of balanced fund.

SPECIALTY BOND FUNDS include convertible bonds, notes, debentures, and preferred stocks that can be converted into a predetermined number of shares of common stock in the issuing company at a set price or exchange ratio. As such, they bear characteristics similar to both fixed-income and equity securities — having one's cake and eating it, too.

BALANCED FUNDS normally have a three-pronged objective: to conserve initial principal, to pay current income, and to promote reasonable long-term growth. The asset mix is made up of bonds, and preferred and common stock. A 50/50 balance of stocks and bonds is typical in balanced fund portfolios.

ASSET ALLOCATION FUNDS are *more flexible* than balanced funds. They may be moved up to 100% into bonds, 100% into stocks, or 100% into guaranteed money market securities, at the discretion of the manager, depending on the manager's outlook. For example, such a fund could hold fixed percentages in several categories such as gold bullion, natural resource issues, Government of Canada T-Bills, various bond categories, and "laddered" maturities, specific stock groups, or Japanese *yen*-denominated issues. They could also shift the percentage of these holdings and their asset categories at any time.

EQUITY-INCOME FUNDS strive for a high level of income from good dividend-paying stocks, such as those of utilities and banks. They are similar to INCOME BOND FUNDS in one respect, that their priority is to maximize income within the portfolio.

GROWTH & INCOME BOND FUNDS combine dividend-bearing stocks and high-yielding common stocks. The dividends from these can vary. They demonstrate a solid historical record of paying dividends.

AGGRESSIVE-GROWTH FUNDS seek to maximize capital gain. Their investments may include smaller company stocks (small-cap funds) of fledgling companies or those industries temporarily out of investor favor.

GLOBAL EQUITY FUNDS offer a worldwide portfolio, including Canadian securities, an easy access to offshore investment. The managers provide the usual record-keeping details for Canadians and the differences in foreign currencies, language, time zone laws and regulations, as well as business customs and practices in the relevant countries.

OPTION OR INCOME FUNDS seek a higher current income by investing in dividend-paying common stocks and premiums from writing covered call options and other conservative options strategies.

SPECIALTY STOCK FUNDS include those issues that provide potential for above-average capital appreciation, with income a secondary objective. Included in this category are NATURAL RESOURCE FUNDS invested in mining, oil and gas, forest products, and associated industries. PRECIOUS METALS OR GOLD FUNDS maintain about two-thirds of their portfolios in gold, silver and other precious metals securities. NATURAL RESOURCES & SPECIALTY FUNDS can also produce exceptionally high returns — and equally spectacular losses. These funds hover near the higher end of our risk/reward spectrum.

> **Stenner's Law #4**: "Risk-free investment" is a contradiction in terms — like a "friendly great white shark."

You guessed it — those funds that represent an escalating degree of risk invariably offer an escalating potential for capital gain. Obviously, this prospect is tempered by the greater speculative nature of this class of mutual fund — what goes around, comes around.

The TSE 300 INDEX FUND portfolio replicates the 300 Toronto Stock Exchange (TSE). In other words, it closely parallels the level of the TSE 300 Index. There are now funds available for most indexes.

INTERNATIONAL EQUITY FUNDS differ from GLOBAL EQUITY FUNDS in that they never hold Canadian securities, but only those of other countries. They offer a racy entry in the equity race. Exotic, fast-moving companies in the Far East, Latin America and Japan often produce unusually large gains and, of course, just as dramatic declines.

SMALL-COMPANY FUNDS are speculative, particularly for the new investor. The stocks in these portfolios are largely untried and often offer high potential with the increased risk. AGGRESSIVE-GROWTH FUNDS are also in this category, although they may be more seasoned performers. Usually because of a rapid growth curve, they trade at prices that are a high multiple of current earnings.

SPECIALIZED SECTOR FUNDS are made up of companies that are often unique and that have positions in new sectors or industries such as health sciences or high technology. They present explosive possibilities to the investor prepared to accept frequent precipitous free falls.

COMMODITY OPTIONS AND FUTURES CONTRACTS occupy the most extreme position in this array of mutual funds. Options carry rights, while futures entail obligations. Calls on the future buying or selling of commodities have created millionaires because of the enormous leverage available. Needless to say, a far greater number of players, like the protagonist in "De Camptown Races," "go back home with their hats caved in."

Table 9.2: Risk/Reward Fund Category Performance shows an average representation of broad categories. There are numerous subcategories, such as those listed in Figure 9.2: Mutual Fund Types.

✦   ✦   ✦

Within this galaxy of mutual funds, managing risk becomes the matching of an investor's particular disposition with the appropriate level of risk/reward. One of the most common practices, often promoted by exuberant mutual fund ads, is that of selecting a fund on the basis of past performance. But an excellent track record is only that — it is not necessarily an accurate forecast at all.

A better strategy is to compile a list of *consistent* performers in an area with which you feel most comfortable, and then refine the selection further with the help of your financial advisor who understands essential economic market analysis, has a good reputation, and a good deal of experience in mutual fund portfolio structuring above all.

TABLE 9.2: RISK/REWARD FUND CATEGORY PERFORMANCE

DESCRIPTION	RISK	RETURN
Latin America	4.4%	53.5%
Canadian Small-Cap Equity	4.3%	52.7%
U.S. Equity	3.8%	46.3%
Canadian Dividend	2.2%	44.2%
Sector Equity	4.3%	43.9%
Canadian Large-Cap Equity	3.3%	43.1%
European Equity	2.6%	42.0%
Oil & Gas	6.1%	36.2%
International Equity	2.9%	32.1%
Canadian Balanced	2.2%	32.0%
International Balanced	2.0%	25.9%
Precious Metals	8.3%	21.4%
Canadian Bonds	1.6%	20.0%
Emerging Markets	3.9%	17.7%
Mortgage	0.7%	14.9%
Asia & Pacific Equity	4.0%	11.1%
International Bonds	1.6%	10.8%
Canadian Money Market	0.2%	8.8%
LSVCC	1.7%	8.1%
International Money Market	0.3%	8.0%
Japanese Equity	4.8%	-2.9%

Legend

RISK: The Standard Deviation (S.D.) of a specific fund category, reflecting a recent 24-month performance period. Highest "S.D." reflects highest risk.

RETURN: Total return over the same 24-month period.

Research adaptation by Peter Loach, Manager of Mutual Fund Research,
Midland Walwyn Capital Inc., and the author

chapter 10

EVERYTHING YOU ALWAYS WANTED TO KNOW ABOUT RISK (AND YOUR ADVISOR FORGOT TO MENTION)

There are risks and costs to any program of action. But they are far less than the risks and costs of comfortable inaction.

— John F. Kennedy

LEARNING TO LOVE RISK

Sometimes taking too much risk is no worse than taking too little. Because in investment, there's no such thing as *no risk*. The more you learn about risk, the more you can benefit.

If you dread picking up the morning paper the day after a market decline in order to check prices, your risk tolerance needs attention. If you've stopped worrying about gloomy headlines about individual companies, you're improving your risk aversion, perhaps because your portfolio is being run by carefully measured and selected fund managers attuned to risk-adjusted past performance. If your portfolio's month-to-month variation is a few points up or down, and you take that with a shrug, congratulations.

It helps to point out that you have history on your side. We've already described how, over a 71-year period, the Dow Jones Index of large-company stocks yielded an *average* annual total return of 10.5%, and small-company stocks returned 12.5%. That doesn't mean that each year was consistent. Large-company stocks fluctuated between a gain of 54% in 1933 and a loss of 43% in 1931. Small-company stocks had an even wider range, gaining 143% in 1933 and giving up 58% in 1937.

There are no guarantees, of course, in the securities markets because total predictability is impossible. But gains and losses lose more and more of their random nature as you look at longer periods. Should you invest in small-cap stocks if your time horizon is as little as five years? Good question. But while such stocks lost money in 21 of the individual 71 years since 1926, they declined in only *nine* of the 66 *overlapping five-year* periods. Extending the holding period to 10 years, small company stocks lost in only two of the 61 overlapping decades. And at 20 years, small-cap stocks made money in every such period without exception.

Although I have also pointed out that standard deviation has been the accepted measure of volatility — that is, indicating how much a given investment varies from its average rate of return — Beta is a much more reliable measure in a *negative* market. The higher the standard deviation, the greater the up-and-down fluctuation. Midland Walwyn Capital, Inc., as well as some other major financial institutions, has a relatively new system of establishing risk/reward in its publications, including the use of standard deviation. Obviously, the raw numbers for standard deviation for a given security or fund are only relevant in comparison with others in their peer group. However, standard deviation is *only one* of a number of important measurements to assist in measuring risk and reward, and even this accepted stalwart is being challenged by new analysis.

Most important is total return, which measures the change in net asset value including dividends and capital gain. In particular, look at the five-year annualized figures, if a fund is that ancient!

But we don't stop there. A fund can be a front-runner one year and decline the following year. We need *consistency* of performance, and here we use a tool known as *decile* rank, measuring a fund against its peer group. A decile rank of #1 means a fund's returns were in the top 10%, a rank of #2 was in the second 10%, and so on. A fund that ranks #3 or #4 or even #5 year after year is probably a better candidate than one that ranks #1 one year and #9 the following year. A reality check for consistency.

Which brings us back to the importance of asset allocation. The goal is not to outguess the world's markets, but rather to compare each fund with its specific peer category, and maintain consistency and total return, together with careful risk-adjusted measurements.

RISKY BUSINESS

To many advisors, risk is like "the devil" to a person of the cloth. Best to leave it out of the text. It is, after all, a negative quantity.

Then why write so extensively about risk?

I'll tell you why. Because considering risk in any investment is as important as considering the role of a grain of sand in the development of a pearl of great value. There are essential ingredients *you* must always consider, even if your financial advisor hasn't. Reward and risk are two of them, equal partners.

Essential Ingredient #1 — The First Difference between Savings and Investment is "Risk." The Second Difference between Savings and Risk is "Reward."

These differences can be expressed as the difference between the *loaning* of and *owning* your money. Holding a stock or equity is your evidence of part ownership in a company. Holding a bond or debenture, like any other loan certificate, demonstrates that you are a creditor of the company. This difference has long-term implications for you. The risk you assume by holding stock may be far greater than that of owning a loan vehicle. Because of that chance, the potential rewards to you are far greater. Or, as we have seen with 40-year lows in interest rates during 1996 and 1997, the risk in *not* holding stocks or stock-based mutual funds may be the greatest risk of all!

In fact, it's worse than that. If you don't undertake managed risk, you lose from the effects of other forces bearing on your no-risk, no-gain investment. Think of inflation. Learn the nature of each risk, and then do what you can to diminish it, before proceeding.

Essential Ingredient #2 — All Investments Carry Risk
"Wealth without risk" is impossible. Worse, it's a fraudulent claim. So Charles Givens' bestseller of that name is a contradiction in terms. It's as inconceivable as considering flight without recognizing the force of gravity. All investors must recognize this principle of success regarding their investments.

Uncalculated risk may not always be an evil force, but it can certainly carry a lot of grief with it.

Essential Ingredient #3 — Risk Is Multifaceted
If you focus first on avoiding risk, and *then* on reward potential, you will succeed. It doesn't work the other way around.

And there are still other chances, against which all your investments must be measured. They include the cost risk, borrowing risk, management risk, inflation risk, tax risk, political risk, and of course the risk of fraud or theft. And then there is the additional risk encompassed in "derivatives" — the "Big D" word!

Derivatives

"Derivatives" has become a buzzword in the financial markets in recent years. In the media, the term tends to be used sensationally and in a derogatory sense, as if they're some sort of financial villain.

Of course, they have been the focus of billions of dollars in losses for certain German industrial firms, Barings Bank of London, and the Orange County administrators in California. Still, the form of the investment is not to blame for their errors. The unrealistic use of those investments in a *highly leveraged* manner caused the downfall of the Orange County administrators.

You can escalate derivatives' risk by not understanding them. It's normal to fear what we don't understand. Ignorance is your greatest danger, just as knowledge is your best protection.

In the recent proliferation of financial instruments, numerous derivatives such as options, futures, swaps and more exotic option-based financial instruments have joined stocks and bonds. They attract investors with their unusual profit potential, entailing extreme leverage. Some derivative instruments are used to *reduce* risk. More on this later.

A derivative is a legal paper asset that derives its value from another asset, known as the underlying instrument. For example, common shares are paper assets that derive their value from the prospective future earnings and underlying assets of the companies that issue them. In fact, with a slight stretching of the imagination, we can even describe a dollar bill as a derivative, though we routinely consider it a tangible asset itself. We do this even though it is not intrinsically valuable. It is no longer backed by gold, as it once was, either.

A futures contract allows you to fix a price today on a security to be delivered in the future. When you take an option on a house, you do the same thing: you fix a price today with a small deposit, promising to take delivery of it at some point in the future. An option contract can give you the right, but not the obligation, to buy or sell a security at a fixed price in the future. If you put a deposit on a Mediterranean cruise for next spring and then decide to cancel, you forfeit your deposit, just as you may forfeit the price of an option.

Naturally, with any such option, if the price drops below the price at which you fixed your future purchase, the option becomes worthless. Think of holding an option ("strike price") on a house at $300,000 when the market sinks its price to $225,000.

Like an option, the value of your equity in a house is only as good as the housing market itself. Before the British Columbia real estate debacle in the early 1980s, many people, believing that happy days would go on forever, used the slender equity in one house to purchase another. With skyrocketing interest rates in 1981–1982 and plunging real estate prices, these ambitious investors saw their margins — just like vanishing option prices — vaporize and wipe them out.

In the case of an option, you usually don't commit a sizable amount of money if you fail to exercise your right. Trading on the equity of your house, particularly your permanent residence, is a dicey business you should enter into with care, and be backed up with sound resources.

Caveat emptor, "let the buyer beware," remains the byword today. Our government goes so far as to protect consumers by permitting many transactions to be declared null and void for a certain period if the buyer can prove a con job. Nonetheless, find out the facts before you undertake any transaction. A good advisor will welcome and encourage your doing so.

Now for the good guys. Mutual fund managers often use derivatives, in the buying and selling of options, to stabilize price movements and so reduce risk within their portfolios. For you as a mutual fund investor, these trading operations can broaden the safety factor on investments within the fund. They can also increase your foreign exposure to as much as 100% in global bonds and stocks (such as in RRSPs and RRIFs) where such exposure is normally limited to the 20% RRSP federal government's Canadian Property Rule. Instead of holding only 20% foreign content inside your RRSP or RRIF, you can shelter as much as 100% because of derivative instruments. (See Table 10.1: Three Uses for Derivative Instruments.)

TABLE 10.1: THREE USES FOR DERIVATIVE INSTRUMENTS

	1	2	3
How Are They Used?	For risk management within a portfolio.	For efficient portfolio management.	To leverage a portfolio's exposure to a market.
Use Permitted?	Permitted by Canadian regulators of mutual funds.	Permitted by Canadian regulators of mutual funds.	Not permitted by Canadian regulators of mutual funds.
Fund Company Use?	Allows portfolio managers to limit market exposures and control the variability of fund performance.	Allows clients to get exposure to foreign markets while staying in 100% RRSP-eligible funds.	None.
Used Elsewhere?	Widely used in the fund management industry and by pension funds worldwide.	Pioneered by Global Strategy and now widely used by other Canadian fund companies.	It is the leveraged use of derivatives that worries regulators.
An Example ...	The manager of a fund has 15% of the portfolio in Japanese stocks, but worries about short-term equity market risk. In the long term, the manager likes the chosen stock list. The manager can cheaply and efficiently "sell" an equivalent exposure to the Japanese market to nearly 0%. When conditions stabilize, the manager eliminates the futures position to restore the original exposure to Japanese shares.	An investor wants 100% exposure to the growing economies of Southeast Asia in an RRSP and chooses a derivative fund. The fund buys, on an unleveraged basis, exposure to the stock markets of Hong Kong, Singapore, etc., using index figures and other permitted derivatives. Because the use of derivatives is on an unleveraged basis, the investor gains exposure to markets in an amount equal to the value of their original investment.	An investor has $1,000 to invest and wants maximum exposure to the Canadian equity market. The investor uses their $1,000 as collateral for a position in the derivatives market ten times that of the amount — that is $10,000. If the market fell by 15%, the investor would lose $1,500 on an original stake of $1,000.

Source: Global Strategy "Strategems"

INFLATION RISK — PROTECT THOSE SHRINKING DOLLARS

Since World War II, inflation (along with deficit spending and national debt) has probably caused the greatest concern to governments, economists, business organizations, and individuals around the world. That inflation has lessened in most countries in recent years is cold comfort to those with memories long enough to recall the flight of the German mark in the 1920s or the more recent trauma of the December 20, 1994, Mexican peso. The more moderate Canadian experience of the 1970s and 1980s witnessed inflation becoming an accepted fact of life.

The Bank of Canada is charged with the responsibility of directing and regulating monetary policy, directly and indirectly determining interest rates and influencing inflation. Through its weekly Treasury Bill auction, it sets the Bank rate (the rate at which the chartered banks may borrow from the Bank of Canada as a lender of last resort) and which is the basis of the Prime Rate and all Canadian interest rates. It also exerts an influential lever on inflation by expanding or contracting the total money supply through open-market operations — buying or selling bonds from or to the chartered banks.

The Canadian central bank's achievement has been substantial in two ways: first, it has indeed contained inflation, which can be easily demonstrated, and second, it has raised public awareness and encouraged our *resistance* to the notion that inflation is inevitable. Many governments in the world are participating in this low interest, low inflation environment.

"By far the most significant achievement [of the Bank]," said Gordon Thiessen, the Bank's governor, in his annual report for 1994, "is the maintenance of a low level of inflation for the third successive year, after two decades of high and unpredictable inflation." Essentially, Thiessen said the same thing in 1995 and 1996, and again in 1997.

For the Bank of Canada, and by inference the federal government, the ultimate objective of Canadian monetary policy is to promote good overall economic performance. Monetary policy, according to Thiessen, can help preserve confidence in the value of money through price stability. Price stability is therefore a means to an end, not an end in itself.

These sound like brave words, political words, yet the methods and the results of the Bank's initiative are real. The Consumer Price Index (CPI) is the most generally accepted indicator of inflation, both in reality and in public perception. The Bank closely follows a core CPI, excluding food, energy and the effects of indirect taxation from its statistics. For its own monitoring purposes, the Bank removes much of the index's short-term fluctuation while closely following its general price movements.

Since 1991, central bank policy has been to contain the CPI fluctuation within a band of 1% to 3%, a strategy that has succeeded. Currently, the target band has been extended to 1998. (Revisit Figure 6.4: The Canadian Inflation Rate and the Consumer Price Index 1986–1996.)

While investors can salute the determined efforts and accomplishments of the Bank of Canada, they should not ignore the continuing effects of inflation. Most economists believe that an inflation rate of less than 2% can produce the healthiest economy. Yet even 2% inflation over time can devastate your program as an individual investor. Inflation has averaged 5% per annum over the last 40 years.

Furthermore, the hacking away of the Canadian deficit has been accomplished at enormous cost to average Canadians and retirees. "Why would a government change the rules [for RRSPs] so as to put greater impediments on private savings for retirement?" asked highly regarded tax expert and lawyer Arthur Drache. "Of course, the answer is quite simple — taxes!"

This is a shocking betrayal by government of its hard-working citizens when the minister of finance had declared loud and clear, "In this budget we are not raising personal taxes. We are not raising corporate taxes. We are not raising excise taxes. In fact, we are not raising taxes."

Third, many Canadians now reaching retirement will receive zero government pension even though they have contributed to the C.P.P. and O.A.S. for many years. Under the proposed new insidious clawback rule, the Senior Benefits plan will be based on "family income" rather than individual income. Instead of the former threshold figure for retirement benefits of $167,000, eligibility will disappear entirely at $78,000.

Garth Turner, former minister of national revenue, in his book *1997 RRSP Guide*, quotes Malcolm Hamilton, pension expert, as saying, "Between the income tax and the new seniors' benefit, you'll be turning some 60 to 70 cents on the dollar over to the government on your retirement savings. To me, this goes beyond the bounds of normal progressivity. This is almost vindictive."

So the next time a government official tells you he's "not raising taxes," just remember we've witnessed one of the greatest tax grabs in Canadian history. I suggest that the government's next announcement should be to privatize many badly managed government agencies and Crown corporations, slash the capital gains tax for all investors (small and big), increase the tax-free dividend credit to allow billions of dollars of investment capital to flow into Canada, and to permit small business to generate thousands of additional jobs for our citizens.

Problem #1 — Inflation

Inflation is not a new phenomenon. The insidious debasement of currency has gone on since coins were first minted in Asia Minor around 600 B.C. Later, unscrupulous governments reduced the precious metal content of coins while reducing their size during the Greek and Roman civilizations. The ruthless Emperor Nero began debasing the *denarius*. Over the following 150 years its silver content shrank by 50%.

As recently as 1946, the U.S. and Canadian governments removed nearly all silver from coins. No doubt, the price inflation since can be related in part to that decision. All Canadian coins today are made of nickel and alloy.

Inflation dramatically influences your investment planning. The average annual inflation increased the total CPI from the early 1970s to the early 1990s by an *annual average* of 6.3%. Individual items for clothing rose in price 3.8%, entertainment 5.3%, transportation 6.0%, housing 6.5%, medical care 8.1%, and education 8.2%. Don't forget, these are *annual percentages*. Translated, housing costs rose by 130% over the period. Thankfully, inflation has moderated in the recent past.

In the securities markets, both stock and bond prices are negatively correlated with inflation and suffer accordingly, particularly in periods of high inflation. In 1981–1982 inflation reached such high levels that interest rates had to rise to more than 20% to afford investors a reasonable return *after inflation* — about 14% at its peak. Naturally, bond prices plummeted while interest rates climbed.

Ongoing inflation smashes industrial companies, whose short-term benefits collapse under the weight of higher costs over the long run. Selling prices rise, with all costs and expenses. Inventories may be written up, and this offsets the rising costs of replacing them. Replacing plant and equipment becomes the most onerous, implying heavy future liability. A sudden rise in inflation can trigger higher company profits in the short run, while it can gut long-term profitability.

To gain some sense of the true effects of inflation during the last half of this century, consider the purchasing price of the Canadian dollar since the early 1940s. Indexing the purchasing price of a dollar as of 1940, that value sank to 58 cents by 1950, to 47 cents by 1960, to 36 cents by 1970, to 17 cents by 1980 to 10 cents by 1990, and to 9 cents by 1996.

Again, inflation affects securities markets in very different ways. A relationship between inflation and various investment categories in the period between the early 1970s and the early 1990s reveals, given an inflation coefficient of 1.0, that single-family homes had a correlation of 0.82, gold 0.59, but domestic stocks were negatively correlated at –0.33, long-term government bonds at –0.61, and long-term corporate bonds at –0.72. In simpler percentages, this means that single-family homes, for example, advanced in price only 82% of the rate of inflation while corporate bonds declined, relative to inflation, by 28%.

The investor in securities is taxed on the inflation rate itself. If you hold a bond with a 6% coupon at a time of 7% inflation, you are earning –1% in real terms, while paying tax at a rate of 6%.

Solution to Problem #1

Gaining access to growth to offset inflation is something like working out on the parallel bars or doing roadwork to offset the potentially harmful strength of the bully next door. You can't remove the threat itself, but you can build up a compensating factor — if you are allowed the time to prepare yourself before the attack takes place.

Long life today does not suggest but *demands* a portfolio amply supplied with equities. Equities can grow old every bit as gracefully as their owner, while the value of fixed-rate securities, as well as some fixed-income securities, can evaporate through inflation and lost purchasing power.

As recently as a couple of generations ago, "retirement" was tantamount to sending out death notices. Once, retirement averaged about seven years, leaving a chunk of assets for the kids and grandkids.

Today, people are living 20 to 30 years longer beyond retirement. The old portfolio, obviously, must be revisited. There is no room for securities that retain their fixed-dollar value as long as they remain invested in the same vehicle and nothing more.

Peter Lynch flies in the face of the traditional portfolio. He asserts that stock portfolios are mandatory, even among seniors of advancing age. "The retirement account," he says, "is the perfect place for stocks, because the money can sit there and grow for 10 to 30 years." You heard Lynch right — the retirement account is the *perfect* place for stocks and stock mutual funds!

Many financial advisors and writers are still grinding out the dogma that Canadian investors should begin shuffling most of their money into bonds and GICs about the time of menopause or the first onset of prostate problems. Consciously or not, these "professionals" pander to conservative investors' worst fears. These advisors, while professing themselves to be "wise," are in fact promoting financial foolishness and huge losses to their clients by telling you that you must lower your expectations of making as good a return as possible as you grow older, and that you must also deliberately bow to inflation and meekly accept your annual tax clawbacking by Revenue Canada.

Problem #2 —Liquidity

Liquidity refers to your ability to exit ("The Exit Factor") an investment at a given time. It does not suggest that such a sale will necessarily be at a set price above, below, or at the price you paid in the first place. Think of your car, which you bought for $20,000. It may have liquidity in the sense that you can sell it readily, even though the used-car "Blue Book" says it's now worth $4,900.

Liquidity's importance is self-evident. Similarly, real estate, bonds or stocks, if there are active markets, may all have liquidity, which is better than having no market at all, but it may prove inadequate if the price isn't right. Of these three particular asset classes, real estate offers by far the least desirable liquidity factor.

Solution to Problem #2

Mutual funds can be sold, at any time, at a price fixed on the total breakup value of the fund portfolio. This is thanks to their great diversification among marketable securities. As in some other specific securities, this cashability does not guarantee parity with what you paid for them. Yet, since the historical trend is upward, given aberrations in the securities markets, chances are that if you have held your mutual fund shares for any reasonable period of time, your cashing in will gain you a satisfactory return.

The large expanse of the holdings of any large mutual fund translates into a substantial leveling effect on their individual market value. Compare this with the locked-in possibilities of real estate, some individual securities, and GICs and other so-called "guarantees." When you lock-up your investments in illiquid assets, you often lock-out golden opportunities.

Problem #3 — Complexity

To the amateur, the securities markets are often scary and overwhelming. Investment securities in general seem huge and unknowable, hopelessly complex, even mysterious. Assessing a stock looks impossibly difficult. Most investors are vitally interested in what is being done with their money, but to varying degrees prefer to stay at a distance, to avoid "getting under the hood." In addition, the ever-increasing array of new investment instruments and technical language confuses most people.

Solution to Problem #3

Mutual funds allow you to participate actively or with disinterest, through buying a fund, or a portfolio of widely diversified funds. And you'll enjoy comparable, results and within the ease of your comfort zone.

Simplicity and convenience are another part of the antidote to complexity. You can buy some of the best financial brains in the world, enjoy *instant* diversification anywhere in the world, all by simply making out a cheque and an application.

Mutual funds are something like today's other packaged consumer goods and services. They are readily available, run totally by professionals, make good sense economically while being widely adaptable, and they can free you for a boat cruise or spending more time with the kids and grandkids.

Problem #4 — Asset Classes

The trouble with asset classes is that class wars can break out often. Did you concentrate your investments in stocks during the great bull market of the late 1980s, only to see the bull turn into a bum steer in October of 1987? Perhaps you felt your advancing years suggested a more conservative stance and you bought bonds in the early 1980s. Then you watched interest rates fly to 20% and fixed-income securities tumble like clay pigeons. Or, you ploughed your money into real estate at exactly the wrong time and watched property values decline while the stock market went bullish.

Solution to Problem #4

Mutual funds give the fund managers plenty of latitude to maneuver. The outstanding feature of a single asset allocation fund is that the fund managers have ample room to diversify the portfolio. Unlike the manager of a normal balanced fund portfolio, they can also alter the makeup of the fund from time to time according to microeconomic or macroeconmic trends. They may at any given time be heavily in equities and light in fixed-income securities, or the reverse, or weighting may be completely shifted from a fully invested position to a substantial (money market) cash position. Or they may return to a completely balanced composition, whatever the circumstances might indicate. The answer is clear: regardless of your age or investment goals, you should *always* have a variety of asset classes in your portfolio.

Problem #5 — Management Risk

Nobody, you may believe, knows your business as well as you do. Managing your private financial business is no different. In broad numbers you may be the best judge, but in the creation of a financial plan you'll encounter areas where you need objective professional expertise for best results. You can't afford to flounder where you insist on maximizing your returns, adjusted to your risk tolerance. If you are floundering instead of managing, you make yourself a sitting duck for every charlatan or incompetent in the financial industry, however well-meaning. There is no such thing as a *single* "all weather" fund manager or financial advisor, automatically steering your portfolio through the worst markets, without any loss potential. Such a scenerio is a fool's paradise. Active asset allocation anyone? That's why I insist on many outstanding, yet different styles of managers.

Solution to Problem #5

Mutual funds take the worry out of being too close to a subject about which you may know too little. So close that you may be in a dangerous position similar to that of the proverbial mouse rolled on by the elephant. The analogy is not inappropriate. The immensity of the mutual fund movement, like that of an elephant, can prove to be an enormous threat as well as a huge ally, depending on how you manage your own situation. Management for hire is widely available, and later we will tell you what to look for in a financial advisor.

Problem #6 — International Risk

The risks involved with international investment are several, and they are compounded by the wide variety of countries with active securities markets. Global investors can earn greater returns in exchange for a given level of risk. Some markets may offer better values than others, giving overseas buyers more opportunities to search for bargains, since all markets are not equally efficient at all times.

The Canadian economy is relatively mature and prone to grow at a slower rate than most. Yet, a mature industry in Canada, such as the cement industry, may be expanding wildly in the developing economies of China, Brazil or Eastern Europe.

The risk element may be reduced in international situations, simply because stock markets don't move in tandem (different economic cycles, correlations) all the time. The relative price movement between markets can be quite low — that is, inefficient — especially with emerging nations such as Chile, Greece, Indonesia, Mexico, the Philippines, Thailand, Turkey or China. There are extra risks when dealing with some emerging markets in contrast with the established international markets. Among these risks are securities regulations, restrictions of foreign investments, currency risk, repatriation of profits, lack of liquidity, accounting differences, fraud and corruption, and a volatile political situation.

FIGURE 10.1: EMERGING MARKETS CORRELATIONS WITH THE U.S. MARKET

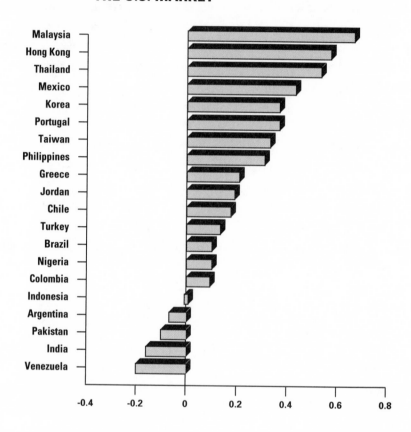

Source: Pictet & Cie

The *correlation coefficient* is a very useful statistical measurement computed from two "time-series" of numbers, such as stock prices in Canada and the U.S. The coefficient gauges how closely the two markets move up and down in relation to one another. A +1.0 correlation represents a perfect positive (same) association. A value of 0.0 shows complete independence between the two markets. This zero correlation means the two markets are totally unrelated.

The closer the correlation to zero between two different markets, the greater the diversification benefit. Time series of stock prices in different countries tend to be positively coordinated, but the coefficient is typically well below 1.0. Researchers have found the relationship between Canada and numerous foreign markets to be 0.5 (50%) or less. This is welcome news to internationally oriented Canadian investors interested in reducing risk.

For example, the U.S.-Canada coefficient of 0.63 (see Table 8.11) compares with the U.S.-Italy figure of 0.42. Seventeen of the 20 world markets (see Figure 10.1) correlate with the U.S. at less than 0.5. The link between the U.S. and Japan, for instance, again referring to Table 8.11, is only 0.32. These charts and the information they demonstrate make a compelling case for the risk-reducing benefits of international diversification.

But with the growing trend toward global business by multinational corporations, the world's economies may become more closely linked and interdependent. This means that the affected markets could move toward higher correlations. It will, however, be a long time before the major markets move toward actual synchronization, if ever, much less the smaller markets. There will always be market inefficiencies and anomalies, and the more the better. The year 1994 provides a recent example. Japan, the world's second largest economy and stock market, saw its stock market rise by 23%, while the TSE 300 Index registered 1%.

Meanwhile, the investor in foreign securities faces certain specific risks, even while diversification often reduces volatility:

1. *Stock Market Risk*: Less-developed foreign markets may not be as closely regulated as the North American markets. Investors in those markets are less protected from trading abuses and other kinds of market manipulation. Many overseas stocks are thinly traded and volatile. They often sell at excessively high price-earnings ratios, making them vulnerable if two things happen: first, their companies begin to lose money, and second, their investors turn sour on them. Country risk and stock market risk often go hand in hand, particularly in developing and emerging nations.

2. *Country Risk*: This covers a variety of economic and political problems, wars and natural disasters, such as earthquakes. This risk is low in the U.S., somewhat higher in Canada with its Quebec Effect, and still higher in a country such as South Africa, with its continuing racial tension. Those who wish to concentrate their investments in one country heighten their exposure to country risk.

3. *Currency Risk*: This arises out of rapid changes in foreign exchange. Such swings strongly affect securities values, sometimes overnight. The devaluation of the Mexican peso on December 20, 1994, led to a huge adjustment in those funds holding securities of that country.

If the Canadian dollar appreciates against the currency in which a foreign investment is held, or denominated, your returns will be adversely affected. Conversely, a declining Canadian dollar would boost the value of your foreign holdings, including international mutual funds. Foreign mutual fund managers deal daily with the yen, pound, franc, mark, peseta, peso, lira, krona and U.S. dollar. Stocks on overseas markets are usually purchased with local money. So a foreign security combines both an investment in a particular stock or bond portfolio *and* a currency speculation.

Currency risk can work for or against you. If the Canadian dollar strengthens (and the particular foreign currency weakens), you incur a loss. If the dollar weakens (and the foreign currency strengthens), you realize a gain.

Currency risk poses no significant problem for long-term investors using a well-diversified international mutual fund. The favorable and unfavorable fluctuations tend to balance out over time.

Some foreign stock and bond mutual funds offer the service of hedging currency risk. Managers can reduce or hedge the threat posed by adverse currency fluctuations with options, futures or forward-contracts, which are particular types of derivatives. Offshore mutual funds can give you two advantages: (1) increase your exposure under RRSP rules from 20% to 100%, and (2) reduce risk and so improve profitability.

4. *Liquidity Risk* in foreign markets may be another danger. The liquidity we take for granted in this continent may not always be available in erratic offshore markets. Consider practical concerns such as the ready availability of financial information and access to current news of all kinds affecting markets and securities. Different reporting standards and these other obstacles can complicate decision-making about stock selection initially, and about buying and selling securities.

Solution to Problem # 6

Mutual funds can be hedged, for example, against currency risks by buying futures options. Holding substantial positions can also diminish problems of liquidity.

As to accessing information and following international financial trends, these professionals have made it their full-time business. Their knowledge and access to wide-ranging contacts give specialist mutual fund portfolio managers a huge advantage over the most informed people dealing with these offshore conditions. So through this professional management you magnify the benefits of investing in these markets while shrinking your risks. The whole idea is to invest in many countries and several asset classes that have a *low* correlation when measuring market cycles between each other. By investing in securities of countries that have low (and different) correlationships, portfolio risk is reduced.

Problem #7 — Capital Losses

Limiting your risk of loss is perhaps most difficult in the securities markets. With no risk at all, you usually lose any chance to realize a profit. The risk you court, though, must be reduced through successful investing.

This we'll call the 20/20 sand-trap, whereby a given percentage decline is not compensated for by corresponding gain. This is no mere word or numbers game. It illustrates the difficulty of coping with losses and the errors we can commit in undoing such loss. (See Table 10.2: A Loss Is Hard to Regain.) You may be so eager to unload a losing investment that you switch into another similarly depressed security. The fallacy is that we often sacrifice quality in such a move, just as you can reduce the quality of your whole portfolio for the sake of taking a profit, particularly if the market is down at the time of redemption.

TABLE 10.2: A LOSS IS HARD TO REGAIN

If you start with a dollar and take a loss, what do you need to break even?

10% loss:	First a	10% loss:	$1.00 - .10 = $ .90
	Need an	11% gain:	$ .90 + .10 = $1.00
30% loss:	First a:	30% loss:	$1.00 - .30 = $ .70
	Need a	43% gain:	$ .70 + .30 = $1.00
50% loss:	First a	50% loss:	$1.00 - .50 = $ .50
	Need a	100% gain:	$ .50 + .50 = $1.00
80% loss:	First a	80% loss:	$1.00 - .80 = $ .20
	Need a	400% gain:	$ .20 + .80 = $1.00

Solution to Problem #7

Mutual funds appreciate in value over time, properly constructed and maintained. This is not always true of other securities. You can best limit loss in this medium. Many components of a fund portfolio may lose value from time to time. Most of those holdings will not. The best way to win back the value you do lose is to use a medium that will overcome those losses, if you allow it the *time* to do so.

Can appreciating risk be healthy? Of course. Consider this observation by Dr. Mark Mobius, a dean of emerging market mutual fund managers: "The perception of risk is very, very important in finding bargains, because if people think something is risky, we could find a bargain."

Which brings us to:

Stenner's Law #5: Whatever is the most difficult thing to do is probably the right thing to do.

chapter 11

ACHIEVING YOUR OWN COMFORT ZONE

Money is the symbol of duty, it is the sacrament of having done for mankind that which mankind wanted. Mankind may not be a very good judge.

— Samuel Butler

ANALYZING REASON AND EMOTION

Risk analysis is portfolio analysis. And analyzing your portfolio includes not only studying its composition but also evaluating the individual securities within it. You have an incredible menu of new investments available from which to choose. A wealth of experts competes for your attention on specific funds, bombarding us daily in the print and electronic media.

The two most obvious factors to be exorcised are *emotion* and *greed*. As one leading fund manager puts it, "Do all you can to rid yourself of emotion in investing while retaining common sense."

Professional people are often so immersed in their own disciplines that they assume that they are equally expert in every other walk of life as well. Those who spend professional lifetimes telling patients or other clients what to do often have great difficulty accepting instruction from professionals outside their own field about their financial care and treatment.

The other deadly potion in investment choice is greed. It, too, must be replaced by common sense. We are frequently misled by ads promising unusual returns, and requiring little capital. Whether we hear of such pie-in-the-sky opportunities through a friend's hot stock tip or it's just a word on the street, the point is that the wrong response within us is to act quickly and foolishly.

When the smoke clears, all we have left is a horrendous tax write-off. "After the kiss," writes W.H. Auden, "comes the impulse to throttle." How do we offset this initial impulse to embrace? How do we convert the irresistible pitch into rationality and prudence in the first place?

First we evaluate the risk factor, or the underlying security of the investment being considered. A federally insured GIC or Treasury Bill has a very high safety factor and an almost nonexistent current value risk factor. At the opposite pole, a commodity contract on margin for copper, corn, or porkbellies has a safety factor so slim and a risk factor so robust that it could wipe out your entire investment, and the benefits to your spouse, kids and aging Dalmatian in a matter of hours.

Second, analyze the profit potential. In GICs or term deposits, you tend to make a modest return. With luck, after tax and the effects of inflation, you may actually take something home. Had you been in GICs during 1993, you would have foregone the opportunity to earn 20% to 40% or, with some funds, as much as 80% or 90% in a few equity mutual funds. Hindsight? Of course. Mutual funds at least supply a chance at good returns, year over year. GICs do not, after tax and inflation. Nor can GICs ever, in a thousand years, increase your capital by a single penny.

Third, measure volatility, or the likelihood of price changes within a single year. Volatility is often referred to as "standard deviation." The visual volatility of a GIC is zero. The volatility of a zero-interest coupon bond could be as much as 25%. A real estate income property could register a 20% volatility, and that of gold might be 50% in a single year. Volatility, obviously, can be both a good and a bad factor, given any time period. But a security with volatility at least shows some signs of life. Where there's life, there's hope of profit potential, provided you understand the risks.

Fourth, consider the income factor related to any investment. If you own a home and live in it, the income you derive from it is nil. If you own 100 shares of stock bought at $10 a share and which yields a dividend of $1 per share, your rate of return is 10%, plus the dividend credit allowed for tax purposes. Or you may receive no dividend, while the stock may increase in price to $20, for a capital gain of 100%, in the first year.

One highly successful investment dealer, when approached by a corporate client seeking financing, always divided the projected revenue of the company by two and doubled the anticipated costs. If the company's profitability *still* looked good at that point, he considered underwriting the company.

HOW SAFE ARE MUTUAL FUNDS?

Having been cautioned on the means of assessing the risks and the safety considerations, you may ask yourself just how safe mutual funds are as a group. There is not a simple answer to this question. Some generalizations can be drawn. To begin with, think of the world's leading banks, telephone and telecommunication systems, most credit-worthy governments in the world, government-insured NHA mortgages, global transportation corporations, insurance companies, commercial real estate companies, textiles and the largest food and beverage industries.

These are themselves quite safe. Safety in mutual funds relates more to the organization of these institutions rather than to ironclad guarantees.

Over time, mutual funds have produced historically superior returns compared to "guaranteed" investments. Mutual fund managers oversee some of the largest private pension plans in the country, including the medical doctors' pensions (mutual fund) plan.

Proof? To our knowledge, there has *never* been a failure of a mutual fund in Canadian history. In other words, the batting average of success among the current 1,500 mutual funds in Canada is essentially 1.000.

LEGAL PROTECTION FOR MUTUAL FUND INVESTORS

Here are some of the criteria of operation for mutual fund managers:

- Each investor must receive a prospectus that details key policies.
- All mutual fund assets must be held by a custodian chartered bank or trust company and be segregated from those of the fund's trustee, custodian and manager.
- A fund broker posts a blanket bond to protect against any potential dishonesty or fraud by employees.
- As one provincial government example, the B.C. government's contingency fund to protect mutual fund assets – and so the investors — from fraud, theft, or dishonest behavior has not been drawn upon once since its inception in 1962.
- The federal government established National Policy 39 in 1995 to standardize securities commissions' regulations. The new national law on mutual fund sales practices is expected soon. Canadian securities administrators have developed a new prospectus and disclosure review system allowing each issuer to deal with a single regulation.
- Qualified financial brokerage firms offer the Canadian Investor Protection Fund (CIPF) for their investors.

MARKET MOVEMENTS AND VALUES

Never interpret a *normal*, healthy market fluctuation whether in bonds, currency, mortgages, real estate, stocks, or interest rates as dangerous to your portfolio. Markets, and securities markets in particular, swing between extremes as they reflect the consensual opinions of millions of investors, institutional and individual, in anticipation of future conditions.

Individual shorter-term market movements have little to do with the current value of securities, except as they depict the average value for those securities. History demonstrates that a market has *always* regained stability following any eccentric behavior, up or down. The lesson of the Principal Group failure in Edmonton in 1987 is also worth remembering. In that huge debacle, individual investors sustained enormous losses to their "guaranteed" term deposits. *The only investors who lost nothing and maintained or were reimbursed their full investment market value were the owners of Principal Mutual Funds.* (See Figure 11.1: The Boring Approach.)

FIGURE 11.1 THE BORING APPROACH*

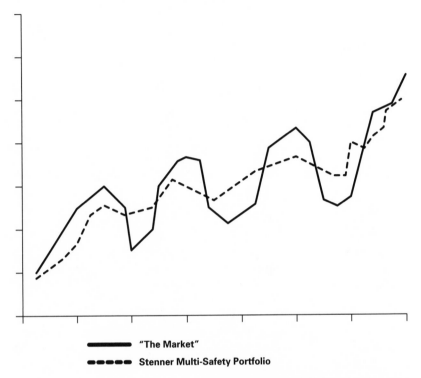

━━━━━ "The Market"

●●●●● Stenner Multi-Safety Portfolio

* theoretical simulated graph, for illustrative purposes only

The Stenner Multi-Safety Allocation System approach to mutual fund portfolio construction seeks to reduce the risk and "chills" that accompany market volatility. Which do you prefer for your nest egg? The boring dotted line (tortoise) approach or the more exciting (hare) solid line experience? "Winning by Not Losing" is what the Stenner Multi-Safety Allocation System seeks to do, structuring a client's portfolio to mitigate risk at every level of the account holdings. We seek above-average, *risk-adjusted* returns.

TACTICAL ERRORS

1. FOCUSING ON THE UPSIDE

Consider the traditional salesperson's approach: "Tom, I've got a stock for you that our research guys think can double in the next two years." Or "how would you like to earn 10%, with your principal guaranteed by the Government of Canada?" Or, "Here's a mutual fund for a sure-fire return of 25% to 50% over the next year, with no downside."

The underlying assumption: "Here is how you will gain if things go well." Any sensible businessperson undertakes an investment based on a plus-or-minus estimate allowing for a reasonable range of possibilities. Yet many investors focus only on the upside.

The antidote to such come-ons is simple. Besides tempering your enthusiasm when looking at the best-case scenario, *always* consider the consequences if your investment were to fail. It's exciting to visualize your $100,000 doubling overnight – it's harder and more rational to figure out how you'll pay the rent or mortgage if that money disappears. Volatility is a two-edged sword.

2. CONFUSING INVESTMENT WITH HOCKEY

"The best defence is a good offence" always worked for the offensive-minded Wayne Gretzky. It's highly suspect advice in the investment world.

In August 1987, as the Dow Jones soared through 2700, nine out of 10 senior Canadian securities analysts in a survey predicted that the market would continue strong for the foreseeable future. Six weeks later, Black Monday saw the greatest stock market crash since 1929. Ninety percent of those top ten analysts were wrong — big time!

Those holding-balanced 50/50 portfolios (half in equity and half in bond investments) would have significantly reduced their risk and immediate losses. Those with fixed-income mutual funds lost nothing in their holdings in the crash. In fact, bonds and bond mutual funds modestly rose in value that day.

3. CONFUSING LUCK FOR TALENT

In the heady 1980s, the stock market rose so strongly that average annual returns on stock and equity mutual funds almost doubled historical norms. In that market you could have made money throwing a dart at the stock quotations page of any newspaper. The same was true for investors in the real estate market from 1987, particularly in B.C.

An entire generation of investors came of age with misconceptions about the markets. The extended real estate boom led our entire culture to believe that land values always go up and that an investor can buy and sell into that form of investment at any time and make a profit. "Rising markets," wrote Lord Keynes, "make quite ordinary men seem wise."

When property values crashed and burned in Vancouver in 1982 and then hunkered down from 1983 through most of 1986, thousands of people lost their homes. Most real estate dropped 50% to 60% in value.

All of which raises the Random Walk hypothesis. It states that a random selection can be just as effective as thoughtful research at any point, based on simple probability alone. In a controlled test, a mouse has a 50% chance of choosing the one of two holes in which a piece of cheese is hidden.

Professor Burton G. Malkiel, in his 1996 book *A Random Walk Down Wall Street,* insists that all markets are passive — that investors already have all the information they need to act. It's just not possible to "beat" the market consistently, his theory proposes.

However, if the markets move randomly, then the assumption has to be that everyone investing in them must operate randomly, too. Human nature is not random.

Individual investors' decisions, sound and unsound, will continue to affect the markets indefinitely. No one can accurately predict the total market supply and demand movements. And markets will always have built-in inefficiencies.

For the investor, the more inefficiencies, the better. These make for profit opportunities as well as improved market stabilities. While some investors will always make good decisions, more of them will make *bad* decisions. Millions of investors of all kinds drive the markets. So much for Professor Malkiel's theory.

In the 1980s, many stockbrokers, realtors and bankers became role models to their clients. In a universe of rising markets, the same advisors could have done better than the cheese-seeking mouse, scoring more than 100% of the time.

Margaret Patel, director of fixed income at Boston Security Counselors, puts the point even more wryly: "If you are at the right place when the market moves, you are either lucky or smart — and it doesn't matter."

So seek ye first a talented financial advisor, fund manager, and management group. If you can't find any of these, warm up your dart-throwing arm or stock up on those lottery tickets.

4. LOSING SIGHT OF BASIC ARITHMETIC

If I tell you I have an investment for you that has the potential to grow 20% in a rising market and lose 20% in a falling market, would I be offering you a break-even situation?

NO! You would lose whichever market came first.

An investment of $100 followed by a rise — taking it to $120 — then a 20% decline, would leave your stock worth $96. If it declined by 20% first — dropping to $80 — and then rose 20%, you would still end up with $96. (Review Table 10.2 for an even more dramatic example.)

The market cannot move both ways simultaneously — unless, of course, you hold several different classes of investments! Avoid the *20/20 sand-trap* so called because it ironically implies perfect vision as well as these percentages.

5. DOUBLING UP TO RECOUP YOUR LOSSES

Your advisor calls to suggest you move from your low-interest-bearing GICs and T-Bills into higher-yielding long-term

"Canadas." Your advisor is talking about 10- to 30-year Government of Canada strip bonds, highly leveraged instruments that could temporarily lose 20% to 30% of their market value if interest rates rise substantially.

Your advisor neglects to remind you that your low-yielding short-term GIC is virtually risk-free. It has full relative value at its maturity whereas a long-term bond exposes you to major capital market loss if interest rates rise during the longer period before the bond's maturity.

Or your advisor may approach you with "I know you want your $10,000 back, but with your long-term government bond, of course you realize that the government guarantees the principal, though only at maturity, in 2010 or 2015. Meantime, the market price varies with interest rates. Your bonds? About $8,000 this morning, give or take —"

And if your bond is "stripped" of its coupon, it's *leveraged*, which incurs more interim market risk.

"— I may have a solution for you. We have a new issue this morning with a very attractive yield. Government bond? Well, no, it's a certain company. But if you were to make a capital gain with this, you could recoup your other loss. I'm suggesting you forego that other losing situation — the long-term Canada — and put the proceeds into this higher-yielding issue. You'll have a good chance to make back all the money we lost. If you give me the okay now, I think I can get you in at issue price."

Ever downward the spiral, downgrading the quality of your holdings to make marginal gains. Not too surprisingly, many investors consider securities markets a no-win game.

INDEX FUNDS: RISKIER THAN YOU THINK!

William E. Donoghue refers to index funds as "the easy answer funds." They seem to offer a way around the hard work of picking securities, market sectors, and individual mutual funds. And they're coming to Canada in a big way. The big brokerage firms and banks are beginning to dish up many different indexes and funds to match. We have stock market indexes, indexed GICs, and dividend indexes or dividend reinvestment programs (DRIPs), the TSE 300 Index, Standard & Poor's 500 Index, Morgan Stanley World Index (you can really buy the world!), the Morgan Stanley European, Asian and Far East Index (EAFE), or the Wilshire 4500 Index, to name a few.

Index funds may appear to be the (easy) answer for the average investor. Note that I said *average*. An index fund simply replicates the performance of that particular market index. Average performers. Are you sure you want to achieve only average? More on this later.

Many academics and the financial media point out that 70% of all mutual funds fail to beat the market averages, so why not buy the index that ensures that you match the average? This may be all right if you don't want to absorb the careful portfolio construction outlined in this book and other excellent works on portfolio strategy. Except for a pesky detail or two. But 30% of all funds *do* beat the index. So if you've really done your homework, you have a 30% chance of surpassing the index's performance. And a few outstanding individual funds have a history of beating their respective indexes by a big margin, consistently. In other words, it's not just a question of beating the index, but by how much?

Then there's that second pesky little detail of bear markets. A well-chosen fund or portfolio of funds should do better in bad markets, increasing their overall performance. And there are a number of Canadian funds that beat the index year after year, and with much less downside risk.

If you buy an index fund and then encounter a bad market, who will be around to advise you to switch to global content or to rebalance in order to stay on course?

Personally, I'll fly with a fund manager as pilot and an excellent financial advisor as co-pilot. Index funds fly without a pilot!

Another argument from the index fund proponents is that they're cheaper, with most having lower management fees. We have demonstrated how no-load (no-advice) funds could cost you more by default than the price of good advice. And management-expense ratios are trivial compared with *risk-adjusted* performance, which can only be achieved with careful selection and a competent advisor. And I'll choose a seasoned investment advisor over a scholarly academic any time when it's the real world we're talking about and not the theoretical world scholars love to inhabit. Especially when we're talking about *real* money—yours and mine.

Further, the index guys will tell you that index funds have Beta factors close to 1.00, so there's little extra risk if you buy, say, the TSE 300 Index. Answer: if risk means anything to you, you can select a number of mutual funds with Betas much lower than 1.00.

But there's more. *Forbes* magazine (April 7, 1997) headlined its cover story: "Index Funds — riskier than you think." Calling index investment proverbial eggs in one basket, author Gretchen Morgenson denied that the S&P 500 Index could outperform active money management. She also pointed out that of the $27 billion invested in mutual funds in the first three months of 1997, 27% went into index funds, compared with 3% in 1994.

Far too much indexing, said Morgenson.

An obvious myth, said Morgenson, was that buying the S & P was tantamount to buying the American economy. It's really a single asset class of 500 weighted large companies. "There's no space in it for the smaller companies that are the *real* engine of U.S. economic growth." Hence the reference to eggs and a single basket.

In fact, *before* management fees, the index beats the active large-cap managers less than half the time, and the small-cap managers only rarely. Canadian index investors are in for a surprise. The sudden trend for indexing creates a self-perpetuating trend. Are the major stocks overvalued? Are the small-caps undervalued? Tough luck, says Morgenson. If you're into "indexing" these days, you are becoming a momentum investor, like it or not. Locked into the large caps and locked out of the small-caps. So the huge weight of new mutual fund investment is increasingly funneled into already overbought big chips. The implications for a value investor are obvious.

Let me illustrate. An index investor in 1982 would automatically have been stashing money into oil stocks, just before their collapse. In 1986, IBM was the largest component of the S&P 500, just before it plunged from $162 to $93. Wal-Mart was the Wall Street darling in 1992, trading at 33 times earnings. Would Wal-Mart rule the world? Over the following four years it fell to 16th place in the index.

In indexes like the S&P, there are continually companies being dropped for "lack of representation," while the new stocks added may have higher price/earnings ratios. The net effect is that S&P investors are buying high and selling low — not what the textbooks recommend. So index investors are not "buying the market." And not the investor, nor the financial advisor nor the professional money manager, but the skewed market content within the index is deciding how much of each stock the investor is buying.

Forbes' Morgenson concludes: "In fact, we suspect index funds have become a *dangerous* placebo, giving many of us the illusion that the stock market is a much safer place than it really is."

A MATTER OF INTEREST

Everything is driven off of trying to find the highest yield and the highest quality.

— Susan Peabody, Senior Vice-President,
Alliance Capital Management

Fixed-income (bonds, mortgages) investors have taken advantage of the precipitous decline in interest rates since 1981, when the Bank of Canada rate peaked at more than 20%, declining to a 37-year low of 3.5% by the end of 1996. A decline in rates provided a once-in-a-lifetime opportunity for these investors to make capital gains profits as the price of fixed-income securities moved in the opposite direction to outstanding interest rates. By that most recent date, declining interest rates pushed up market values for most bonds, mortgage securities, and the mutual funds that held them.

A fixed-rate GIC investor locking in higher interest rates during this period might be tempted to gloat over the current fixed-income markets. He shouldn't. Their investments have *market* value — and will be worth less in purchasing power when they cash them in at future maturity dates. In other words, if you bought a car for $30,000 and agreed not to sell it for five years, you might delude yourself four years later that it was still worth $30,000 in today's dollars, but this is not so.

Similarly, bondholders need not worry about market losses on paper as a result of interest rate fluctuations, *if* they mean to hold these securities to their maturity, when they can recover their full face value.

Here are five distinct strategies for obtaining a regular income from fixed-income securities in a time of rising interest rates and market price declines.

Hedging Your Bets

1. Purchase fixed-income funds that specialize in buying securities at below par value and holding them to maturity, assuming that the bond's coupon meets the fund's requirements. Any fluctuation in the bond's prices as interest rates vary is irrelevant. By staggering the maturity dates of these securities, the manager will be able to reinvest in other securities to make up for interest rate variations.

2. Minimize your risk of capital loss by shortening the term-to-maturity. Investors in fixed-income mutual funds as well as those in GICs and individual bonds can follow this strategy. This tactic is especially helpful if you have a good mutual fund portfolio manager who structures and restructures the portfolio when and as you need it. Ask your financial advisor or institution how the fund's portfolio has been structured to *protect* against big losses.

3. Purchase funds holding convertible preferred shares or convertible debentures of good quality companies. This is one means of having your cake and eating it, too. Most often the

preferred "trades off" the common stock, its price influenced more by the level of the underlying common share than by prevailing interest rates. Meanwhile, you enhance your investment's security by holding the senior instrument. If projections of continued economic growth in Canada are correct, the near future will mean continuing strong stock markets, and therefore well-guarded capital gains for convertible securities.

4. Purchase funds that buy *retractable* preferred shares or debentures (unsecured bonds) as long as their market prices are below their retraction prices and the time to the dates of retraction is not too distant. The company can recall retractable securities, whereas the investor can "convert" convertibles at his option, into common shares, prior to the future retraction date. Several Canadian dividend and income mutual funds employ a retractable strategy extensively in the structuring of their portfolios.

5. You can build a very conservative fixed-income bias into your portfolio, designed so that you profit from bond market movements in *both* directions. Many other bond funds are suited primarily to an environment of falling rates. This type of fund routinely moves to lock in a current price by agreeing to sell bonds at a future delivery date. Later, before the bond delivery date, the manager may buy the bonds at what was anticipated to be lower prices to close out the settlement of the original sale. The investor profits on the *spread* between the original sale price and the lower price of the purchase. Such a fund can benefit from changing bond prices whether interest rates are rising or falling. This gives the fund greater ability to preserve and enhance the investor's principal. This type of fund also qualifies as an RRSP and RRIF investment, an added attraction.

Investing to profit from rising interest rates involves a similar type and amount of risk as buying bonds in the hopes of profiting from falling rates. Professional fund managers practice both. Any investor can use all five of these strategies to advantage.

DIVIDEND GROWTH — NO TRIVIAL PURSUIT

You've got to own the Wal-Marts of this world when they are bringing a good high rate of return and ploughing it back into growth.

— William Berger,
former chairman Berger Associates, Denver

One way to approach equity investment is to commit yourself to dividend-paying stocks. It's a matter of emphasis. Like other stocks, these often take advantage of rising markets. They also tend to protect your investment more on a market downside. In a way, they take *some* of the risk and anxiety out of stock investment — a great bonus.

An intelligent investor sees the dividend payout as the true value of a stock, rather than fluctuating earnings or the prospect for capital gain that may be linked to those fluctuations.

"All you own when you own a common stock," says William Berger, former chairman of Berger Associates of Denver, "is that stream of earnings — what they can earn on this year's retained earnings that they don't pay out to you."

In other words, the emphasis should be placed not on income or growth per se, but on the *growth of income*. No income stream grows as steadily or as substantially as dividends from blue-chip corporations in Canada and the U.S. Note that dividend income continues to outstrip inflation.

For the winner in the equity market, the rewards can be significant. Solid investment need not be exciting, but it can be. The thrill of the hunt, the joy of discovery, the lasting satisfaction of financial victory, all of these can surpass winning on the playing field, because this financial endeavor is *real*. And *tangible*.

We emphasize a value-based approach to equity investment, using a stock's dividend as a benchmark as the primary measure of its value. Market price in isolation means little to an investor, so we need a means of measuring whether the price of a given stock is high or low, or just about where it should be. Too often the dividend, the most tangible source of return, is underestimated even by those who put money into the market with the clear rate of return in mind. In simplest terms, a company's stock represents the value of that business.

With the dividend-yield approach, the price of a stock is primarily driven by its yield. When a higher dividend yield is available, investors will buy it, eventually pushing the price up to a point that the dividend yield loses its attraction. So rather than looking at the price cycles of a stock, the company's products, market strategy or other factors, look *first* at its dividend-yield patterns. You can learn to buy and sell on the basis of these yields, as they move within parameters that you or your money manager have determined. The dividend yield sends very clear signals that a share's price is too high relative to its yield, too low or on the move. There are exceptions to this rule — the huge 1995–97 bull market the Dow Jones Index has achieved, for one.

A dividend is a distribution of the net earnings of a company to its shareholders and its owners, after all operating expenses, funds retained for various purposes, and taxes are deducted. There may be various classes of preferred stock, which most often receive a fixed dividend, in percentage terms. Common stock holders receive dividends that may vary from time to time, according to decisions made by the board of directors. Dividends are most often paid in cash, but can also be paid in the form of additional shares of stock.

Appreciation in the value price of a stock in the open market may be spectacular, if inconsistent, subject to the whims of the market, and anything but certain. Dividends are real and tangible.

There are three basic measures of share value: dividend yield, price/earnings ratio, and price/book value ratio. The dividend yield reveals most about a *company's* health, in addition to producing regular, reliable income. Price/earnings and price/book value ratios reveal more of conditions of the *market* than that of the company itself. (Revisit Figure 8.4: A Canadian Comparison.)

A consistently rising dividend dramatically reveals a company's profitable progress as well as any available indicator and reliably predicts its future growth.

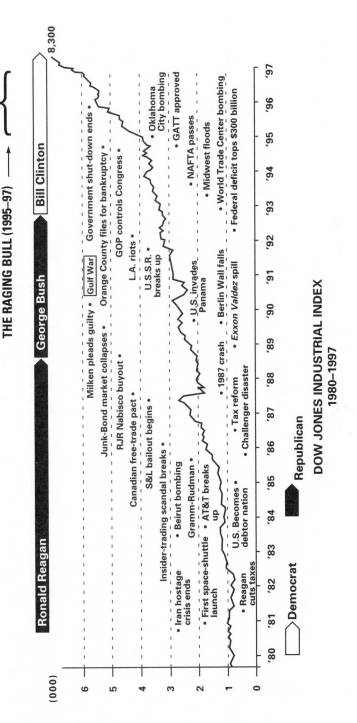

FIGURE 11.2: THE RAGING BULL.

THE RAGING BULL (1995–97)

Ronald Reagan | George Bush | Bill Clinton

- Iran hostage crisis ends
- First space-shuttle launch
- Reagan cuts taxes
- U.S. Becomes debtor nation
- Beirut bombing
- Gramm-Rudman
- AT&T breaks up
- Insider-trading scandal breaks
- S&L bailout breaks begins
- Canadian free-trade pact
- RJR Nabisco buyout
- Junk-Bond market collapses
- Milken pleads guilty
- Challenger disaster
- Tax reform
- 1987 crash
- Exxon Valdez spill
- Berlin Wall falls
- U.S. invades Panama
- U.S.S.R. breaks up
- L.A. riots
- GOP controls Congress
- Orange County files for bankruptcy
- Government shut-down ends
- World Trade Center bombing
- Midwest floods
- NAFTA passes
- GATT approved
- Oklahoma City bombing
- Federal deficit tops $300 billion

Gulf War

Republican
Democrat

DOW JONES INDUSTRIAL INDEX
1980–1997

(000)
6
5
4
3
2
1
0

'80 '81 '82 '83 '84 '85 '86 '87 '88 '89 '90 '91 '92 '93 '94 '95 '96 '97

8,300

Source: The Wall Street Journal

> **Stenner's Law #6**: Dividends, like your blood pressure reading, usually tell the truth.

Taxable income in your hands is often a mixed blessing because of the long arm of Revenue Canada. That tax reality is unavoidable in the case of interest income, but dividend income, although not primarily tax exempt or deferred, is *tax-preferred*. Unlike the income you receive from any interest-bearing instrument, such as bonds, insurance annuities, GICs, or T-Bills, dividend income from Canadian corporations receives a gentler tax treatment, through a federal tax credit on such dividends. Gentler by a significant *30% to 34% tax-free credit*, depending on which province you live in and your own top marginal tax bracket.

This incentive encourages Canadians to invest in common and preferred shares of Canadian companies, such as banks, utilities and industrial companies. It is the after-tax return on their investments that determines their ultimate performance, and therefore the real measuring stick for an investor. A Canadian taxpayer can retain between 27% and 37% more from dividend income than from interest income. That adds up over 10 to 20 years!

(See Table 11.1: The Dividend Tax Credit in Action and Table 11.2: Dedicated 1995 After-Tax Returns.)

TABLE 11.1: THE DIVIDEND TAX CREDIT IN ACTION

	DIVIDEND INCOME	vs.	INTEREST INCOME
Cash Dividend	$1,000		$1,000
Gross-up	$ 250		-----
	$1,250		$1,000
Federal tax @ 29%	$ 363		$ 290
Dividend tax credit	$(167)		-----
Basic federal tax	$ 196		$ 290
Federal surtax @ 8%	$ 16		$ 23
B.C. provincial tax @ 52%	$ 102		$ 151
B.C. provincial surtax @ 30%*	$ 30		$ 45
TOTAL TAX	**$ 344**		**$ 509**
AMOUNT RETAINED AFTER TAX	**$ 656**		**$ 491**

* Over $5,300 B.C. tax

TABLE 11.2: DEDICATED 1995 AFTER-TAX RETURNS ON $1,000 OF CANADIAN INVESTMENT INCOME*

PROVINCE	CAPITAL GAINS	DIVIDENDS	INTEREST	INT./DIV. FACTOR**
Alberta	$654.50	$686.00	$539.30	1.272
British Columbia	$593.80	$634.30	$458.40	1.384
Manitoba	$622.00	$636.70	$496.00	1.284
New Brunswick	$614.80	$653.10	$486.30	1.343
Newfoundland	$615.00	$653.40	$486.70	1.343
Nova Scotia	$622.75	$660.32	$497.00	1.329
Ontario	$601.10	$640.80	$468.10	1.369
P.E.I.	$622.70	$660.30	$497.00	1.329
Quebec	$603.00	$612.70	$470.70	1.302
Saskatchewan	$610.40	$634.90	$480.60	1.321
Average Canadian	$616.01	$647.25	$488.01	1.327

* For investors in the top tax bracket by province
** For equivalent after-tax yields

NET INCOME ON ONE DOLLAR†

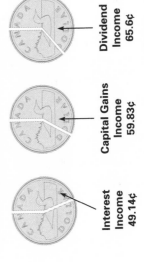

| Interest Income 49.14¢ | Capital Gains Income 59.83¢ | Dividend Income 65.6¢ |

† B.C. figures based on investors in top tax bracket for 1996 (52%)

Source: Midland Walwyn

You would need a 9.38% yield from an interest-bearing security to match a dividend yield of 7%. That's a saving of 34%!

THE IMPORTANCE OF TIMING

Another dimension to equity income, of course, is timing. Solid mutual fund investment can eliminate many of the problems and errors inherent in trying to guess the market.

During a 25-year period, if you had possessed infallible foresight, you could have played the following market highs: May 14, 1969; March 13, 1974; October 5, 1979; January 6, 1984; October 9, 1989; December 29, 1993 and December 1995. And no doubt you would have made a bundle.

The next best thing to being an infallible prophet would have been to buy a good growth fund and stick with it. The Templeton Growth Fund in the 25-year period 1971–95 produced an *annual* rate of return of 17.1% if you had picked *the worst* time of each of the 25 years to invest $5,000 per year on the exact day the stock market touched its *highest* point each year. Had you made that investment once a year in the same fund in each of the 25 years at *the lowest* point in the year, you would have achieved 17.8% annually. A difference of only 0.7% for all your trouble! (Revisit Table 6.3.)

The message seems to be that, without trying to play the market with infallible timing, you could achieve nearly as satisfactory a result simply by investing in a superior global equity growth fund and exercising patience.

PART III

PUTTING IT ALL TOGETHER

chapter **12** | # TAKING CONTROL OF YOUR FINANCIAL FUTURE

It's impossible to produce superior performance
unless you do something different from the majority.

—Sir John Templeton

THE MONEY GAME

At this stage you're a player sitting on the bench, waiting to go into the game. Before you run into the action, you have to develop a winning mentality; in our case, a winning *money mentality*, made up of equal parts of attitude, lack of a prejudicial point of view, effort and persistence. An indifferent attitude toward the mysteries of investment, taxation and financial planning can only handicap you from the beginning.

I've had prospective clients tell me, "I'm the original kiss of death. I'm like the character in the *L'il Abner* cartoon strip who goes around with a cloud over his head. As soon as I invest, the market will drop. I've never made a dime in the market. I guess I'm the sort of person that should keep my money in the bank and hope the bank doesn't burn down."

This is enough to render such a person totally incapable even of breaking even. So much of investing depends so much on your state of mind, on your judgment and ability to follow through with action.

For a start, say goodbye to "luck." Whatever its metaphysical or psychosomatic ingredients you can't *count on it. It will neither help you nor run against you.*

The business of learning and understanding specific investment products, portfolio composition, and tax strategy is difficult enough without surface impediments such as a bad attitude toward financial matters and any dependence on luck. You want to be receptive to any and all productive ideas and concepts, without imposing irrelevant thoughts or attitudes on the process.

Prejudice impedes success just as much as attitude. Occasionally, a prospective client has said, "Please don't confuse me with facts." This tells me their minds are already made up about how and where they want to invest their money.

Another response that I often face is "Better to be safe than sorry." This always baffles me. Proper investment posture involves neither extreme safety nor an apologetic attitude.

Those who cling to "safety" as an objective, embracing high taxation, inflation and "safe" guaranteed instruments, court the eventual disaster of running out of purchasing power in their retirement years, and eventually out of money. Understanding the truth of a balanced investment philosophy can set you free from this sort of financial bondage and dependence. Don't succumb to delusions of security.

Coming off the bench and moving into the money game with winning potential requires concentrated effort. Learn everything you can about the investment industry and its processes, pay close attention to details, especially as they affect you, and recognize the importance of timing, just as you do in other areas of life.

Time, training and *temperament*: If you lack *any* of these three "Ts", make sure you have an experienced professional advisor standing behind your bench to coach you. Lose the egotistical idea that nobody knows better than you do about your own money matters. It's a big world — we all need help.

> **Stenner's Law #7:** There is no such thing as free mutual fund advice.

THE COST OF "FREE"

In investment, the security you buy for "free" will almost always cost you money. You can lose income, capital gains and purchasing power. Recently, new clients of mine told me they had previously purchased "no-load" mutual funds through their bank. In one case in particular, this client had made about 9.5% over the previous 12 months. I showed him that the fund in the same peer group category I had recommended for most of my clients had earned 23.1% in the same period. He gulped, "So that 'no-advice fund' really cost me 13.6% in the past 12 months." I added, "My clients tend to stick with me over the years. So, with a mutual fund portfolio purchase which I design for long-term flexibility for them, my clients pay zero to invest their money (no front-end charge typically), they can withdraw up to 10% free each year, and typically after six or seven years there is no early redemption fee. Further, they never pay a commission transfer within any of these mutual fund family groups."

The no-load mentality has become a syndrome. A preponderance of mutual fund media advertising in both Canada and the United States preaches no-load as an article of faith. Rather, I view this subculture as an appeal to base motives—the abdication of common sense. *As America (and Canada) slept, you might say, somebody has changed the price tags.* And there is that element in many of us (perhaps all of us) that seeks a *deal* at whatever cost in quality. If you like to buy flawed or inferior merchandise at flea markets because they are to be had at drop-dead prices, go ahead. But don't delude yourself that in the same way you can really save money with no-load mutual funds. Because you will be sacrificing true value in advice, or selection. To the often heard, "a deal is a deal," one might counter, "When is a deal not a deal?" The answer we think is, "When the deal is a no-advice deal."

FIGURE 12.1: WHO HAD THE BETTER ADVICE?

AVERAGE HOLDING PERIOD
FOR EQUITY FUNDS

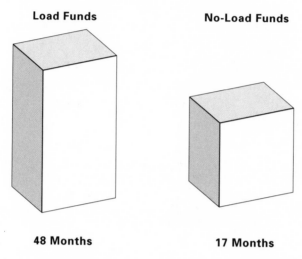

Load Funds	No-Load Funds
48 Months	17 Months

Source: Dalbar Surveys

NOTE: In a Dalbar survey, conducted from January 1984 to September 1993, the average holding period for all "load" funds was 48 months; the average holding period for "no-load" funds was only 17 months. Conclusion: the most recent measurement between "load" and "no-load" has been during the longest run-up in the Dow in history, so we haven't had an opportunity to see how many no-loaders will jump ship at the first sight of a significant bear market.

I have also known non-investors who have left their funds in a savings account, simply because they didn't want to pay the reasonable commission necessary to invest properly. This inverted thinking will cost them much more in many lost opportunities.

Enthusiasm is the important ingredient in any investor's makeup. The flip side is that you must avoid *other people's* enthusiasm! Heeding it could lead you to financial ruin. Sincerity and honesty are not at issue here. Guard against the *unsupported* opinion of other people. Remember the old Wall Street truism: "Those who know don't talk; those who talk don't know."

As important as enthusiasm is *persistence*. That means continuing toward your investment objectives even if you have not reached any of your goals. You must be able to ride out all the phases of a market. Learn to rejoice on upswings, catch your breath on level ground, and accept downdrafts for what they are — times for readjustment and base-building for the next advance. Accept that market corrections are as common as snow in January. (See Table 12.1: A History Lesson.)

TABLE 12.1: A HISTORY LESSON — SHARP CORRECTIONS ARE NORMAL!

	Routine Decline (5% or more)	Moderate Correction (10% or more)	Severe Correction (15% or more)	Bear Market (20% or more)
Number of times since 1900	318	106	50	29
How often to expect this	About three times a year	About once a year	About once every two years	About every three years
Last time it happened	March 1997	July 1996	March 1994	October 1990
Average loss before decline ends	11%	19%	27%	35%
Average length	40 days	109 days	217 days	364 days
Chance of decline turning into a bear market	9%	27%	58%	100%

Source: The Wall Street Journal

You'll also need the quality of *decisiveness*. Consider making a decision a privilege. Procrastination and indecisiveness go hand in hand — not wanting to decide, you put off making the decision, be it large or small. Yesterday is history, tomorrow is a promise. Only today is legal tender.

Consistent indecision amounts to deciding *not* to act, which usually hurts you. Many people exhibit little or no caution in investing. *Overcaution*, the opposite condition, is just as bad and often worse.

Good judgment comes from experience, and experience . . .
[well] that comes from poor judgment.

— Simon Bolivar Buckner

CONTROLLING YOUR (IN)SECURITY

Long before retirement is even within reach, complex questions confront you. How much money will you need to get by, especially if you live much longer than you expect? Will your RRSPs, pensions, investments and savings sustain you? How much *is* enough?

You need to reduce these questions to their essence and establish realistic goals. Next, you need to determine the two necessary ingredients required to go on — working out a time frame in which to operate and a total cost figure representing what you'll need getting to and throughout your retirement.

Between figuring out the time period and identifying how much money you'll need, calculating the cost is the more difficult. A competent financial planner can set up a sophisticated computer program to take your best estimates and work out what your retirement needs will be and how much you'll have to save by the time you retire to be financially secure.

TABLE 12.2: REQUIRED RETURN TO MEET CERTAIN OBJECTIVES AFTER MARGINAL TAX RATES AND INFLATION

Nominal Return* Required to Meet Investment Objectives at Varying Rates of Taxation and Inflation

MARGINAL TAX RATES

Investment Objective	26% Inflation		40% Inflation		50% Inflation	
	3%	5%	3%	5%	3%	5%
Maintain Purchasing Power	4.054%	6.757%	5.000%	8.333%	6.000%	10.000%
Double Real Value in 30 Years	7.213%	9.915%	8.896%	12.229%	10.675%	14.675%
Double Real Value in 20 Years	8.820%	11.287%	10.878%	13.921%	12.705%	16.705%
Double Real Value in 10 Years	13.753%	16.456%	16.962%	20.296%	20.355%	24.355%

*Nominal rate of return *before* taxation and inflation.
** Real value means net return *after* inflation

Source: Dunwoody

NOTE: Marginal tax rates have assumed a B.C. taxpayer at 3 various income levels.

FROM:	RATE	USED
** $0 – $29,950	26.35%	26%
** 29,950 – 53,665	40.30%	40%
53,665 – 59,180	44.36%	
** 59,180 – 62,193	49.47%	50%
62,193 – 73,208	50.92%	
78,208 and over	54.17%	

Marginal tax rates vary slightly between provinces due to differing provincial tax rates and high income surtaxes.

Be aware that electronic fortune-telling is an imprecise science, depending as it does on estimates and projections of many variables and unknowns. If you're looking ahead 10 years, think back over how much your personal financial conditions have changed over the *past* decade. It's amazing how far off estimates for the future can be from reality. Accept that you have to begin with some sort of estimate as a starting point. You might build in a comfortable margin, such as investment setbacks in a given year or two, and bulk up your cost-of-living projections to offset this inaccuracy.

Deciding the big question of how much annual income you will need to live in your retirement years may be a relatively simple projection. Distorting this picture will be externals, such as the imponderable factor of inflation, both before and after retirement.

The number of years you (and your partner) will live is guesswork at the best of times. (See Table 12.2: Required Return to Meet Certain Objectives.) You're looking for some solid means of perpetuating the income you'll need.

Bottom line on the income side is: How much will your government and employee pension, RRSPs and other income-producing investments pay you after taxes and after inflation? The one thing we all know is that governments are quickly shifting the heavy burden of your retirement onto *your* shoulders.

This process will reveal the wonderful compounding effect of interest, dividends, and capital gains, and how choosing correctly among investments can make the difference between life and death in your own comprehensive retirement plan.

In brief, you might go at it as follows:

1. Forecast as well as you can your spending requirements in the first year of your retirement.
2. Forecast your *after-tax* income from all sources.
3. Deduct your projected expenses from your retirement income and determine the surplus or shortfall, if any, that you'll have to make up with income from your non-RRSP and non-pension investments.
4. Finally, calculate the amount of investment capital you'll have to accumulate by your target retirement date to produce this income, to make up the difference between that after-tax income and those expenses.

From this total, determine how much you have to invest each year to meet or exceed that target. This is where your financial advisor comes in, to apply a *present-value* approach.

You may find that retiring early may enable you to save less than the amount you'd need if you retired later. Allow that, in the latter case, you would live as a retiree longer and, at first glance, you might seem to require a larger retirement pot. Factor in the latest clawback-adjusted income tax benchmarks, too; together these can wipe out your government pension plan income.

The opposite can also be true. The income you'll need in your early years of retirement may be exceeded by your investment income. This you can reinvest, adding it to your retirement fund before you reach 60 or 65, continuing to allow it to grow.

You may even be able to do both — withdraw income and still accumulate capital. Look at Figure 12.2: A Systematic Withdrawal Plan, devised by Templeton Growth Fund Ltd. Note that from $100,000 invested over 25 years, despite withdrawals totalling $364,000, more than $650,000 remains! Or what's so bad about a $100,000 investment in late 1981 into Trimark Fund, having monthly income withdrawals of $825 over the past 16.7 years ($155,925), with a June 30, 1997 account value of $682,825 left over? That's performance! See Table 12.3: Trimark Fund — Systematic Withdrawal Plan.

FIGURE 12.2: A SYSTEMATIC WITHDRAWAL PLAN*

This is an example of an assumed net investment of $100,000 made in Templeton Growth Fund Ltd., on January 1, 1977. $750 cash withdrawn monthly, indexed to inflation. At December 31, 1996 this monthly amount equalled $2,050. Income dividends of $52,065 and capital gain dividends of $215,270 have been reinvested.

STANDARD PERFORMANCE DATA

Average annual compounded rates of return for Templeton Growth Fund Ltd. for the period ended December 31, 1996:

1 Year	3 Years	5 Years	10 Years	15 Years	20 Years	Since Inception
18.4%	12.0%	17.1%	12.4%	15.5%	17.1%	15.4%

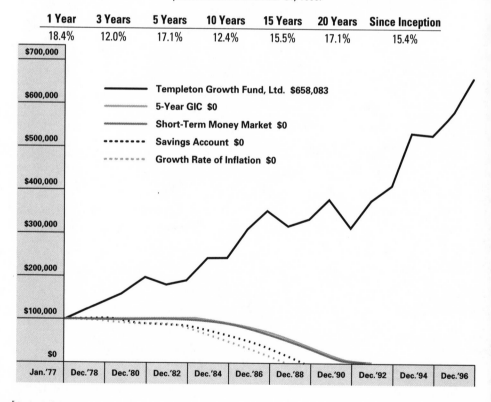

Indexed

Source: Templeton

FIGURE 12.2: A SYSTEMATIC WITHDRAWAL PLAN (cont'd.)

Date	Cumulative Indexed Withdrawals	Dividends Reinvested Each Year	Total Shares Remaining	Net Asset Value Per Share	Remaining Market Value	5-Year GIC	Short-Term Money Market	Savings Account	Growth at Rate of Inflation
01-Jan-77	$–	$–	8,237.232	$ 12.14	100,000	100,000	100,000	100,000	100,000
31-Dec-77	9,397	7,191	8,117.973	14.73	119,578	99,582	98,179	96,677	98,778
31-Dec-78	19,621	1,685	7,827.946	18.81	143,482	98,950	95,794	93,400	96,364
31-Dec-79	30,771	4,320	21,681.508	7.59	164,563	98,393	97,842	91,925	94,124
31-Dec-80	43,047	12,187	21,844.335	9.06	197,910	98,728	98,722	90,285	91,663
31-Dec-81	56,836	3,835	20,729.429	8.81	182,626	101,130	104,355	91,320	88,189
31-Dec-82	72,098	13,675	20,673.480	9.28	191,850	101,177	104,580	87,039	80,535
31-Dec-83	88,241	4,438	19,627.614	12.24	240,242	96,349	97,995	76,489	67,699
31-Dec-84	105,081	11,844	19,285.973	12.80	243,003	90,412	91,484	64,817	53,150
31-Dec-85	122,583	18,567	19,418.165	15.88	308,360	81,882	81,971	50,514	37,629
31-Dec-86	140,812	23,159	19,696.162	17.77	350,001	70,769	70,474	34,585	20,627
31-Dec-87	158,833	9,582	19,187.736	16.44	345,446	57,814	56,474	16,498	2,148
31-Dec-88	179,619	10,103	18,654.199	17.89	333,724	42,539	41,015	0	0
31-Dec-89	200,383	7,832	72,082.434	5.30	382,037	25,125	28,087	0	0
31-Dec-90	222,129	9,847	69,474.887	4.46	309,858	4,889	4,050	0	0
31-Dec-91	245,082	14,193	67,798.541	5.58	378,316	0	0	0	0
31-Dec-92	268,374	28,111	68,769.145	5.98	411,239	0	0	0	0
31-Dec-93	292,066	18,818	68,188.538	7.81	532,552	0	0	0	0
31-Dec-94	315,847	18,081	67,497.512	7.84	529,180	0	0	0	0
31-Dec-95	339,940	21,860	67,263.629	8.60	578,487	0	0	0	0
31-Dec-96	364,283	27,027	67,634.453	9.73	858,083	0	0	0	0
TOTALS	$364,283	$267,335	$67,634.453	$9.73	$658,083	$0	$0	$0	$0
GAINS IN 20 YEARS					$922,366	$195,155	$194,612	$157,312	$162,529

It's tougher to retire at 55. You have fewer productive years left in which to build up a pool of funds you would otherwise accumulate through a pension and increased salary from ages 55 to 65, usually the financial peak of your working years.

You can break down the difference between retiring at 55 and at 65. Assume that you received increases of about 5% a year between 55 and 65. At age 65 your income would therefore be about 60% higher than it was a decade earlier.

By the time you leave the work force, you would accordingly have had 10 more years of service, say 35 years instead of 25, which comes to 40% more. Your pension would have grown through two factors: your income would be 60% higher, and you'd have 40% more in years of service.

This double-barreled effect on the pension base in later working years drastically affects your retirement fund. By retiring at age 65, you'd have 2.25 times as much pension as you would have received at age 55, simply because you worked 10 more years. As opposed to the, say, $40,000 a year you would have received at age 55, you might find that working those extra 10 years could boost your pension to $90,000 a year!

Retirement planning is hard, tedious work. And you have to do it, especially if you want to avoid poverty in your retirement, or a severely restricted way of life. There's no escape — the ultimate responsibility for developing your investment income is *yours.* Some thoughtful person in mid-life crisis expressed it this way: "When the baby boomers start to retire in the next decade, and with fewer younger workers available to pay for our government pensions, guess who will support us? Us."

To complicate retirement and pension planning even more is the unprecedented smorgasbord of investment options available: employer-defined benefit or money purchase pensions, severance packages, Canada Pension Plan, Old Age Security, RRSPs, RRIFs, LIFs, LIRAs, stock option plans, deferred profit sharing, 1,500 separate mutual funds, GICs, stocks, bonds and other investment securities, real estate proceeds, business ownership, and so on.

TABLE 12.3: TRIMARK FUND — SYSTEMATIC WITHDRAWAL PLAN

This is an example of a *Trimark Systematic Withdrawal Plan*. The purchaser of the plan invested $100,000 at the inception of *Trimark Fund* on September 1, 1981, and withdrew $825 each month, beginning on October 1, 1981.

Date	Total Annual Withdrawal	=	Return of Capital	+	Capital Gain (Loss)	Cummulative Total Withdrawals	Distributions Reinvested Each Year	Annual Tax Liability at 40%	Trimark Fund Account Value	Comparative Plan Value at 10% Return	Annual Tax Liability at 40%
01-Sep-81	$ 0		$ 0		$ 0	$ 0	$ —	$ —	$ 96,000	100,000	$ —
31-Dec-81	2,475		2,534		(59)	2,475	0	0	98,620	100,817	1,317
31-Dec-82	9,900		9,471		429	12,375	1,352	464	122,827	100,463	3,818
31-Dec-83	9,900		5,993		3,907	22,275	15,778	4,056	155,387	100,073	3,804
31-Dec-84	9,900		6,580		3,320	32,175	5,962	1,983	146,894	99,644	3,788
31-Dec-85	9,900		5,785		4,115	42,075	1,381	403	189,855	99,172	3,771
31-Dec-86	9,900		4,516		5,384	51,975	19,477	744	199,443	98,653	3,752
31-Dec-87	9,900		4,848		5,052	61,875	32,011	801	186,289	98,082	3,731
31-Dec-88	9,900		6,310		3,590	71,775	23,657	1,242	218,228	97,454	3,709
31-Dec-89	9,900		6,159		3,741	81,675	18,412	1,853	242,821	96,763	3,683
31-Dec-90	9,900		7,129		2,771	91,575	25,082	8,395	209,377	96,003	3,656
31-Dec-91	9,900		7,432		2,468	101,475	3,649	1,829	257,673	95,167	3,626
31-Dec-92	9,900		6,151		3,749	111,375	6,629	3,113	321,107	94,247	3,592
31-Dec-93	9,900		5,003		4,897	121,275	26,998	9,569	410,854	93,235	3,555
31-Dec-94	9,900		4,551		5,349	131,175	13,914	5,779	461,593	92,123	3,515
31-Dec-95	9,900		4,266		5,634	141,075	29,985	10,686	527,630	90,899	3,470
31-Dec-96	9,900		4,200		5,700	150,975	7,015	3,815	594,553	89,552	3,421
30-Jun-97	$4,950		$1,943		$3,007	$155,925	$ —	$ —	$682,825	$ 88,936	$ —

Source: Trimark Mutual Funds

Leave no stone unturned in your own financial planning. Examine all the specific financial media. Study the particular risk attached to each investment: inflation, interest rates, reinvestment, liquidity, market, credit, economic, political, and currency exchange. And in creating your strategy, make sure you understand the *combined income* and *threshold clawback* rules so there are no more nasty surprises, courtesy of Revenue Canada.

> **Stenner's Law #8**: Without measured risk, there can be no reward, because one is a function of the other.

For a practical example of how this works, consider the fact that an ultra-conservative investor can obtain a very secure, virtually pure stream of reliable monthly dividend income from a preferred dividend mutual fund. And thanks to the federal dividend tax credit, an 8% distribution of this type translates into approximately a 10.2% after-tax yield (34% better). And that's not locked in!

As for the reinvestment of the proceeds from an RRSP, rolling them into a Registered Retirement Income Fund (RRIF) is usually far superior to an annuity. A RRIF keeps the control of your money and the rate of return with you, and gives you far greater flexibility and investment choice. The income derived from a RRIF compared to an annuity can amount to thousands of dollars more, depending on the size and time period involved. Even in planning this specific area of your life, the greatest thing about measured risk is superior reward!

THE GREAT FINANCIAL PLANNING FLAW

The traditional calculation of required retirement income is inadequate, according to Professor Moshe Milevsky of the Schulich School of Business at York University in Toronto. To rely on a fixed rate of return, says Milevsky, ignores the random nature of returns and places retirees at risk.

"That is not a prudent way to plan for retirement," says Milevsky, "because investors can never earn a constant rate of return."

In addition, it gives investors a false sense of security, believing that fixed-income investments alone can provide an adequate nest egg. Instead, Milevsky and colleagues Kwok Ho and Chris Robinson have developed what they term "probabilistic financial planning."

Conventional financial planning includes four major considerations: (1) how much money will be needed at retirement, less that which will be provided by Canada Pension Plan and Old Age Security; (2) the amount the retiree expects to save and invest annually prior to retirement; (3) the number of years to retirement; and (4) the anticipated rate of return during that period.

The flaw, according to Milevsky, lies in the assumption of a constancy in (4), or a fixed rate of return. Such an assumption, say 10%, can be subject to a standard deviation of more than 18%, theoretically capable of producing an annual rate of return anywhere between 40% and -20%. Milevsky aims with the "probabilistic financial planning" system to minimize shortfall risk and maximize the probability of reaching retirement goals.

The solution, says Milevsky, is in choosing random returns rather than fixed rates of return, in addition to changing investment strategy from time to time — deciding to retire later, adjusting to a lower standard of living in retirement, increasing savings and investment, or taking on more risk. The last strategy brings the argument to the equity markets in general and mutual funds in particular. Over a time horizon of 30 or 40 years, Milevsky points out, the risk of equity market loss reduces literally to zero, while the risk of fixed-income investment providing sufficient value increases over time, as I have consistently pointed out because of the "guaranteed loss" due to static principal, inflation and taxes.

A "buy and hold" philosophy, according to Professor Milevsky, constantly outperforms all other strategy, so why should investors with a 30- or 40-year time horizon act as if they have a 30-day horizon? Or, over 20 years, the major stock markets have shown that virtually all market *risk* to one's capital has been wrung out to *zero*.

Planners or individuals should examine the long-term track records of mutual funds, concentrating on average year-over-year returns for the last 15 years. Look at the standard deviation for the fund during that period. It will determine the pattern of historical returns for that fund, and provide a better picture of what an investor can realistically expect over the long term, rather than relying on a fixed rate of return.

I heartily concur, of course.

THE VALUE OF MUTUAL FUNDS IN ESTATE PLANNING

Mutual funds offer a little known but extremely valuable benefit not available with individual stocks, bonds, real estate, mortgages and other investment categories. I refer to the ease of estate-planning settlement.

Upon your death, investment securities such as interest-sensitive strip bonds, other fixed-income vehicles, market-sensitive convertible bonds, and convertible preferred stocks will be frozen in the estate probate period and can only be changed with the permission of the courts. This could be a time-consuming process with added legal expense, and in the meantime there may be good market reasons for altering such holdings because of changing conditions.

When you buy a mutual fund, on the other hand, you don't merely purchase a bundle of individual securities — you are purchasing shares in the fund that owns individual securities on behalf of all the shareholders. In the event of the death of a fund shareholder, mutual fund shares are frozen within the estate, but *not* the securities that are in the fund's portfolio. Portfolio managers are free to buy and sell as market conditions dictate. So while the fund in the hands of an individual deceased shareholder are frozen, the specific securities in the portfolio are not. A mutual fund manager, in other words, provides professional management of the assets during the settlement of the estate, which often takes several years.

A second major estate advantage offered by a mutual fund—as opposed to individual securities — is the ease with which an estate can be divided with no disruption of the portfolio balance or its diversification. Assume that you have four heirs, whom you wish to share equally as beneficiaries, and that the securities in the estate consist of 10,000 shares of, say, Fidelity Canadian Growth Company Fund. Each heir would receive 2,500 shares and there would be no disruption in the diversification within each of the four inherited portfolios.

Each beneficiary would still own an exact proportionate share of 100 to 150 stocks, professionally selected and managed as if they still belonged to one person. (Had the deceased held the portfolio in the form of individual securities, it would require liquidation in order to divide the portfolio equally.)

Another significant advantage of a mutual fund with respect to estate planning is that it allows you to choose professional managers, some of the best anywhere in the world, for those who are dependent on you.

chapter **13** | # THE RRSP: THE GREAT CANADIAN TRADITION

Tax-sheltered funds, bonds, and stocks will explode in value. Mortgage or RRSP? There is no contest.

— The Honourable Garth Turner,
Former Minister of National Revenue

Our history is strewn with major government initiatives — of Ottawa getting it wrong. So it's refreshing to talk about the Registered Retirement Savings Plan as a conspicuous exception. The RRSP is as singularly Canadian as the *Bluenose*, maple syrup, William Kurelek's paintings or the CanadArm.

Canadians can invest in RRSPs over the years leading up to their retirements. The tax on the amounts deposited over those years is compounded along with the principal and interest, and is tax deferred. In other words, the money in an RRSP — the principal plus contributions plus interest — compounds tax free. And an RRSP can grow very quickly, as many Canadians have discovered. See Table 13.1: The Increasing Advantage of Tax Deferral Over Time.

TABLE 13.1: THE INCREASING ADVANTAGE OF TAX DEFERRAL OVER TIME

Investment of $500 per quarter at 10% annual return compounded quarterly with a 30% tax rate after-tax value at the end of the period

Duration of Investment	Regular Taxable Account	Tax Deferred Account	Advantage of Tax Deferral
10 Years	$28,617	$ 29,591	3.4%
20 Years	$ 85,897	$ 98,934	15.2%
30 Years	$200,548	$275,014	37.1%

THE NEW REALITY

Canadians have always been diligent savers (if not investors!), squirreling away almost double the per capita level of their American neighbors. As the highest taxes in North America and employment insecurity have laid siege to Canadians' disposable income and declining interest rates have tarnished most of our "guaranteed" savings, this rate has slipped over the past decade.

A new class of reluctant investors has emerged — "GIC refugees" — who have backed, often willingly, into the brawny arms of market-oriented investments, particularly mutual funds.

To remind you of a few facts we all face today:

Canadians are living longer. In the late 1890s, the average lifespan was 48 years. Today, men live an average of 80 years, and women an average of 83 years. In the past, for those few who could ever afford to retire, their retirement might have been just a few years. Today, many retiring seniors anticipate 20 to 30 years, sometimes longer. This retirement period may even approach the length of time we spend in the labor force.

Employment. Since the early 1970s, North America has endured a series of recessions. These have pummeled the employment prospects of many older men and women. Technology in the automation age continues to advance and more traditional industrial production to recede. This one-two punch in the workplace has meant mixed blessings for workers in the 45-to-55 age group. They head the vanguard accepting early retirement, often to make way for younger employees at lower pay scales. They also must scramble to organize their finances to support themselves, willingly or otherwise, much sooner than they had planned.

Interest rates. In 1996, interest rates declined to their lowest level in 36 years. Many observers believe North America may have entered a 50-year cycle of lower interest rates. Even the high point of the current cycle will fall substantially short of the 20% level we saw in 1981. In financial terms, investors who have depended up to now on interest-based investments may have to accept relatively low returns for some years to come.

Real estate is another key factor in the new RRSP reality. Canadians who once depended on the equity they had accumulated in their homes to finance their retirements have been rudely awakened. The boom in British Columbia real estate, for example, came to a halt in 1993-94.

Inflation. Many Canadians nearing retirement grew up in a climate of continuing inflation (about 5% per annum over the past 40 years) and know they must factor it into every transaction. The remarkably low level of inflation since 1991 should not lull you into believing inflation has been permanently weakened and that your savings will be adequate in the future. Even a low level of inflation, say 2%, can erode savings over time, converting a 5% yield into 3% without a trace. This "invisible tax" hits everyone.

Serious political, financial and demographic developments at work today could also seriously interfere with your retirement income strategy. For example, current and future federal governments will continue their big squeeze on hard-working Canadians with bullet-biting measures — hiking taxes, raising the official retirement age from 65 to 70 years, cutting Canada Pension Plan payments, reducing contributions to RRSPs or taxing the earned profits on these plans. Changes would blast the efforts of anyone planning for retirement. These people will have to purchase investments promising to offset these developments with higher income and capital appreciation performance.

Finally, *the baby boomers* will upset the entire economic world as we know it when they shift en masse from the work force to retirement, from production to consumption at an earlier age than any generation before them. No one can accurately predict the final effect on the North American economy. Economists point to the mushrooming effect of senior boomers traveling, buying vacation properties, and happily spending their money rather than bequeathing it to their children. They predict this will be an immense stimulus to the service sector, retailing, and the hospitality industries. Gloomier observers forecast inflationary pressures that will seriously erode the value of our savings.

CRUNCHING THE RETIREMENT NUMBERS

How much will your own retirement cost? At an annual inflation rate of just 3%, if you're earning $30,000 now, you'll need $40,317 to enable you to retire with equivalent purchasing power in 10 years, or $54,183 in 20 years. If you're earning $60,000 now, figure on $80,635 in 10 years and $108,367 in 20, just to keep pace with today's dollar value.

The best recommendation is to minimize risk and maximize reward with securities held around the world in professionally managed mutual funds and tucked into your retirement assets.

But, the question naturally arises: If foreign investments are by definition prone to greater risks than domestic ones, why should you concern yourself with maximizing foreign content within an RRSP, RRIF or other non-registered investments?

Two reasons. Historically, foreign components in an RRSP increase your overall return. Second, investing globally allows you to spread, therefore reduce, the volatility of your overall portfolio and the risk.

Almost 98% of the world's bond and equity markets exist outside Canada. (See Figure 13.1: World Market Trading.) Over the past decade, the investment securities of foreign countries have earned substantially higher returns with less risk.

FIGURE 13.1: WORLD MARKET TRADING

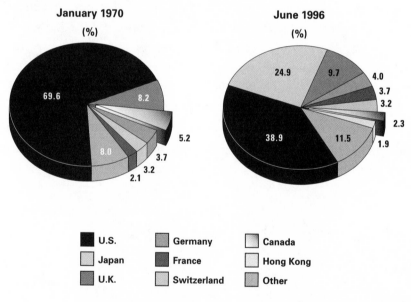

Source: *Morgan Stanley*

Morgan Stanley, the Wall Street financial house, compiles a World Index of equities. Over the past 10 years, that index has shown a return of more than 17% annually. If you had committed your entire RRSP investments to Canadian stocks on the Toronto Stock Exchange 300 Index, your annual return for the same 10 years would have averaged 10.1%, and with higher standard deviation (i.e., more risk).

Now that so many foreign countries have active securities markets, and with it different degrees of volatility from one country to the next, you can take advantage of the Canadian Property Rule. You can weight investment holdings in rising economies and avoid those in declining ones.

The federal government's Canadian Property Rule limits foreign content in RRSP investments to 20% of your ACB (Adjusted Cost Base) or *net* cost. However, indirectly, through certain Canadian funds, you can obtain as much as 100% effective exposure to foreign markets in the United States, Europe, Asia or Latin America by the use of financial instruments known as *derivatives.* These instruments include foreign currency-denominated bonds of Canadian government issuers, covered call options, and futures contracts. Several Canadian registered foreign mutual funds can give you instant global diversification, including foreign-currency management protection for or against the Canadian dollar within your RRSP. (See the discussion on derivatives in Chapter 10.)

So why is foreign content invaluable in your RRSP? According to the above indexes, it has produced more than 50% higher profits over a recent 10-year period than purely domestic investments have, and it offers you greater safety through broader diversification.

MAKING ANNUAL CONTRIBUTIONS

I'm often asked about the importance of making an annual RRSP contribution. I always respond with this question: "If you're in a top provincial and federal marginal tax bracket, where else can you achieve as much as 54.16% (B.C.) in a guaranteed "rate of return" on your money as soon as you deposit it? If you make a $10,000 RRSP contribution at a top marginal tax bracket of, say, 54.16%, you gain an income tax cash rebate of $5,416! And, you get to take your 54% tax rebate and invest that back into your RRSP.

TABLE 13.2: RRSP QUICK REFERENCE SUMMARY
(After the 1996 Budget)

MAXIMUM RRSP CONTRIBUTION LIMIT

1996-2003	–18% previous year's Earned Income up to $13,500 less PA
2004	–18% previous year's Earned Income up to $14,500 less PA
2005	–18% previous year's Earned Income up to $15,500 less PA

EXAMPLES OF EARNED INCOME

Employment income
Net income from self-employment
Net rental income
Alimony/maintenance received
(under certain circumstances)
CPP/QPP disability benefit
(not regular CPP/QPP)

DOES NOT QUALIFY AS EARNED INCOME

Investment income
Taxable capital gain
Ltd. partnership income
Death Benefit
Retiring Allowance
Pension or DPSP income
RRSP/RRIF/OAS/CPP/QPP

FOREIGN CONTENT LIMIT

Foreign investments in each RRSP cannot exceed 20% of plan book value *(each plan, not total of all plans)*

SPOUSAL RRSPS

- ***Since 1993 common-law spouse is a spouse for all tax purposes***
- Direct your contribution to spousal plan; you claim deduction
- May contribute to spousal plan until spouse's 69th birthday *(providing you have contribution room)*
- Plan and plan assets are owned and controlled by spouse

WHERE TO GET PERSONAL CONTRIBUTION INFORMATION

- "Notice of Assessment" which follows tax return *(shows RRSP limit + unused deduction room since 1991)*
- Revenue Canada General Enquiry # and TIPS line also provide annual limit *(Government blue pages of phone book under Revenue Canada)*
- Employers report PA *(Box 52 of T4; Box 34 of T4A)*

REFUNDS ON DEATH

- may be rolled to spouse's RRSP, **If no surviving spouse:**
  - may be rolled to RRSP of physically/mentally infirm child who was **dependant of deceased**
  - may be added to taxable income of child who was dependant of deceased, or used to buy fixed-term annuity to age 18

OTHER SPECIAL RRSP ROLLOVERS

- Spouses can directly transfer between plans due to legal separation/divorce

Retiring allowance may be rolled to **own** RRSP, **not** spousal *(limit of $2,000/calendar year of employment up to and including 1995 **plus** $1,500/year of employment up to and including 1998, when employer contributions to RPP/DPSP did not "vest" in employee; no rollover allowed for 1996 and future years of service).*

THREE YEAR WITHDRAWAL RULE ON SPOUSAL RRSPS

Withdrawals are "attributed" back to you for tax purposes if you've made contributions to any spousal plans in calendar year of withdrawal or in 2 previous calendar years

- Does not apply while living apart due to manage breakdown
- Only applies to RRIF income **in excess of RRIF minimum**
- Rolling funds from spousal RRSP to RRIF creates spousal RRIF

RRSP CARRYFORWARD

- Can carry forward unused contribution room indefinitely (*to age limit*)
- Can also contribute now but carry tax deduction forward (*to shelter income in a later year; possibly reduce clawback of government benefits*)
- Retiring allowance is **not** eligible for carryforward treatment

CONTRIBUTING SECURITIES THAT YOU ALREADY OWN

(*Making contribution to self directed RRSP "in kind" rather than in cash*)

- Contribution = fair market value of securities at time of contribution
- Deemed disposition of securities when contribution made
- Capital gains taxable but cannot use capital losses

HOME BUYER'S PLAN

(*Withdrawal maximum $20,000 from RRSP*)

- Cannot have occupied own or spouse's home for 5 years
- Must complete form T1036 "Applying to Withdraw an Amount Under the Home Buyer's Plan"
- Must repay minimum 1/15th of total per year, report on Schedule 7 with tax return or T1037 if tax return not filed (*defaults added to taxable income*)
- If you withdraw funds from an RRSP under the Home Buyer's Plan within 89 days of contributing to the RRSP, part or all of your RRSP contribution may not be tax-deductible

$2,000 OVERCONTRIBUTION (*lifetime limit*)

- Only if you reached at least age 18 in preceding year
- Overcontributions in excess of $2,000 subject to 1% per month penalty
- No RRSP deduction and withdrawals taxed (*to claim offsetting deduction taxpayer must prove it was "accidental"*)

SWAPPING SECURITIES FOR CASH

(*Swapping non-registered securities for cash in self-directed RRSP*)

- Cash received = fair market value of securities swapped
- Cash not added to taxable income, no tax withheld
- Capital gains taxable but cannot use capital losses

TAX WITHHELD ON RRSP WITHDRAWALS

(*for RRIFs, tax withheld only on withdrawals in excess of minimum*)

	Quebec (lump sums only)	Other provinces
$5,000 or less	21%	10%
$5,001 – $15,000	30%	20%
$15,001 +	35%	30%

Courtesy Thérèse Giroux, C.F.P., R.F.P., Retirement and Estate Services Planning Manager, Midland Walwyn

In addition to that $5,416 cash rebate, where else can you receive a 100% tax-free compounding of your money each year to age 69 and substantial tax-free compounding beyond that age? (Your residential home, while tax-free when you sell it, permits you no tax rebate.)

Assume an 8% annual return on just $2,500 in *annual* contributions over 35 years. The tax-sheltered RRSP would be worth $430,777 at year 35. A non-RRSP accrual over the same period would be worth $92,062 at the end of the same period — at a 50% tax level, this comes to almost one-fifth of the RRSP total. And the RRSP accumulation rolled into an income option such as a Registered Retirement Income Fund (RRIF) continues to compound tax-sheltered too. You are taxed on only the annual income portion.

Gambling on the dreams of future retirement income can be a financial tragedy. According to Environics Research, only an estimated 51% of Canadians who qualify to invest in RRSPs are expected to contribute to RRSPs for the 1997 tax year, up from 34% in 1996. The average planned contribution for 1997 is $4,275, up from $4,075 in 1996. The most favored investments for RRSPs again in 1997 are mutual funds (56%), GICs and term deposits (only 27%), stocks and bonds (23%), and savings accounts (22%).

You can no longer put off such contributions in favor of paying your mortgage — do both! Use your annual RRSP tax rebate to reduce your mortgage each year.

RRSPs AND CAPITAL GAINS

There's another major advantage to your RRSP in terms of tax deferral. Unrealized (not sold) capital gains outside your registered plan continue to shelter your investment from taxes while the plan's funds keep on compounding in value. You pay tax on only 75% of your capital gains when you realize, or cash, them. Inside your RRSP, you pay no tax for many years on your unrealized capital gains under current tax law. And, if you decide to transfer capital gains from one fund to another (sell one, buy another), no capital gains tax is charged against that capital gain disposition.

SELF-DIRECTED RRSPS

The Myths of Self-Directed RRSPs

Many people have said to me, "I'm just not knowledgable enough about investment markets to self-direct my RRSP." What puts people off is the term "self-directed." The government should have called it the "Flexible RRSP" so that people would not be so intimidated.

My strong advice is this: Everyone who has an RRSP account over $5,000 should have it tucked away in a self-directed plan. These plans are no longer just for the well-heeled where trustee fees used to approach $1,000 annually. A typical trustee fee these days is $125 to $150 annually. If you're 50 years of age or older, you can get that fee cut in half if you are a member of the Canadian Association of Retired Persons. I know that's true of my clientele at Midland Walwyn, so you should ask your advisor about your annual registered trustee fee.

But don't get hung up on the trustee fee. It's the least important element of your investment decisions. Instead, concentrate on the terrific services offered with a self-directed plan. By the way, the annual membership fee for CARP is only $10 per couple. There are many excellent benefits to being a member, memberships now being over 330,000 strong and growing under Lillian Morganthan's energetic leadership. If you're a baby boomer (age 30–49), make sure you apply for membership in the Canadian Association of Baby Boomers (CABB).

The Benefits of a Self-Directed Plan

The benefits of a self-directed plan are many. First, you get to combine all of your RRSP or RRIF investments under one umbrella, so that you have control of your retirement future.

Consolidation eliminates the pressure and time loss transferring from one trustee to another to take advantage of a better investment. Your trustee acts on your behalf and that of your financial advisor.

Second, think of "self-directed" as maximum *flexibility* for managing your portfolio. Take advantage of a professional advisor while you maintain ultimate control.

Third, your self-directed plan permits you to hold many different types of mutual funds, numerous individual securities, GICs and your mortgage as well. You can choose among hundreds of different "family group" mutual funds to suit your personal investment needs. Most Canadian stock shares and government and corporate bonds (including Canada Savings Bonds) can be held inside your RRSP, with any income distribution to be reinvested tax free.

You can also hold your own or an institution's mortgages inside your plan.

Four, contributions to your RRSP/RRIF need not be in cash. Investments that are outside your RRSP can be used as contribution and are known as contributions-in-kind. In addition, you can alter some of your registered investments to switch from one mutual fund to another with a different manager, or use your GIC to buy a stock. This procedure is known as a conversion. You can even swap investments outside your RRSP for investments inside, providing they are eligible and of the same value. *That's flexibility.*

Five, one of the greatest advantages of a self-directed plan is the allowable portion that can be held outside of Canada, currently 20% of *book* value. International investments have historically improved the value of your RRSP/RRIF and most certainly should be part of your retirement strategy.

Six, valuing your foreign content (adjusted cost base) each month for each separate investment plan is a huge service provided by most trustees and financial institutions. If you have more than one RRSP, foreign content is not based on the consolidating of all your RRSPs into a single "self-directed plan," even if your financial advisor is providing all the direction.

FOREIGN CONTENT RULES IN AN RRSP

Revenue Canada allows individuals to invest a percentage of each registered account in foreign content assets without penalty. However, if the foreign content in a self-directed account exceeds 20% of the account's total book value, a 1% penalty tax will be calculated on the excess amount. "Book value" is the original adjusted net invested "cost" you paid for your mutual fund. The foreign property rule for registered plans is calculated on book value, not market value. (See Table 13.3.)

The trustee is responsible for calculating the book value of each account. The calculation for book value for each investment is the average cost per share multiplied by the number of shares in the account.

For example, if an account holder purchased a fund in 1992 for $4,000, another fund for $4,000 in 1993, a third fund for $6,000 in 1994, and a fourth fund for $6,000 in 1995, the maximum foreign content allowable without penalty in the account is $4,000, or 20% of the original cost.

It is important to remember that transactions change the book value of an RRSP. For instance, purchases, reinvested funds and share transfers increase book value. Redemptions, trustee fees taken from holdings, share transfers out of holdings, and conversions and switches decrease book value.

Based on book value, the trustee or financial institution calculates the foreign content of all accounts on an ongoing basis. Notification is sent to the account holder if a transaction has taken place that may cause the foreign content limit. Steps must be taken to rectify the situation before month-end when a penalty would be applied.

There is no grace period possible in which to make corrections. If a registered account's foreign content exceeds 20% at any month-end, the financial institution is required to withhold the corresponding foreign content penalty and pay it to Revenue Canada in March of the following year. Revenue Canada requires that the tax can be taken from within the registered account. It cannot be paid from outside of the account under any circumstance.

Since foreign investments often pay higher dividends, you may wish to keep your RRSP's foreign content level slightly below 20% in order to stay within allowable limits. You could also invest dividends from foreign mutual funds into Canadian-content mutual funds. With RRIFs, keep foreign content limits in mind as funds are depleted by payouts.

It's in the investor's best interests to load up on foreign exposure inside registered plans. But our bone to pick with Revenue Canada is that we are restricted to a 20% limit on the adjusted cost (book value) RRSP/RRIF assets. This means that 80% of RRSP/RRIF assets are invested in less than 3% of the world's markets! We hope that Revenue Canada will one day increase the foreign content permitted in RRSP/RRIF holdings or remove the restrictions altogether. This would give Canadians the opportunity to accumulate much more retirement wealth which, after all, eventually will be taxed 100% by Revenue Canada when the income is withdrawn from the plan.

TABLE 13.3: ADJUSTED COST BASE

Trade Date	Trans. Type	Amount $	Share Price	No. of Shares	Share Bal	Average $/Share	Book Value	20% Foreign Content
Jan 97	PUR	$4,000	$8.00	500	500	$8.00	$4,000.00	$800.00
Feb 97	TSF IN	150	10.00	15	515	8.06	4,150.00	830.00
Mar 97	PAC	120	10.00	12	527	8.10	4,270.00	854.00
Mar 97	FEE	−39	9.75	−4	523	8.10	4,236.30	847.26
Apr 97	RED	−50.25	10.05	−5	518	8.10	4,195.80	839.16
May 97	DIV	29.30	9.80	3	521	8.11	4,255.10	845.02

Source: M.R.S. Promotional Materials

Breaking the 20% Foreign Content Barrier for Your RRSP

For some years now, studies have proven that having more than 20% foreign content inside your RRSP/RRIF actually increases your profit substantially while decreasing your portfolio risk. A study by Ibbotson & Associates shows that historically, say from 1970 to 1995, a 25-year period, a portfolio that combined 68% international stocks with 32% Canadian stocks would have increased your *average* annual return by *more than 3% per year without adding any risk.*

Using this performance illustration, if you'd had 100% of your registered investment (or non-registered investment, for that matter) plans in equities as represented by the TSE 300 Index (Canadian stocks), you'd have had an excellent return of 11% compounded annually over that 25-year period.

If, however, you'd been permitted to hold 68% of your investments in foreign stocks as measured by the Morgan Stanley World Index, you'd have earned 14.% per year over the same period.

Translated into dollars, a $10,000 single investment over that 25-year period for the "Canadian only" investor would have accumulated a total portfolio value of $135,855. The globally diversified investor with 68% foreign stocks and 32% Canadian stocks would have accumulated a portfolio worth more than $275,000. That's *double* the total wealth to enjoy in your retirement with zero additional risk.

Strategy #1

Your first strategy to break the 20% barrier is to own a Canadian mutual fund that internally uses its 20% foreign content plus an RRSP-eligible foreign fund. This gets you $36,000 invested in foreign assets without trespassing on Ottawa's 20% limits in respect to $100,000 of RRSP proceeds. Now you're holding 36% foreign content, not 20%.

Strategy #2

This strategy involves 100% RRSP-eligible foreign funds. These funds are unique, Global Strategy having been the first mutual fund company in Canada to introduce them about a decade ago. These funds can be called "derivative" or "synthetic" RRSP/RRIF funds. Typically, they will invest 80% of their investment portfolios in Government of Canada and/or provincial Treasury Bills, and the remaining 20% in futures and options contracts of international securities, and in various global indexes. These might include the EAFE Index (European Asian Far East), the Standard & Poor's 500 Index, or the Hang Seng Index in Hong Kong.

These "derivative" fund portfolios are able to mimic fully invested foreign funds while at the same time complying with Revenue Canada's 20% maximum foreign content rule. You could use these unique funds to gain effective foreign exposure up to 100% inside your registered plan. That said, I don't recommend that much foreign content inside your RRSP. You should have some portion in Canadian securities.

So much for international equities inside your plan. You can also purchase foreign currency bonds, up to 100% foreign content, inside your registered plan. For example, our federal and provincial governments and Canadian companies often issue bonds that are denominated in other currencies, such as the Hong Kong dollar, U.S. dollar, Japanese yen, Swiss francs or German marks.

Obviously, we need foreign investment to help us finance our deficits. The truth is that a lot of foreigners don't like the risk associated with our Canadian dollar-denominated securities, so they buy our bonds in their currencies. These bond securities are 100% eligible for RRSPs and RRIFs! The 20% foreign content rule of Revenue Canada doesn't care what currency a security is stuck in— only the originating country.

Strategy #3

Another barrier-breaking strategy is to buy a mutual fund that holds bonds issued by the World Bank. The Canadian government is a signatory to the World Bank and therefore these securities are deemed to be Canadian property. These bonds are typically denominated in major foreign currencies.

For years, I have recommended substantial holdings of my clients' registered plans to access much more than 20% foreign content to obtain not only better gains but to reduce overall risk.

You can access several excellent international balanced funds that qualify for this treatment. (See Figure 13.2: 100% Eligible Foreign Funds for Your RRSP/RRIF.)

FIGURE 13.2: 100% ELIGIBLE FOREIGN FUNDS FOR YOUR RRSP/RRIF

Fund Name	Fund Type	Fund Name	Fund Type
International Equity Funds		**International Bond Funds**	
Diversified Europe Fund	EurEqu	Dynamic Global Bond Fund	IntBd
Universal World Growth RRSP Fund	GloEqu	Guardian International Income	IntBd
20/20 RSP Int'l Equity Allocation Fund	GloEqu	Admax World Income Fund	IntBd
Talvest Global RRSP Fund Inc.	GloEqu	C.I. Global Bond RSP Fund	IntBd
C.I. Global Equity RSP Fund	GloEqu	Altamira Global Bond Fund	IntBd
Diversified Asia Fund	FarEast	Spectrum United RSP Int'l Bond	IntBd
Diversified Japan Plus Fund	FarEast	Talvest Foreign Pay Canadian Bond	IntBd
Diversified Latin America Fund	EmLat	AGF RSP Global Income Fund	IntBd
Diversified World Equity Fund	GloEqu	20/20 Foreign RSP Bond Fund	IntBd
Admax Global RRSP Index Fund	GloEqu	Fidelity RSP Gobal Bond Fund	IntBd
Atlas American RSP Index**	USEqu	Atlas World Bond Fund**	IntBd
Atlas International RSP Index**	GloEqu	Universal World Income RRSP Fund	IntBd
CIBC International Index RRSP**	GloEqu	Guardian Foreign Income Fund	IntBd
CIBC U.S. Index RRSP Fund**	USEqu	Diversified Foreign Bond Fund	IntBd
International Balanced Funds		BPI Global RSP Bond Fund	IntBd
BPI Global Balanced RSP Fund	InBal		
Universal World Balanced RRSP	InBal		
C.I. International Balanced RSP	InBal		
Guardian International Balanced	InBal		
Strategic Value Global Balanced RSP	InBal		

** Date: March 1997

Source: Midland Walwyn

For example, note the investment policy of Global Strategy's (Rothschild) Diversified Bond Fund. "The fund seeks to maximize return primarily through exposure to high-quality debt securities of government and *supra*national entities (such as the World Bank) worldwide. The fund may hold debt securities or options, futures, forwards and other similar investments to achieve this exposure. The currency exposure of the fund is managed with a view to protecting returns from risk of foreign currency declines, as well as to enhancing returns."

Equity-wise, let's look at Global Strategy's Diversified Asia Fund to get a glimpse of its investment policy: "The fund seeks long-term growth of capital through effective exposure to the equity markets of Asia, including Hong Kong, Singapore, Malaysia, Korea, Thailand, Taiwan, Indonesia and the Philippines, as well as China, India, Sri Lanka and Pakistan. The fund invests in equity securities, options, futures, forwards, and other instruments that provide this exposure."

This type of investment expertise is promised by Global Strategy in its global RSP fund, RRSP foreign bond, Japan RRSP, RRSP Europe fund, RRSP Latin America, and U.S. Equity RRSP fund.

Imagine—you can even get U.S.-dollar denominated stripped World Bank bond coupons with some 100% Canadian RRSP derivative bond funds!

Take advantage of the 20% barrier-breaking strategies for foreign content inside your registered plans. You have a unique opportunity to grab potentially higher returns with less risk!

FIGURE 13.3: THE RRSP MOST LIKELY TO SUCCEED (1997)

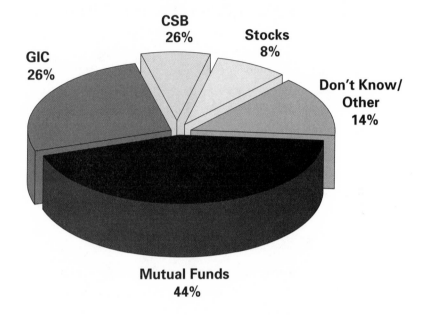

Source: Marketing Solutions

chapter **14** | # EVALUATING BULLS, BEARS AND ADVISORS

The best investors are like professional socialites. They arrive early and make sure that they depart well before the end, leaving the mob to swill the last tasteless dregs.

— The Economist (London)

It's time to talk turkey about the two most important subjects to you as an investor in mutual funds. Up to this point we've talked all around them — retirement, the New Reality, inflation, taxes, portfolios, safety, risk, interest and dividends, RRSPs and RRIFs — we've even talked about bull markets. Now let's focus our attention on: (1) how to choose mutual funds, and (2) which may be more important, how to choose a financial advisor who specializes in mutual funds.

YOU ARE KNOWN BY THE COMPANIES YOU KEEP

1. Choosing a Particular Mutual Fund

How do you size up a particular mutual fund? We're not here discussing choosing the particular *type* of fund — T-Bill, fixed income, equity or whatever. Let's say you've already done that and decided that a good equity fund is right for you. But how do you analyze the *quality* of that fund, and by implication, that fund's manager?

A number of fund managers are highly talented and can generate above-index returns — and even more important, *risk-adjusted* returns in nasty markets. The real issue is, can you identify those managers *today* who will significantly outperform other funds in their peer group over the next five to 10 years?

You can find much of the information you'll need in order to evaluate a fund in its per-share table, one of the most useful parts of a mutual fund's prospectus. This table contains data over the past 10-year period or the fund's life, whichever is shorter. (Most are much shorter.) Analyze a mutual fund's performance according to its total return and volatility.

Measuring a Fund's Quality

Look first at the total return, especially if income is important to you. There are three components of total return from a stock fund:

1. Dividends from net investment income
2. Distribution from net realized gain, and
3. Net increase (or decrease) in net asset value (such as computing total returns).

The MANAGMENT-EXPENSE RATIO (MER) helps you determine a fund's efficiency and cost effectiveness. This is the ratio of its total expenses to its average net assets. The expense ratio has nothing to do with sales (brokerage) commissions. An expense ratio can vary anywhere from 0.4% to 3.5%. The lowest, or most economical, ratio is found among the plain-vanilla stock market index funds and money market funds. But, "expense ratio" should *never* be the key criterion in deciding which fund to buy. Superior management and portfolio quality are the critical factors to consider. A possible exception to this rule might be in measuring expense ratios for certain bond funds.

Small, aggressive-growth funds that employ leverage and incur high interest costs often report the most expensive ratios. They also tend to report some of the highest returns. Mutual funds that invest internationally also tend to demonstrate higher expense ratios than domestic portfolios do because of the greater research they do and the other costs associated with foreign investing. Stock funds generally have higher MERs than do fixed-income funds.

The INCOME RATIO is produced by the net investment income divided by average net assets — like a dividend yield to a stock. This ratio focuses exclusively on income. For equity (stock) funds that concentrate on capital appreciation, this number could be very low, perhaps zero. Conversely, for income-oriented equity funds (such as preferred dividends) or balanced (stocks and bonds) funds, the ratio could be 3% to 4%.

PORTFOLIO TURNOVER RATE measures the amount of buying and selling the fund's management does. Compare the current portfolio with those of a year ago, five years ago, and even 10 years ago, noting how much turnover took place. This will give you some idea of how aggressive the manager is in his approach and his ability to react to changing markets. How do you interpret the numbers? A 100% turnover implies that the manager holds each stock or bond for one year, on average. A 50% turnover means that positions are held for about two years, 200% for six months, and so on.

Also check the growth in the total asset figure over time. This suggests how popular this fund is with new investors. That may not be the last word on its quality — the public is rarely right in its choice of financial markets — but a solidly growing fund gives the manager more strength with which to take advantage of investment opportunities.

TRANSACTION COSTS: These are other, more important cost factors than brokerage commissions and more difficult to document:

Dealer spreads: Every stock has a bid price and an ask price. Typical costs are 10 cents per share paid by a fund's brokerage commission. "Spread" can be the largest cost component.

Transaction size effects: A manager who trades frequently can cost you substantial profits. For example, if a stock is thinly traded and the manager wishes to sell a large block in a hurry, he or she will incur adverse price impacts, beyond the usual spread. For this reason, investors *may* be better off with funds that trade less. It's less costly. The opposing argument, naturally, is that such a conservative fund may perform less impressively. Bottom line — it's how much your fund *pays* you. The cost can often be irrelevant.

Conduct as much ratio analysis as you can, price-earnings, dividend payout ratio, standard deviation, and Beta measurements. Look at the fund's track record, during bad markets, such as 1994, as well as good markets, such as 1995–96. Did it decline as much or less than the industry in bear markets?

In a larger sense, perhaps the best method of analyzing a mutual fund is to look at the fund manager's performance, and then decide whether that manager's style and that performance match is what you're looking for, what you expect for *future performance*. We can look at performance under several headings:

Value — Both you and the mutual fund manager look for stocks trading below their real value, or at a price below those of competitors within the same industry. In the extreme, value investors don't even consider the level of stock market indexes, but buy or sell when they see few or many "values" in those markets.

Growth — The ideal for growth investors, sometimes referred to as "momentum" investors, is to find companies with a record of superior earnings growth and the likelihood of that trend continuing. Where this happens, investors sometimes add to a successful earlier investment. Usually, such a growth stock will pay a small dividend or none at all. This could mean either it has outgrown the payout or has not yet declared one.

Check whether the company makes a point of justifying its current levels of the stock and much more. A stock may appear high on fundamental analysis, but the manager may have reason to expect further growth. Clues may lie in aggressive management, an unusually strong momentum, marked leadership within its industry, or some unusual or unique product or service. Roger Babson once said, "The ideal investment is one where demand must grow but supply can't." Think of urban waterfront property! (See Table 14.1: Growth vs. Value.)

Sector — Sector investors (or fund managers) choose an area of the overall economy or industry that is slated to grow at a rate far faster than others. Then they assemble a portfolio around that sector, typically composed of the securities of a narrow-sector industry. While the type of companies included will vary, invariably stocks will be the favored vehicle. Narrow-sector-type funds include gold, health sciences, and telecommunications.

TABLE 14.1: GROWTH VERSUS VALUE

	Best Equity Funds for Falling Inflation	Best Equity Funds for Rising Inflation
	GROWTH INVESTING	VALUE INVESTING
FOCUS	Emphasis on companies and industries in stage of rapid growth with earnings momentum.	Emphasis on companies and industries whose market values are low relative to share value measures based on earnings, dividends or assets.
COMPANY CHARACTERISTICS	• Rapid and increasing growth in sales and earnings. • Low or no dividends. • Typically high price-to-value measures such as price-to-book, price-to-earnings.	• Often unglamorous, out-of-favor businesses. • Low price-to-earnings and measures such as price-to-book. • High-dividend yields.

TABLE 14.1: cont'd

	Best Equity Funds for Falling Inflation	Best Equity Funds for Rising Inflation
	GROWTH INVESTING	**VALUE INVESTING**
RISK	• Tend to be more volatile, higher Beta stocks. • Prices can move up or down substantially with small changes in expectations or actual earnings performance relative to expected performance.	• Tend to be less volatile, low Beta stocks. • It may take considerable time for the market to recognize value. • Upturns in company performance may not occur.
RETURN	• High capital appreciation. • Little or no dividend income.	• Capital appreciation. • High dividend income.
PERFORMANCE PERIODS	• Tend to perform better on a relative basis when the economy is slightly down.	• Tend to perform better on a relative basis during middle to late stages of an economic recovery.
SAMPLE COMPANIES	• Healthcare • Communications • Biotechnology • Pharmaceuticals • Technology • Specialty retailing	• Transportation • Automotive • Machinery • Forest products • Insurance • Oil and gas
OTHER NAMES	• Glamor • Emerging company • Emerging markets	• Contrarian • Out-of-favor • Neglected

SETTING YOUR OWN INVESTMENT STYLE

An investment style may follow one of three different approaches, such as growth, blend, and value, or may mix more than several management styles. Investment fund managers may also apply a single style, such as *top down*, or macroeconomic, whereby they survey the general economy with an eye to the most outstanding industry or industries, followed by the selection of the leading companies' stocks within those industries. Logically, then, *bottom up,* or microeconomic, investing entails searching widely for stocks that represent better than average *value* or the potential for growth.

Sometimes a manager uses the two strategies together, applying top-down procedures used to identify the leading industries and then bottom-up analysis to choose the leading stocks within those industries.

The expression "spread-lending" is often used in traditional banking. You have, no doubt, experienced it, in any case. Mutual fund managers may buy and sell bonds when they spot bond issues out of line with the rest of the market. This is *spread trading.* The objective is to make a profit on the spread, and possibly to improve yield without giving up safety. And here the profit accrues to the benefit of the lowly shareholders, not to the bank.

To cite a single mutual fund outstanding for its performance, the Templeton Emerging Markets Fund was formed to join the Templeton stable as recently as September 1991. In its first year it grew 36.2%, followed by a two-year performance of 29.3%. Measured at its third year, overall annual performance was 82%. Even in 1994, a terrible year in the market, the fund managed just a modest loss of about 4.8%.

The fund's manager, Dr. Mark Mobius, who is also Templeton's managing director for the Far East division in Hong Kong and Singapore, describes how he managed the fund:

> Throughout the bull market, the Fund was able to provide investors with excellent returns, and has also weathered the correction well. Why? First, the Fund was not heavy in Asia. Second, the Fund maintained a high cash position of 26.7%, a combined result of new investors into the Fund and our difficulty in finding securities that meet our bargain criteria. And third, the Fund's portfolio was broadly diversified geographically and by sector.

All of which might be summarized as: Look for a fund that does well in bad markets because of (1) strong cash position, (2) stringent bargain criteria, and (3) broad diversification.

Templeton Growth Fund, the flagship of this group of funds, was created in November 1954. Over its 43-year life, it has averaged an annual yield of 15.6%. (Figure that on a compound basis!) In the past 20 years its annual return has averaged 19.0%, and its past five-year average is 13.7%.

"International equities," says Mark Holowesko, now manager of the fund, "continue to offer opportunities as recent market declines have priced equities at attractive levels."

The message: *Professional fund managers get their kicks, their excitement, from declining markets, not bull markets.* For example, the volatile movement of equity markets between February and May 1997 created a fund manager's paradise! You can appreciate this perception in a fund manager. For an individual investor, it is probably best to "leave the driving" to them. It can be very difficult and nerve-wracking to be positive in a negative, growling, bear market environment. To take the contrary view and have the courage to buy when everyone else is selling is exceptionally hard to do.

A FUND OF KNOWLEDGE

There are certain things you learn that are accumulated from the mistakes you make .... I define portfolio managers by the number of bear markets they've lived through.

— Richard Hoey, Chief Economist,
Dreyfus Corporation

2. Choosing a Financial Advisor

Legal structures and federal and provincial regulatory bodies, such as securities commissions, form major safeguards to the investor. For example, management companies and individuals involved with mutual funds are prohibited from engaging in personal transactions with the funds they handle. Consider your choice of a financial advisor as important as your choice of any other professional — doctor, lawyer, engineer, accountant. You will be entrusting this person with your lifetime of hard-earned savings for careful nurturing.

First, your advisor must bring to your service an excellent reputation. That should not be too difficult to check. You may try to find out who some of his clients are and contact them. However, even if you obtain several letters of recommendation from "happy" clients, that doesn't really tell you anything. Anyone can produce a "happy client" letter. Talk with local bankers, accountants and brokers. Even if they don't know the advisor you're considering personally, they'll often know his reputation and the firm he works for.

This person should instill confidence in you from your first meeting. You'll sense this through personal appearance, bearing and conversation. Be prepared to stick with that person through several major market shifts as you watch how you both respond to market dynamics and to each other. Ask straightforward questions.

Besides directing the course of your investment, an experienced financial advisor can also coordinate your whole financial picture, and act as a quarterback for a team that may include your accountant, banker, lawyer, stockbroker and insurance agent. He can act as your general practitioner in a group of specialists.

A measure of a competent financial advisor is the company he keeps. Or rather the *companies*. Ask the candidate how many mutual funds are represented in their practice. If the answer is only one group of funds, he cannot be an unbiased financial planner. A creative planner should be free to select among the best funds and plans available in the market so he can match your particular situation.

A good advisor will ask you a lot of searching questions and in addition give you a written questionnaire to fill in. Rather than take offence, be honest and cooperate fully in this process. The more he knows about your preferences, fears, prejudices, values and goals, and of course your net worth, the better you can design and maintain a good financial plan.

*　　*　　*

I mentioned the advisory team of banker, lawyer, accountant, broker and insurance agent. Are these other professionals qualified planners? While each member of this team we have designated is a specialist, you wouldn't ask your financial planner to draw up your will. Why ask a banker or a lawyer to do something for which they may have little or no training? Having said this, there are many financial advisors and/or planners who come from *all* of these professions.

Indeed, many thousands of the best-trained financial advisors with the largest brokerage and full-service firms in Canada do not use the term "financial planner." The majority of these professionals have at least one university degree in disciplines such as commerce, economics, law, accounting, and so on. While the possession of a degree does not make a top financial advisor, the degree does indicate that the individual has the ability to master a discipline.

On the other hand, there are a number of outstanding members of the financial community who, though not possessing collective academic degrees, have excelled in their industry through deep, practical market experience, which is probably the single most important attribute a qualified advisor can have.

Further, a financial advisor with a brokerage firm must now pass not only the rigorous Canadian Securities Course exam and the Representative's Conduct Manual exam, but he is also required to sit for the Certified Investment Manager's exam in addition to attaining the new Certified Financial Planner designation. And no, it doesn't matter specifically how a financial advisor is compensated. What does matter is that the advisor discloses and presents that information to you so that there are no surprises down the road. Full disclosure is the key. Any potential conflicts of interest or bias towards certain financial products should be mentioned by the advisor.

WHY YOU NEED A PRO

If you are a pro, do you really need a pro? In my experience, many professional people — physicians, lawyers, accountants, educators, engineers — fully appreciate the experience and specialized knowledge that a financial advisor or a fund manager has devoted to a career. On the other hand, some professional people may find it difficult to take the advice of a professional outside their own profession.

Professional financial management for the individual can be obtained in two ways. An investor with a sizable amount of money — say, $250,000 or more — may turn his investment account over to an investment manager or firm, who will assume complete control of the account for a stated fee — perhaps 1% to 2% annually of the total accumulated value. He acts with complete discretion, consulting with his client as he goes along. This type of arrangement is generally known as a "WRAP" account.

The client deposits funds with a bank or broker as custodian, through whom the advisor will operate, and the advisor obtains a signed discretionary agreement from the client. Regular confirmations of transactions are sent to the client, together with a regular report on the progress of the account as to gains, losses and general performance, the same as with a regular mutual fund portfolio. Naturally, the client can terminate the arrangement at any time.

Letting the professionals do it for you adds up to a lot of pro power for your hard-earned money, and certainly less worry. Here's why. What follows is a short excerpt from a column I wrote, published by the *Vancouver Sun*, March 4, 1996:

> International stock and bond fund managers often provide active foreign currency managed portfolios. A sudden change in interest rates in a foreign country can affect the perceived strength of its currency and its relationship to other world currencies.
>
> In the case of equity mutual funds, currency risk over time is typically much less than market risk and world-wide

it accounts for about 15% of the total stock market risk. With bonds, however, the currency risk may become the principal risk experienced.

What can you do to benefit from the diversification of international investing and possible higher returns while minimizing the currency exchange risk?

First, invest internationally with the longest-term money you have. For example, a 10-year period will reduce the exchange risk that may be seen in shorter periods, such as in 1995 with the Japanese yen and the German mark.

Second, invest in funds that cover many countries. The risk of a world stock index compared to a single country currency risk should be much less.

Third, some funds hedge part or all of their foreign currency exposure, providing a degree of insurance against significant [currency] losses. This is a specialized game best left to the judgment of a successful international money [mutual fund] manager.

chapter 15

GETTING *THE* LOAD OFF YOUR MIND

It's not the bulls and bears you need to avoid —
it's the bum steers.

— C. Hillis

There has been much written and advertised recently on the subject of "no-load" funds (on which you pay little or no commission), as if acquisition fees were one of the most important considerations in buying mutual funds. This is misleading information, and its dissemination can be laid at the door of media journalists. In a word, blindly buying "no-advice funds" at somebody's urging, whether that of journalists or irresponsible agencies, can be an expensive process for the unwitting investor — by default.

THE NO-ADVICE FUNDS

The "no-load" mentality has become a syndrome. A preponderance of mutual fund media advertising in both Canada and the United States preaches no-load as an article of faith. There is that element in many of us (perhaps all of us) that seeks a deal at whatever cost in quality. But don't delude yourself that you can really save money with no-load funds, because you will usually be sacrificing true value in continuous personalized advice, service and selection.

More than once, I have asked a prospective client the question, "What kind of mutual funds do you have at the bank?" The answer is usually, "I'm not sure, but I think they're no-load funds."

Using no-load funds is part of the larger consideration of whether or not you employ a financial advisor. A 1996 poll of 1,000 investors by Princeton Survey Research Associates for the Investor Protection Trust (IPT) indicated that 67% of "knowledgeable" investors use or have used a financial broker. Those designated "somewhat knowledgeable" responded 44% in favor of using a financial broker, while of the "not too knowledgeable" category, only 27% chose not to go it alone. (The categories of "knowledgeability" were established with an eight-question test of the investor's factual understanding.)

FIGURE 15.1: INVESTOR BEHAVIOR WITH FINANCIAL PROFESSIONALS

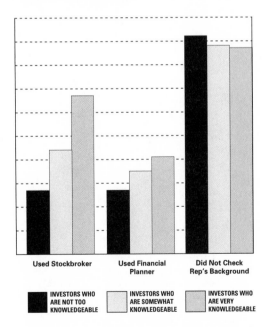

Source: Investor Protection Trust/Princeton Survey Research Associates

If investors were better informed about the true nature of no-load funds, it's likely that the percentage of those seeking advice would be even higher. In the Princeton poll, 35% of all investors said no-load funds have no sales or other charges, and 26% didn't know.

I am not suggesting for a moment that "no-load" funds are inferior to load funds. I am stating that by far, the majority of investors need to depend on full-time, independent financial advice through all market conditions — and that "true value" typically comes with a (*contingent* only) deferred-cost arrangement.

In a *Financial Post* column (February 1994), Bruce Cohen wrote:

> Do no-load funds provide a free lunch? Maybe. There's no sales commission but you face two non-monetary costs. The first is the lack of personal service. The second cost is that no-load groups tend to lag in launching niche funds. If you want to be leading edge, you'll likely go load.
>
> How can no-load funds sell units without a commission? Phil Armstrong, president of Altamira Investment Services Inc., explained this at the firm's annual conference. To attract a new client, he said, his [Altamira's] advertising and phone costs are about the same as a sales [brokerage] commission.

But Cohen's arguments represent only a small justification of the investor's avoiding the *no-load trap*.

An experienced financial advisor typically costs the shareholders of a mutual fund only the total of *a fraction of 1%* per annum via the management fee of the mutual fund. And the whole question of commissions and other fees has little relation to the potential profitability of a given mutual fund portfolio, and therefore of its shareholders. Many financial advisors who specialize in mutual funds provide their clients with a great deal of value-added advice and service, dealing not only with mutual funds but with related financial instruments and services — financial planning, portfolio reviews and re-balancing, retirement and estate planning, investment and relevant tax planning, and expert

RRSP/RRIF advice. There is usually a *very substantial cost* to providing this service that is borne heavily by your advisor, staff and firm. Many of these excellent advisors also network with other professionals such as lawyers, bankers, accountants and bankers, to make sure your overall financial plan is executed professionally. Often, many of these services are provided free by the financial advisor.

The Load Funds

There are mutual funds with relatively high (perhaps too high) commission rates, some with nominal rates, and some with no commission at all. No-load funds refer to the latter group. There are also front-end loads (commissions), and back-end (deferred or trailing loads) that are *contingent* charges only, based on a declining scale each year the fund is held, typically reducing to zero over a six- or seven-year period.

With the back-end (DSC — deferred sales charge) funds, you can usually get as much as 10% of accumulated value *free each year*, and virtually *unlimited commission-free transfers* into other funds within each family group. In reality, your back-end or deferred fund purchase *becomes a no-load fund* over time, but without sacrificing the enormous benefits of ongoing financial advice and many other services.

Don't allow the load to confuse you about the real issue here — making money. Don't be caught up in the mania of forsaking solid professional money management because a fee is two-tenths of 1% more at one fund than another.

The protagonists of no-load funds, buttressed by much of the financial press gallery in Canada, have framed the debate of load versus no-load in the wrong terms. According to this faction, the argument goes this way: the central issue over a lifetime of investing is *which* funds you bought. And everything else being equal, a no-load fund should outperform a load fund (they say), if only because of the difference of the load.

But success almost always results from the quality of the ongoing advice the investor gets (load fund) and does not get (no-load fund).

In other words, the no-load investor saves the commission but pays the vastly more costly penalty of no advice. The Dalbar Research studies claim to prove this fact.

In Chapter 12, I refer to a new client of mine who had purchased a large portfolio of funds at his bank — then I learned the true cost of his no-load funds. His balanced fund at the bank returned 9.5% in the year, while my most recommended balanced fund produced 23.1% in the same period. The client lost 13.6% in profits by default.

There is no correlation between low or no commission rates and investment fund success. The truth is doubtless the reverse, as the highly regarded Dalbar Institute study has shown, over a wide range of fund types. Yet the media constantly advocate the no-load myth, as if picking a "superior" fund is the critical issue, and not the subsequent management of the portfolio.

Most "load" portfolios allow virtually unlimited free (no-commission) transfers within each family group. Many of these "families" contain at least 30 distinct categories of funds. As such, there is no reason why an alert investor should ever pay a sales fee, because after several years deferred-load funds can actually become no-load, as mentioned earlier.

Perhaps the no-load advocates confuse *investment* returns with *investor* returns.

The Investment Company Institute of America (ICI), through two recent studies concerning shareholder redemption decisions and shareholder perception of investment risk, discovered (1) that investors who buy funds through a compensated professional advisor do better — make critical mistakes less often — than investors who buy no-load funds on their own, and (2) that risk is one of the most misunderstood principles of investing and an investor's family history greatly influences his investment behavior and tolerance of risk.

In any event, the ICI study of redemptions contradicts the hypothesis that the investor who foregoes professional advice will behave rationally and commit no more critical errors than the investor guided by a professional advisor. In fact, no-load full redeemers are *twice* as likely to sell their fund shares within two years of purchase as those who take advantage of financial advice (during the time-frame studied). They violated the first rule of investors in mutual funds, and in particular equity funds: *give them a chance to work*. Give the long-term uptrend time to do its inevitable work. "The more you chase the 'holy grail' of short-term performance, the less you achieve in long-term results," says Walter Cabot, president of the Harvard Management Company. (Review Table 12.1: A History Lesson: Sharp Corrections Are Normal!)

THE ILLUSION OF PAST PERFORMANCE

One outgrowth of the media's obsession with no-load is its pre-occupation with past performance as the sole requirement for investing success. Preoccupation with "track record" also sets the investor up for failure! Assessing past performance requires an exhaustive amount of intensive research to derive any useful impli-cations from it for today's and tomorrow's markets.

Why? The reliance on past performance encourages the investor's worst instincts. Faced with the formidable job of investing in today's volatile markets, investors will exhibit a deep emotional need to con-clude that two-plus-two-equals-four. Life is rarely like that.

Some authorities express stronger opinions. "Performance fig-ures," according to Dean LeBaron, president of the highly respected U.S. fund firm Batterymarch Financial, "are worthless. They have zero predictive value."

An investor's preoccupation with published track records no-load funds, and the latest management-expense ratios (MERs) will often set up the investor for a fall. Investing is not a one-variable equation. The past returns produced by a fund manager are, of course, impor-tant, but only meaningful if you consider *how* he produced them. You buy a manager when he's in the doghouse. A good manager is aggressive in *bad* markets, where the biggest opportunities exist. How consistent is the manager's performance measured against his specific peer group? How did this manager do in a bear market when measured against his peers?

We are the first to admit that *risk-adjusted* past performance is a key element of past performance. So are Beta and standard deviation. But, before we dare to become "predictive" about all of these past performance numbers, may I state that there has to be much economic and market trend research done for each fund before slotting in the past performance numbers. Do we believe in carefully studying past performance? You bet! Do we make this our sole criterion for predictive returns in the future? You bet we don't!

Track record and past performance can frequently send precisely the wrong message to investors. Every fund manager's style will sometimes go completely out of sync with the market, just when he may have the best record in town.

Selecting the best possible fund for your individual purposes will likely eclipse the amount you pay at the outset or later in the form of commission. I have had clients, usually beginners, refuse this advice and lose out on thousands of dollars of potential gain. Such people expect something for nothing. And, more often than not, they receive *less* than nothing.

Buying a fund with a current or potential sales charge attached to your advisor doesn't guarantee investment success, of course. As Nick Murray has said, in his own inimitable fashion, "We know that the mutual funds an investor buys *have virtually no effect on the long-term investment return*. What does determine his returns and his success is *what the investor does with his mutual funds after he buys them*: the appropriate investment process is a continuum, not a snapshot of depositing your money." Note Murray's emphasis on what the investor does with his mutual funds *after* he buys them.

GOING BACK TO THE BASICS

Guideline #1: Learning to Screw Your Head on Backwards

Instead of looking for the equity mutual fund that will double in value over the next three to four years, *try to find the investment that will go down in value only half as much as the overall market during a decline, preferably because of external market conditions.* How your portfolio performs in a declining market is much more critical to your ultimate success than how it performs in a rising market.

This principle goes against most people's natural impulses, and against every traditional rule of marketing and selling. Your broker or banker would never call you to say, "I have an investment for you that will only go down half as much as the market if we have a sell-off."

That would be to admit that markets do go down as well as up, an admission that some financial advisors are loathe to make — except in comforting retrospect, such as discussing 1929 or October 1987's Black Monday. How can you sell someone on an investment's potential for a smaller loss? Well, the excellent financial advisor does do just that.

Guideline #2: Grasp the Meaning of Risk and Reward

All successful investors must come to grips with risk. Remember, reward always comes with its shadow — measured risk. You can't have one without the other.

Guideline #3: Prudent Investing Can Be Peacefully Dull

As one of my clients said, "But Gordon, isn't your investment style awfully boring?"

I answered, "If making above-average returns most years is boring, if reducing risk is boring, if sleeping peacefully at night is boring (well, most nights), if helping my client reach that goal of a retirement home on the back nine of a golf course, then I'm all for boredom!"

My axiom is that mutual funds offer no crap tables, one-arm bandits or floor shows — casinos do. Investing in the securities markets means investing in quality. (See "Stick to Your Principles" in Chapter 17.)

chapter 16

THE WORLD IN YOUR WALLET: INVESTING GLOBALLY

The emerging markets are greater in number and offer a wider choice. These markets offer the portfolio investor a new frontier.

— Dr. Mark Mobius

HOME TRUTHS

In the nationalistic, insular Canada in which many of us grew up, certain truths were held to be self-evident. One of them was the slogan, "The dollar that goes the farthest is the one that stays at home."

But as the century progressed, we began to be aware that as a nation of investors we had boxed ourselves in. A typical deal in the mid-fifties, say in the petroleum industry, usually saw Canadian investors opting for the funded debt while American carpetbaggers walked off with the equity. This happened by more than design — Canadians preferred to hedge their bets by taking the high road.

The decades since have seen Canadians gradually becoming equity conscious, but here the age-old patriotism has seemed to linger. It hasn't fully dawned on Canadian investors that the successful nations — formerly Britain, then the United States, and latterly Japan and Germany — have been those that have deployed their entrepreneurial capital all over the world. They've been owners, not loaners, primarily.

We are told that Canada is one of the world's best places to store all our hard-earned cash, and that we'll reap the rewards of investing in GICs, government guaranteed CSBs, and guaranteed insurance annuities. The bottom line is that, unlike buying a Mazda or a BMW, investing abroad brings earnings and capital gain home to your Canadian bank account. Your money *does* go further by leaving home. The distinction is important. Offshore investment by Canadians has the same effect as bringing tourists to Canada to spend their fat $1.40 dollars, deutsche marks or yen.

But parking our savings on a national scale in savings accounts and GICs has contributed nothing to our monetary strength abroad. In fact, those savings have historically lost ground against the rising cost of living, early taxation of our income, and the relentless erosion of the Canadian dollar's value against that of the U.S. dollar.

In a 1993 market survey, Canada was considered the best place in the world to invest — *after* Austria, Denmark, Germany, Norway, Singapore, Malaysia, the Netherlands, France, Sweden, the United States and Switzerland. We placed number 18 out of 20 of the world's established markets. The Morgan Stanley World Index demonstrated that over a 25-year period, the TSE 300 appreciated an average of 10.2% annually. It was exceeded by the stock exchanges in Hong Kong (22.1%), Japan (17.5%), Switzerland (14.7%), the U.K. (13.9%), France (13.3%), Germany (13.1%), and the U.S. (12.4%). (Review Figure 8.5: Morgan Stanley World Index.)

Apart from quality markets in terms of investor attractiveness, there is the matter of volume. According to Morgan Stanley, while Canada represented about 5.2% of the world's securities market trading in 1970, this has shrunk to less than 3% today.

The tired truth must be stated here, that despite reductions in deficits, our national debt still needs to be dealt with. Governments, provincial as well as federal, have to make a real effort, more than political posturing.

We're not out of the woods yet, despite our government's determination to destroy the average hard-working Canadians' retirement dreams by taxing us literally to death. Successful Canadians are being punished for succeeding. Our deficit may be coming down, but our taxes are soaring; for example, a top marginal tax bracket of over 54% (federal and provincial); a complete loss of all "guaranteed" government pension income to thousands of our citizens thanks to the massive "clawback" provisions and "combined" household income "fat tax." We have watched our international credit standing deteriorate and witnessed the steady decline of the Loonie against the U.S. dollar and other currencies.

During the Meech Lake Accord, Stephen Jarislowsky, one of Canada's top pension fund managers, said that the inevitable result of a failure to reduce deficits and debt could be to "make cash, real estate, annuities, bonds . . . worthless in relatively little time."

He referred to the necessity of recognizing Canadian economic realities that, "pushed into the background by useless debates, are becoming only too real." Then he predicted a 40% chance of a run on the Canadian dollar that could drop it below 68 cents U.S. The "prophecy" nearly came true in the summer of 1993 when the Canadian dollar dipped briefly to 69 cents.

The deficit situation has improved substantially since that statement was made, brought about by a more buoyant Canadian economy, the Bank of Canada's containment of inflation, and an improved world situation. It is *not* because of any substantial improvement in our government's attack on the deficit and debt situation through reduced spending! It is the "tax to the max" program of our citizens; a hammer blow against the average hard-working taxpayer and senior citizens. The chickens, while they have not yet come home to roost, will still be shuffling nervously toward the henhouse for some time in the future. Over-taxing our citizens to achieve deficit reduction is wrong.

On the positive side, every day, we Canadians, investors or not, are becoming more keenly aware of the global society around us. We see how interdependent we are on the mushrooming technology and entrepreneurship of other countries. We drive German and Japanese cars, listen to and watch stereos, radios and television sets from Taiwan and Korea, wear sneakers, blouses and shirts with labels from Thailand and Brazil and China. Almost all the advanced technology we use, from communications and information systems to the cars in our driveways, comes from outside our country.

The only real recourse for Canadian investors is to invest globally for greater returns, a wider range of opportunity, and — bottom line — making our investment dollars go further abroad while paradoxically staying at home with us individually.

We have seen how, over the past 25 years, market indexes in Europe, Australia and the Far East have shown much better returns than those within Canada. The added strategy of having a good portion of your assets in foreign-currency denominated securities can protect your money and RRSPs and RRIFs. This strategy qualifies under the Canadian Property Rule established by the federal government for registered plans. You can now invest up to 100% of your RRSP/RRIF in securities worldwide, specifically through the use of derivative mutual funds in both fixed-income and equity categories.

Now you can deploy your investment funds in such ways as to assure yourself of strong international growth in bonds, equities and guaranteed cash equivalents. Geographical diversification is simply good sense. Whether in real estate, mutual funds, stocks, bonds, collectibles or art, any prudent investor will imitate your grandmother's habit of not putting all her eggs in one basket.

As discussed in the context of international risk ("Problem #6" in Chapter 10), investing worldwide reduces risk to your entire portfolio. On any given day or in the short term, many of the world's securities markets move in the same direction or sympathetically. This correlation appears highest over a short term. Over a longer period — say, three to five years — these markets move in greater non-correlation to one another. This is what investors crave — inefficiencies in markets. This is the stuff of opportunity. Less risk — more profit.

WORLDS OF OPPORTUNITY

Today, there are more than 50 stock markets worldwide, and many of the world's best, and often largest, companies are based outside the U.S. and Canada, such as Volvo, Bayer, Siemens, and the Japanese railroads. By investing solely in North American securities markets, the contemporary investor excludes:

- all 10 of the world's largest banks
- all 10 of the world's largest construction and housing companies
- 8 of the 10 world's largest engineering companies
- 8 of the 10 world's largest chemical companies, and
- 7 of the 10 largest automotive companies.*

Also, if you choose to invest only in Canada, you invite higher levels of risk.

The choice available to investors in foreign mutual funds has exploded into several categories. *Single-country* funds invest in companies within a single nation, such as Germany, Japan, Korea, China, Mexico, India and, recently, Russia. Such a fund, taken singly, can be quite risky — at least as risky as the economy it buys into.

Regional funds invest within a major region, such as in Europe, the Americas, Asia, the Pacific Rim or Latin America.

International funds typically invest anywhere outside Canada. Most hold positions in a wide assortment of countries. *Global funds*, on the other hand, may invest both in Canada and abroad. A typical global portfolio commits more than half of its assets to non-Canadian markets. The capability of moving more heavily into Canadian stocks is what gives these funds their potential edge over the international variety. This distinction is lost on most investors.

Some foreign portfolios specialize even further. They might focus on small international stocks or those in a specific sector —

---

* I am indebted to Randall-Helms International, Inc. for quantifying these modern facts of life.

health sciences, telecommunications, financial services, resources or technology.

The Japanese stock market offers a good long-term example of the benefits and risks of investing in a single nation. Japanese companies now represent nearly one-quarter of the world's stock market value, second only to those of the U.S. Japan has more than 2,500 publicly traded companies and eight stock exchanges.

Anyone who bought shares in Japan Fund after it went public in 1962 and held that position was richly rewarded. From that point through 1989, the compound annual return of the Japanese market was 22.4%, compared to 9.3% for U.S. stocks.

The Japanese market has been highly volatile. The Nikkei Index of stocks, representing the Tokyo Stock Exchange equivalent of the Dow Jones Industrial Index, gained 29% in 1989, hitting an all-time high of 38,916 on the last trading day of that year. Then the index headed into a prolonged decline. By the summer of 1992, the Nikkei had fallen more than 60% below its record high of three years earlier. It corrected modestly to about 20,000 by the end of 1996.

In August 1992, after its six-year low of 14,309 (63% below its December 1989 peak), the Nikkei reacted favorably when the Japanese government announced plans to bolster the sagging economy. Within several weeks, the market had regained more than 25% on this news. In spite of all the problems in Japan, we mustn't forget that in 1994 it was the only stock market in the world to merit investment. It posted about a 23% gain. How's that for a non-correlation?

Wide, unpredictable fluctuations of different markets, even a major market such as Japan's, emphasize why you should avoid concentrating a stock portfolio within any single country. Diversify, diversify, diversify.

International small-cap funds can be included as an attractive small-asset allocation (say, 15%) within your portfolio. Smaller companies, whether in Canada, the U.S., or elsewhere, often have above-average growth potential. Correspondingly greater roller-coaster potential? Perhaps. But since *international small-caps* rarely move in sync with those here at home, you add another layer of diversification within the same asset class to your portfolio.

A CENTURY OF CHANGE

Sir John Templeton, the first and leading global investor in stocks, was born into a poor family in Tennessee in 1912, when the uniform unskilled wage was 10 cents an hour. Today, the average North American factory worker earns more than a hundred times that. Here is Sir John, on record.

> In my lifetime, real consumption per person worldwide — that is, the standard of living in real goods — has more than quadrupled. It's the first time in history that such a quadrupling has occurred in the span of a single person's lifetime. Also, in my lifetime, to choose but one significant detail, the number of miles of paved highway in North America has increased over a hundred times. So has the number of people who own automobiles.
>
> In 1912, North America had no color film, refrigerators, radios, transcontinental telephones, traffic lights, talking movies, plastics, nor man-made fibers. Even after the great boom culminating in the Crash of 1929, there were still no airlines, Xerox, fax machines, sports broadcasts, antibiotics, herbicides, nylon, no frozen foods, no TV, no transistors, no lasers, no computers, no nuclear energy, no man-made satellites in space.
>
> The people of the world now benefit from using more than a hundred times as much electricity than they did a century ago. Through scientific development, enormous improvements have been made in the quality of vegetables and crops and also in the quantity produced on each acre of farm land.
>
> Indeed, 50% of all discoveries in natural science have been made in this century. In North America alone, more than $160 billion was dedicated to research and development in a single year. That is more in one year than in the total expended on scientific research in all the world's history before my lifetime.

There is a huge multiplier effect in human opportunity and human consumption. With life expectancy doubled over the past two centuries, so will the consumption of goods and services increase. Stock markets representing those goods and services can only rise over time. Increases in gross national product will be reflected in higher sales volumes, higher profits and dividends, and usually higher share prices.

The previous bull market that peaked in October 1987 saw the price of stocks triple. Its successor, in the midst of which we find ourselves in late 1997, has been even more extensive.

There are, of course, specific risks inherent in offshore investment, particular to each country involved. These must be examined carefully and balanced against their unusual potential rewards. A competent financial advisor can acquaint you with these areas of risk, to enable you to make the right decisions. When you invest in reliable foreign mutual funds, your fund manager has already taken those risk factors into account.

EMERGING ECONOMIES

Part of the value of offshore investment stems from the fact that emerging economies are likely to expand more rapidly than those of North America, simply because they are at the stage, in many cases, that we were 50 years ago. If we look at North America in the 1940s, we can imagine a road map for the growth of these emerging growth nations. And if we say that the standard of living worldwide will quadruple in the next 40 years, we can only guess at the multiple that will apply to the emerging nations. (See Figure 16.1: Emerging Markets Life Cycle and Figure 16.2: Telephone Lines.)

Investing offshore can mean one of the best means of maximizing such an opportunity, while reducing risk. And mutual funds represent the best means of doing so.

FIGURE 16.1: EMERGING MARKETS LIFE CYCLE

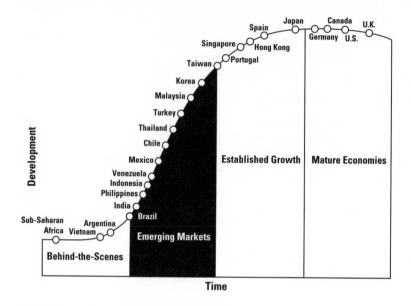

FIGURE 16.2: TELEPHONE LINES

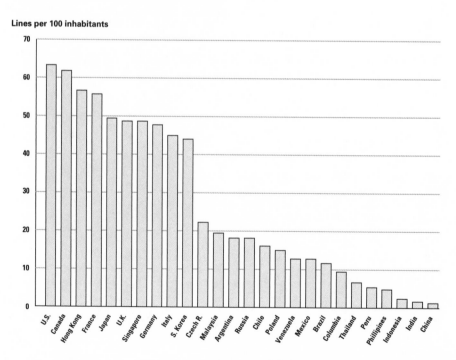

Source: Global Evaluation and Statistical Review

MEASURING INVESTMENT VALUE

What if it were possible to construct a graph or a computer screen displaying every conceivable investment you could imagine, and which would also show you at a glance the strengths, weaknesses and mediocrities of each? Or, what if such a matrix could be constructed so you could evaluate and compare each of about 30 to 40 categories and types of mutual funds?

It is possible to lay out such a matrix. First, however, review Figure 9.2, the simple risk/reward chart depicting numerous fund types in ascending risk order.

The matrix presented in Table 16.1 depicts various broad asset classes on the left-hand vertical axis, with the headings across the top representing the important investment criteria. This enables you to determine at a glance that government bonds for example, provide literally zero risk, moderate monitoring time, and 100% liquidity, while real estate represents moderate risk, moderate monitoring time, and a liquidity factor on average of, perhaps, 10%.

Table 16.2 is similar to Table 16.1, except that it sets the asset classes off against a range of risk/reward, rather than other investment criteria. You can tell at a glance, for example, that government bonds are low in risk and medium low in reward, whereas mutual funds are medium low in risk and medium high in reward.

Table 16.3 lists the various types of mutual funds on the left hand vertical axis and ticks them off according to the various investment criteria we have already discussed. This is possibly the most useful of these matrixes for the mutual fund investor, since these values are often hinted at or alluded to, but rarely depicted graphically. The mutual fund investor, for example, can determine that a dividend fund, while moderate in risk and good in inflation protection, can also provide a high after-tax income feature for investors in a certain tax bracket. These relative values, it should be pointed out, are to a degree arbitrary and based on my personal experience and judgment.

TABLE 16.1: MATRIX OF ASSET CLASSES/INVESTMENT CRITERIA

ASSET CLASSES	CRITERIA VOLATILITY	RISK	CAPITAL GAIN/INCOME	LIQUIDITY	INFLATION PROOF
CASH	0	0	0	100%	0
T-BILLS	Slight	0	Slight	100%	0
GOVERNMENT BONDS	5%–20%	0	10%–15%	100%	0
CORPORATE BONDS	10%–20%	Slight	10%–20%	100%	0
PREFERRED STOCKS	25%	Moderate	5%–15%	100%	0
COMMON STOCKS	25%+	Moderate	5%–25%	100%	Moderate
ANTIQUES	10%–25%	Moderate	10%–40%	50%	Good
REAL ESTATE	20%+	Moderate	5%–25%	Varied	Good
FOREIGN SECURITIES	15%+	Moderate	5%–25%	100%	Moderate/Good
EQUITY MUTUAL FUNDS	25%	Moderate	5%–25%	100%	Excellent
GOLD & COMMODITIES	0%–500%	Very High	0%–250%	75%–100%	0

Source: Author's interpretation of Ronald W Adly, The Investment Evaluation.

TABLE 16.2: ASSET CLASSES: COMPARATIVE RISK/REWARD

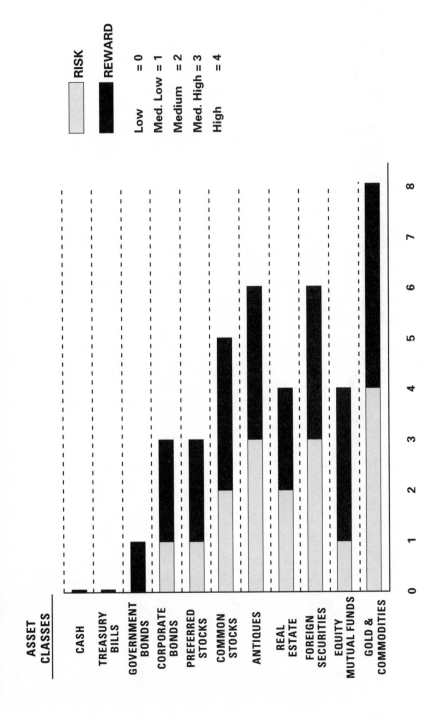

TABLE 16.3: MATRIX OF MUTUAL FUND TYPES/INVESTMENT CRITERIA

CRITERIA FUND TYPES	VOLATILITY	RISK	CAPITAL GAIN/ INCOME	LIQUIDITY	INFLATION PROOF
T-BILL/ MONEY MARKET	0	0	Low	100%	0
GOVERNMENT BOND	Low	0	Medium	100%	Low
FIXED INCOME	Medium	Moderate	Moderate	100%	Low
BALANCED FUND	Low	Moderate	Good	100%	Moderate
DIVIDEND FUND	Low	Moderate	Good	100%	Good
GROWTH FUND	Moderate	Moderate	High	100%	High
INTERNATIONAL BOND	Medium-High	High	High	100%	Variable
INTERNATIONAL GROWTH	High	High	High	100%	High

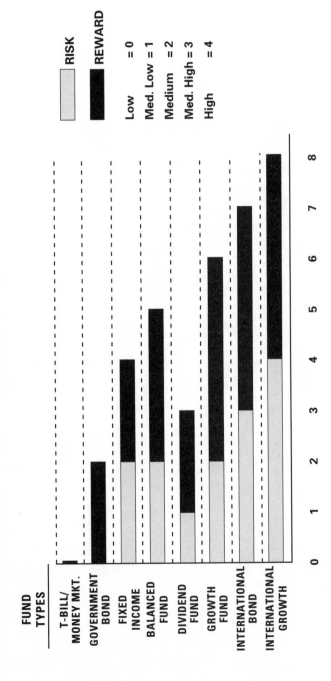

TABLE 16.4: MUTUAL FUND TYPES: COMPARATIVE RISK/REWARD

FUND
TYPES

T-BILL/
MONEY MKT.

GOVERNMENT
BOND

FIXED
INCOME

BALANCED
FUND

DIVIDEND
FUND

GROWTH
FUND

INTERNATIONAL
BOND

INTERNATIONAL
GROWTH

RISK

REWARD

Low   = 0
Med. Low = 1
Medium   = 2
Med. High = 3
High   = 4

Source: By the author.

Table 16.4 shows the same basic mutual fund types in the vertical axis, here matching them against very general comparative levels of risk and reward rather than other investment criteria. This table demonstrates in particular the relative slings and arrows that await you as a prospective investor in each type of mutual fund, as well the most notable attractions of each.

By necessity, this discussion must be limited to a brief overview. Effort has been made to remove some of the confusion and complexity over investment asset classes and mutual fund types, and to highlight in simple terms their relative attraction to a wide variety of investors. Construction of this group of tables has been simplified to make rough comparisons only. The main point is that you must focus on specific objectives as an investor. Also, numerous other categories have been omitted; for example, dividend funds can be common share dividends or highest quality preferred share dividends. Real estate funds are not mentioned, nor are asset allocation or mortgage funds.

RISK-ADJUSTED RETURNS

In the investment industry's ongoing pursuit of performance, we require another very important qualifier related to our matrix of risk/reward (Figure 16.4). That is the relatively recent study of risk-adjusted returns, or the measurement of risk *relative* to performance. That is, what is the cost of performance in a given fund in terms of the risk taken to achieve it? This system takes raw percentage returns and adjusts them by a factor related to a given norm.

One of the generators of such a system, Byron Wien, chief U.S. stock strategist at Morgan Stanley & Company, recently told the *Wall Street Journal*, "now absolute performance is king, and we think that's wrong."

This milestone of past performance risk/reward measurement, the *risk-adjusted measure,* was pioneered by Franco Modigliani, Nobel prize laureate and professor emeritus at Massachusetts Institute of

Technology, and others. It tells investors whether the performance they achieve in a mutual fund is worth the price. That is, it adds a qualitative dimension to the quantitative measure of performance. For example, the accompanying table produced by Morgan Stanley depicts the 10-year average returns (raw percentage) of each of seven mutual funds, ranging from 19.2% down to 12.2%. After applying the risk-adjustment factor (the volatility adjusted to the benchmark Standard & Poor's 500 Index), the ranking of the seven funds was greatly altered. For example, the top fund, AIM Constellation, with a raw yield of 19.2%, sank to fourth place with 14.5% once the risk-adjusted factor was taken into account. (See Table 16.5: The Mutual Fund "Risk" Question.) The system introduces a useful qualification to the simple measurement of performance.

Closer to home, compare the relative positions of the top 10 Canadian equity funds before and after a risk-adjusted factor. (See Table 16.6: Top Canadian Equity Funds.)

TABLE 16.5: THE MUTUAL FUND "RISK" QUESTION

Selected funds ranked and reranked adjusting for risk

ANK	FUND (Morningstar Rating[1,2])	10-YR. AVG. RETURN	RISK-ADJUSTED RETURN	RISK-ADJUSTED RETURN
1	AIM Constellation (*****)	19.2%	14.5%	4
2	T. Rowe Price New Horizons (****)	16.3	13.4	6
3	Fidelity Magellan (****)	16.2	14.9	3
4	20th Century Vista Investors (**)	15.2	11.9	7
5	Vanguard Windsor (***)	14.0	13.8	5
6	Fidelity Puritan (****)	12.5	15.7	2
7	Income Fund of America (****)	12.2	16.9	1
	Standard & Poor's 500 Stock Index	**15.2**		

According to 10-year return.

Morningstar's risk-adjusted rating ranks funds from one to five stars, five being the best, one the worst.

Source: Morgan Stanley Equity Research, Morningstar, Wall Street Journal

TABLE 16.6: TOP CANADIAN EQUITY FUNDS

TOP 10	3-YEAR ANNUAL COMPOUND RETURN	TOP 10	RISK-ADJUSTED 3-YEAR RETURN
AIC Advantage Fund	23.7%	Ivy Canadian Fund	4.68
Navigator Value Investment Retirement	22.2	Cundill Security Fund	4.6
Phillips, Hager & North Vintage Fund	19.2	Optima Canadian Equity Fund	3.93
Tradex Equity Fund	17.4	AIC Advantage Fund	3.86
Optima Canadian Equity Fund	17	Phillips, Hager & North Vintage Fund	3.83
Equitable Life Segregated Common Stock	16.9	Navigator Value Investment Retirement	3.78
Scotia Excelsior Canadian Growth	16.8	Equitable Life Seg Common Stock	3.4
McLean Budden Pooled Canadian	16.7	Tradex Equity Fund Ltd.	3.34
AltaFund Investment Corp.	16.1	Standard Life Ideal Equity Fund	3.32
Phillips, Hager & North Pooled Pension Trust	15.7	Bisset Canadian Equity Fund	3.22

Source: BellCharts Inc.

STAR WARS: ADJUSTED PERFORMANCE AND CONSISTENCY

Seemingly, every book, periodical and mutual fund research publication is currently engaged in its own entry into the "star wars" contest in recommending which funds beleaguered investors should choose.

There is much to commend this starry-eyed research, and many investors from economics professors and chartered financial analysts to the general public accept such a quick-fix mentality. A glance at the latest Top 10 funds is seen as enough to complete a portfolio. Instant gratification can be achieved in ten minutes. Is a five-star fund necessarily the best (or even among the best)?

The best public research on mutual fund performance records is undoubtedly provided by Morningstar Inc.'s Mutual Funds rating service in the U.S. You might well ask: "Gordon, why are you citing this organization when it doesn't survey any Canadian-registered funds?" My answer is simple: Canadian investors need the best possible research advice they can obtain. I want you, as an investor, to appreciate fully how complex and difficult successful investing is. And as *Stenner on Mutual Funds* goes to press there are several excellent and relatively new Canadian research groups springing up across the landscape which, while not yet of the quality of Morningstar, are on the right track toward carefully refining newer methods to assist Canadian mutual fund investors in understanding what they're buying and why.

Let's look at Morningstar. Like other rating organizations, it employs an investment style matrix that applies *two* ratings within each of nine "boxes" of a matrix. (See Tables 16.7 and 16.7A.)The first rating is that of *risk*, expressed relative to that of the average fund in its category (peer group). The average risk score for the category is set equal to a factor of 1.00. For example, a risk score of 1.35 for a specific fund means that the fund has been 35% riskier than the average fund within its category for a measured period.

TABLES 16.7 AND 16.7A: INVESTMENT STYLE MATRIXES

EQUITY STYLE BOX

Risk		Investment Style		Median Market Capitalization
	VALUE	BLEND	GROWTH	
LOW ○	Large-Cap Value	Large-Cap Blend	Large-Cap Growth	LARGE
MODERATE ○	Mid-Cap Value	Mid-Cap Blend	Mid-Cap Growth	MEDIUM
HIGH ○	Small-Cap Value	Small-Cap Blend	Small-Cap Growth	SMALL

Within the equity style box grid, nine possible combinations exist, ranging from large-cap value for the safest funds to small-cap growth for the riskiest.

FIXED-INCOME STYLE BOX

Risk		Maturity		Quality
	SHORT	INTERMEDIATE	LONG	
LOW ○	Short-term High Quality	Intermediate-term High Quality	Long-term High Quality	HIGH
MODERATE ○	Short-term Medium Quality	Intermediate-term Medium Quality	Long-term Medium Quality	MEDIUM
HIGH ○	Short-term Low Quality	Intermediate-term Low Quality	Long-term Low Quality	LOW

Within the fixed-income style box grid, nine possible combinations exist, ranging from short maturity–high quality for the safest funds to long maturity–low quality for the riskiest.

Sorce: Morningstar Inc.

The other major component in the star ratings, the *return* figure, measures a fund's performance compared with the average of other funds in its investment category. After adjusting for any maximum sales loads or fees, Morningstar calculates and rates the excess return for each fund, typically against the 90-day Treasury Bill return benchmark.

To determine a particular fund's star rating for a given period, the fund's *risk* score is subtracted from its *return* score. The resulting number is then plotted along a bell curve to determine the fund's rating for each time period. If the fund scores in the top 10% of its broad investment category, it receives five stars (highest). If it checks in within the next 22.5%, it receives four stars (above average). A place in the middle 35% receives three stars (average), and within the next lowest 22.5% two stars (below average). The bottom 10% are awarded one star. The star ratings are recalculated monthly.

In my opinion, the greatest shortcoming of the star ratings, particularly that of the five-star rating, is that investors tend always to buy anything that is five-star because they believe it's unequivocally the best and will do as well for them in the future.

"Morningstar's analysis of funds and statistics is impressive and it deserves kudos," argues Mark Hulbert, astute editor of *The Hulbert Financial Digest*, which tracks American money letters. "The five-star ranking system has changed over the years, and now Morningstar says it is simply historical about how funds have done on a risk-adjusted basis, and is *not* prospective."

But let's get it from the horse's mouth: "The five-star rating is a double-edged sword," says Joe Mansueto, Morningstar founder and chairman. "It's a valid way of evaluating funds on a risk-adjusted methodology to find those that have achieved the best returns for a given level of risk. It ferrets out all-weather funds that have done consistently well. But it gets abused when people think of it as the be-all and end-all. Consider it a nice entry point to a whole host of items to look at, but definitely not the end point."

Why do I dwell on the discussion of an American rating system? Because, for all of its shortcomings, it remains superior to anything in Canada. And this type of data can be extremely useful in the hands of a professional investment advisor who can use this information as a framework within which to place the current methods of research. A five-star rated fund, for a number of reasons, might be rejected in the face of new, more timely information. Or, such information could confirm other pertinent data and point toward a buy or sell. At most, the star rating deals with *past performance only* and even that is measured by certain biases that are sometimes quite controversial and built into the risk-reward score.

"We're a five-star fund" is one of the proudest statements that a U.S. portfolio manager ever makes, meaning that the fund has received that Morningstar rating. You'll see this claim in many advertisements by U.S. fund companies. Does a five-star rating really mean anything? Well, yes and no. But in any event, this kind of advertising has been seeping into Canadian mutual fund advertising, research, and best-selling mutual fund books, driving the popularity of five-star-rated funds.

This "star war" in Canada is becoming big business. Used professionally, it can provide extremely useful information in aiding an investor to choose specific mutual funds. Used by a novice and interpreted as some sort of accolade, it can be misleading and dangerous to that investor's financial health.

For anyone relying heavily on any Canadian or American five-star or "$5" past performance yardstick to predict future performance, I must draw your attention to a January 1997 column in the *Wall Street Journal's* "Smart Money" magazine, entitled "Which Morningstar Rating Is For Real?", by Walecia Konrad.

"The idea," said Konrad, "was to stop using nebulous fund categories such as 'equity income' or 'growth and income,' which have long been a part of the mutual fund lexicon but don't really tell you very much about how a fund operates."

So, Morningstar recently began organizing funds based on their investment style (value, growth or a blend grouping) and the size of funds they favor (large, medium or small). Now you've ended up with some formerly classified "growth" funds becoming "mid-cap blend" funds, and aggressive-growth funds being reclassified to "large-cap growth."

That's reasonable enough. I would say "It's about time!" But here's where it starts to get tricky. In addition to its new manager style category of rating, Morningstar will continue to use its famous "five-star rating system" for funds, which is based not on these new, more accurate smaller categories, but on how these funds perform against much larger, broader groups.

The result: a small-cap value fund may get a five-star ranking for beating its peers (which is really what counts), but only two or three stars because small-cap value funds may have been among the worst funds overall. No doubt fund marketers will pick whichever ranking makes them better, leaving investors to wonder which data is reliable.

Steve Savage, head of Value Line, Morningstar's arch-rival in the fund-rating wars, complains, "If a manager chooses a style that performs *poorly*, he'll be rewarded, since all the other managers who have chosen better-performing assets are removed from the rankings."

The biggest losers seem to be "balanced" or "hybrid" funds, which typically contain a mix of bonds and stocks. Morningstar used to have a five-star rating for this separate category; now they're lumping all balanced funds into either equity or bond categories. This seems to be a little unorthodox, if not vexatious and misleading.

The message? When selecting any mutual fund as a candidate for your portfolio, make sure you don't rely too heavily upon any past performance chart. Past performance ratings can often give you invaluable information. But you must be clear as to the *interpretation* of that data and how the ratings people are biased.

And it's another strong reason for selecting a financial advisor who *specializes* in mutual fund portfolio construction and who has a solid grasp of capital markets and their intricacies.

FIGURE 16.3: TYPICAL MORNINGSTAR STYLE MATRIX

Fidelity Large-Cap Stock

	Ticker	Load	Yield	SEC Yield
	FLCSX	None	0.4%	—

Mstar Category
Large Growth

Investment Style
Equity
Average Stock %

Prospectus Objective: Growth
Fidelity Large-Cap Stock Fund seeks long-term growth of capital.

The fund normally invests at least 65% of assets in equity securities of companies with market capitalizations of $1 billion or more. It may, however, invest the balance in companies with smaller market capitalizations. Investments may include common and prefened stocks, convertible securities, and warrants. The fund may also invest in securities of foreign issuers.

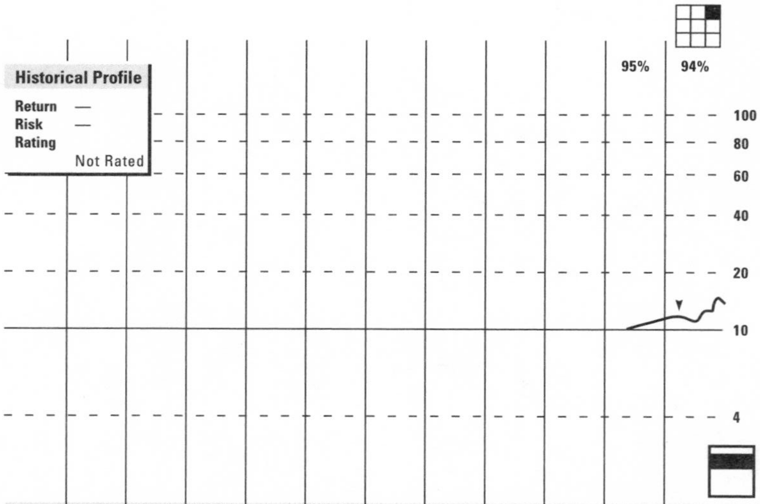

Historical Profile
Return —
Risk —
Rating Not Rated

Growth of $10,000
III Investment Value $000 of Fund
— Investment Value $000 S&P 500

▷ Manager Change
▷ Partial Manager Change
▲ Mgr Unknown After
▼ Mgr Unknown Before

Fund Manager(s)
Thomas Sprague. Since 04-96. BS, Cornell U. 1979. MBA, Wharton 1989.

Manager's Investment Style
New manager Sprague looks for big companies with good prospects for high earnings growth selling at low P/Es for their growth rates. Sprague is willing to overweight certain sectors.

Performance Quartile
(within category)

History	1985	1986	1987	1988	1989	1990	1991	1992	1993	1994	1995	1996
NAV	—	—	—	—	—	—	—	—	—	—	11.05	12.51
Total Return %	—	—	—	—	—	—	—	—	—	—	10.80*	21.55
+/- S&P 500	—	—	—	—	—	—	—	—	—	—	-2.54*	-1.40
+/- Wilshire LG	—	—	—	—	—	—	—	—	—	—	—	-5.40
Income Return %	—	—	—	—	—	—	—	—	—	—	0.30	0.42
Capital Return %	—	—	—	—	—	—	—	—	—	—	10.50	21.13
Total Rtn % Rank Cat	—	—	—	—	—	—	—	—	—	—	—	36
Income $	—	—	—	—	—	—	—	—	—	—	0.03	0.05
Capital Gains $	—	—	—	—	—	—	—	—	—	—	0.00	0.80
Expense Ratio %	—	—	—	—	—	—	—	—	—	—	—	1.30
Income Ratio %	—	—	—	—	—	—	—	—	—	—	—	0.70
Turnover Rate %	—	—	—	—	—	—	—	—	—	—	—	—
Net Assets $mil	—	—	—	—	—	—	—	—	—	—	78.8	111.7

Performance 12-31-96

	1st qtr	2nd qtr	3rd qtr	4th qtr	Total
1989	—	—	—	—	—
1990	—	—	—	—	—
1991	—	—	—	—	—
1992	—	—	—	—	—
1993	—	—	—	—	—
1994	—	—	—	—	—
1995	—	—	8.61	3.36	10.80*
1996	5.25	3.69	4.64	6.44	21.55

Trailing	Total Return %	+/- S&P 500	+/- Wil Large Grth	% Rank All	Cat	Growth of $10,000
1 Yr	21.55	-1.40	-5.40	14	36	12,155
3 Yr Avg	—	—	—	—	—	—
5 Yr Avg	—	—	—	—	—	—
10 Yr Avg	—	—	—	—	—	—
15 Yr Avg	—	—	—	—	—	—

Tax Analysis

	Tax-Adj Return %	% Pretax Return
3 Yr Avg	—	—
5 Yr Avg	—	—
10 Yr Avg	—	—

Potential Capital Gain Exposure: 6% of assets

Bear Market Performance

	Worst 3 Month Period 1987-91	Worst 3 Month Period 1992-96
Fund	—	—
+/- S&P 500		
+/- Category Avg		

Decile Rank (5-year period) — Worst ... Best

Operations

Address	82 Devonshire Street Boston, MA 02109
Telephone	800-544-8888
Advisor	Fidelity Management & Research
Subadvisor	FMR (U.K.)/FMR (Far East)
Distributor	Fidelity Distributors
States Available	All plus PR
Report Grade	A-
Income Distrib	Semi-annually
NTF Plans	Fidelity

Risk Analysis

Time Period	Load Adj Return %	Risk All	%Rank Cat	Mstar Return	Mstar Score Risk	Morningstar Risk-Adj Rating
1 Yr	21.55	—	—	—	—	—
3 Yr	—	—	—	—	—	—
5 Yr	—	—	—	—	—	—
10 Yr	—	—	—	—	—	—
Average Historical Rating						

*1=low, 100=high

Category Rating (3 Yr)

Other Measures	Standard Index S&P 500	Relative S&P 500
Alpha	—	—
Beta	—	—
R-Squared	—	—
Standard Deviation	—	—
Mean	—	—
Sharpe Ratio	—	—

Return: Not Rated
Risk: Not Rated

Investment Style

SIZE: Large / Med / Small
STYLE: Value / Blend / Growth

Diversification Value for Portfolio Types

Large Cap	Small Cap	Bond	Balanced	Diversified

Minimum Purchase	$2500	Add: $250	IRA: $500
Min Auto Inv Plan	$2500	Systematic Inv: $100	
Date of Inception	06-22-95		

Expenses & Fees

Sales Fees	No-Load		
Management Fee	0.30%/+0.52% min.(G)+(-)/0.20%P	max./0.27%	
Actual Fees	Mgt: 0.62%	Dist: —	
Expense Projections	3Yr: $42	5Yr: $72	10Yr: $158

Total Cost (relative to category) Average

	Stock Portfolio Avg	Relative S&P 500
Price/Earnings Ratio	26.5	1.13
Price/Book Ratio	5.3	1.08
Med Mkt Cap $mil	9,177	
Foreign %	3.4	0.37

Portfolio Analysis 10-31-96

Total Stocks: 152   Total Fixed-Income: 0

Share Chg (04-96) 000	Amount 000		Value $000	% Net Assets
-6	19	IBM	2,415	2.28
-4	22	General Electric	2,166	2.04
6	24	Merck	1,792	1.69
-4	25	Aetna	1,679	1.58
19	27	Adaptec	1,614	1.52
8	24	Cisco Systems	1,483	1.40
2	44	Toys 'R' Us	1,480	1.40
25	30	Sears Roebuck	1,470	1.39
12	24	American Home Products	1,447	1.36
17	10	Intel	1,428	1.35
10	13	Allstate	1,407	1.33
3	25	NationsBank	1,367	1.29
4	15	Columbia/HCA Healthcare	1,343	1.27
18	38	Owens-Illinois	1,334	1.26
0	86	Philip Morris	1,332	1.26
-3	14	FNMA	1,319	1.24
7	34	British Petroleum (ADR)	1,313	1.24
0	10	Ascend Communications	1,294	1.22
20	20	Bank of New York	1,225	1.16
11	37	Linear Technology	1,191	1.12
12	36	American Express	1,110	1.05
-5	24	Bergen Brunswig Cl A	1,098	1.04
35	35	Tyco International	1,075	1.01
0	22	Eastman Kodak	1,074	1.01
7	13	CUC International	1,057	1.00
32	43			

Special Securities

% of assets 10-31-96

Private/Illiquid Securities	0
Emerging-Markets Secs	0
Options/Futures/Warrants	No

Composition

% of assets 10-31-96

Cash	7.5
Stocks	92.5
Bonds	0.0
Preferreds	0.0
Convertibles	0.0
Other	0.0

Market Cap

Giant	33.2
Large	34.8
Medium	30.3
Small	1.8
Micro	0.0

Sector Weightings

Sector Weightings	% of Stocks	Rel S&P	5-Year High	Low
Utilities	0.0	0.0	—	—
Energy	7.9	0.9	—	—
Financials	11.1	0.7	—	—
Ind Cycls	14.7	0.9	—	—
Cons Dur	3.3	0.8	—	—
Cons Stpls	6.2	0.6	—	—
Services	14.0	1.1	—	—
Retail	11.56	2.2	—	—
Health	15.6	1.5	—	—
Tech	15.8	1.3	—	—

Source: Morningstar 1997 Mutual Fund 500

THE MORNINGSTAR PAGE LEGEND

1. "Analysis" features written analysis of the reasons behind a fund's successes and failures

2. "Historical Profile" shows at a glance how a fund has balanced risk and return.

3. "Portfolio Manager(s)" explains who's responsible for a fund's performance, with profiles that include work experience, education and other funds managed.

4. Performance quartile graph has year-by-year boxes with a dark line showing where the fund ranked.

5. "Risk Analysis" shows how a fund measures up using a variety of measures, including Morningstar risk, Beta, and standard deviation.

6. "Investment Style" box helps you understand a fund's true investment strategy.

7. "Investment Criteria" describes the fund's investment policies and objectives.

8. "Performance" presents five years of quarterly returns. Trailing total returns for as many as seven time periods tells you if a fund leads or lags the pack.

9. "Tax Analysis" gives tax-adjusted returns and potential capital gains exposure.

10. Performance graph indicated growth of $10,000.

11. "History" lets you examine up to 12 years of statistics, including comparisons with market benchmarks, to see if the fund is a proven long-term performer.

12. "Investment Style Historical" boxes tell whether the fund follows a consistent strategy or one that changes with market conditions. You can check where it sat in the style box at the start of each calendar year.

13. "Average Stock Percentage" lets you evaluate what percentage of assets a fund has invested in stocks during each calendar year to discover if its current position is the norm or an aberration.

14. "Portfolio Analysis" reviews a fund's top stock or bond holdings to find out what's driving its performance.

15 "Sector Weightings" shows how assets are divided among 10 sectors.

16 "Special Securities" explains whether a fund can and does own derivatives and other complex illiquid securities.

17. "Operations" list nuts-and-bolts information about the companies that operate and distribute the fund, including general information about fees and services.

NOTE: Your financial advisor can secure *most* of this information for you with Canadian-registered firms.

Source: Morningstar Inc.

DO YOU KNOW BILL SHARPE?
(OR, SHARPENING YOUR PENCIL)

Nobel Prize Laureate William F. Sharpe, inventor of the Sharpe Ratio, a tool for measuring risk and reward, sums up the value of Morningstar's rating system, despite its limitations, as follows: "Before I'd invest in a fund, I would want to have read the Morningstar material."

RISK ADJUSTMENT AND PERFORMANCE CONSISTENCY

The addition of *risk-adjustment* to the raw performance evaluation is dealt with elsewhere, but obviously it adds a second dimension to the evaluation of a given fund relative to its brothers and sisters.

But there is really a third dimension — performance *consistency* over time. Some 12 years ago, through my former organization, Stenner Financial Services Ltd., my senior staff and I developed a comprehensive proprietary Mutual Fund Performance Consistency Survey to aid the investor in just such a selection process. That survey grouped funds into 15 separate categories on a risk/reward scale that identified the objective of each fund and the degree of price fluctuation or risk expected of each, based upon the consistency of historical performance.

It was my perception at that time that the Stenner Performance Consistency Survey was a pioneering effort and, to my knowledge, close to unique in the industry. Since that time, other organizations and individuals have developed similar and more exhaustive systems. Two notable recent Canadian examples, in addition to Morningstar, Value Line and BellCharts, Inc., as already mentioned, are the Midland Walwyn Capital Inc. Proprietary Fund Research system and the FundLine Index devised by Eric Kirzner and Richard Croft in their recent book, *The FundLine Advisor*.

The Stenner Performance Consistency Survey did not attempt to help investors unerringly pick the top performance winners in a given year; rather, it was designed to help attain consistently above-average results, while avoiding unpleasant surprises. Through a screening process, and drawing upon rate-of-return statistics of hundreds of funds meeting high standards of quality and availability, the survey selected the top performance funds from 15 peer groups, which were then arranged on a risk/reward scale from "1" (ultra-conservative money market funds) to "15" (speculative cyclical gold stock funds). Of course, today's universe of mutual funds provides many times the number available at that time.

Consistency was then studied by tracing the selected funds through one-year, three-year, five-year and 10-year periods, constructing up to 121 moving average calculations per fund, noting the consistency of each fund's performance (i.e., within the top quartile for all periods, the top half of the group for all periods, or for various annual periods). Such a risk/reward scale is presented in Table 16:6. Remember, this quarterly study was performed, and the ratings assigned, *in October of 1986*!

BellCharts Inc. produces what is arguably one of the most comprehensive information systems on mutual funds available in Canada. It combines fresh information with more detailed responses from a wide variety of fund managers, prospectuses and other financial publications.

Perhaps arbitrarily, BellCharts divides its "book" into 14 categories within three broad asset classes. So as not to confuse the reader, let me reiterate that throughout this section we refer to the numbers of mutual fund categories variously anywhere from a dozen to 40 or more, sometimes for clarity and simplicity, sometimes to illustrate that many fund types are almost infinitely dividable into sub-species.

Pal-Trak is also an excellent research software package offering some insights and interpretations of fund data not always emphasized in other formats.

The bottom line on mutual fund research in Canada is definitely improving and Canadian investors and advisors are the beneficiaries of this intelligence, even if we do copy the Americans much of the time!

TABLE 16.8: STENNER PERFORMANCE CONSISTENCY SURVEY

Stenner Financial Services Ltd.
"The Navigator" October 1986 edition

RISK/REWARD SCALE

MODERATELY AGGRESSIVE

CANADIAN STOCK FUNDS

		1 Year	3 Years	5 Years	10 Years
	Industrial Growth	11.3	13.7	18.5	20.0
	Industrial Pension	14.2	15.1	19.2	17.7
@	Investors Retirement Mutual	8.0	10.9	10.9	13.4
	London Life Equity	11.5	13.4	14.9	16.1
	MONY Equity	12.6	15.1	20.0	17.7
	Mackenzie Equity	14.7	15.5	16.0	16.8
***	Maritime Life Growth Fund	22.6	18.4	15.6	17.0
	Montreal Trust RSP Equity	15.5	10.2	11.2	14.0
	Mutual Equifund	17.8			
	National Trust RSP Equity	17.4	13.3	13.2	14.9
**	Phillips, Hager & North RSP Fund	22.1	14.6	14.6	15.4
*	Phillips, Hager & North Canadian	21.0	14.0	13.5	18.4
@	Pacific Growth	12.1	5.5	8.5	12.8
	Principal Growth	16.8	12.0	8.6	14.1
	Principal Canadian	19.0			
	Prudential Growth Fund of Canada	15.7	13.2	12.4	14.5
***	Royfund Equity	27.9	21.0	15.9	18.9
@	Royal Trust "C" Fund	6.3	8.5	10.2	13.3
	Templeton Canadian	15.7	9.8		
@	Timvest Growth	12.7	12.8	9.7	13.4
	Trimark Canadian	8.7	15.1	18.0	
*	United Venture Retirement	20.4	15.4	12.3	19.4
***	Universal Savings Equity	17.4	15.9	18.3	18.5
@	United Accumulative Retirement	12.4	10.0	10.8	14.2

ALL ELIGIBLE FOR RRSP

NB:

	1 Year	3 Years	5 Years	10 Years
Highest Return in Group	28.7	21.0	20.0	22.0
First Quartile Break	20.7	16.7	17.1	19.0
Mean Rate of Return	15.5	13.2	13.7	16.6
Third Quartile Break	10.4	9.7	10.2	14.2
Lowest Return in Group	4.7	4.7	4.3	12.8
Number of funds surveyed	45	42	40	38

NB:
**** *Consistent FIRST QUARTILE performance for all periods.*
***Consistently in TOP HALF of performance results for all periods.*
**Consistently in TOP HALF for latest 1, 3 & 5 year results only.*
Performing in TOP HALF for 1 & 3 years only.
@*Consistent BELOW AVERAGE results relative to peer group.*

Figures represent compound annual rates of return with all income and capital gains dividends, if any, reinvested in additional shares/units. All rates of return are for cumulative periods ending September 30/86.

Source: Stenner Financial Services Ltd.

BellCharts summarizes its fund classes and categories as follows:

Balanced
• Canadian
• International

Bond
• Canadian
• Short term and mortgage
• U.S. and international

Equity
• Canadian
• Canadian dividend
• Canadian small- to mid-cap
• Emerging markets and Latin American
• European
• Far East
• Global
• Specialty
• U.S. and North American

By using BellChart's Floating Bar Charts (see Figure 16.5), an investor can compare at a glance the past performance of a particular mutual fund with the performance of all other (peer group) funds with similar objectives. Each *floating bar* represents the returns of 90% of the funds in that category for the particular time period. Five percent of the funds in the category had superior performance; 5% had performance below the bar. "*X*" marks the performance of the fund being compared to the rest. The square is the performance of the benchmark. The *median* fund is shown by a line extending from the bar. All funds included are ranked in performance in *four equal quartiles*.

BellCharts also divides its commentary on fund performance into some nine different management styles, most of which at one time or another are combined in some fashion by most fund managers.

Those broad investment styles are: Value, Growth, Sector, Blend, Top-down, Bottom-up, Combination, Interest Rate Anticipation, and Spread-Trading.

Midland Walwyn's proprietary "Fund Research" document is an excellent quarterly review of hand-picked fund recommendations covering about a dozen fund categories. It is produced by a staff headed by Peter Loach and Scott Barlow. The top 15% of holdings of each fund are listed, as well as industry sector allocations, the percentage of stocks, bonds, cash and/or other securities, key statistical information including Alpha, Beta, Sharpe Ratio, R-squared, mean, standard deviation and skewness. Quartile performance is charted for up to 10 years with a snapshot of items such as the relevant index comparison with each fund catalogued, recent 12-month income and capital gain distributions in dollar and percentage returns. Worst month and 12-month figures illustrate downside risk. Midland Walwyn's "Fundmate"™ indicates a correlated substitute for each buy recommendation, and a further "complement" choice is suggested. There is a manager's style box, as well as a comparative management-expense ratio cost per $100. Brief background commentary accompanies each fund reviewed, with each fund's policy statement.

Gordon Pape's *Buyer's Guide* substitutes dollar signs ($) in place of stars, with a similar purpose.

The FundLine devised by Richard Croft and Eric Kirzner starts with the assumption of the need for diversification and attempts to quantify an expected rate of return for a given level of risk, the ideal of course being a lower-risk portfolio generating above-average returns. While stated differently, it arrives at substantially the same conclusion as my Performance Consistency Survey did some years ago.

It is suggested that the average investor be aware of these evaluation systems, just as my risk/reward matrices earlier in Chapter 16 may be highly useful. But for detailed application, as in any other self-administered evaluation, it's recommended that you consult your financial advisor.

FIGURE 16.4: BELLCHARTS, INC. SAMPLE PAGE

20/20 DIVIDEND FUND

INVESTMENT PROFILE

INVESTMENT OBJECTIVE

To provide superior returns with reasonable risk in a combination of Canadian dividend income, capital appreciation and interest income through investment in common and convertible preferred shares.

PORTFOLIO MANAGEMENT

Fund Sponsor: 20/20 Funds Inc., founded in 1985, is in the business of providing investment fund products and services in Canada. It has 20 funds, $2.6 billion in assets under management, and 171 employees. Its name was changed from 20/20 Group Financial in March 1995.

Investment advisor: Connor, Clark & Lunn is a Vancouver-based money management firm specializing in the management of pension funds and mutual fund portfolios and currently manages more than $7.8 billion of assets. The company has been in operation since 1982 and among its clients are Chrysler Canada Ltd., The Molson Companies Ltd., McDonald's Restaurants of Canada Ltd. and Petro Canada Ltd.

Portfolio manager: Gordon McDougall (Connor, Clark & Lunn) is the president and director. He holds an MBA from the University of Pittsburgh, a B.Comm from Sir George Williams University and a CFA from the University of Virginia. He has 26 years experience in the investment industry and has been associated with 20/20 for 10 years.

EQUITY – CANADIAN DIVIDEND

PERFORMANCE

RATING

Performance: ★★★★
Volatility: AV+
Std. deviation: 2.51
MER: 2.00

LEGEND
Fund X
Benchmark □
Median —

ANNUAL PERFORMANCE

	1986	1987	1988	1989	1990	1991	1992	1993	1994	1995
Annual return	10.1	1.8	13.9	17.8	-5.1	15.1	1.0	26.3	.4	16.3
TSE 300 Total return	8.9	5.9	11.1	21.4	-14.8	12.0	-1.4	32.6	-0.2	14.5
Quartile	1	2	1	2	3	2	3	1	1	1
Annual rank	2	7	3	2	11	8	11	5	5	5
Funds in group	11	13	15	15	16	16	17	21	22	35
Compound return	9.4	9.3	10.2	9.7	8.4	11.4	10.5	13.8	8.1	16.3
Compound rank	1	3	1	2	3	2	3	4	4	5
Assets ($M)	.000	10.7	9.0	8.7	13.6	24.6	29.2	41.5	50.7	132.0
Capital gains	.000	.000	.000	.000	.000	.000	.000	.000	.000	.000
Income	.632	1.600	.441	.403	.661	.387	.320	.198	.193	.335

Chart scale: 30, 20, 10, 0, -10

INVESTMENT STYLE

VALUE	BLEND	GROWTH	SECTOR
BOTTOM UP		TOP DOWN	

PORTFOLIO BIASES

	EXPECTED VOLATILITY
Small cap ☐☐☐	Generally > than the market
Mid cap ☐☐☐	Generally = to the market
Large cap ☐X☐	Generally < than the market ☐☐X
Industry sector	
Environment	EXPECTED TURNOVER
Ethical	Less than 30%
Index	30% to 100% X☐☐
	More than 100%

PORTFOLIO CHARACTERISTICS

The fund invests primarily in common stocks with high dividend yields. The manager uses an asset allocation strategy - adjusting the weight of two asset classes - Canadian stocks and cash.

PORTFOLIO MIX

Assets	Current mix	Allowable range
Foreign	12.0	0-20%
Domestic	82.0	0-100%
Cash	6.0	0-100%

PORTFOLIO COMPOSITION

Top ten securities	% of portfolio
Bombardier Inc	5.0
Alcan Aluminum Ltd	5.0
Magna International Inc.	6.0
Imasco Ltd	6.0
NOVA Corporation of Alberta	6.0
Bank of Montreal	6.0
Royal Bank of Canada	6.0
Bank of Nova Scotia, The	6.0
Quebecor Printing	5.0
IPL Energy	5.0

Total securities held: N/A
Average number of securities held: 26-50
Capital gains: Annual
Income: Monthly
Composition date: December 31, 1995

ASSET ALLOCATION

▨ Financial Services	20.0%
▨ Industrial products	17.0%
☐ Oil and Gas	10.0%
▨ Consumer products	10.0%
▨ Pipelines and utilities	8.0%
▨ Other	33.0%

RISK AND RETURN SCATTER GRAPH

Three-year average annual compound return

Standard deviation

FACTS AND FUNDAMENTALS

Fund sponsor: 20/20 Funds Inc.	**Notes:** ~
Telephone: (905) 339-2020	**Sales fee:** Choice
(800) 268-8690 Fax: (905) 339-3863	**Front-end maximum:** 9.0%
Funds in family: 20	**Deferred during:**
RRSP/RRIF eligibility: 100%	**Year 1:** 6.0% **Year 6:** 1.5%
Minimum initial investment:	**Year 2:** 5.5% **Year 7:** Nil
RRSP: $500	**Year 3:** 5.0% **Year 8:** Nil
Non-RRSP: $500	**Year 4:** 3.5% **Year 9:** Nil
	Year 5: 2.5% **Thereafter:** Nil
Minimum subsequent investment: $25	**Management fee:** 1.5%
Periodic investment plan: Yes	**Fees to switch between funds:** Free from Money Market. Otherwise 2 free transfers per year, thereafter $25 per transfer.
Minimum investment: $25	
Minimum subsequent investment: $25	**Withdraw under systematic plan:** None.
Systematic withdrawal: Yes	
Minimum holdings: $5,000	
Minimum withdrawal: None	**RRSP fees:** None.

Source: BellCharts Inc.

FIGURE 16.5: BELLCHARTS FLOATING BAR CHARTS

DYNAMIC DIVIDEND GROWTH FUND

Dividend Income

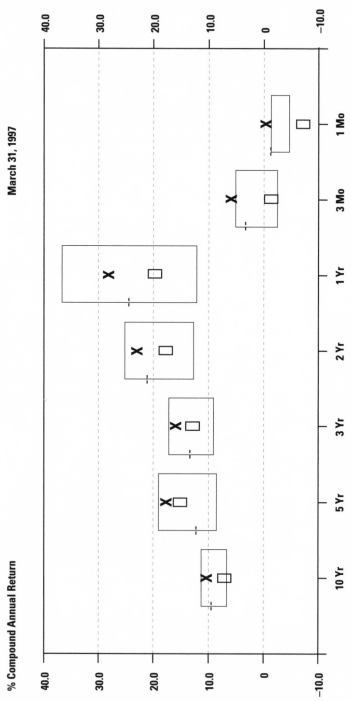

March 31, 1997

% Compound Annual Return

LEGEND:

5th Percentile	10.9	19.3	17.3	26.6	37.0	4.0	–1.0
95th Percentile	7.3	8.9	9.2	13.8	13.5	–1.6	–3.4
1st Quartile	10.5	14.6	15.4	23.1	29.9	2.6	–1.4
Median	8.15	11.3	12.4	19.7	22.8	1.5	–2.2
3rd Quartile	8.1	10.1	10.2	15.7	18.7	1.0	–2.6
DYNAMIC DIV GROWTH X	8.5	14.4	14.7	22.0	25.8	3.0	–1.8
Rank	6	6	7	10	13	7	13
Number of Funds	13	17	22	31	33	39	39
TSE300 Total Return	7.8	14.2	13.0	19.0	20.1	–0.8	–4.8
Quartile	2	2	2	2	2	1	2

Objective: High current income and safety of capital principally through Canadian dividend-paying securities.

Sponsor: Dynamic Mutual Funds

FIGURE 16.6: MIDLAND WALWYN FUND RESEARCH SAMPLE

Canadian Equity — FUND RESEARCH

All Data: March 31, 1997

AIC Advantage Fund (II)

Fund Objective & Approach

The investment objective is to maximize return in a manner which is consistent with the preservation of invested capital. The focus is on a select number of quality businesses with excellent long-term prospects.

Portfolio Management

The fund's lead manager is Jonathan Wellum. Mr. Wellum holds two master's degrees and the CFA charter. Michael Lee-Chin, AIC chairman and chief strategist, and Neil Murdoch, are also advisors to the fund.

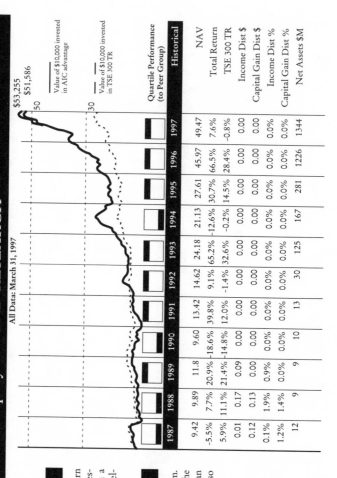

	1987	1988	1989	1990	1991	1992	1993	1994	1995	1996	1997	Historical
	9.42	9.89	11.8	9.60	13.42	14.62	24.18	21.13	27.61	45.97	49.47	NAV
	-5.5%	7.7%	20.9%	-18.6%	39.8%	9.1%	65.2%	-12.6%	30.7%	66.5%	7.6%	Total Return
	5.9%	11.1%	21.4%	-14.8%	12.0%	-1.4%	32.6%	-0.2%	14.5%	28.4%	-0.8%	TSE 300 TR
	0.01	0.17	0.09	0.00	0.00	0.00	0.00	0.00	0.00	0.00	0.00	Income Dist $
	0.12	0.13	0.00	0.00	0.00	0.00	0.00	0.00	0.00	0.00	0.00	Capital Gain Dist $
	0.1%	1.9%	0.9%	0.0%	0.0%	0.0%	0.0%	0.0%	0.0%	0.0%	0.0%	Income Dist %
	1.2%	1.4%	0.0%	0.0%	0.0%	0.0%	0.0%	0.0%	0.0%	0.0%	0.0%	Capital Gain Dist %
	12	9	9	10	13	30	125	167	281	1226	1344	Net Assets $M

Quartile Performance (to Peer Group)

$53,255
$51,586

Value of $10,000 invested in AIC advantage

Value of $10,000 invested in TSE 300 TR

Commentary

The fund's strategy is based on three basic themes which manager Jonathan Wellum believes will become increasingly important in the coming years. (1) The re-structuring of the household balance sheet from short to long-term investments, (2) a sustainable low-interest-rate environment and (3) demographics.

The first and most important trend for the fund is the switch by households from interest-bearing investments to longer-term higher-risk equity strategies in order to provide a comfortable retirement. The primary beneficiaries of this trend include mutual fund companies such as AIC Advantage top holdings Trimark and Mackenzie Financial and also financial services companies such as Fairfax Financial and Newcourt Credit. The expected lower interest rate speed up this process by decreasing returns on formerly popular instruments such as CSBs and GICs. Demographic trends imply that an increasing percentage of the population in the developed world will be saving for retirement.

Wellum looks for companies that will experience exponential earnings growth as a result of one, or a combination of these trends. The financial services portion of the fund will comprise a minimum of 40% of the fund's assets.

The remainder of the fund is composed of solid, industry-leading, well managed companies which will provide stability and modest growth for the fund. Examples of these include CanWest Global, Franco-Nevada and Loblaws.

Portfolio Composition

Company	% Total Assets
Short Term (Cdn)	9.10
Fairfax Finl Holdings	7.87
Franco-Nevada Mng	7.81
Trimark Financial	7.60
MDS Inc Class B	7.48
Mackenzie Financial	7.37
Loblaws Cos	6.40
Other Assets	5.87
CanWest Global	5.76
Thompson Corp	5.55
Dundee Bancorp	5.30
Coca Cola	4.94
Newcourt Credit	4.68
Berkshire Hathaway	3.47
AGF Management	2.92

Sector Allocation

	% of Holdings
Financial	42.3
Comm	11.3
Gold & Silver	7.8
Consumer	7.5
Merchandise	6.4

Statistics

Alpha	0.1
Beta	2.3
Sharpe Ratio	18.0
R-Squared	0.6
Mean	1.439
Standard Deviation	4.959
Skewness	(1.21)

Composition

Stocks	85.03
Bonds	0.00
Cash	9.10
Other	5.87

Downside Risk

Worst Month	
October-87	-26.099
Worst 12 Months (ending)	
September-90	-26.399

Fundmate ™ / Correlation

		Correlation
Substitute	Bisset Canadian Equity	0.70
Complement	Cundill Security	0.12

Performance as of March 31, 1997

	Q1	Q2	Q3	Q4	Total
1993	9.9%	11.1%	9.7%	23.4%	65.2%
1994	-5.5%	13.9%	5.9%	1.5%	-12.6%
1995	-1.4%	17.8%	0.7%	11.7%	30.7%
1996	15.0%	7.3%	15.8%	16.5%	66.5%
1997	7.6%				7.6%

	Total Return	Value of $10,000
3 Mo	7.6%	$10,761
6 Mo	25.4%	$12,540
1 Yr	55.8%	$15,581
3 Yr	29.4%	$21,657
5 Yr	27.4%	$33,601
10 Yr	16.2%	$44,688

Manager Style

Large — Small
Value — Growth

MER per $100

$2.55

Group Average $2.19

Source: Midland Walwyn

FIGURE 16.7: THE THREE DIMENSIONS OF MUTUAL FUND EVALUATION

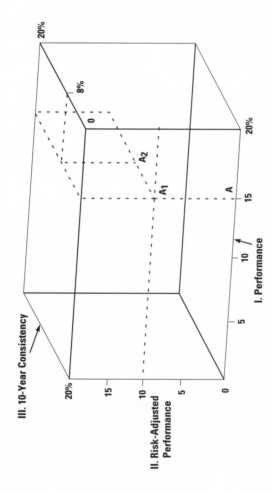

A — Performance = 15%

A₁ — Risk-Adjusted = 10%

A₂ — 10-Year Consistency = 8%

A DIFFERENT KIND OF (SHOOTING) STAR

So far in this section we have been describing various methods by which mutual funds are evaluated. Of the three important dimensions, the first two are *quantitative* in nature (mutual fund performance and performance over time), and the third is *qualitative* — risk adjustment in relation to a norm or average. In this "star" evaluation system, all three dimensions are to a degree constant: they evaluate the present situation, past performance (short and long), and to a degree they predict future performance. On this basis, a portfolio can be established through the cooperation of the investor, his financial advisor and the fund manager.

The process of ongoing monitoring, reallocation, reporting and review is a moving process rather than the fixed-telescope science of asset allocation. We might call it a shooting star system.

One leader in this new field is Mackenzie Financial Corporation, a large mutual fund family group of funds with its STAR (there's that "S" word again). Since 1987, Mackenzie has been a leader in this dynamic field. It works like this: If the balance of a client's individual fund holdings shifts due to different growth rates for different mutual funds, the portfolio is *automatically* informed as to content changes of his portfolio. And the financial advisor/dealer provides a quarterly update informing the client of all changes made and why. This exhaustive review and reallocation are done to keep the client updated. This STAR moving review and rebalancing is performed at a modest annual fee, usually about 1/10th of 1%.

However, some investors may contend that this is a cookie-cutter approach that is unsuitable for their individual purposes. A second concern raised is that only seven funds are utilized for this management system and each of these funds is limited to Mackenzie funds. A further concern is that a computerized system is only as good as the information that it receives. That's probably all true, but there could be some real benefit for tucking a little of this methodology into your portfolio.

chapter 17

PROSPERING DESPITE JANUARY AND TAXES

The cleverly expressed opposite of any generally accepted idea is worth a fortune to somebody.

— F. Scott Fitzgerald

THE JANUARY EFFECT

Short-term volatility in the market creates contrarianism of a sort. In any efficient securities market, prices generally reflect all past and current data, and the consensus of most investors about conditions six to nine months in the future. While these general influences prevail, price changes within the market should be random and unpredictable, and seasonal patterns, at least before the fact, should *not be* easily understood. The more uncertainty, the better for profit potential.

The "January Effect" (or "Year-End Effect") refers to the abnormally high returns in the first month of the new year compared to those of any other month. For several reasons, to be outlined shortly, small-company stocks often generate such above-average returns. January is not necessarily a good month for large-cap blue chips.

Studies show that as much as 50% of this bulge often takes place in the first week of the month. Smaller firms can average a 5% to 10% return; larger companies can average about 2% to 3%. Both numbers easily surpass the average weekly returns for the year, more often than not.

The likelihood of this superior market performance in the first month of the year has been so widely documented over decades of stock market history, at home and globally, that today we ask how and why, rather than "Is the January Effect real?" In fact, there are a number of explanations.

First, there is *tax-loss selling*. In December, stock prices often tend to fall as investors bail out of poorly performing stocks before the year-end, in order to take advantage of capital losses and the resulting tax deductions. The January Effect itself is part of a rebound phenomenon as stocks often return to their normal levels under normal bidding in the new year. Many foreign stock markets and other asset classes, such as corporate bonds, confirm this consistency.

Second, there is the *psychological effect*. The turn of the year promises a clean slate for those embarked on government, business and consumer budgeting. It may even coincide with mutual fund managers' performance evaluations.

So *window dressing* is a huge component in the overall January exercise. Some portfolio managers, like coaches fielding their best athletes, are anxious to unload speculative or undesirable stock selections before year-end and the publication of their annual reports to shareholders. Once they've sent the annual report to the printers, they may return to their old tricks, reacquiring their pets in the new year. In fact, investors at all levels resolve to clear out their losers and invest in what they perceive are winners. This has an enormous cumulative effect.

Third, in a burst of *investigative journalism*, many financial publications routinely glow with bullish investment articles and enthusiastic corporate outlooks at year-end, as the rest of us are declaring our own New Year's resolutions — to quit smoking, to spend more time with our families, and even to impose new quotas for business performance on ourselves.

Fourth, *dividend policy* can distort what is really happening. Stocks paying high dividends or those showing outstanding capital gains may bring abnormally high returns in January, while low dividend-payers show abnormally low ones.

Fifth, *cash flow patterns* at the end of the year emphatically contribute to the January Effect. Many people may invest their bonuses and holiday gifts at this time, and make year-end pension plan contributions.

The huge influx of annual *RRSP contributions* begins to happen at this time, too. As concerns about funding retirement grow larger, so too do RRSP contributions.

And finally, of course, there is the *holiday effect*. Stocks perform unusually well before Christmas and New Year's, thanks partly to blue-chip window dressing. The cup that doth cheer but not inebriate makes all price-earnings ratios look good.

All of which is not to assume that all mutual funds share in this burst of market activity. Many conservative managers confine their buying to fundamental value, based on underlying strength, according to the likelihood that they will perform well over a full business cycle of four to six years, regardless of the market's ups and downs.

Mind you, the sound investor, whether institutional portfolio manager or individual investor, responds to this cavalry charge by applying his own brand of contrarianism, buying when others sell and selling when others buy.

INVESTING QUITE CONTRARY

When I use the term "contrary," I don't mean "ornery" or "cantankerous." "Contrarian investing" is a strategy that involves pursuing a value or other style approach driven by your own hard arithmetic and sound judgment.

While I don't recommend it, such a strategy in January could lead the brave investor to move counter to advancing markets. *Could*—not necessarily. Sensible contrarianism means more than moving against the crowd. It means moving in a logical way that the multitude may not discern.

On the day John F. Kennedy was assassinated and the stock markets around the world unanimously went into free-fall, a prominent Vancouver broker consistently bought stocks — blue chips, red chips, white chips. He bought Bell Telephone, CPR, oil stocks and moose pasture. If it failed to move, he saluted it; if it moved, he bought it. He bought himself and his firm into exhaustion.

Within the next two or three trading days, with the knee-jerk reflex of stock markets after such arbitrary reaction to such a shock, numerous markets of the world bounced back up. He sold out his long positions and made a fortune. "I zig when they zag," captures the spirit of the true contrarian.

Perhaps the supreme expression of contrarianism for a Canadian is to believe in the Canadian future, especially as an investment vehicle. We have been a nation of self-deprecators, or at least a nation whose people invariably believe that the products we make are, by definition, inferior to those made in Stuttgart, Pittsburgh or Japan.

Japan is an interesting object-lesson for us. In 50 years, that nation has transformed its image from poor quality "Made in Japan" goods to world-class mechanical and technological superiority. Imitative, yes, but excellent.

Alex Christ, chairman of Mackenzie Financial Corporation, chose Toronto over his home in Rochester, New York. He forged both the giant financial enterprise he now heads and substantial fortune for himself. "I was born in the U.S. by accident and moved here for opportunity," he says. "If I didn't think Canada was the best kept secret in the world, I wouldn't stay here."

Sir John Templeton, as usual, said it even better: "It takes patience, discipline and courage to follow the 'contrarian' route to investment success: to buy when others are despondently selling, to sell when others are avidly buying."

SHEDDING TAX — NOT TEARS

*Next to being shot at and missed, nothing is really quite
as satisfying as an income tax refund.*

— F.J. Raymond

A monster lurks in Revenue Canada's tax rate schedule that many Canadians may not fully appreciate. It can devastate your personal financial planning. It's the Bracket-Creeper Monster, who hides out in the fine print of RevCan's tax schedule and likes to feed on inflation. Your higher income over the past decade has pushed you into a higher tax bracket. There both taxation and inflation combine forces to erode your hard-earned money.

Is tax-free income a thing of the past? Believe it or not, Revenue Canada actually gives its blessing to *real tax-free income* from several investment sources. The first approved source is the dividend tax credit. Dividends received by individuals from Canadian tax-paying corporations qualify for a 34% tax-free "gross-up"—net to you as investor.

There's a reason behind this seeming largess. Unlike bond interest, which is a pre-tax item, Canadian corporate dividends are paid out after corporate taxes. The funds you receive as dividends have already been taxed. So the tax credit in the hand is worth considerably more than interest income in the bush.

A true preferred-dividend mutual fund is an excellent vehicle for securing the dividend tax credit. It gives you unique capital and income stability and works with high-quality stocks, quite often investing in floating-rate, exchangeable and retractable preferreds.

For those investors subject to full taxation, every $1.00 of dividend equals about $1.30 to $1.34 of interest income after tax, depending upon your province of residence. In 1996, such a fund's cash payout yield approximated 9%, or an after-tax equivalent of about 11% in interest income. You can receive these dividends monthly or quarterly, depending on the type of dividend mutual fund you choose.

First, when revenues and taxable income rise, corporate demand for preferred stock tends to increase. This is another feature of these funds. Your investment goal is to preserve your capital and generate a stable, high-quality stream of tax-efficient dividend income, even as prime rates rise. This is particularly true in utility stock-based securities and in funds containing convertible issues.

Second, we must stress the 25% tax-free income you can receive from capital gains dispositions. Third, by deferring unrealized capital gains you can accumulate huge tax-preferred gains.

And there are other, broader means of minimizing your taxes, all legal and legitimate. Many of the people who come to my door ignore the most visible tax-free gifts that are right in front of them. I often ask them, "Do you really enjoy paying all that income tax on purpose?"

A low-income earner with no other income but that of preferred dividends enjoys one of the most outstanding tax benefits. He can receive as much as $22,625 in dividends free of tax! For senior citizens, the allowable amount increases to as much as $24,000.

In 1987, C.I. Mutual Funds, a leading Canadian mutual fund, established what was at the time a unique investment vehicle for Canadian investors, its C.I. Sector Fund. This instrument gives investors access to 21 of the group's funds without incurring immediate capital gains and, therefore, taxation. The C.I. Sector Fund is itself an open-end mutual fund with 21 different classes of special shares, each devoted to one of C.I.'s corresponding C.I. funds. These special "shares" can be transferred to any of the other "classes" (i.e., 21 different "funds") without creating a taxable disposition on the profit on the capital gain at the time. These "disposed of" capital gains are not taxed for up to a 20-year period. Only dividends declared are subject to tax each year and enjoy the dividend tax credit provision.

Naturally, once you redeem any of your capital gains in the C.I. Sector Fund, you create a taxable disposition, like any other mutual fund.

TABLE 17.1: TAX-DEFERRAL BENEFITS COMPOUND

Poor tax planning can make a significant dent in net returns. As the table below demonstrates, it is not only the amount of tax, but also the timing which determines the after-tax value of your investment. In this example, each $100,000 investment earns an annual return of 12% which is compounded over 20 years.

AFTER-TAX VALUE

End of Year	Interest Income (50% tax paid annually)	Capital Gains (37.5% tax paid annually)	Capital Gains (37.5% tax deferred)
0	$100,000	$100,000	$100,000
1	106,000	107,500	112,000
2	112,360	115,563	125,440
3	119,102	124,230	140,493
4	126,248	133,547	157,352
5	133,823	143,563	176,234
6	141,851	154,330	197,382
7	150,363	165,905	221,068
8	159,385	178,348	247,596
9	168,948	191,724	277,308
10	179,085	206,103	310,585
11	189,830	221,561	347,855
12	201,220	238,178	389,598
13	213,293	256,041	436,349
14	226,090	275,244	488,711
15	239,656	295,888	547,357
16	254,035	318,079	613,039
17	269,277	341,935	686,604
18	285,434	367,580	768,997
19	302,560	395,149	861,276
20	320,714	424,785	964,629

Less tax on disposition (at 20-year level)

	n/a	n/a	($324,236)

After-tax value

	$320,714	$424,785	$640,393

The calculations are used for the puroses of illustrating the effects of tax-deferred compounding and are not intended to reflect the future value of any mutual fund or returns on investment in any mutual fund.

Source: C.I. Sector Fund

TABLE 17.2: A SAMPLE C.I. SECTOR FUNDS INVESTMENT

Mr. and Mrs. Smith invest $10,000 and keep that investment. If their Sector Fund shares earn 12% per year, doubling every 6 years:

Year 1 Investment = $10,000

	Taxed at 40%	Tax-Deferred
Year 6 Value	$15,176	$19,738
Year 12 Value	$23,032	$38,598
Year 18 Value	$34,954	$76,899
Year 24 Value	$53,048	$151,786

Mr. and Mrs. Smith still pay tax if they redeem their Sector Fund shares. However, their tax-deferred value of $151,786 after 24 years minus the 40% tax payable is still $91,071 — compared to a traditional after-tax investment value of $53,048.

1. An investor who buys and holds — capital gains continue to expand year after year, tax deferred.
2. An active investor who trades frequently — capital gains taxes are deferred until Sector Fund shares are redeemed.
3. An investor who frequently re-balances a portfolio due to changing investment objectives — capital gains taxes are deferred until redemption.

Sector Funds are structured as mutual fund corporations, and not as traditional mutual fund trusts. The individual funds are deemed classes, thereby allowing the transferability of tax deferred. This is not possible within a traditional fund family, where capital gains are deemed taxable upon transfer from one fund to another.

Source: C.I. Sector Fund

Thanks to this ability to move around from one mutual fund to another, you can actively manage your portfolio according to market developments, buying and selling within the C.I. Sector Fund without incurring immediate tax obligations through any capital gains. Mind you, the tax is deferred, not wiped out. This difference in retaining and accumulating capital helps you tremendously over time. You can make capital gains inside the special classes of shares, so you pay no tax on your various *internal* redemptions.

There are a handful of other mutual fund companies now offering this special class share arrangement, including AGF, BPI and GT Global. But this idea is not for everyone. You will need to examine each structure very carefully, be in a substantially high tax bracket, and consider your cash flow and other financial arrangements before you embark on this kind of structure.

You win on so many fronts — flexibility, wide diversification and access to widely acclaimed money management firms while deferring the tax you pay, which can amount to substantial monies. You therefore have the use of the government's tax money during the period of deferral — it and your capital compounded together.

As the famous humorist Will Rogers might say today, death alone is certain, while taxes are (sometimes) negotiable.

MUTUAL FUNDS AND THE TAX COLLECTOR

In *The Economist* (31 May 1997), the title of an article about Russia caught my eye: "Disappearing Taxes." I think the writer should have called the article "Disappearing Tax Collectors" when he revealed that, in 1996, 26 tax collectors were killed in Russia; 74 were injured; six had been kidnapped; and 41 had their houses burned down. Dangerous work!

In Canada, where we tax-paying citizens are annually punished with one of the industrialized world's most insulting and regressive personal tax bites, being a tax man with Revenue Canada is merely an unpopular, rather than dangerous, profession.

Mutual funds help people escape paying a lot of taxes. But, in this almost perfect of all major investments, that little word "tax" keeps popping up. We pay tax on profits of our realized capital gains; on a portion of our dividend income; on bond and mortgage income (whether we need the income or not); and on certain annual mutual fund distributions, such as when our portfolio manager trades profit for capital gains dividends.

The good news is that you can do something to substantially lower your yearly tax exposure to mutual fund profits. But you must never let the potential tax tail wag the economic dog. Sound economic basics are first; tax considerations are the second or even third most important factors.

Before we get to the nitty-gritty of mutual fund tax benefits from both an investment point of view as well as a tax-reporting task, let's zero in on the tax fatigue that most hard-working and retired citizens alike are experiencing.

There has been much noise from our politicians about deficit cutting and how Canadians are on-board with a policy of debt reduction. It's as if a tax break for honest, toiling citizens would drive the debt again and increase the deficit. This, in my opinion, is nonsense.

The truth is that higher taxes distort the way we spend, save and invest. Taxes change the relative prices not only of the goods and services we buy, but also affect our jobs. Patrick Luciani, in *The Financial Post Magazine*, wrote: "Each one of these [tax] changes distorts the allocation of resources, making the economy a little less efficient and productive. And the higher the marginal tax rate, the higher the distortion."

Luciani tells us that economists have always known about this hidden, deadweight loss, but are only recently realizing what a big threat it is to the average Canadian. To illustrate what is meant by "dead weight," if you've ever flown in a twin-engine plane, and one engine dies out, you'll get an idea of what the pilot must do to compensate for the weight of that useless engine, hanging heavily on the wing.

Bev Dahlly, professor of economics at the University of Alberta, tells us just how damaging the effects are of increased taxes. He suggests that the cost to our Canadian economy of raising a single dollar of taxes ranges from a low of $1.40 in Alberta to a high of $2.00 in Quebec. "The average for Canada is around $1.66, meaning that for every dollar the government raises in taxes, the equivalent of only about $0.60 is returning to the economy."

To return to Patrick Luciani, "Critics of lower taxes argue that

Canada ranks 14th among the 25 biggest industrial nations in terms of taxes as a percentage of gross domestic product. That's fine as far as it goes, but since 80% of all our exports go south of the border, the U.S. is really the only constituency that matters as far as comparing tax rates is concerned."

In other words, we are the second worst of the 25 largest industrialized nations after taxes on income, profits and capital gains are combined.

Our tax picture gets even worse when we compare our marginal tax rates in Canada. In British Columbia, for example, the average taxpayer with annual earnings of just more than $59,000 will hit the top marginal tax rate of 54.16%. U.S. taxpayers have to earn $200,000 (U.S.) before paying the top tax rate of 39%. And that's the top tax rate for just a few states; most states are less. So when you adjust the U.S. dollar amount for Canadian currency, that's $270,000 of annual earned income before the top tax rate kicks in.

And you still consider Ottawa your friend?

Think about this. The Fraser Institute in Vancouver has provided some insightful conclusions drawn from their research. They tell us that after three decades of steadily creeping income taxes and surtaxes, top marginal tax rates have been falling around the world. For OCD countries, Luciani cites the Fraser Institute studies as showing the average tax marginal rates fell from 61% to 44% by 1991. From 1980 to 1990, more than 50 countries reduced their top rates for fear of the serious damage they were doing to their economies. The study showed that even Sweden, once the model for all socialist democrats around the world, cut its marginal rates drastically from 80% to 50%.

Yet Canada insists on moving in the opposite direction. Our falling deficit is not, as clearly the majority of Canadians think, entirely the result of government efficiency or cutbacks, but rather due to increased revenues from the high taxes we pay (not to mention higher "employment insurance" payments). Only 16% of the $25 billion Ottawa shaved off the deficit by the end of the year was due to lower spending.

Despite relatively low and stable interest rates, people on fixed or low incomes are faced with the daunting task of having to live on much less money.

Where people do have the power to do something about this situation is through investing in mutual funds. There is a mutual fund product for every taxpayer and investor, regardless of risk personality, that offers tax benefits, including bond funds, balanced funds, high-yield income funds and equity funds.

Maximizing Your Tax Benefits

How important is it, when you buy mutual funds, to worry about how "tax efficient" your funds are?

Truthfully, not very.

Robert Arnott, a strong proponent of "tax-managed investing," states, "For short-term investors, tax strategy won't make any real difference." Tax efficiency have a substantial impact on after-tax returns, but several professional studies demonstrate that it will add up to a meaningful amount only if you stick with one fund for 20 or 30 years.

Arnott admits, "tax-minimization strategies are often in conflict with the aim of making the most money possible." To illustrate this point, a fund manager may change the timing of a portfolio transaction so that it will, or will not, show up in the current tax year. He may sell a position in the fund at a loss, even if he would otherwise want to sit tight and watch the stock appreciate. He may do these things, even if they run counter to his investor's intuition.

Harold Evensley of the investment management firm of Evensley Brown Kaly & Levitt in Coral Gables, Florida, says "Swell, but what if the price goes up over the course of those 31 days?" [referring to an investor selling for a tax loss and repurchasing the fund 31 days later to avoid an "artificial transaction"].

"Does the money saved on taxes make up for the 'opportunity cost' imposed by being out of the [fund] for a month? And even if it does, if the manager is good at doing his job, don't the strategies amount to putting a world-class gymnast into a strait jacket?"

Another recognized expert on the subject states, "The arguments for tax-focused investing . . . are generally not legitimate within the real world." Simply put, the time spent obsessing about tax efficiency would probably be better spent determining which mutual funds are likely to deliver higher pre-tax returns.

In an article published in *The Globe & Mail* Gordon Powers concluded that "Tax efficiency is no excuse for mediocre returns. Many top-performing funds do very well despite the amount of taxable income they produce."

When you buy a fund, it is a very individual matter. But, there are so many variables from a tax efficiency point of view, that many times, it just doesn't matter. It is true that the greater a fund's portfolio turnover rate, the more likely capital gains will be distributed annually, instead of being built up over time and reflected in your fund's net asset value. Or, you may expect to have a lower income tax bracket in the year (even December) in which you buy the fund and you plan to have a considerably higher tax bracket in the following year. You can see that it would be to your advantage to buy the fund near the end of the year and receive the capital gain distribution at the lower tax bracket, instead of waiting until the next year, when you will be taxed at a higher rate.

When it comes to selecting what fund you want to purchase and when, it's wise to consider the potential tax benefits, but not to be myopic about it. The major point is to select funds for their economic characteristics, risk-adjusted history, and personal suitability.

When it comes to calendar year-end purchases, it still might be wise to heed John Templeton's oft-quoted words, 'When's the best time to invest? When you have the money.'

STICKING TO YOUR GUNS

In a confusing world of possibilities for your investment dollars, remember these essentials stemming from the guidelines listed at the end of Chapter 15:

1. Avoid the "instant gratification" syndrome common to our generation. Smart investors never allow this sentiment to interfere with long-term successful money management. Never confuse the short term with the long term. Long term means years, not weeks. Instant coffee, instant Internet, fax machines and fast food all have their places in our technological society. Never apply the same standards to long term in this very serious world of money management.

2. Don't trade into lower quality in order to obtain a moderate short-term increase in yield.

3. Generally, buy on rumor and sell on news. The market is always one jump ahead of you. By the time you read it in the newspaper, it's probably too late to act on information. Or, better still, let your fund manager worry about the rumors and the news.

4. Before making any investment, consider the consequences of being wrong — and how those consequences would affect you.

5. Think of currencies as common shares, where the earnings per share are expressed in each country's balance of payments. The international level of inflation on currencies serves as a barometer for investors, since it measures a nation's economic health.

6. Don't fear a bear market. Have faith. Be enthusiastic, resourceful, knowledgeable and ambitious. Recognize the opportunities. Franklin D. Roosevelt's famous dictum, "The only thing we have to fear is fear itself" was more than an idle political slogan. Faith undergirds everything that is good in our society. It forms the sinew of all prosperity and success in every endeavor of life.

7. The market is not just a fluctuating index — it is a series of extremes in both directions. By taking advantage of those extremes, the prudent investor can improve on the reality in between. This is our key to beating the indexes—a truly managed portfolio.

8. The stock market is a barometer of what is expected to happen, usually within six to nine months, not a thermometer reflecting present conditions.

9. As a general rule, bull markets tend to last from three to four years. Bear markets tend to last between a year and 18 months.

10. If you're hoping rather than believing, it's probably time to sell.

chapter 18

UNLOCKING THE POWER OF MUTUAL FUND DYNAMICS

The railroads made some good money. But the people who made even bigger money were the people along the right of way.

— Ralph Wanger, Acorn Fund

MARKET STABILITY

Who rides on the back of a tiger may find it difficult to dismount.

— Chinese proverb

Some market observers have recently raised this question: Does the massive influx of billions of dollars invested by mutual funds into securities pose a threat to both free market movement and price stability?

In Canada, the total assets of mutual funds have increased from $5 billion to about $250 billion between 1980 and 1996, and in the U.S. from $58.4 billion to almost $3 trillion over the same period. Financial institutions, including mutual funds, wield an increasing influence over the securities markets through the sheer size of their holdings. Given a bear market panic, some observers worry that mutual fund holders could seek redemptions on a large scale, thereby bringing on what one financial writer refers to as "market mayhem."

A rash of mutual fund redemptions following the crash of October 1987 did add to the widespread sell-off. This run was relatively short-lived. You might wonder if a run on mutual fund holdings might be possible, like the run on bank deposits by customers in the 1930s. My personal experience during the worst market crash since 1929 (October 19, 1987) was that only 2% of all of our clients cashed their funds out.

I believe, in fact, that the huge public participation in securities markets through mutual funds is a stabilizing influence, not a destabilizing one. And a market crash of any magnitude because of a concerted spate of redemptions by mutual fund holders is unlikely, according to reliable evidence.

According to Daniel Bachman, U.S. director of short-term macroeconomic services at WEFA Group, a study of household behavior indicates that such an eventuality is highly unlikely. "The move into mutual funds by households," he says, "is part of a long-term trend. Households are reorganizing their portfolios after the defeat of inflation." (Review Figure 1.3 that illustrates the increasing percentages of household assets and mutual funds in Canada for the last 15 years.)

For years, the fear of inflation inhibited mutual fund investment in favor of more conventional savings and investment vehicles. The demise of double-digit inflation in the 1980s gave the mutual fund industry major impetus.

Bachman concedes that bear markets might trigger temporary fund redemptions, exacerbating the sell-off, but low current bank yields would almost certainly force most mutual fund holders to think seriously about retaining their funds. He traces the inverse correlation (opposite behavior) between high interest rates and the pace of mutual fund investment. Between 1952 and 1965, U.S. households maintained nearly 40% of their assets in mutual funds and other securities. From the late 1960s through the 1970s, that level of household investment dropped steadily with the oil and inflation shocks of the latter decade. By the decade of the 1980s, households held only slightly more than 20% of all their assets in mutual funds and other securities.

By the end of 1994, with the specter of inflation largely subdued in people's minds, 32% of all household assets were held in mutual funds and other securities, well up from the depths of the inflation-ravaged 1970s and 1980s, but still far below the level of the 1950s. Bachman clearly relates this movement to prevailing inflation: "The household movement out of stocks was clearly the result of the bout of inflation in the 1970s. During that period, real returns on stocks and bonds appeared low, while real returns were highest on bank deposits, particularly in the 1980s."

And looking at the meteoric growth in mutual fund investment from 1980 to the present, the growth can certainly be seen to parallel that inflation trend. Today, a continuation of the trend seems highly likely: "As it becomes more clear that another period of double-digit inflation and extreme Fed tightening is unlikely, households are moving back to previous portfolio allocations," Bachman predicts.

In fact, he projects household assets in securities and mutual funds to reach $9.5 trillion by the year 2000, or 35% of all household assets. Such a constant growth of such household accumulation can only be seen as a huge stabilizing factor in the securities markets, because individual investors — and therefore mutual funds — are less fickle than other institutional investors. "There is no evidence that individual investors react faster to market movements than professionals," adds Bachman. "In fact, the opposite is more likely."

Professional traders and portfolio managers have access to information more quickly, are faced with meeting quarterly objectives, and therefore are less likely to buy and hold. When markets turn downward, they can react more quickly, dumping large positions.

One weakness in Bachman's reasoning is that mutual fund managers are every bit as professional as other institutional traders and portfolio managers, and therefore, his inclusion of mutual funds with individual investors (as set off from professional investors) may be somewhat inaccurate. The attributes he assigns to the professionals could also be attributed to mutual fund portfolio managers. However, while fund managers are professionals, they are highly influenced by the collective wishes of their shareholders.

Furthermore, among the fund manager group, there is a significant number of "value method" fund managers, who are well known for their philosophy of buying and maintaining their positions "forever." As such, this group perhaps acts more like individual investors.

Periods of market volatility coincide with lower levels of individual stock holdings, which Bachman equates somewhat with mutual fund holdings. In the earlier decades illustrated, when individual holdings accounted for more than 80% of stock holdings, the (S&P 500) standard deviation (risk) was 1.4%. As the proportion of individual holdings declined in the 1970s, market volatility increased to 2.0%. Now that trend has reversed, with individual holdings remaining the same, but mutual fund holdings have doubled while standard deviation has declined.

Individual stockholders and, in particular, mutual fund holders, bring more stability to the markets — a comforting, statistical fact. What has, been happening in the U.S. is to a very large degree happening in Canada. In fact, Canadians are buying more mutual funds than Americans on a per capita basis.

WORKING WITH THE PROS

If you buy the same securities as other people, you will have the same results as other people.

— Sir John Templeton

Several times I have referred to the three Ts of successful investing — Time, Training and Temperament — identified by Venita Van Caspel in her book *Money Dynamics for the 1990s*. Only you can decide whether or not you possess the right mix of these to invest profitably in your own future. If not, your first and most important investment is finding an experienced and compatible financial advisor.

Once you've decided to take the plunge after all this soul-searching and more tangible research, consider the following three "ambushes." If you can avoid or overcome these, you're ready to actually select your mutual funds — at long last!

HOW *NOT* TO SELECT A MUTUAL FUND

AMBUSH #1 — THE LATEST RAGE

The uninformed investor may ask, "What stock or mutual fund is hot right now?" A sensible question. Fads in the market come and go like seasonal fashions.

In the late 1960s, we had the high-tech "onics" craze, when almost every new stock or mutual fund issue carried the suffix "onics." Since many funds at that time concentrated on such stocks, they were the hottest investment topic of that period.

In the early 1970s, many portfolio managers were characterized as "gunslingers." They favored aggressive investing over prudence. The result was a rash of hot high-tech funds, attracting astronomical amounts of money at that time. The year 1983 saw the launch of many high-tech funds, as the craze for technology stocks reached its peak following the bull market of August 1982. Since 1995, we have experienced a prolonged bull market in the high-tech sector. And there's little question this particular sector will continue to be potentially very rewarding as well as very volatile.

Unfortunately for the novice, investment themes become hottest, and most dangerous, at their peak, with an inflow of investment capital coming at precisely the worst time. "Onics" stocks started to drop just when sales of those funds were at their peak. The great bear market of 1973–74 followed closely on the heels of the boom. Technology funds went into a protracted eclipse shortly after the launch of most high-tech funds.

This chasing of declining fads is as regular as the emerging of crocuses each spring. Amateur investors seem to return for more punishment with the same regularity. A 1995 *Business Week* article pointed out that betting on the past performance of a specialty or "sector" fund could violate the principle of diversification. In addition, hot stock groups often accelerate upward over a short period. Then they tend to linger. Buying a fund whose specialty has already been discovered by professionals and has moved to the front of the pack is likely to be a losing game.

Avoid the latest-rage ambush. Set your own investment goals carefully and precisely, keeping your sights firmly focused on those objectives and not being swayed by current fads or crazes. The returns from hot stocks or funds are always tempting. Treat them as an illusion because they are usually of short duration. Like a nova, they shine with the most impressive brilliance just before they disappear.

AMBUSH #2 — THE PERFORMANCE CULT

Many investors fall prey to last year's top-performing funds. It makes no sense to invest in funds just because they have recently been superior performers. Most often, they don't continue as such. Consider yesterday's superior performers as today's sub-performers.

A review of that one year-to-year performance rank of equity funds produced this startling fact. A well-known mutual fund firm's product ranked *second* in the U.S. fell to 385th spot the next year. Another well-regarded fund firm's product ranked 203rd in the first-year performance measurement, and 12th in the second year. Now, both funds were listed in the same equity category, and both had superior national recognition and reputation. But the difference in performance between the two funds was dramatic. Why? Different companies, different management styles, different policies. The important point is that a great deal of detailed information about each fund would have been vital, especially for a novice investor, who would have gotten clobbered buying into the former fund.

Often, the novice investor chooses a fund from the performance charts in the newspapers — yet there is no correlation between the fund rankings of one year and the next. Only a long-term horizon should be used as a performance indicator.

Always resist instant gratification — apply your personal style and discipline consistently.

AMBUSH #3 — HAPHAZARD SELECTION OF FUNDS

Since all mutual funds are mistakenly perceived to perform well, some investors conclude that they can build a good portfolio by selecting its components at random. Be forewarned — the range of performance in funds is exceedingly wide, so these investors run the danger of selecting a below-average fund and suffering a long-term loss.

How do you avoid this ambush? Maintain a clear idea of your own risk/reward personality and your precise investment goals. Is your interest primarily in steady current income or reduced taxes or long-term capital gain? Or is it a combination of the three? Will you accept a reasonable near-term fluctuation in order to achieve superior long-term goals?

Finally, construct a common-sense model of asset allocation for your portfolio. Understand the basic characteristics of each fund product. Assign specific percentages of each asset class and market sector according to your risk/reward personality.

And — the point can't be overemphasized — secure the advice of an experienced, knowledgeable financial advisor. This is the most important asset you can acquire.

PSYCHING THE BUSINESS CYCLES

How do different mutual fund asset categories perform during different business cycles? And why ask this question?

Simply, because it pays to know, generally, which market phase we're in at any given point in the overall cycle. This is the *active* part of the strategy behind the Stenner Multi-Safety Allocation System.

A typical business cycle has four major phases:

- Phase One is the early recovery stage, as the economy expands and inflation is low or declines.

- Phase Two is the late recovery stage, when the economy grows and inflation may rise or begin to rise.
- Phase Three is marked by stagflation. The economy slows and inflation and interest rates are still high or rising.
- Phase Four brings recession. The economy slows even more and inflation and interest rates begin to decline again.

Expect your risk profile to shift with these economic changes. You might consider adjusting your total assets during each phase by 10% to 20% — never all.

CHERRY-PICKING YOUR MUTUAL FUNDS

There are two vital principles to follow in choosing funds. First, examine the historical data. Second, attempt to personalize mutual fund management so you can select that management's investment style. Make sure your financial advisor sifts thoroughly through a great deal of strategic past and current research information. Do your homework.

Your targets are those funds that aim for *above average* and *consistent* results. Mutual funds that are above average rank consistently in the top half of all available funds in their peer group (Canadian bond funds within all Canadian bond funds, and so on). We refer to those in the top 25% to 50% as falling into the top first or second quartiles.

At a minimum, a fund must rank consistently above the 50th percentile on a year-to-year basis. Avoid those funds whose managers may, for example, achieve the top decile one year (top 10%), sink to the bottom quartile (bottom 25%) the next, the second quartile (top 50%) the following year, the seventh decile (bottom quartile) in the fourth year, and then the top quartile (top 25%) in the fifth year. These funds should not win your favor over funds that have ranked consistently in the first or second quartile.

Consistency derives from a psychological aspect of investing. Contemplate two hypothetical aggressive equity funds. Both have appreciated by 50% over three years. Fund A rose 40% in value in the first year, declined 5% in the second, and appreciated 15% in the third. Fund B rose 22% in value in the first year, 17% in the second, and 11% in the third. Both funds appreciated by the same percentage over those years. Which one provided a better "comfort level" to its investors?

Superior Fund B increased its value steadily while Fund A behaved more like a roller-coaster. By embracing consistency you save yourself the grief of chasing after the latest fad in funds that are here today and gone tomorrow.

Now, as to examining the historical data, you neglect this step at your peril. This tedious and meticulous screening process may have reduced your selections to about 8% to 10% of the whole universe of mutual funds; that is, only 8% to 10% of the current stable of funds available to Canadians, or about 140 specific mutual funds from all asset categories.

We'll look first for data that reveals consistency and above-average returns on funds within each category. At a minimum, we should look at records for a period of three years, five years being even better. Beyond five years, it is difficult to assess the value of the data — vast changes have taken place in global environments, securities markets, and in investment philosophies that have driven fund managers. Not to mention changes in the portfolio managers themselves.

We'll review the year-by-year performances of funds, too, not just their cumulative (total) returns. The Fund A and Fund B comparison illustrates why. *Cumulative* returns, whether for a three-, five-, or 10-year period masks our ability to measure *consistency* of performance.

In this overall appraisal, no more than about 90 acceptable mutual fund candidates would qualify for our consideration. That's less than 7% of all the bond and stock funds available in Canada, whether domestic or international; small, medium or large cap; value, growth or blended style.

We're about halfway to our objective now by identifying above-average performers. Now, let's discuss the individual manager. You want to know what makes the manager of a given mutual fund tick. What is his unique investment style?

Anyone can discover the fund's basic investment policy or objectives by reading its prospectus. Consider an "aggressive-growth fund." The term "aggressive growth" covers a broad range of investment styles — small-cap (capitalization) stocks, emerging growth companies, turnaround situations, deep cyclical stocks, high-technology issues, over-the-counter juniors, or new issues.

Rarely will you be able to find this kind of in-depth information about a fund manager in your quest. Annual reports often include fund managers' personal reviews of their funds' operations, which is a good place to start. And you can ask your financial advisor, who should be well versed in the funds with which he deals and may be able to secure the latest information regarding the current portfolio status of any fund.

HOW DO YOU KEEP YOUR PORTFOLIO CURRENT?

I refer to re-balancing your portfolio as "weeding your fund garden." Monitor changes in your personal objectives, and be prepared to consider percentage changes in your asset arrangements, changes in sector placement, changes in domestic and foreign sectors, changes in currency weightings and, as a result, changes in your specific mutual fund choices.

Changes in	Require Modifications in
Personal objectives	Broad asset allocation/specific asset allocation/sector allocation/mutual fund selection
Broad asset allocation	Specific asset allocation; sector allocation and mutual fund selection
Specific-based allocation	Sector allocation/mutual fund selection
Sector allocation	Mutual fund selection
Mutual fund selection	Individual mutual funds

THE ILLUSTRATED PORTFOLIO

Refer back to Chapter 7 where we describe the first six levels of our seven-tier selection process. We now provide the seventh level — the specific funds with our model portfolio.

Before reproducing our "exploded" illustrated Stenner Multi-Safety Allocation portfolio model, we'd like to remind you that this is a single, hypothetical portfolio of mutual funds only, based on certain broad assumptions. Any number of such models is possible, depending on changing conditions such as the economy, market conditions in other countries, inflation, the various securities markets, and the individual disposition of you as an investor, as communicated to your financial advisor. This illustrated portfolio construct is not intended as a specific recommendation to the reader, nor should it be construed in such a manner. Each investor must determine for himself, or in conjunction with an advisor, the suitability of any mutual fund portfolio selection.

FIGURE 18.1: STENNER MULTI-SAFETY ASSET ALLOCATION

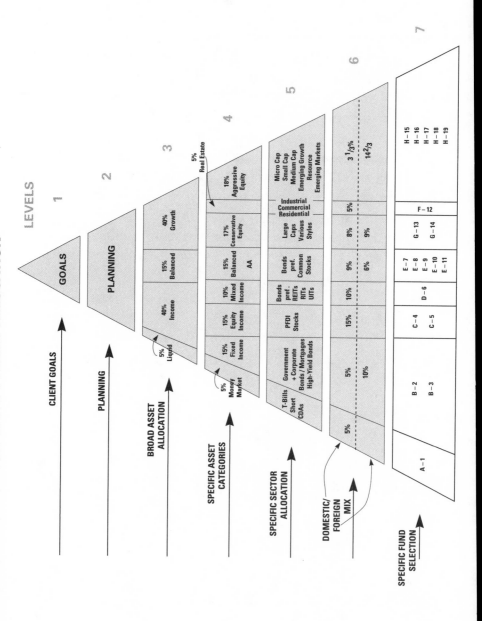

FUND SELECTION LEGEND

A – 1 INDUSTRIAL CASH MANAGEMENT	E	– 7 GLOBAL STRAT INC – 8 FIDELITY CDN AA – 9 GUARDIAN CDN BAL	– 10 AGF 20/20 AMER TAA – 11 20/20 EUROPEAN AA
B	– 2 GUARDIAN INTERNATIONAL INCOME – 3 TRIMARK ADVANTAGE BOND	F – 12 DYNAMIC REAL ESTATE EQUITY
C	– 4 AGF 20/20 DIVIDEND – 5 C.I. MONARCH DIVIDEND	G	– 13 AIC ADVANTAGE II – 14 FIDELITY EUROPE
D – 6 GUARDIAN MONTHLY HIGH INCOME	H	– 15 20/20 AGRESSIVE SM – 16 DYNAMIC GLOBAL RES – 17 20/20 LATIN AMER	– 18 TEMPLETON EMERGING MKTS – 19 FIDELITY FAR EAST

THE STENNER $300,000 PORTFOLIO
(UNLOCKING THE SECRETS OF THE PYRAMID!)

TABLE 18.1: THE STENNER MODEL $300,000 PORTFOLIO

Specific Representative Mutual Fund (Non-registered) Selections for a $300,000 Portfolio

A Money Market Funds — 5%

Fund 1: Industrial Cash Management Fund	$15,000
Alternates:	
– Guardian Short-Term Money Market Fund	
– Bentel Goodman Money Market Fund	

B Fixed-Income Funds — 15%

Fund 2: Guardian International Income Fund	$22,500
Fund 3: Trimark Advantage Bond Fund	$22,500

C Equity Income Funds — 15%

Fund 4: AGF (20/20) Dividend Fund	$22,500
Fund 5: C.I. Monarch Dividend Fund	$22,500
Alternate:	
– Dynamic Dividend Growth Fund	

D "Mixed-Income" Funds — 10%

Fund 6: Guardian Monthly High-Income Fund	$15,000
Fund 7: BPI High-Yield Income Fund	$15,000
Alternates:	
– Atlas High-Yield Fund	
– G.T. Global Growth & Income Class Fund	

E Balanced/Asset Allocation Funds — 15%

Fund 8: Global Strategy Income Plus Fund	$12,000
Fund 9: Fidelity Canadian Asset Allocation Fund	$12,000
Fund 10: AGF 20/20 European Asset Allocation Fund	$11,000
Fund 11: AGF American Tactical Asset Allocation Fund	$10,000
Alternates:	
– Guardian Growth and Income Fund	
– Trimark Fund	
– Universal World Balanced Fund	

F Real Estate Funds — 5%

Fund 12: Dynamic Real Estate Equity Fund	$15,000
Alternate	
– Dynamic Canadian Real Estate Equity	

G Conservative Growth Equity Funds — 17%

Fund 13: AIC Advantage II Fund/AIC Diversified	$25,000
Fund 14: Fidelity European Growth Fund	$26,000

Alternates:
- C.I. Hansberger Value Fund
- Trimark Fund
- Templeton Growth/Ivy Canadian (Large Cap)

H Aggressive Growth Funds — 18%

Fund 15: AGF (20/20) Aggressive Small Companies Fund	$10,000
Fund 16: Dynamic Global Resource Fund	$11,000
Fund 17: Templeton Emerging Markets Fund	$11,000
Fund 18: 20/20 Latin America Fund	$11,000
Fund 19: Fidelity Far East Fund	$11,000

Alternates:
- Global Strategy Small-Cap
- BPI Canadian Small-Cap Opportunities

RATIONALE FOR PORTFOLIO FUND SELECTIONS

Our client is seeking a safety-first, panic-proof, risk-mitigating, worry-free, long-term portfolio for growth of capital and good income.

Fund 1: INDUSTRIAL CASH MANAGEMENT FUND is selected for its consistently high money market and government Treasury Bill content and performance. Added to this is the free cheque-cashing service to enable a client to draw cheques against his account.

Fund 2: GUARDIAN INTERNATIONAL INCOME is an international bond portfolio providing currency low-risk hedging, primarily in foreign currency-denominated bonds, with a term-to-maturity primarily mid-term (6 to 10 years). Investment advisor is Kleinwort Benson (Kleinwort Guardian Overseas Ltd.) in London, England. Income distribution is quarterly.

Fund 3: TRIMARK ADVANTAGE BOND invests in all areas of the Canadian fixed-income market with no restrictions on investment quality.

Fund 4: AGF (20/20) DIVIDEND holds a key position in my equity income category. This has a low portfolio turnover rate of 30% or less, and you can anticipate above-average capital gains with low annual tax dispositions, and some monthly dividend and interest income from common and convertible preferred shares. Primary emphasis is on stable and large-cap securities.

Fund 5: C.I. MONARCH DIVIDEND is relatively new. Jonathan Baird is the portfolio manager; he is a former co-manager of two Dynamic Funds. I believe he will continue to occupy a top or second quartile position.

Fund 6: "Mixed Income" is my "Stenner-hybrid" designation of a brand new category of income funds. Several are available. GUARDIAN MONTHLY HIGH INCOME is designed to provide a high level of predictable, monthly, after-tax income while employing the risk-control strategies for which Guardian is known. In terms of fluctuation or volatility, I place this category of funds somewhere between preferred shares and common equity, which I believe creates an important new category. Currently, the fund is comprised of non-perpetual preferred shares, common shares, corporate bonds and unit investment trusts (UITs), the latter offering income from the real estate and resource industries. These funds typically employ RITs (Royalty Income Trusts) and REITs (Real Estate Investment Trusts) to secure a level of monthly income.

Although you can buy individual RITS, REITs and UITs, I believe you can more advantageously acquire several of these popular and different classes of alternative "high income," tax-preferred, pre-packaged, popular income vehicles within one or two professionally managed mutual funds. The Guardian Fund is just one of this new breed of mutual funds.

Fund 7: BPI HIGH-YIELD INCOME is my next selection in this mixed-income sector, investing both in RITs and using covered call option writing to generate call premiums. This strategy is unique.

Fund 8: TONY MASSIE'S GLOBAL STRATEGY INCOME PLUS FUND belongs in our specimen portfolio in the balanced category. He's known as a win-by-not-losing manager. This fund aims at high total return consistent with preserving capital. It invests in a full range of income-producing investments such as bonds, preferred shares, dividend-paying common shares, short-term debt obligations, and certain risk-reducing derivative instruments. Tony's a "nibbler," tending to take small but frequent profits. BellCharts show this fund's risk and return scatter-graph as "low-risk/high return."

Fund 9: FIDELITY CANADIAN ASSET ALLOCATION is another type of balanced fund. Its first year of operation, 1995, saw it ranking number 1 in Canada among all 134 domestic balanced funds, with a two-year average of just over 22% per annum. Not too shabby. I respect managers Dick Habermann, Alan Radlo and Ford O'Neil. A great addition to our portfolio. In the 1996 and 1997 editions of *Gordon Pape's Guide to Mutual Funds*, Mr. Pape gave this fund a very low rating. In 1995 and 1996, I gave this fund a high recommendation to my clients, based on my research into the change of managers. The result? Fidelity Canadian Asset Allocation ranked number 1 of all balanced funds in Canada in 1995 and number 2 in 1996. Not bad!

Fund 10: 20/20 EUROPEAN ASSET ALLOCATION. Now part of the outstanding AGF organization, this fund combines the high potential of the European market with the versatility of asset allocation management.

Fund 11: AGF (20/20'S) AMERICAN TACTICAL ASSET ALLOCATION FUND rounds out my balanced sector, offering U.S. bond, stocks, and guaranteed short-term notes. Barclays Bank of England has taken over the management of this excellent low-risk high performer with Wells Fargo in San Francisco. It has the best risk-reduction record of any fund in its category.

Fund 12: In its first full year in business, DYNAMIC REAL ESTATE EQUITY FUND made brilliant gains for its shareholders. Is this enough reason to include it inside this portfolio? No. But this sector has a relatively low correlation with North American stock markets. If you add a North American sector that moves in lock-step with the stock market only 50% of the time, you've chosen an excellent risk-mitigator, a relatively non-correlated security.

This real estate equity fund is the only one of its kind in Canada. It seeks current income and long-term capital growth through a globally diversified portfolio of publicly traded real estate and equity securities. The fund is positioned to take advantage of the improving cycle of all classes of North American real estate. As real estate assets continue to recover following a severe and prolonged down cycle (British Columbia excepted), there is upward pressure on values to approach replacement costs. The fund is most recently invested in office, residential and hotel assets, primarily in the U.S. Sunbelt with selected Canadian securities being increased recently. Unlike owning real estate directly, investors in this fund can redeem their shares at any time.

When was the last time you "owned" real estate where you were guaranteed the saleability of your holdings and could buy on demand (within several days)?

Fund 13: Moving into the conservative growth sector, dare we have a portfolio without an AIC fund in it? I think not. If AIC ADVANTAGE II does only half as well as its other sibling, AIC ADVANTAGE, it'll be a great winner. The fund focuses on investment in the financial management services sector (not banks) with emphasis on owning companies such as Trimark Financial, Mackenzie Financial, Dundee Bankorp, AGF Management and Berkshire Hathaway — Warren Buffett's company. It's a toss-up between AIC ADVANTAGE II and AIC DIVERSIFIED, a slightly more conservative fund.

Fund 14: FIDELITY EUROPEAN GROWTH belongs in the international portfolio within this sector. With excellent risk-adjusted top-quartile returns compared to its peers, this portfolio invests in long-term growth in equities in Europe, the U.K. and Eastern Europe. BellCharts places it in the "low risk/high return" area of its scatter-graph. An excellent selection, permitting exposure within Europe.

Fund 15: AGF (20/20) AGGRESSIVE SMALL COMPANIES FUND means entry into the aggressive-growth sector. This is a really high turnover (200% to 300%) fund, associated with Richard Driehaus Capital Management in Chicago. Bill Anderson manages this exciting fund with Brendan Kyne. Heavy in technology, basic materials (cast in concrete, anyone?), health care and consumer cyclicals, these guys maintain a pretty hot deck. It's important to take a position here, in our small-to-medium-cap segment.

Fund 16: An exciting new fund, DYNAMIC GLOBAL RESEARCH, deserves a spot inside this specimen portfolio. This fund has made spectacular early gains since its inception, and global demand for nat-ural resources remains high, fueled by infrastructure development in Asia, Latin America and other emerging markets. Currently, precious metals, building material companies, base metals, pulp and paper, and oil and gas companies are trading back at low multiples. Stronger com-modity prices should enhance corporate profits. This section of disci-plined allocation gets a key global market segment.

Fund 17: Does TEMPLETON EMERGING MARKETS FUND deserve a part in this portfolio? Yes! Probably a larger portion than I'm assigning it, especially as Dr. Mark Mobius is the manager in global emerging markets. Expected portfolio turnover annually is less than 30%. A buy-and-hold value manager, Mobius emphasizes value-style hold-ings in many nations, and low stock market capitalizations. Risk-adjusted, both as to standard deviation and Beta, it doesn't get any better than this.

Fund 18: 20/20 LATIN AMERICA is managed by Peter Gruber, Globalvest Management. With a value, bottom-up style, and low portfolio turnover, he invests mostly in Latin American securities with superior growth potential, medium- and large-cap stocks. The fund is currently heavily weighted in Brazil.

Fund 19: FIDELITY FAR EAST FUND: K.C. Lee is an exceptional manager, at times standing head and shoulders above most of his peers. He provides superb, consistent management in Asia. As manager of FIDELITY FAR EAST, he targets long-term growth principally in South-east Asian companies in Hong Kong, Korea, Singapore, Malaysia and Thailand.

BUILDING A FIRM FOUNDATION

What has my conservative-balanced investor achieved within this prescribed mandate?

First, reduced volatility and therefore reduced risk within the entire portfolio. Second, an efficient, exceptionally diversified portfolio, in terms of safety and stability. Third, above-average, consistent results over the longer term.

This is a panic-free, multi-correlated, multi-level, multi-asset, multi-manager "all-weather" investment portfolio that lets you sleep well at night and should also let you eat well in your retirement. Remember, our style is not to outperform all the market indexes in some or even most years.

And we wholeheartedly subscribe to the researched conclusion that 80% to 90% of all returns are gained through asset allocation factors rather than market timing. Time in the market is what's important, not timing.

The portfolio matches the client's personal balanced philosophy of risk-reward, and it is totally flexible. It is easy to look after, since there are only 19 positions to monitor instead of 30 or 40 individual stocks, 10 to 30 bonds, and several GICs, or other fixed-rate cash investments. This portfolio has all the characteristics and strengths to cope with a volatile, complex investment environment. It is relatively simple and straightforward and, we suggest, the ultimate in risk aversion and safety.

Our portfolio provides indirect ownership in hundreds of stocks (corporations), bonds, money market securities, real estate, mortgages and commodities. Our Stenner Multi-Safety Allocation System balances different themes, not one or two, as in a traditional brokerage portfolio. Which type of portfolio is better equipped for today's complex marketplace? The investor can alter any of these sector allocations or change, adjust or modify his or her personal goals with a phone call. In many cases there will be no commission fees involved, either.

Through its several distinct and disciplined levels of diversification, a Stenner System portfolio provides the following multi-layered safety factor paradigm introduced in Chapter 7:

1. Each investment within our carefully constructed portfolio is itself diversified.
2. We've achieved a far greater degree of diversification than is possible in a traditional, individual securities portfolio with our active allocation system (multi-asset, multi-class, multi-sector, multifund structure), which identifies and captures literally every major and minor asset class, type of security, and market sector.
3. Diversification is achieved by investing in a cross-section of funds with distinct and complementary investment styles or themes. No one fund bias or school of thought can dominate or control the success or failure of our portfolio as a whole. Instead, the portfolio draws on the combined, totally independent experience of 19 full-time professional fund managers. A third significant layer of year-round protection is achieved by further diversification with different manager styles: value, growth, sector, blend, top-down, bottom-up, interest rate anticipation and spread trading.
4. Recognition of the importance of currency management is a discipline in itself. This separates the Stenner system from the traditional stock-bond portfolio approach, as demonstrated in the recent U.S.-Canadian dollar versus the yen and deutsche mark (1996). Securities markets are becoming

increasingly volatile and complex, and highly inflammatory events, such as the Japanese financial crisis or the actions of Quebec separatists, can continue to disrupt our markets in new ways. These conditions can only create uncertainty. The overriding advantages and safety factors of our System of fund investing will also become even more apparent to individual investors. The unquestionable record of success displayed by multifund investing, notably its defensive and stable characteristic in declining markets, speaks for itself. With its ability to deliver what other investment strategies cannot, this form of investing suits most investors, regardless of their experience, the size of their holdings, or their ages. This "multifund" investment approach was reportedly initiated in the mid-1970s, but today it is being used by many pension funds.

※　　※　　※

Mutual funds are still a new form of investment. I believe they and their exploding popularity can put you in the best position in the global boom that many observers predict. By working the portfolio system in this book, you'll have prepared yourself with the right attitude, and the right tools, as well as the knowledge to enter this brave new world of investment. My system equips you to build your own financial success over the long term, with the help of a trusted, independent advisor.

Familiarize yourself with the potential risks and rewards of each of the financial choices you face. Then develop your own careful strategy to take full advantage of the future. It promises excitement and reward to those who seize the opportunities before them!

And remember, if you're a conservative investor, you can balance your entire portfolio to be very conservative. If you're an average investor, you'll construct an average risk-reward portfolio. If you're an aggressive investor, you'll construct your fund allocation aggressively. And there are many themes, variations and combinations in-between.

I hope I've helped you to see that the best investments in the world are not guaranteed, unless they are *"guaranteed" to fluctuate!* Clearly, no investment is "guaranteed" when measured against the major risks. This book is dedicated to *your* financial success. No doubt, after reading through *Stenner on Mutual Funds*, you may think that this book is all about risk. It isn't. It's really about reward!

GLOSSARY

Accrued interest: Interest accrued on a bond or debenture since the last payment of interest.

Acquisition fee: *See* **Load.**

Aggressive-growth fund: A mutual fund that seeks maximum capital gains, usually being fully invested in stocks.

All-weather fund: A mutual fund that performs in both good and bad markets.

Alpha: A measure of a mutual fund's performance in relation to its volatility.

Analyst: This term usually refers to a research specialist employed by a brokerage or other institution, who follows a specific industry or group and makes recommendations accordingly.

Annual report: A review that mutual funds and other public companies must publish annually by law, presenting their financial results for that period.

Appreciation: The increase in the value of a security or other asset over time.

Asset allocation fund: A mutual fund that is balanced in a variety of investments but in which the manager may vary that balance in relation to the markets.

Average: *See* **Index**.

Averaging down: Adding to an investment at a lower cost. *See* **Dollar-cost averaging**.

Back-end load: A charge incurred when certain mutual fund shares are sold. Also known as deferred charge or trailer fee.

Balanced fund: A mutual fund that contains fixed-income and equity holdings to provide a mix of safety, income, and growth — typically, the stock/bond ratio may approximate 60% to 40%. Differs from an asset allocation fund in that the manager does not rebalance holdings as frequently or to as great a degree.

Bank rate: The minimum rate at which Bank of Canada makes short-term loans to chartered banks and other "money market jobbers." This rate is set at one-quarter of 1% above the average weekly tender rate of 91-day Treasury Bills.

Bear market: A market characterized by sinking values or which may remain depressed.

Beta: A measure of a mutual fund's volatility relative to a Beta of 1, which is assigned to an index such as the TSE 300. A Beta of 1.20

indicates fluctuation 20% over the average. Beta may be used as a measure of risk.

Bid (or redemption) price: The price at which mutual fund shares are redeemed, usually equal to the net asset value per share.

Blue chip: A stock of a well-established company, usually listed on a major exchange and having paid dividends consistently for many years.

Bond: A certificate evidencing indebtedness by a govenment or corporation to the holder. A fixed interest rate is paid, and the bond has a stated future maturity date for repayment of the principal. Bonds rank senior to stocks as to payment of interest and principal.

Bond fund: A mutual fund that invests exclusively in fixed-income debt securities — bonds, debentures or notes issued by companies and governments. Bonds are secured by a mortgage; debentures are issued on the general credit of the company.

Broker: A person who buys and sells securities for the investing public, usually for a commission.

Bull market: A consistently rising market (the opposite of a bear market).

Bottom-up investing: A strategy whereby a fund manager looks first at specific companies, then at the industry or group. A top-down investor considers the industry first, then selects leading stocks within such a group.

Business cycles: The broad movements of the economy through growth, peaking, recession, bottoming out and resumed growth. Growth phases of cycles may last as much as four years or more, while recessions are typically of shorter duration.

Callable: A feature whereby the issuer of a security may elect to redeem it.

Canada Savings Bonds (CSBs): A nonmarketable government security, first issued in 1946, which is nontransferable but which may be cashed at full value plus accrued interest at any time.

Capital: This term refers to either all the assets and financial resources a company employs to produce its products, or the total assets of an individual or organization.

Capital appreciation fund: A mutual fund that maximizes capital gain by investing in growth securities. A mild version of an aggressive-growth fund.

Capital gain: A synonym for capital appreciation or growth in value. With mutual fund holdings, such gains are taxable at a lesser rate than that of regular income.

Cash flow: A company's net income for a period, prior to deducting depreciation and amortization and deferred income taxes.

Central bank: The agency that acts as fiscal agent for a national government. In Canada, the Bank of Canada is the central bank.

Closed-end fund: A mutual fund that has a fixed number of shares outstanding, as compared with most funds, which are open-ended and continually buy and sell their shares on a daily basis.

Co-efficient: A change denoting an interrelationship, such as between a market price and the index of such prices over time (e.g., Beta co-efficient).

Common stock: A share in the ownership of a company, with unlimited potential for growth and dividend payments if the company's earnings continue to grow.

Compound interest: Interest that is paid on and added to the principal. In other words, interest is paid on interest as well as principal.

Consumer Price Index (CPI): A price index that tracks the cost of living by measuring the prices of a given basket of consumer goods.

Contrarian investing: An investment strategy that goes against the mainstream by buying securities when most investors are selling, and selling when most are buying.

Convertible securities or funds: These kinds of securities can be exchanged for other securities in the same company under certain conditions. They thus provide the holder with an option.

Current yield: Dividends or interest paid to investors as a percentage of the current value of the security.

Defensive stock: A stock that has a record of stability even in poor markets.

Deferred sales charge: *See* **Back-end load.**

Derivatives (financial): Intangible investment instruments, such as an option or future, that depends on the value of an underlying tangible security, such as an option to buy a house. Financial derivatives may carry expanded risk, but they may also be valuable tools in the hands of a skilled fund manager.

Diversification: The strategy of spreading investment over a wide variety of holdings, the prime example of which is a mutual fund or a group of funds.

Dividends: A form of income paid to investors in common or preferred stock.

Dollar-cost averaging: A strategy of investing a fixed amount at fixed intervals, lowering the average cost, since the investor acquires more shares when unit prices are lower.

Dow Jones Industrial Average: The most widely recognized index: 30 blue-chip stocks listed on the New York Stock Exchange.

Efficient Markets Theory: *See* **Random Walk Theory.**

Equity: This term usually refers to ownership in a company, evidenced by common or preferred stock. Mutual funds so invested are referred to as equity funds.

Event risk: The risk that a bond will lose value due to certain situations relating either to the company or the general economy.

Expense ratio: The measure of a mutual fund management's expenses relative to net assets. Large funds tend to have lower expense ratios.

Fair-weather fund: A mutual fund that does well in a bull market but poorly in a bear market.

Fixed-income fund: A mutual fund that is largely invested in bonds and preferred stocks, or other debt instruments such as mortgages, providing the holder with a regular fixed rate of return.

Foul-weather fund: A mutual fund that does very well in bull markets and reasonably well in a bad market.

Front-end load: A commission paid by the investor at the time of purchase.

Foreign fund: An international mutual fund that invests only in securities outside of Canada, as distinct from a global fund, of which the holdings may include Canadian securities.

Fund manager: This term can refer to a company that manages an individual mutual fund, but more often refers to the individual who is responsible for a single fund within a family group.

Global fund: *See* **Foreign fund.**

Growth fund: A mutual fund that invests in companies that appear to have good growth characteristics.

Hedge fund: A mutual fund that may sell short or write options in order to protect its other investments.

Income fund: A mutual fund that has the primary objective of generating a high level of income, such as from bonds, debentures or stocks with a high payout.

Index: A market model, made up of selected securities, such as the TSE 300 or the Dow Jones Industrial Index.

Index fund: A mutual fund that invests in the securities contained within an Index, such as the TSE 300. In other words, the fund will replicate, and perform equally as well — or poorly — as the Index.

International fund: Same as **Foreign fund.**

Investment company: A company that pools investors' funds and invests them in securities. Mutual funds are a particular, open-end example of such a company.

Junk bonds: Bonds of a quality lower than that of investment-grade bonds, which compensate by offering a higher rate of return.

Leverage: A term with several meanings. It can mean buying securities by borrowing money to do so, or it can mean a company's "leveraging" its equity by issuing funded debt. A homeowner who uses the equity in his house to buy another is also leveraging.

Limited partnership: An investment group composed of a general partner, who manages a project, and the limited partners, who may be many, who invest in it, and whose liability is limited to the amount of their investment.

Liquidity: Generally, the readiness with which an investment may be converted to cash. This does not imply a guaranteed price level.

Load: Charges or commission paid by mutual fund investors, which may vary from 1% to 8%.

Long term: In the bond market, this refers to securities with a term of more than 10 years to maturity.

Management fee: A charge by an investment advisor or fund manager, usually less than 1% per annum.

Money market: The market for short-term obligations of governments with maturities of three years or less, and of corporations or financial institutions with maturities of one year or less.

Money market fund: A mutual fund that invests in debt securities of less than a year to maturity.

Moving average: The price of securities averaged over a period and entered on a graph as an indicator of a market's general direction.

Mutual fund: A company that invests pooled investments, its peculiarity being that it issues and redeems shares on a daily basis.

Net asset value: The value per share of a fund: the total net assets divided by the number of shares outstanding.

Net worth: The value of a corporate entity or an estate after deducting all liabilities.

No-load fund: A mutual fund that requires no sales commission. Its shortcomings in quality and advice may more than offset its economy of acquisition.

Option: Any call on a future purchase (or a "put" on a future sale), at a set price within a fixed time period.

Over-the-counter market: A market for an unlisted security, usually conducted verbally between brokers or dealers.

Portfolio: The investment holdings of a company or individual.

Portfolio manager: May mean either a fund manager who is responsible for running a mutual fund's holdings, or an advisor who maintains an individual client's investments.

Preferred stock: This security has two characteristics: it normally carries a fixed rate of return, but it ranks senior to common stock. Many variations include convertible preferreds, which may be converted into common stock.

Premium: The excess of a security's price over its net asset value. A bond with a high coupon will trade at a premium in a period of lower interest rates.

Price-earnings ratio: A ratio that expresses the relationship between a stock's price and its earnings per share after taxes.

Prime rate: The rate charged by chartered banks to their most credit-worthy customers.

Prospectus: An official document outlining all relevant information about the security or fund and observing the principal of full disclosure. It is required by law concerning any new issue of securities to the public.

Prudent man rule: The general principle that the investment should be such as an ordinary but informed individual would observe when investing for another to whom he felt morally bound. In Canada, this may also include a list of securities which have been approved by a provincial government or the federal government.

Quotation: The market price of any security, usually indicating the highest bid and the lowest offering price.

Rally: Usually a brief but brisk rise in the general price level of a market.

Random Walk Theory: The theory that all stock prices are unpredictable and random because all factors are recognized by the market price, in other words, that such a market is efficient.

Real Estate Investment Trust (REIT): A company that invests in real estate or lends to real estate companies.

Registered Retirement Income Fund (RRIF): A registered retirement vehicle that allows the systematic withdrawal of funds previously invested in an RRSP beginning no later than the 69th calendar year of the registrant.

Registered Retirement Savings Plan (RRSP): A financial plan registered and administered directly or indirectly by a bank, trust or insurance company, credit union, mutual fund or brokerage firm, under which an investor can invest in a retirement fund over time and defer taxes on such deposits until retirement.

Risk: Either the measure of volatility of a security or the possibility of loss.

Risk-averse: An individual who has a low level of risk tolerance.

Risk tolerance: An individual's preparedness to accept potential loss.

Sector: Stocks or other securities within a particular industry.

Securities and Exchange Commission (SEC): The federal agency in the U.S. that administers securities legislation. In Canada, such administration is vested in each individual province.

Selling short: The sale of a security that is not owned, with the expectation that it may be purchased later at a lower price, and therefore yield a profit.

Standard deviation: The variance of a stock or mutual fund's degree of fluctuation above and below its own average. (Beta measures such fluctuation relevant to the whole market's average.) Such variation is usually considered a risk factor.

Strip bonds: *See* **Zero coupon bonds.**

Tax-loss selling: The selling of a security to generate a loss for tax purposes.

Term deposit (Certificate of Deposit, or CD): An instrument issued by chartered banks or other deposit-taking institutions, carrying a fixed rate, which cannot be cashed before maturity without the payment of a penalty.

Top-down: An investing strategy whereby the investor considers first the general economy, then the industry and individual company. (See **Bottom-up** for the reverse strategy.)

Total return: Profit or loss realized by a mutual fund, including capital gain, interest or dividends, expressed as a percentage of the original value of the assets.

Transfer agent: An agency, usually a trust company, that acts as custodian of records for a mutual fund or other public company.

Treasury Bills (T-Bills): Short-term obligations offered by the Bank of Canada as fiscal agent for the federal government's short-term financial requirements. They may be 91 days, 180 days or a year in term. Instead of carrying coupons, they are offered and traded at a discount to provide a predetermined yield-to-maturity.

Turnover ratio: A measure of the trading activity of a mutual fund. A turnover rate of 100% is the equivalent of a complete turnover of the portfolio in the course of one year. More aggressive mutual funds obviously have higher turnover ratios.

Volatility: A market characteristic of a security which describes swings in price. It is often associated with relative risk, although it does not inherently imply risk.

Yield-to-maturity: The calculated yield of a bond, given its current price, its rate of return and the length of time-to-maturity.

Zero coupon bonds: Bonds that do not carry coupons, but are sold at a discount from face value and will appreciate in value as they approach maturity.

BIBLIOGRAPHY

Ady, Ronald W. *The Investment Evaluation* (New York: Prentice Hall, 1984).

Bank of Canada, 1991. "Targets for reducing inflation: Announcements and background material," *Bank of Canada Review* (Spring): 3-21.

_____. 1993-94. "Statement of the Government of Canada and the Bank of Canada on monetary policy objectives," *Bank of Canada Review* (Winter): 85-86.

Basso, Thomas F. *Panic-Proof Investing* (New York: John Wiley & Sons, Inc., 1994).

Bogle, John C. *Bogle On Mutual Funds* (New York: Irwin, 1994).

Boroson, Warren. *Keys To Investing In Mutual Funds* (New York: Barrons Educational Services, Inc., 1992).

Canadian Securities Institute. *How To Invest in Canadian Securities* (Toronto, 1986).

Chevreau, Jonathan. *1996 Investor's Guide To Mutual Funds* (Toronto: Key Porter Books, 1996).

Croft, Richard and Eric Kirzner. *The FundLine Advisor* (Toronto: HarperCollins, 1996).

Dent, Harry S., Jr. *The Great Boom Ahead* (New York: Hyperion, 1993).

Downes, John et al. *Dictionary of Finance and Investment Terms, 3rd edition* (New York: Barrons, 1995).

Foot, David K. *Boom, Bust and Echo* (Toronto: Macfarlane Walter & Ross, 1996).

Forman, Dr. Norm. *Mind over Money* (Toronto: Bantam, 1988).

Fredman, Albert J., and Russ Wiles. *How Mutual Funds Work* (Englewood Cliffs, N.J.: New York Institute of Finance).

Gadsden, Stephen. *The Authoritative Guide to Understanding Mutual Funds* (Toronto: McGraw-Hill-Ryerson, 1994).

Gibson, Roger C. *Asset Allocation* (Chicago: Irwin, 1996).

Graham, Benjamin and David L. Dodd. *Security Analysis* (Toronto: McGraw-Hill, 1934).

Grant, John. *Handbook of Economic Indicators* (Toronto: University of Toronto Press, 1992).

Griffeth, Bill. *The Mutual Fund Masters* (Chicago: Probius Publishers, 1995).

Hirsch, Michael. *Multifund Investing: How to Build a Higher Performance Portfolio of Mutual Funds* (New York: Dow Jones Irwin, 1987).

Hulbert, Mark. *The Hulbert Guide to Financial Newsletters* (Chicago: Dearborn Financial Publishing, Inc.).

Hunter, William T. *Canadian Financial Markets, 3rd edition* (Toronto: Broadview, 1991).

Investment Company Institute. *Mutual Fund Fact Book, 1993 edition.*

Laderman, Jeffrey M. *Business Week's Guide to Mutual Funds, 3rd edition* (New York: McGraw-Hill, 1993).

Lederman, Jess and Robert A. Klein. *Global Asset Allocation* (New York: John Wiley & Sons, 1994).

Luciani, Patrick. "The Case for Cutting Taxes," *The Financial Post Magazine* (May 1997).

Lynch, Peter with John Rothchild. *Beating the Street* (New York: Simon & Schuster, 1991).

_____. *One Up on Wall Street* (New York: Simon & Schuster, 1993).

Malkiel, Burton G. *A Random Walk Down Wall Street* (New York: W.W. Norton, 1996).

Mamis, Justin. *The Nature of Risk* (New York: Harper & Row, 1994).

McLuhan, Marshall. *Understanding Media* (Toronto: Signet, 1964).

Morgenson, Gretchen. "Index Funds — Riskier Than You Think," *Forbes Magazine* (April 7, 1997).

Moynes, Riley. *The Money Coach* (Toronto: Copp Clark, 1996).

Pape, Gordon. *Gordon Pape's 1997 Buyer's Guide to RRSPs* (Toronto: Prentice Hall, 1996).

Powers, Gordon. "How tax efficient is your mutual fund?", *The Globe and Mail* (20 February 1997).

Pring, Malcolm J. *The All-Season Investor* (New York: John Wiley & Sons, 1992).

Rosenberg, Claude N. *Investing with the Best* (New York: John Wiley & Sons, 1986).

Schabacker, Jay. *Jay Schabacker's Winning in Mutual Funds* (New York: AMACOM, 1996).

Stern, Aaron, M.D. *Me: The Narcissistic American* (New York: Ballantine, 1979).

Taylor, John H., Ph.D. *Building Wealth with Mutual Funds* (New York: Windsor Books, 1993).

Turner, Garth. *Garth Turner's 1997 RRSP Guide* (Toronto: Key Porter Books, 1996).

_____. *2015: After the Boom* (Toronto: Key Porter Books, 1995).

Tyson, Eric. *Mutual Funds For Dummies* (Foster City, California: IDG Books, 1994).

Van Caspel, Venita. *Money Dynamics For the 1990s* (New York: Simon & Schuster, 1988).

Yanni, Nicholas. *W.C. Fields* (New York: Pyramid Publications, 1974).

Zimmer, Henry B. *Making Your Money Grow: A Canadian Guide to Successful Personal Finance, 3rd edition* (Toronto: Collins Publishers, 1989).

INDEX

A

Adams, Sherman, 18–19
after-tax yield, 242–43, 255
AGF Group, 122, 168, 367–73
AIC Advantage, 367, 372
Algoma Steel Corp., Inc., 142
Arnott, Robert, 351
asset allocation, 51–53, 104, 106, 108, 110, 116–21, 169, 215
Atlas Group, 122,131

B

Bachman, Daniel, 356–58
BPI High Income Funds, 122, 131, 134–35, 348, 368–70
Bank of Canada, 74, 79, 81–82, 107, 188, 209–210
Baring's Bank, 5, 205, 304
BellCharts, Inc., 152–59, 318, 327–28, 330–35
Berger, William, 239
Beta Factor, 191–92, 235, 300
Beutel Goodman Money Market Fund, 368
Black, Conrad, 41
Black, Herbert, 84
Black Monday, 33, 100, 309, 356
blue chips, 150
Bolsa Mexicana, 169
"Boring Approach", the, 228–29

B.C. Telephone, 93, 186
Buffett, Warren, 92
bull (and bear) markets, 90–91, 354
("The Raging Bull"), 241
Business Week, 360
business cycles ("Psyching the Cycles"), 361–62

C

Cabot, Walter, 299
Canada Pension Plan, 61, 66, 210, 258, 260, 267
Canada Savings Bonds, 8, 44, 67, 73, 83, 303
Canadian Deposit Insurance Corporation (CDIC), 44–45, 56, 72
Canadian Investor Protection Fund (CIPF), 8, 72, 227
Canadian Investment Fund (CIF), 17
Canadian Property Rule, 207, 268, 293
Canadian Securities Course (CSC), 291
Canadian Securities Institute (CSI), 108–09, 291
Chant, Dr. John, 44
Christ, Alex, 343
CIBC Wood Gundy Securities, Inc., xxviii
C.I. Group of Funds, 4, 122, 168, 345–47, 367–69
C.I. Sector Fund, 265, 345–47
Cohen, Bruce, 45, 296

commission rates, 297
commodities options, 84
compounding, 29, 127, 255
Consumer Price Index (CPI), 80, 82, 180,
    188, 210–11
contrarianism, 342–43
Cook, Peter, 61–62
correlation, 170–74, 218
correlation coefficients, 170, 218
Croft-Kirzner FundLine, 327, 331

D

Dahlly, Professor Bev, 349
Dalbar Institute, 183, 250, 298
deferred sales charge (DSC), 76, 298
demographic investing, 58
Dent, Harry S., Jr., 57
derivatives, 205–08, 269, 278
DesMarais, Paul, 41
diversification, 6, 29, 32–38, 140, 171
dividends, 78, 142, , 152–53, 239–40
dividend payout ratio, 147
dividend tax credit, 242–44
dollar-cost averaging, 77–78, 185
Donoghue, William, 235
Dow Jones (Index), 23, 53, 73, 88, 148, 203,
    230, 246, 307
Dynamic Mutual Funds, 122, 367–69, 372

E

efficient markets theory, 191, 231
Evensley, Harold, 351
estate planning, 262–63

F

Federal Reserve Board, 107
Fidelity Group of Funds, 263, 367–69,
    371–72
Financial Post, 349
Foot, Professor David K., 13, 57–60
Forrett, Patrick, 174
Fraser Institute, The, 350
Fried, John, 95
front-end load, 249

G

Gabelli, Mario, 143
Gates, Bill, 24, 92
Givens, Charles, 205
Global Strategy, 122, 168, 174, 208, 277,
    280, 367–69, 371
Globe and Mail, 61, 352
Granville, Joe, 21
Greenspan, Alan, 107
Griffeth, Bill, 18, 31
Griswold, Merrill, 19
Gross, William, 31
G.T. Global, 348, 367
Guaranteed Investment Certificates (GICs),
    36, 43–44, 67, 130, 138–39, 179, 213–14,
    225–26, 232–34, 237, 242, 258, 265, 274, 303
Guardian Group of Funds, 122, 192,
    367–70

H

Hansberger, Thomas, xvii–xix, 69
Hirsch, Michael, 100, 112, 116–18
Hoey, Richard, 289
Hopewell, Lynn, 92

I

Ibbotson Associates, 95
index funds, 233–34
inflation, 79–82, 178, 188, 209–11, 266
interest rates, 74–75, 161, 180, 186–90, 266
Investment Company Institute of America
    (ICI), 9–16, 36–39, 183, 298
Investment Funds Institute of Canada
    (IFIC), 9–16, 63
investment funds, see mutual funds

J

January Effect, 163, 340–42
Jarislowsky, Stephen, 40, 304

K

Kirzner, Eric and Richard Croft, 327, 331

L

LeBaron, Dean, 299
leverage, 62, 77–78
liquidity, 7,83, 140, 213, 221
Luciani, Patrick, 349–50
Lynch, Peter, 6, 19, 40, 93,125, 213

M

Mackenzie Financial Corporation, 122, 339, 343
Malkiel, Professor Burton G., 231–36
Mamis, Justin, xxiii
management expense ratios, (MERs), 283–84, 299
Massachusetts Investors Trust (MIT), 18
Midland Walwyn Capital, Inc., 128, 203, 279, 327, 336–37
Milevsky, Professor Moshe, 260–62
Mobius, Dr. Mark, 222, 288, 302
Monarch Dividend Fund, 367–68, 370
Morgan Stanley, 171–74, 268, 303, 316–17
Morgan Stanley World Index, 160–61, 234, 277, 303
Morgenson, Gretchen, 235–36
Morningstar, Inc., 183, 317, 319, 327
Murray, Nick, 152, 300
Multiple Solutions, 4
mutual funds (types), 129, 154–59, 164–69, 193–201, 366–68

N

National Council of Real Estate Fiduciaries (NCREIF), 95
Nesbitt Burns, xxviii
New Reality, 42, 64, 67
New York Stock Exchange (NYSE), 162
Nikkei (Tokyo Stock Exchange Index) 169, 307
Nippon Telephone, 43
no-load funds, 249, 294–99

O

Old Age Security (OAS), 258, 261

P

Pape, Gordon, 328
Pattison, Jimmy, 41
performance consistency
Plender, John, 64, 65
Powers, Gordon, 352
preferred stock, 141
price-earnings ratio, 146
Principal Group, 43, 228
Prudent Man Rule, 43, 177
Putnam, Mr. Justice Samuel, 177

R

Random Walk Hypothesis, 114, 191, 231–32
RBC Dominion Securities, Inc., xxviii
Real Estate Investment Trusts (REITs), 130, 196
RRIFs, 85, 131, 207, 238, 260, 272–81, 305
RRSPs, 59, 85, 115, 131, 207, 210, 238, 254, 260, 264–281, 305, 342
Revenue Canada, 213,242,260, 275, 344, 347
Reichmann brothers, 41
Richards, Dan, 4
Richardson family, 41
risk adjustment, 229, 300, 316, 327, 338
risk-reward (evaluation), 67, 70, 71, 193–95, 200–01, 203, 301, 313, 315
risks, (bond) 133–37, (equity) 175–86, (general) 35, 106, 188–222
Royalty Income Trusts (RITs), 130, 196

S

Schabacker, Jay, xxviii
ScotiaMcLeod, Inc., xxviii
Scratchley, Arthur, 32
sector allocation, 110, 366
Securities Exchange Commission (SEC), 182–83
Seniors' Benefits, 210
Standard & Poor's (S&P), 73, 95, 144, 167, 234
Statistics Canada, 11–12, 61, 81
Stenner's Laws, #1– 41, #2 – 43, #3 – 63, #4 – 199, #5 – 223, #6 – 242, #7 – 249, #8 – 260
Stenner Multi-Safety Allocation System, 19–20, 35–37, 93, 99–100, 104, 229, 361, 365, 375

Stenner Performance Consistency
    Measurement, 328–29
Sterling, Bill, 59–60
Stern, Aaron, 42
Sumitomo copper scandal, 5, 84, 206
systematic withdrawal plans, 256–58

T

tax defferal, 346
tax (general), 30, 70, 85, 346–47, 350–51
tax-loss selling, 344
Templeton Group of Funds, 88–89, 94, 244,
    255–56, 289, 367, 369, 373
Templeton, Sir John, 17, 19, 31, 87, 247,
    308, 343, 352, 358
Thieme, Heiko, 100
Thiessen, Gordon, 107, 209
Toronto Stock Exchange (TSE), 114,
    149–50, 167, 169, 199, 219, 278, 303
Trimark Funds, 122, 131, 256, 259, 367–69
Turner, Honorable Garth, 59–60, 138,
    211, 264
20/20 Sand Trap, the, 232

U

Unit Investment Trusts, 130

V

value investing, 69
value method, 358
Van Caspel, Venita, 6, 79, 358
Vega, Joseph de la, 5
volatility, 46, 48–49, 70, 74, 225–26

W

Wallace, Peter, 128
Wall Street Journal, 241

Z

Zedillo, President Ernesto, 137